Protecting Farmlands

Protecting Farmlands

Edited by

Frederick R. Steiner

Washington State University
Pullman, Washington

and

John E. Theilacker

County of Lake Planning Department
Lakeport, California

AVI PUBLISHING COMPANY, INC.
Westport, Connecticut

Frontispiece
Suburban growth is best shown in this comparison of an area in Santa Clara County, California, that was predominantly agriculture in 1950 (*top photo*) and by 1978 was covered with highways, housing developments, and industry (*bottom*). Photos courtesy of USDA-Soil Conservation Service.

© Copyright 1984 by
THE AVI PUBLISHING COMPANY, INC.
250 Post Road East
Westport, Connecticut

Library of Congress Cataloging in Publication Data
Main entry under title:

Protecting farmlands.

The majority of papers in this vol. are from 2 previous publications: the 1st from the proceedings of a conference entitled "Farmlands preservation—the state of the art," held at Washington State University, Nov. 12–14, 1979, and the 2nd from "Farmland, food, and the future," published by the Soil Conservation Society of America (1979)
   Bibliography: p.
   Includes index.
   1. Land use, Rural—United States—Addresses, essays, lectures.   2. Land use—United States—Planning—Addresses, essays, lectures.   3. Agriculture—Economic aspects—United States—Addresses, essays, lectures.
4. Soil conservation—United States—Addresses, essays, lectures.   5. Food supply—United States—Addresses, essays, lectures.   I. Steiner, Frederick R.
II. Theilacker, John.   III. Farmlands preservation—the state of the art.   IV. Farmland, food, and the future.
HD256.P76   1984   333.76'17'0973   84–297

ISBN 0-87055-452-2

Printed in the United States of America

A B C D E   3 2 1 0 9 8 7 6 5 4

Contents

List of Contributors		**xi**
Preface		**xiii**
Introduction		**xv**
Part I	**Overview of Farmlands Protection**	**1**
Chapter 1	**The Loss of U.S. Cropland: Whose Issue Is It?**	**3**
	James M. Jeffords	
	The Emerging Perspective	4
	No Longer One Question	5
	The Facts of Farmland Conversion	5
	The Role of the Federal Government	7
	Can We Meet the Challenge?	8
Chapter 2	**Public Involvement in Land-Use Planning**	**9**
	Joanne Barnes Jackson	
	Legislation Concerning Citizen Involvement	10
	Four Theorems of Public Participation	11
	Applications for Farmland Preservation	12
	Conclusions	14
	References	14
Chapter 3	**Farmland Protection: Legal and Constitutional Issues**	**15**
	John C. Keene	
	Major Classes of Approaches	15
	Legal Problems in Regulatory Programs for Protecting Agricultural Land	15
	Legal Problems Arising Out of the Use of the Taxing Power	36
	Legal Problems Arising from Programs for Acquiring Interest in Land	39
	Legal Problems Arising from the Use of the Spending Power to Protect Agricultural Land	40
	Conclusion	43
Chapter 4	**The Ethical Dimension of Farmlands Protection**	**45**
	R. Neil Sampson	
	Problems Amid Plenty	45
	Stress on the Land Base	46
	The Value of the Land	50
	References	52

Chapter 5   Farming on the Urban Fringe   55
              Roger J. Blobaum
              Regional Food Plans as Public Policy   57
              Putting Together a Metropolitan Food Plan   57
              Conclusions   61
              References   61

Part II   Local Approaches for Farmlands Protection   63

**Chapter 6   Three Guidelines for Communities
              in Protecting Farming   65**
              William Toner
              The Agricultural Community Should Play a Central Role
                in the Design, Development, and Application of Local
                Plans and Regulations to Save Farms and Farmland   65
              Rely on Conventional Planning Tools and Techniques,
                but Use all Tools at One's Disposal   68
              Keep in Mind That the Flip Side of Agricultural
                Preservation Is Urban Development   69
              Conclusion   71
              References   71

**Chapter 7   Local Approaches to Farmland Preservation:
              A Rural Renaissance for Zoning   73**
              Jack Kartez
              Agricultural Zoning   73
              Density Limits without Uniform Lot Size Provision   74
              Special Agricultural Use Provision Problems   75
              State-Mandated Agricultural Zoning   75
              Need for Rural Zoning Literature   77
              References   80

**Chapter 8   King County's Purchase of Development
              Rights Program   81**
              John Spellman
              Agriculture in King County   81
              Why Save Farmland in King County?   83
              History of the King County Program   84
              Provisions of the King County Program   84
              Rationale for the PDR Approach   85
              The Crucial Elements for Acceptance   87
              Recent Events   87
              Since 1982   89
              References   90

**Chapter 9   Agricultural Land Preservation in
              Whitman County, Washington   91**
              William R. Wagner
              Impacts of Concern   91
              Geological History   91
              Land-Use Planning History   92
              Current Land-Use Strategy   93

Land-Use Management Improvements Still Needed   94
Summary   95
Reference   95

Chapter 10   Techniques for Protecting Prime Agricultural Land: Zoning Applications in York County, Pennsylvania   97

William J. Conn
Introduction   97
Evaluation of Agricultural Zoning Techniques   99
Application of Zoning Approach   102
Evaluation of This Zoning Approach   107
References   108

Chapter 11   Corn Suitability Ratings: A Method of Rating Soils for Identifying and Preserving Prime Agricultural Lands in Black Hawk County, Iowa   109

Sonia A. Johannsen and Larry C. Larsen
Introduction   109
Physical Characteristics   109
History   111
Urbanization and the County's Attempt to Control It   111
Development of Corn Suitability Ratings as a Tool
  in County Zoning   112
The Application of the Corn Suitability Ratings and
  Land Use   119
Experience and Impact of Using Corn Suitability Ratings   124
The Present Status of the CSR in Zoning in Black Hawk
  County   125
References   126

Part III   Middleground and State Approaches for Farmlands Protection   129

Chapter 12   Farmland Conservancies: A Middleground Approach   131

Charles E. Little
Deed Restrictions in Pennsylvania   131
California Coastal Conservancy   133
Canadian Examples   135
French SAFERs   136
Nongovernmental Programs   138
Defining the Middle Ground   140
Issues and Options   142
References   144

Chapter 13   Wisconsin's Farmland Preservation Program   147

James A. Johnson
Introduction   147
How the Law Works   148
What Have We Learned? How Has Local Government
  Responded?   153
Where Are the Major Problems?   157

	Conclusion	158
	References	159

Chapter 14   Oregon's Agricultural Land Protection Program   161
Ronald Eber

	Introduction	161
	Oregon's Land-Use Program	161
	The Agricultural Lands Protection Program	162
	Summary	167
	Author's Note	168
	Appendix 1: Goal No. 3—Agricultural Lands	168
	Appendix 2: Incentives and Privileges to the Property Owner within an Exclusive Farm Use Zone	169
	Appendix 3: Statutory Provisions Related to the Exclusive Farm Use Zone and Special Farm Use Assessment	169
	References	170

Chapter 15   Protection Efforts in the Northeastern States   173
Mark B. Lapping

	Policy Responses: The First Generation	173
	Policy Responses: The Second Generation	176
	Policy Responses: The Third Generation	179
	Conclusion	180
	References	181

Chapter 16   Property Tax Relief Programs to Preserve Farmlands   183
Richard W. Dunford

	Rationale for Property Tax Relief Programs	184
	Types of Property Tax Relief Programs	186
	Effectiveness of Property Tax Relief Programs	190
	Elements of an Effective Farmland Preservation Program	192
	References	193

Part IV   Federal Involvement in Farmlands Protection   195

Chapter 17   The Changing Role of the Federal Government in Farmland Retention   197
W. Wendell Fletcher

	Agricultural Land: A Significant National Resource	198
	The Objectives of Change	200
	The Federal Role in Transition	202
	Current Status and Future Policy Options	207
	References	209

Chapter 18   Evolution of Land-Use Policy in the U.S. Department of Agriculture   211
Norman A. Berg and Warren T. Zitzmann

	Some Early Activities	211
	After World War II, Renewed Interest in the Land-Use Issue	214

USDA's Concept of the Land-Use Issue   215
Development of a Secretary's Memorandum on
    Land Use   216
Seeking a USDA Focus on Land Use   218
Reconciling Two Schools of Thought on
    Agricultural Land   219
Actions in Response to the Prime Lands Seminar   220
An Updating of USDA Policy on Land Use   221
References   223

Chapter 19   The National Agricultural Lands Study (NALS)   225

Robert J. Gray
The Program of Study   226
Public Participation and Information   228
Findings, Conclusions, and Recommendations   229
Summary   231
Reference   232

Chapter 20   SCS Important Farmlands Mapping Program   233

Raymond I. Dideriksen
Inventory Program Products   235
Inventory Program Status   238
Prime Farmland Contributions to Food and Fiber
    Production   238
Summary   239
References   240

Part V   International Farmlands Protection Efforts   241

Chapter 21   Canadian Provincial Farmland Protection Programs   243

C. E. Bray
Agricultural Land Production Potential   244
Loss of Agricultural Land through Urbanization   247
Legislative Initiative   249
Land-Use Programs   250
Land Tenure Programs   254
Conclusions   259
References   260

Chapter 22   The European and International Experience with Farmland Protection: Some Inferences   263

Dallas Miner, Martin Chorich, and Mark B. Lapping
No Common Approach   264
Some Pertinent Examples   265
Conclusion   272
References   272

Chapter 23   Farmland Protection in the Netherlands   275

Frederick R. Steiner
Framework for Physical Planning   277
Making National Policy   277
The Provincial Role in Planning   278

Municipal-Level Planning   279
Protecting Farmland   280
Farmland-Related Problems   280
The Land Reallocation Program   282
The Land Consolidation Process   283
Extent of Land Consolidation   284
Reclamation of New Land   285
Lessons from the Dutch Experience   287
References   290

Annotated Bibliography   **291**
Index   **307**

List of Contributors*

Berg, Norman A., American Farmland Trust, Washington, DC 20036

Blobaum, Roger, Roger Blobaum and Associates, Route 4, Box 3, Osceola, Iowa 50213

Bray, Carol E., Food Research Institute, Stanford University, Stanford, California 94305

Chorich, Martin, London School of Economics, London, England

Conn, William J., York County Planning Commission, York, Pennsylvania 17402

Dideriksen, Raymond I., 131 Antler Road, Greenville, North Carolina 27834

Dunford, Richard W., Department of Agricultural Economics, Washington State University, Pullman, Washington 99164

Eber, Ronald, Department of Land Conservation and Development, Salem, Oregon 97310

Fletcher, W. Wendell, Office of Technology Assessment, U.S. Congress, Washington, DC 20510

Gray, Robert J., American Farmland Trust, Washington, DC 20036

Jackson, Joanne Barnes, 4811 Trinity Place, Philadelphia, Pennsylvania 19143

Jeffords, James M., U.S. House of Representatives, Washington, DC 20515

Johannsen, Sonia A., Black Hawk County Board of Supervisors, Waterloo, Iowa 50703

Johnson, James A., Wisconsin Department of Agriculture, Trade and Consumer Protection, Madison, Wisconsin 53713

Kartez, Jack, Program in Environmental Science and Regional Planning, Washington State University, Pullman, Washington 99164

Keene, John C., Department of City and Regional Planning, University of Pennsylvania, Philadelphia, Pennsylvania 19104

Lapping, Mark B., School of Rural Planning and Development, University of Guelph, Guelph, Ontario, Canada N1G 2W1

Larsen, Larry C., Zoning Administration, Black Hawk County, Iowa Northland Regional Council of Governments, Waterloo, Iowa 50703

Little, Charles E., American Land Forum, 5410 Grosvenor Lane, Bethesda, Maryland 20814

Miner, Dallas, National Oceans Service, U.S. Department of Commerce, Washington, DC 20230

Sampson, R. Neil, National Association of Conservation Districts, Washington, DC 20005

Spellman, John, Governor, State of Washington, Olympia, Washington 98504

Steiner, Frederick R., Program in Environmental Science and Regional Planning and Department of Horticulture and Landscape Architecture, Washington State University, Pullman, Washington 99164

*Addresses as given are current

Toner, William, Department of Environmental Planning, Governors State University, Park Forest South, Illinois 60466

Wagner, William R., Oregon District Four Council of Governments, Corvallis, Oregon 97333

Zitzmann, Warren T., Soil Conservation Service, U.S. Department of Agriculture, Washington, DC 20013

Preface

Two previous publications provide the major source of the papers in this volume. The first was the proceedings of a three-day conference entitled Farmlands Preservation—The State of the Art held at Washington State University, November 12–14, 1979. Only a limited supply of these proceedings were available and they are no longer in print. The second was "Farmland, Food, and the Future" published by the Soil Conservation Society of America (1979). The material from both publications has been updated for this volume.

The purpose of the conference was to bring together farmers, elected officials, educators, conservationists, planners, attorneys, and other individuals interested in the issue of the protection of farms and farmland. These decision makers at the county, regional, state, and national levels heard what was being done across the United States to protect farmland. Rather than concentrate on why the loss of farmlands has caused many individuals to become alarmed, the goal of the conference was to focus on successful approaches.

Many individuals and groups helped with the farmlands conference. The Office of Environmental Education of the then U.S. Department of Health, Education and Welfare; the National Association of Counties; and Washington State University's Conference Center provided financial support of this effort. Walter Bogan, Julia Lescuex, Robert Weaver, Edward Thompson, Jim Havens, Freda Semingson, Steve Gibbs, and Donna Zimmer were instrumental in providing this support. The cooperation of the following individuals was also important: William Wagner, Norm Hatley, Jim Henning, John Henley, Jr., and especially the late Harry Wegner of Whitman County, Washington; Washington Governor John Spellman; Pat Dunn then of King County, Washington; and Representatives Mike Kreidler, Roger Van Dyken, and Otto Amen of the Washington State House Agriculture Committee. Also, U.S. Representatives Thomas Foley (Washington State) and James Jeffords (Vermont) and former Senator Warren Magnuson (Washington State) and their staffs were quite helpful. Chuck Hinde and Dale Harrison of KWSU radio were responsible for broadcasting the entire conference live and, as a result, some 21,000 rural people who could not attend were reached. Rich Hagood and the Partnership for Rural Improvement helped finance the publication of the proceedings.

The Soil Conservation Society of America's publication, from which four chapters were derived, concentrated more on the broader aspects of farmlands protection. The Soil Conservation Society of America, founded in 1945, is a nonprofit scientific and educational association dedicated to advancing the science and art of good land use. Its 15,000 members worldwide include researchers, administrators, educators, planners, technicians, legislators, farmers and ranchers, and others with an interest in the wise use of land and related natural resources. Most academic disciplines concerned with the management of land and related natural resources are represented.

"Farmland, Food and the Future" was prepared in cooperation with a seven-member project advisory committee. The members of that committee included Pierre Crosson, Resources for the Future, Inc.; R.I. Dideriksen, Soil Conservation Service; Robert G. Healy, The Conservation Foundation; Walter E. Jeske, Soil Conservation Service; Charles E. Little, American Land Forum; Dallas Miner, Office of Coastal Zone Management; and R. Neil Sampson, National Association of Conservation Districts.

Three of the following chapters appeared in neither the conference proceedings or the Soil Conservation Society book. Chapters 12 and 23 appeared first in the *Journal of Soil and Water Conservation* in a different form and Chapter 21 was solicited directly from the author. Three of the chapters from the conference at Washington State University were also adapted for articles in the *Gonzaga Law Review, Natural Resources Journal*, and the *Journal of Soil and Water Conservation*. These chapters were in turn readapted for this volume. In addition, some of the chapters also appeared in different forms in various publications of the National Agricultural Lands Study. This study was a result of action taken by the Carter administration and is explained in Chapter 19.

We would like to acknowledge the ongoing support of both the College of Agriculture and Home Economics and the Program of Environmental Science and Regional Planning, Washington State University. In particular, Jack Robbins, Bill Funk, Ken Brooks, Ken Struckmeyer, Al Pettibone, Paul Rassmussen, and Betty Musick have been helpful. Doris Birch and the Word Processing Center of the College of Agriculture and Home Economics have done all the typing and retyping for which we are extremely grateful. Lonnie Kennedy helped with some of the graphics. The Bureau of the Information and Documentation Centre for the Geography of the Netherlands contributed several maps and the Soil Conservation Service provided several photographs.

We appreciate the encouragement and guidance of AVI Publishing Company. We owe special thanks to our wives, Anna-Ostrowska Steiner and Kathy Theilacker, for their understanding and love.

Frederick R. Steiner
John E. Theilacker

Introduction

If one were to make an analysis of the most intrinsically suitable regions for supporting agriculture on the planet Earth, one would find an inordinate percentage of the most suitable in the Northern Hemisphere. Europe and North America contain large regions possessing a productive combination of climate, topography, and soils for farming. This ecological advantage has been fully utilized by the cultures of Europe and North America. Agriculture has provided the bedrock for Western civilization.

Yet agriculture is a threatened resource. Robin Best (1979) reports that nearly all the countries of the European Economic Community experienced a fairly substantial loss of agricultural area during the decade from 1961 to 1971. On the other hand, urban development increased. Most of the agricultural loss was in cropland. This loss occurred even though most European nations have rather strong land-use controls.

In Canada, which presently supplies 10% of the world's food, 4,531,643 acres (1,835,315 hectares) of farmland were lost between 1961 and 1976 (MacGregor 1980). This loss occurred while large areas of land were being developed for agriculture in the western provinces. Most of the land loss has been in the eastern provinces; Ontario alone has lost 5,000,000 acres (2,025,000 ha) since 1951. Although a federal land-use policy was first proposed by the Trudeau administration in 1974, no federal action has yet been taken, though several provincial and local governments have moved to protect farmland.

The most dramatic losses of farmland have occurred in the United States. According to the Soil Conservation Service, the United States loses 20,000 acres (8100 ha) of its agricultural land each week, representing a loss of over 3 million acres (1,215,000 ha) per year. Throughout the past decade, an area the size of the states of Vermont, New Hampshire, Massachusetts, Rhode Island, Connecticut, New Jersey, and Delaware combined has been converted into new housing developments, industrial complexes, shopping centers, highways, water reservoirs, and other uses (U.S. Congress 1980). Federal land-use legislation was first proposed in the early 1970s and more specific federal farmlands protection legislation was first proposed in Congress in 1979 and 1980. In 1981, Congress passed the Farmlands Protection Act. In addition, there has been action taken by the executive branch of federal government and some states and local governments have adopted farmlands protection programs.

The World Conservation Strategy (1980), prepared jointly by the International Union for Conservation of Nature and Natural Resources, the United Nations Environment Programme, and the World Wildlife Fund, gave top priority to reserving good cropland for crops. According to the authors of this report:

> In view of the scarcity of high quality arable land and the rising demand for food and other agricultural products, land that is most suitable for crops should be reserved for agriculture. This will reduce the pressure on ecologically fragile marginal lands which tend to degrade rapidly beyond their productive capacities. However, this require-

ment may conflict with urban, industrial, energy or transport policy. There are many examples of prime farmland drowned by dams or lost to airports, roads, factories or housing. Without careful planning and zoning, human settlements sited in farming areas are bound to encroach on farmlands as they expand. Such conflict should be anticipated and where possible avoided. Since it is not possible to resite high quality cropland but it is possible to be flexible about the siting of buildings, roads and other structures agriculture as a general rule should have precedence (International Union for Conservation of Nature and Natural Resources 1980).

While many publications have addressed the issue of the loss of agricultural land, "Protecting Farmlands" concentrates on various approaches for agricultural land retention. The focus is on the United States, though several international experiences are included. This volume is intended for use by people interested in protecting agriculture. Protecting farmland is an interest of local, state, and federal government officials, farmers, weekend gardeners, agribusiness managers, and laborers. Also, farming is a way of life for many people. As well, agriculture is a factor in many economies, whether in the United States, Canada, or abroad. It is time for agriculture's importance to become explicit in the minds of all people in the United States. Successful land-use planning practices on all levels can slow the rate of farmland conversion to other uses, providing time for a renewed look at agriculture's importance both in our lifetime and in our children's.

James Jeffords (Chapter 1) asks whose issue the loss of United States cropland is? Although the issue of agricultural land depletion via conversion has been widely reported, "experts" continue to dispute the severity of this resource loss. Recent evidence supporting this issue focuses on the amount of readily convertible land for tillage; increasing world population and the corresponding increase in the world food demand; availability of exportable food products for continuing the United States' balance of trade; and the decreasing probability for advanced agricultural technology counterbalancing the loss of cultivatable land. Congressman Jeffords asserts that directions in negating this loss point toward mediation of high impact rural growth and change, the need to protect the diversified structure of agriculture, and the development of new approaches to protect farmland.

Joanne Jackson (Chapter 2) reviews public awareness of major land-use issues. She insists that effective land-use planning entails public awareness. Legislation dealing with public information and public participation has recently increased on federal, state, and local levels. Jackson presents four general principles to guide planners in developing positive public awareness of land-use issues: honesty, the clear presentation of alternatives, an understanding of impacts, and a knowledge of the people affected. Each of these applies to the protection of farmland as well as other land-use issues.

John Keene (Chapter 3) reviews the important legal aspects of farmland protection. The recent upsurge of agricultural land retention programs calls for a serious look into the legal aspects on which these programs should be based. Many suburban municipalities have initiated comprehensive growth management programs that allow for development while protecting agriculturally and environmentally significant land areas. Safeguards to building a legally supportive farmland protection program concern the prior consideration, through inclusion, of state and local agriculture-related policies in comprehensive data gathering and planning. A balance of developable land must be provided for the continuation of beneficial growth including ample provision for low and moderate income housing.

Neil Sampson (Chapter 4) explores the ethical dimension of farmland protection. As he points out, the search for a land ethic in America is not new or novel.

It has been the basis for the conservation movement from the beginning. Sampson believes a new land ethic must be a product of education and social evolution. It cannot be written, legislated, or imposed on people.

Roger Blobaum (Chapter 5) maintains that efforts to preserve farmland on the urban fringe must also work toward protecting the family farm as an enterprise of local importance. Blobaum promotes the creation of a metropolitan food plan similar to growth management plans for urban areas. Through the intention of its elements, this plan would accomplish a three-way connection among the economic viability of small farms, the preservation of farmland in the urban fringe, and the food needs of urban consumers.

Part II of "Protecting Farmlands" presents local approaches for farmland protection. William Toner (Chapter 6) suggests three guidelines to be applied to programs for maintaining farms and farmland: ensuring the success of a farmland preservation program means that the agricultural community must play a central role throughout; conventional planning tools and techniques have proved successful in protecting farmland and may be even more effective when combined; and ensuring that farmland is protected requires the provision for satisfying urban development needs as well. In the course of his examination of local farmland protection programs, Toner discovered that most successful programs shared these basic planning guidelines.

Jack Kartez (Chapter 7) maintains that the emergence of farmland protection as a major planning objective has spurred a renaissance of innovations in zoning as planners struggle to mold conventional zoning techniques into a workable tool for rural counties. Rural agricultural counties must rely on the exercises of the police power through zoning, rather than on expensive development rights purchase techniques. In recent years, rural counties have encountered common problems and discovered similar solutions in efforts to adapt zoning (a primarily urban concept) to rural conditions. Three examples of problems and solutions are identified here: innovative density limits in agricultural zoning districts; special use provisions needed in agricultural zones; and trends in state provisions for local agricultural zoning.

Although development rights programs may be too expensive for rural counties, they may be the only alternative for urban counties wishing to protect farms and farmlands. John Spellman (Chapter 8) reviews the purchase of development rights program in King County, Washington. Through the enabling ordinance, various priorities for purchases were established and designated. Lands designated to the highest priority are those threatened by development, thereby falling into the first round category, and so forth. The value of the development right is determined by subtracting appraised value of the farm from its value at its fair market price. The development rights solution is permanent, yet benefits the farm community economically by compensating the farmer while consequently lowering the price of the farmland so that young people and others can afford to enter the field.

In contrast to urban King County is rural Whitman County, also in Washington. William Wagner (Chapter 9) reviews agricultural land preservation in Whitman County, where grains, legumes, and beef cattle are the primary agricultural products. The sale of these commodities supports the local economy of 15 small towns and 20,000 people. It also contributes to the economy of the major town of the county, Pullman, which has a population of 23,500 and is the home of Washington State University. The preservation of agricultural land is favored for the immediate reason that conflicting land uses tend to negatively impact the income potential of individual farmers. On a broader plane, the Palouse region, of which Whitman County is the center, is a highly productive dryland farming area, which will remain an important agricultural area long after energy and irrigation problems seriously impact marginal and irrigated farmland elsewhere.

Somewhere between the rural character of Whitman County and the urban character of King, is York County, Pennsylvania. William Conn (Chapter 10) reviews York County's approach for protecting prime agricultural land. York County was experiencing an increase in the conversion of small family farms into subdivisions. County officials searched for a protection technique that was simple and quick and could be understood and implemented by the county's municipalities. Development rights, easements, and tax programs do not meet those criteria. However, zoning regulations do.

Black Hawk County, Iowa, also uses zoning regulations based on a combination of factors. Larry Larsen and Sonia Johannsen (Chapter 11) discuss the cornerstone of that program, corn suitability ratings. This method was developed using soil classification types with crop productivity for the purpose of identifying and preserving the best land in the county.

The third part of "Protecting Farmlands" focuses on middleground and state approaches. Charles Little (Chapter 12) reviews middleground approaches between traditional zoning and expensive development rights programs. These approaches may be applied through action at either the local or state level. The Wisconsin farmland preservation law is innovative because it combines tax relief for farmers with incentives for local governments to adopt agricultural preservation plans and exclusive agricultural zoning ordinances. James Johnson (Chapter 13) illustrates the program's uniqueness, in that preservation is achieved with traditional land-use tools, and implementation is at the local level.

Oregon is another state with a unique program to protect farmland. Ronald Eber (Chapter 14) shows how the protection of farmland is connected to Oregon's statewide planning program. The people of Oregon have determined that it is in the state's interest to protect the resource foundation of its largest industry, agriculture. Mr. Eber briefly explains Oregon's land-use program; sets forth the seven major components he believes are essential to any effort to protect agricultural lands and how Oregon's program addresses these; and finally makes some more general comments and observations on Oregon's experience in implementing its program since 1974.

Mark Lapping reviews the experience of northeastern states in Chapter 15. Professor Lapping reviews the changes in farming that have occurred during the past century in the oldest agricultural region of the nation. He shows how the number of farms, the total land in farms, and the percentage of total land area in farms in the region have all decreased. These changes are linked to evolving policy regarding farmlands.

Richard Dunford (Chapter 16) reviews state tax relief programs. Farmers located along the urban fringe and other areas affected by development pressure often have the ability to reduce that pressure through differential assessment of property value. Forty-eight states have some type of current use-value assessment program available for farmland owners. However, the success of these programs, unless accompanied by additional measures to protect farmland, appears to be limited to strongly rural areas or highly productive agricultural regions.

The fourth part concentrates on the federal government's involvement in farmland protection. The changing role of the federal government in farmland retention is reviewed by Wendell Fletcher (Chapter 17). In recent years, mounting concern about the loss of farmland has resulted in increased federal activity. Both Congress and the executive branch have begun to adopt new federal policies that could facilitate retention of high quality agricultural land in the future.

Norman Berg and Warren Zitzmann (Chapter 18) review the evolution of land-use policy in the U.S. Department of Agriculture. The USDA was involved in land-use issues long before the initiation by Congress of action for land-use planning in the early 1970s. In 1973 the USDA began a program of developing their interests through regional workshops on planning functions and the formation of statewide land use committees. Through further action, the USDA initiated a mapping program conducted by the Soil Conservation Service for the identification of the nation's "important farmland." Furthermore, the USDA reaches into rural areas through a network of qualified people competent in protecting natural resources.

A National Agricultural Lands Study was initiated by President Carter. Robert Gray (Chapter 19) explains the interagency cooperation of this study, sponsored jointly by the secretary of the USDA and the chairman of the Council on Environmental Quality with support from nine additional federal departments and agencies. The study relied heavily on public involvement and existing data. Its final report was made to the president in January 1981.

Raymond Dideriksen (Chapter 20) explains the SCS Important Farmlands Mapping Program. Prime farmland accounts for a large share of the cropland acreage of the United States and is more productive than nonprime farmland. In light of this, the SCS has begun to inventory those areas containing farmland of national importance (prime and unique) and of statewide and local importance. The mapping inventory provides a list of soils that qualify as prime farmland and important farmland maps, as well as statistical data on prime farmlands for both the county and state levels.

The final part focuses on the international experience in farmland protection. Five Canadian provinces (Manitoba, Saskatchewan, Alberta, British Columbia, and Ontario) have developed land-use and tenure programs. These programs are designed to protect farmlands for future agricultural production, maintain the family farm, and perpetuate the owner-operator rather than tenant-operator form of tenancy. Land tenure patterns in many provinces are changing as the number of farms operated by full owners declines. Carol Bray (Chapter 21) reviews how provincial legislation can check the reallocation of agricultural land to nonagricultural uses.

Dallas Miner, Martin Chorich, and Mark Lapping (Chapter 22) show how several European nations, Israel, and Taiwan, which are undergoing the sort of urban sprawl common in America, have taken measures to preserve agricultural land. Frederick Steiner (Chapter 23) focuses on the efforts of the Netherlands. The Netherlands provides an especially interesting example of a nation approaching farmland protection because it is densely populated yet highly productive agriculturally.

The thrust of all the chapters is toward the wiser use of agricultural land resources. This goal may be accomplished on a variety of jurisdictional levels by many means. A helpful starting point is an understanding of successful approaches for the protection of farmland.

References

Best, R. 1979. Land-Use Structure and Change in the ECC, *Town Planning Review* **50**, 395–411.

International Union for Conservation of Nature and Natural Resources. 1980. "World Conservation Strategy," prepared in cooperation with United Nations Environment Programme and the World Wildlife Fund, Gland, Switzerland.

MacGregor, R. 1980. The Vanishing Land, *MacLean's* pp. 46–53 (May 12).

U.S. Congress. 1980. Agricultural Land Protection Act, *Congressional Record* **126**, (February 6 and 7).

Part I

Overview of Farmlands Protection

1

The Loss of U.S. Cropland: Whose Issue Is It?

James M. Jeffords

The jigsaw puzzle is beginning to come together.

Out of many differing perspectives regarding agricultural land issues, and from recent local and national studies of the problems, causes, and potential solutions, a broad and helpful composite is beginning to emerge.

That composite I believe will at last help America decide what actions are needed at what levels. It has been put together with the help of many Americans who are not traditional allies.

A few of the puzzle pieces have been set in place by farmers and ranchers who want to continue in agriculture, but face strong pressures to sell out and to let the land serve some other community purposes. Other pieces have been fitted on the board by landowners who see in any farmland preservation movement the specter of federal intervention in land-use decisions. They fear losing their greatest financial asset, their equity in the land. Other puzzle pieces have been added by conservationists who are alarmed by the possibility of America's running out of enough farmland, a strategic and irreplaceable resource.

A few sections have been assembled by people who look at the expanse of American land or at aggregate charts or tables and are convinced that land could never be a limiting factor in food and fiber production.

Fiercely competing for some puzzle pieces at the edge are people who believe in energy production and question the need for spending extra dollars for reclamation, and other people who fear the effects of mining and mining boom towns on agriculture or who are suspicious that new-fangled biomass plantations may seriously impact on agriculture.

Finally, a few corner pieces have joined together by citizens who already have formed farmland retention programs, and by state and federal officials who are aware that some of their actions may have had a negative impact on agriculture.

No, the picture is not yet complete. Yet it is far enough along that, despite differing interests and views, we need to begin arriving at enough of a consensus to act responsibly.

The Emerging Perspective

What is the composite view? Do we have a farmland crisis today? The answer is no.

But that is the same answer you would have received ten or 15 years ago if you had asked if there were an energy crisis.

Had we begun dealing with that issue before it became a crisis, the difficulties our nation, and much of the world, faces today could have been alleviated. We waited too long. We began floundering for solutions only after we began to feel the severe impacts of dwindling traditional energy sources. We had to pass up some of the best solutions because it was too late.

I want to help our nation avoid a similar crisis in farmland productivity. We do have time to act in a reasonable manner. We have some time to alter the course, in ways that will not compromise the legitimate interests or concerns of any group of Americans.

We are seeing the permanent shift of up to 3 million acres (1,215,000 ha) of farmland a year to other uses. We have 24 million acres (9,720,000 ha) of reserve farmland, or potential cropland. That reserve provides a buffer. It is diminishing rapidly, but it is still large enough to allow us to begin addressing the issue in a reasonable way, to protect America's ability to produce sufficient food and fiber without infringing on legitimate individual rights.

We have a 6 in. (152.4 mm) average layer of topsoil. That is not much; it is less than half of what our first settlers discovered and used. But we do have time to begin rebuilding that productive soil without regimenting America's farmers into a maze of bureaucratic regulations from Washington, D.C., or from a state capital.

However, we must take advantage of the time margin available to us. We must not wait until prices for food and fiber products are unreasonably and uncontrollably high, or until serious regional or national shortages occur for some products.

We must not wait until businesses that serve and supply agriculture are forced to close because there are too few rural customers.

We must not wait until the strategically important food and fiber exports of the United States are jeopardized, crimping our balance of trade and our efforts to promote world peace.

We must not wait until the standard of living for middle-income Americans is substantially lowered because a much higher proportion of family income needs to be spent on food. The cost to taxpayers of programs to meet the nutritional needs of low-income Americans would rise out of sight.

If America does wait too long, the only solutions available will be drastic ones: solutions that will trample the rights of individual landowners and rural residents, and solutions that still may jeopardize our role as the world's breadbasket.

So whose issue is farmland retention?

It is an issue of supreme importance to everybody who shops for food, or grows or sells food. It deserves the attention of everyone who works for local, state, or federal government. It deserves the attention of those who want to limit the size and influence of government. It deserves the attention of everyone who lives close to productive farmland, or on it, as well as those who have little or no agriculture nearby. It is the issue of every taxpayer.

No Longer One Question

Farmland retention is an issue that must be treated in the broadest possible economic, social, and environmental context rather than as a single question. The supply and condition of farmland are affected by numerous complex and often indirect variables.

As stated in a recent U.S. Department of Agriculture (USDA) report on the structure of agriculture:

> There have been a number of fundamental changes in the environment in which farmers produce our food, feed, and fiber. One of these basic changes is that agriculture is no longer—if it ever was—an isolated part of the economy whose problems could be addressed separately without consideration of the influences of other forces on farming and the effects of the farm economy on the rest of society. The connections among the various parts of the U.S. economy and the various parts of the world have become so much broader and so much more direct that it no longer makes sense to think about our agriculture (as an isolated segment).

The USDA study found that

> Even the programs which were designed to protect the farm sector accelerated and continue to reinforce trends that push families out of farming, keep new farmers out, and concentrate control of the resources that produce our food into the hands of fewer persons.

All Americans have the responsibility to see that these trends are reversed, and that all sectors of American society are treated fairly. We must *minimize* the need for expensive federal programs to repair natural resource mistakes, and *maximize* the number of food-and-fiber production options that remain available to cope with an uncertain future.

Let me underscore the point that all parts of American society deserve fair treatment.

In our free society, it would be counterproductive and contrary to our American ideals to stifle legitimate rights of those who own land and those who produce food, or to centralize in Washington, D.C., the powers traditionally reserved for state and local government.

If we fail to optimize agricultural productivity, because we have not worked to minimize land conversion from agriculture and to maximize soil conservation, then food prices will rise substantially, particularly if high farm exports continue.

The impacts will not be shared equally by the public, however. The poorest one-fifth of American households spend about 40% of family income on food, while the one-fifth who have the highest incomes spend only about 10% on food.

Thus, rising food costs would have a much greater impact on disadvantaged families, and would impede efforts to improve living standards and to reduce federal outlays on assistance programs.

The solution, then, requires that all segments of our society work together to slow the unnecessary loss of productive agriculture.

The Facts of Farmland Conversion

Although conversion of agricultural land is clearly a national problem, it is one that can be most clearly recognized and dealt with at the regional, state, and local levels. National statistics are helpful, but are mainly an accumulation of factors that are not identical in all parts of the country.

Local solutions are likely to be the most effective, where those solutions are forthcoming.

In New England, the conversion of farmland to nonagricultural uses already has been so widespread that the region imports over 80% of its food. The result? By the best projections food prices are 10–15% higher than they would be if commodities were produced in New England.

Florida lost nearly 15% of its agricultural land base in just one 10-year period.

In Michigan, 8 million acres (3,240,000 ha) of farmland would be required to fill the state's estimated needs for agricultural production in the year 2000. Yet even now, far less than that acreage is in production, and if recent trends continue, farmland acreage in Michigan will drop to about 4.7 million acres (1,903,500 ha) by the year 2000, a 41% shortfall.

In the state of Washington, one county well suited to agriculture and having a strong demand for food and fiber predicts that agriculture there will gradually disappear, unless new farmers can make money after amortizing their startup costs.

Other states and localities have provided similarly disturbing testimo-

Fig. 1.1 Subdivision south of Vallejo, California, which has completely incorporated valley lands and is encroaching on the dairy in the background.

ny. Local government officials and community leaders have begun to recognize the dangers to their communities. They have begun to recognize the need for local communities to take the lead in setting their own goals and priorities, based not just on the supply of available land, but also on a careful evaluation of their total agricultural environment.

The Role of the Federal Government

As a member of Congress, my own primary involvement in this issue has been to work for a constructive federal role.

That is not, and should not be, the lead role. Even from a Washington, D.C., perspective, it is clear to me that the federal government is too remote from local situations and perspectives to exert strict controls that could be fair, constructive, and reasonable. The agricultural environment in Monkton Landing, Vermont, is too different from the agricultural environment in Dade County, Florida. Even if congressmen and bureaucrats were the most brilliant people on earth, a premise that is increasingly subject to challenge, we could not devise and implement a detailed agricultural policy that makes sense for both of these localities.

But that does not mean Washington, D.C., can or should ignore the problems. Agricultural productivity is, after all, a national challenge of enormous consequence. The challenge for the federal government then is to find and carry out a role that will be helpful without being intrusive. Local leaders of farmland protection efforts repeatedly have told us in Washington, D.C., that they need help. Even at the local level, where problems are fairly clearly defined, addressing the issue in a meaningful way is a complex task. Technical help is needed, and information must be assembled, before an informed local decision can be made. What steps have been tried by other communities which are similar to ours? Have these steps been successful or not? What would be the likely financial cost? Arriving at technically sound answers to questions such as these is beyond the resources of many local communities.

What is more, many ideas for agricultural land retention have not been adequately tried in all types of communities. A town or county with an extremely limited tax base is justifiably reluctant to risk substantial local resources in order to serve as a guinea pig. Federal assistance for pilot projects, which would have a negligible impact on the federal treasury, could vastly increase the information base which communities need in order to make their own local decisions.

A constructive federal policy would include the following components:

1. Minimize the impact of federal programs on the conversion of productive agricultural land.

2. Reassess federal farm programs, reshaping them to encourage sound conservation practices rather than providing financial incentives for destruction of topsoil.

3. Inventory the problem on a national scale, to fit together the remaining unassembled puzzle pieces and provide a more sound national perspective on the extent of the problem and the time frame available for reversal of destructive trends.

4. Inventory the solutions that have been tried by various states and localities, and objectively evaluate the success or failure of those efforts.

5. Provide financial assistance to communities that wish to try novel or untested approaches as pilot projects, to add to the body of valuable information needed by other communities in order to make informed decisions.

6. Encourage communities and individuals to set goals and priorities that respect natural resources, and to plan in accord with natural systems.

7. Provide technical assistance to states and communities in determining the amount of agricultural land they will need in order to produce needed goods and sustain agriculture-related business and industry.

8. Achieve better coordination among agencies and among the various levels of government so that they do not work at cross purposes.

Can We Meet the Challenge?

Farmland retention is an issue that is frustrating to deal with, because the problems and solutions are so complex. There is no magic wand to wave or a single new federal law that can solve the problem once and for all. The ultimate solution, if there is one, can come only through interaction of virtually all segments of American society and all levels of government.

That will happen only through some sort of national awakening. Most Americans give relatively little thought now to the decline of our nation's farmland. The issue must be brought into the nation's consciousness, the way the problems of air and water pollution were brought into the national consciousness in the early 1970s. Perhaps another Earth Day, with an emphasis on farmland, is in order.

We can head off rude awakenings if we act in time.

I am encouraged by the growing number of community leaders and government officials at local and state levels who have promoted constructive action. As a group, they are the people who can and should be the leaders of this effort.

Congress, as a whole, has been less willing to exercise foresight and to deal with problems until they become crises. But constructive action there will continue to be among my own highest legislative priorities. In the 95th and 96th Congresses, I began with a concurrent resolution about the importance of agricultural land, on which I had 76 original cosponsors. A Senate version, led by Senator Hatfield, had more than 35 cosponsors. I will continue to try to provide the linkage between farm policy and farmland retention. Other legislation is needed to address questions of research, tax and other incentives, technical information and educational initiatives, and interagency coordination as well as strengthened overall agricultural policy.

The role of Washington, D.C., is a small one compared to the combined efforts at the state and community levels, but positive congressional action is essential to the overall solution.

The challenge is tremendous. But it is achievable. A large enough portion of the puzzle has been put together so that all of us who take the trouble to look at it should be able to arrive at a reasonable consensus as to what our respective roles should be.

We have little time. Let us begin now, while that is still true.

2

Public Involvement in Land-Use Planning

Joanne Barnes Jackson

It is possible that every generation since the Industrial Revolution has considered itself the victim of great change. Certainly this generation has reason to think so. Some of the profound changes it is facing are closely related to increased population and competition for scarce resources; others have their roots in the historic tradition of popular control over government. Since the uses of land are the visible interface between a population and its resources, many of the changes taking place today are expressed in how land is used and public attitudes toward these uses. (The term "population" is used here in the widest possible sense: it means not only people, but also the philosophy and the culture of those people.)

"Land use" is one of those terms that seems to have sneaked into the American vocabulary in the 1960s. Although the term is self-defining, it is not yet a household word. Even those of us who use the term daily use it in a variety of ways. My colleagues frequently debate the question of land use and marinas. Are marinas a land use or a water use? Can one use the term "land use" to refer to both land and water uses? For the purposes of this chapter, the term "land" will be used to refer to any part of the earth's surface. Land-use issues, therefore, are issues concerning the ways in which people employ land, and land-use planning pertains to premediated decisions to use land, hopefully, wisely.

Land-use planning generally involves establishing a list of land uses that the population of a given area needs or desires. Consideration is given to future needs and desires as well as present ones. When this selection of land uses is completed, planners make an inventory of the land to determine its capabilities. Then the desired land uses are matched with the available land and a plan is made. This last step has traditionally involved a large, detailed map or a series of maps (Geddes 1968 orig. 1915; Lynch 1962; McHarg 1969). The success of the plan must be judged by its degree of implementation. No matter how technically sound, or even brilliant, an unimplemented plan is a failure of one variety or other.

This type of land-use planning is relatively new. Although planning seems to have played a part in human actions from the very beginning, land-use planning for regions did not become an issue until populations became large enough to produce conflicts over how land was to be used. This occurred at different times in different parts of the world. Town and country planning in England, for instance, is usually traced to the Industrial Revolution (Benevolo 1971). As population increased, labor became more specialized, so that people who earned their living doing one thing (manufacturing light bulbs, for example) had little knowledge or contact with individuals who made their living differently (by farming, say). This has resulted in the children of light bulb manufacturers thinking that oranges are produced in plastic bags in a factory on the other side of town and that french fries come from a factory in the far north, near where ice cream is made. The children of the farmers believe that light bulbs grow on bushes in the south. Although this is an exaggeration, the point is that we cannot assume that even adult light bulb manufacturers and adult potato farmers, no matter how well intentioned, will agree with each other about land-use decisions. They are almost certain to express different views if they ever find themselves at a planning meeting or a public hearing concerning land use.

This kind of controversy is not new. I imagine that anyone who is involved with land-use planning has witnessed, if not taken part in, similar disagreements. Yet these kinds of disputes are bound to continue, and perhaps to grow more vehement, as more and more members of our highly specialized society seek direct citizen involvement in land-use decisions when they become disenchanted with administrative decision making.

Legislation Concerning Citizen Involvement

Votes have never been a particularly effective means for citizens to control government. As popular disillusion with government has increased, legislative and executive responses have been to provide citizen involvement programs, as well as access for and accountability to citizens. The Federal Administrative Procedure Act of 1946 is frequently cited (e.g., Rosenbaum 1976) as the beginning of our present citizens participation practices. This act, with its amendments, was the first to make public hearings mandatory. The trend was continued in the Freedom of Information Act of 1966 and the National Environmental Policy Act of 1969 (NEPA). Both these later acts established new information and accountability obligations for federal agencies and gave citizens the right to have these obligations judicially enforced. So, although NEPA did not mandate the public to be aware of major federal land-use issues, it did require planners to be aware of and accountable to the public. Almost every piece of federal environmental legislation passed since NEPA (for example, the recent clean water, clean air, coastal zone, and surface mine reclamation legislation) has had increased provisions for public information and public participation programs. This type of requirement is also seen at the state and local levels.

The emphasis on public participation has reached almost alarming proportions. I recently saw a Request for Proposals calling for training of public participation program leaders. The scope of work indicated quite clearly that the sponsoring agency was not particularly interested in having program leaders deal with the issues that might arise in public participation programs. Rather, the agency was primarily concerned with increasing the leaders' ability to manipulate the participants through a variety of subtle psychological techniques. Though I find this approach distasteful, it is not surprising that public participation programs are moving in this direction. All types of government agencies have learned that they must deal with direct citizen involvement and that a citizen or group of citizens can veto a project they do not like. This can be done either by direct opposition or by slowing a project down until it becomes economically unfeasible.

A planning colleague of mine is so painfully aware of this problem that he frequently daydreams about doing land-use plans for large totalitarian countries. When questioned, he explains that these countries are bigger than the state he is currently planning for, and, more importantly, that the authoritarian form of government makes implementation of any plan infinitely easier than in the United States.

The conclusion to all of this is simply that given our form of government and current legislation, the public must be involved in land-use planning and they should be involved in a positive fashion that will facilitate equitable decisions.

The methods that can be used to help bring about this idyllic state of affairs vary from region to region and project to project, but there are some general principles for increasing positive public awareness of any project. The theorems presented below should aid in the establishment of wiser land-use practices.

Four Theorems of Public Participation

My experience as a planner and a consultant has led me to formulate four basic principles of public participation. I will present each of these theorems, and then apply them to the issue of farmland preservation. The first theorem is basic: "Be honest and straightforward." Almost all plans contain elements that are offensive to at least one segment of the population. Too many planners try to deny this. If you bend the truth, someone in your vast, but not always visible, audience will see what you are doing. If that person or those persons are opposed to the program you are proposing, they can, and probably will, use your truth bending as an example of your general unreliability.

This first theorem has a collateral concept. Not only must one be honest, but the project must be necessary. This means that one must know and be able to demonstrate that whatever project or plan one is proposing is better than not doing the project or plan. Many land-use planners include what is called the "null or do nothing alternative" in their presentations. The null alternative portrays what will happen if no plan is made or intervention attempted. Needless to say, the difference between the plan and the null alternative should be obvious to all. Theorem 2 is "Know your public." If one wants your public to be aware of and responsive to the plan or program, one must know who will be affected by a plan or a proposed course of action, and one must be able to recommend strategies that will lessen any potential negative impacts. Knowledge of citizens' rights and responsiveness to citizen desires are fundamental to democracy. If public policy ignores public preferences, the motivation for compliance is lost.

Knowing the public also means being aware of how the decision making process operates in your region. This is not always as obvious as the diagrams in political science textbooks indicate. In most areas, seemingly unimportant social organizations (for example, garden clubs) distribute information, usually verbally, and help mold public opinion.

The third theorem is "Know the cultural attitudes that may bear on the project." This theorem is related to the second one. There are countless examples of doomed plans and projects that were predestined to fail because the planners did not recognize and assimilate into their plans the underlying values of the people they were dealing with.

The fourth theorem is "Public awareness of land use increases with negative impacts from land use." This theorem explains why so many public participation programs have attracted only those who are opposed to the proposed projects. Although there are all kinds of possible positive and negative impacts associated with various projects, direct negative economic impacts will claim the most public attention and action. Recent increases in the price of gasoline prices are an example of this. We have all heard for years that we should conserve gas by driving cars that give better gas mileage, yet most Americans did not buy more efficient cars until gas prices rose abruptly.

Applications for Farmland Preservation

These four theorems should be the cornerstone of any public awareness or public participation project or program. Their general applicability to farmland protection programs is presented below. Let us go back to Theorem One: be honest and straightforward and certain that your project is necessary and worthwhile. Those of you who work with farmland preservation may be scrupulously honest, but are you convincing your public that the protection of farmland is necessary? What will happen if farmlands are not preserved? Will the conversion of farmland to other land uses result in serious adverse economic impacts? Will these impacts be greater than the adverse economic impacts that will be sustained by protecting farmland?

To those not directly involved in farmland preservation, the answers to these questions are not obvious. For example, I remember long and complicated passages in economics textbooks dealing with government aid to farmers (Samuelson 1970). Although I never fully understood the policies, I remember being quite convinced that the result of most agricultural policy meant the Americans paid taxes to ensure that they would have to pay higher prices for food. Since "Economics" is one of the best-selling textbooks of all times, it would not be surprising if many others shared this view.

Even if giant surpluses are a thing of the past, there are other aspects of the need for farmland preservation that must be made clear to citizens. Are we really losing farmland as fast as some experts claim we are? And is that loss irrevocable? Small-scale farming is attracting considerable interest. Books on the subject (Langer 1972; Kains 1973; Thomas 1976) indicate that the typical 1-acre suburban lawn in most parts of the United

States can be converted to vegetable gardens that will sustain a family of four. The public needs to know that these strategies will not work before it believes that the loss of farmland is irrevocable.

Honesty also requires that the distinction between family farms and large-scale agribusiness be acknowledged. Because the family farm occupies a cherished space in American folklore, farmland preservation efforts often try to capitalize on the image of the happy wholesome farm family even when larger-scale agribusinesses are the benefactors. At the very best, this type of approach is guilty of mixing metaphors.

The second theorum stressed knowing your public. Who will benefit from your plan, who will suffer from it? This may be the most difficult part of a planner's job. The planner must not only know all segments of his or her public and their relationship to their land, but also be able to devise strategies to mitigate the suffering of those adversely impacted by the proposed change. I recently heard of a county in an eastern state that tried to implement a series of ordinances designed to protect the agriculture of the county. Those responsible for the ordinances anticipated full public support. However, they found themselves facing serious opposition because most of the land being farmed was not owned by farmers, but by speculators interested in development.

Theorem three is concerned with values that may influence a project. Since this theorem is the least tangible of the four, let me present an example.

Recently, I completed a report for an eastern state that attempted to determine the potential for development for over 100 different land uses. The list of land uses was well balanced and nine land uses were considered in the harvest section. ("Harvest" was used as a major category instead of agriculture so that we could include commercial fishing.) The physical and economic requirements of each type of land use were presented in detail. Since the study was aimed at determining the development potential of currently undeveloped areas, the definition of an undeveloped area proved to be the source of considerable disagreement. Although there were a number of objections, the state officials finally decided that farmland is undeveloped land even though eight types of agriculture were presented in the study as potential types of development.

This type of myopia is common. The American idea of progress frequently means that farmland is not considered a real land use; rather, it is viewed as an interim use, something that occurs prior to development. Progress (with a capital "P") will "improve" farmland, transforming it into houses, streets, factories, and the like. This false perception has been strengthened by many departments of community and regional planning that came into being in the post-World War II building boom. While they talked about ecology and the specter of uncontrolled growth, these schools sent many graduates out to transform pastures into subdivisions.

The fourth theorem states that public awareness increases with negative impacts. This theorem can be used to explain the popularity of farmland preservation plans among farmers. It also predicts that urbanites will support farmland preservation plans nationally when we see national food prices rise as a result of scarcity; or that they will support local farmland preservation when transportation costs make food grown in other regions prohibitively expensive. Price increases due to price supports or middleman profits will not produce sympathy for farmers or farmlands protection.

In areas where there is a severe shortage of housing or chronic unemployments, the situation may be somewhat more complicated. Most people, it seems to me, would prefer to have a job or a place to live in the location of their choice rather than have relatively inexpensive food grown locally. If this is true, perhaps farmland preservation should be considered on a regional basis only where the benefits of such programs can be made comprehensible to the people of that region.

Conclusions

America's vastness has fostered a complacency about land. The sheer size of the country has allowed us to treat land casually. But, the threat of famine and increased conflicts over food are very real and have been discussed at length (Borgstrom 1967 and 1971; Meadows 1972; Meadows 1974; Brown 1974; and Ophuls 1977). However, many of farmland preservation projects I know have either floundered or failed.

Land-use planners can play a major role in changing complacent attitudes toward land and in preserving farmland. There must be changes made in the perception of farmland, one that recognizes farms as an important land use, if such land is to be preserved. But it may not be easy. The process of gaining broad-based public support can be long and tiresome. It requires keen minds and hard work. It also requires honesty, the clear presentation of alternatives, and a thorough understanding of the impacts. Yet the future appears to be promising. Attitudes and practices do seem to be changing. The recent concern over energy has shown us that public opinion and actions can change quickly. Although it is reassuring to know that Americans can respond to crisis, it seems wiser to plan to avoid crises when we can.

References

Benevolo, L. 1971. "The Origins of Modern Town Planning" (J. Landry, Tr.) MIT Press, Cambridge, MA.

Borgstrom, G. 1967. "The Modern World at the Edge of Famine." Collier, New York.

Borgstrom, G. 1971. "Too Many: An Ecological Overview of the Earth's Limitations." Collier, New York.

Brown, L.R. 1974. "By Bread Alone." Praeger, New York.

Geddes, P. 1968. "Cities in Evolution: An Introduction to the Town Planning Movement and to the Study of Cities." Harper Torchbooks, New York.

Kains, M.G. 1973. "Five Acres and Independence." Dover Publications, Inc., New York.

Langer, R.W. 1973. "Grow It!" Avon Books, New York.

Lynch, K. 1962. "Site Planning." MIT Press, Cambridge, MA.

Meadows, D.L., et al. 1974. "The Dynamics of Growth in a Finite World." Wright-Allen, Cambridge, MA.

Meadows, D.H., et al. 1972. "The Limits to Growth." Universe Books, New York.

McHarg, I.L. 1969. "Design with Nature." Natural History Press, Garden City, New York.

Ophuls, W. 1977. "Ecology and the Politics of Scarcity: Prologue to a Political Theory of the Steady State." W.H. Freeman, San Francisco.

Rosenbaum, N.M. 1976. "Citizen Involvement in Land Use Governance: Issues and Methods." The Urban Institute, Washington, D.C.

Samuelson, P.A. 1975. "Economics," 8th Ed. McGraw-Hill Book Co., New York.

Thomas, S. 1976. "Backyard Livestock." The Countryman Press, Woodstock, VT.

3

Farmland Protection: Legal and Constitutional Issues[1]

John C. Keene

Major Classes of Approaches

This analysis of the legal aspects of agricultural land protection is organized according to the four major powers that are available to state and local governments: regulation, taxation, acquisition of interests in land, and the spending power. Regulation embraces zoning, subdivision regulation, pollution control, growth management, and the creation of agricultural districts. Governments enact tax incentives or otherwise shape their tax laws so as to reduce the pressure that taxes often create to convert farmland to noncrop uses. Several states and units of local governments have adopted programs for purchase of the development rights for agricultural land and the topic of land banking has received considerable attention in recent years. Finally, local governments may use sewer moratoria, control over provision of utilities, and capital improvement programs to deflect development from agriculturally important areas.

Legal Problems in Regulatory Programs for Protecting Agricultural Land

Is the Program Authorized by State Enabling Legislation?

The first question that must be answered by any farmland regulatory program is whether it is authorized by appropriate state legislation. Most agricultural municipalities lack a home rule charter and therefore have

---

[1]This chapter is a revision of an article with the same title which appeared in 15 *Gonzaga Law Review* 621 (1980) (and is printed here with the permission of the editors of *Gonzaga Law Review*), and a chapter in "The Protection of Farmland: A Reference Guidebook for State and Local Governments," Robert Coughlin and John Keene, senior authors and editors; J. Dixon Esseks, William Toner, and Lisa Rosenberger, authors, National Agricultural Lands Study Report, published by the U.S. Government Printing Office in 1981. The research covers developments occurring before June 1981.

only those powers that are expressly or impliedly delegated to them by the state legislature. The zoning enabling acts of most states, which are modeled after the Standard Zoning Enabling Act,[2] have sufficiently broad enabling language to make it probable that a court would construe them to authorize agricultural zoning. However, it may still be advisable to secure an amendment to a state's enabling act specifically permitting such a regulatory program as was done recently in Pennsylvania and New Jersey.

Several states, with Hawaii, California, Oregon, and Wisconsin the most notable examples, have enacted laws permitting or requiring such zoning. Others, such as New York, Maryland, Virginia, Illinois, and Minnesota (for the twin cities region) have authorized the creation of agricultural districts upon the petition of a sufficient number of farmers in a particular area.[3] At the local level, without any specific enabling act authorization, small municipalities have experimented with very large minimum lot size fixed and sliding scale area-based allocations combined with small residential lot size and exclusive agricultural zoning ordinances. The fixed area-based allocation technique includes the so-called quarter/quarter method that permits a farmer to reap some of the financial gain resulting from rising land values without severely disrupting agricultural operations. The farmer is permitted to develop 1 acre (0.405 ha) for a single family home for each 40 acres (16.2 ha) he owns. The sliding scale area-based allocation approach is a variation on the quarter/quarter idea. A farmer is allowed to develop individual lots but the number is determined according to a sliding scale under which the number of homes permitted per acre decreases as the size of his holding increases. For instance, Peach Bottom Township, Pennsylvania, adopted a sliding scale which permits one single family unit for the first 7 acres (2.84 ha) and one unit for each additional 50 acres (20.25 ha) up to a maximum of 19 for tracts of over 830 acres (336.15 ha).

In conclusion, the first step in the development of a regulatory program for protecting agricultural land is to determine whether it is authorized by enabling legislation. It appears that most uses of zoning for this purpose can find support in the typical enabling act, but it may be a desirable form of insurance to secure appropriate amendments expressly approving it.

Is It in Accordance with a Comprehensive Plan?

The draftsmen of the first zoning enabling act, passed in New York in 1914, as well as those of the Standard Zoning Enabling Act, realized that a comprehensive plan was an essential link between general police power objectives and regulations applicable to specific properties within each zoning district.[4] Any municipality that is embarking on a farmland protection program should undertake a comprehensive planning study on which the program will be based. This study should analyze trends in agricultural use, the importance of farming to the municipality's economy, and include soil and open space studies, and a review of state and

---

[2]U.S. Department of Commerce, *A Standard State Zoning Enabling Act* (rev. ed. 1926), reprinted in ALI, *Model Land Development Code* (tent. draft 1968).

[3]*See* Keene, John C., et al., *The Protection of Farmland: A Reference Book for State and Local Governments* (U.S. G.P.O.), 1981.

[4]*See* S. Toll, Zoned American 171, 233 (1969).

regional policies concerning agriculture and agricultural land preservation, as well as a more traditional examination of the factors that would be considered in a traditional growth management study. The comprehensive plan should be amended to reflect the findings of these analyses and the new farmland policies. Unless this is done, the municipality exposes itself to the risk of a successful attack by a landowner whose land had been zoned for development but is now restricted to agricultural use, on the grounds that the rezoning is not in accordance with the comprehensive plan.

One of the leading cases on the comprehensive plan requirement is *Udell v. Haas.*[5] The plaintiff's land had been rezoned from commercial to residential use, causing at least a 60% drop in value. Finding that the town had adopted a developmental policy that envisioned that the area where the plaintiff's land was located would be used for commercial development, the court held that the rezoning was not in accordance with a comprehensive plan. The court emphasized that the plan is the essence of zoning and provides the basis for a rational allocation of land use.

In recent years some state legislatures have enacted statutes that require local governments to adopt comprehensive plans.[6] Such a requirement was involved in the Oregon Supreme Court's decision in *Baker v. City of Milwaukie*, in which the court held:

> In summary, we conclude that a comprehensive plan is the controlling land-use planning instrument for a city (or county). Upon passage of a comprehensive plan, a city (or county) assumes a responsibility to effectuate that plan and conform prior conflicting zoning ordinances to it. We further hold that the zoning decisions of a city (or county) must be in accord with that plan and a zoning ordinance which allows a more intensive use than that prescribed in the plan must fail.[7]

Thus, as more and more states strengthen the role of comprehensive planning in land development regulation, it becomes increasingly important that local governments prepare an agricultural land protection program based on sound ecological, economic, and demographic data, and a careful articulation of state and local agricultural policies. If they fail to do this they run the risk of having agricultural zoning declared invalid for failure to meet the requirement that it be in accordance with a comprehensive plan.

Is There a Taking without Just Compensation?

If we assume that an agricultural land regulatory program is properly authorized by enabling legislation and is in accordance with a comprehensive plan, the principal constitutional hurdle it will have to surmount is the challenge that it constitutes a taking without just compensation. Whether such a program relies on exclusive agricultural zones or very large minimum lot sizes, it will often have the effect of significantly reducing the market value of the land so limited. Legal doctrines in this area are in a state of flux and legal commentators have developed several different theories, none of which is completely satisfactory.[8]

---

[5]21 N.Y. 2d 463, 235 N.E. 2d 897, 288 N.Y.S. 2d 888 (1968).
[6]Fishman, R., ed., Housing for All under Law 325–410 (1978).
[7]271 Or. 500, 533 P. 2d 772, 779 (1975).
[8]*See*, e.g., F. Bosselman, D. Callies, & J. Banta, *The Taking Issue* (1973); Kusler, Open Space Zoning: Valid Regulation or Invalid Taking?, 57 *Minn. L. Rev.* (1972). The basis of the issue is, or course, the interpretation of the requirements of the fifth amendment to the United States Constitution.

The Starting Point: Pennsylvania Coal Co. v. Mahon

The starting point in contemporary "taking" analysis is the 1922 decision of the U.S. Supreme Court in *Pennsylvania Coal Co. v. Mahon*.[9] The special circumstances of the case and the fact that Justice Brandeis dissented from Justice Holmes' decision suggest that it warrants careful analysis. The plaintiff, Mahon, sought an injunction to prevent the coal company from mining under his property in such a way as to remove its support and cause subsidence of the surface and his house. The coal company had sold the surface rights to the property to Mahon's predecessor in title in 1878 but had reserved the rights to remove all the coal underneath the surface, and its grantee had waived all claims for damages resulting from the mining of coal. Mahon claimed that the Kohler Act took away the coal company's right to mine under a residence owned by another party where such mining would cause subsidence of the surface. The trial court found that mining under Mahon's property would cause subsidence but denied an injunction since it destroyed the coal company's absolute right to remove its coal. The Pennsylvania Supreme Court reversed and granted the injunction, holding that the statute was a legitimate exercise of the policy power.

Justice Holmes identified the property interest involved as the right to mine coal and found that the Kohler Act destroyed that right by making it commercially impracticable to exercise it. He found that since the case involved a single private house and the threatened damage was not common or public, the coal company's activity of mining coal was not a public nuisance. He held that with respect to the Mahon's individual claim the public interest was not "sufficient to warrant so extensive a destruction of the [coal company's] constitutionally protected rights."[10]

Moving to broader questions raised by the Kohler Act that had been argued in the courts below, Justice Holmes held that the provisions that prohibited mining under streets and cities where the right to mine coal without providing support had been reserved were also unconstitutional. They destroyed the right to mine without having to provide support, which had been recognized by Pennsylvania courts as an estate in land. He reasoned that if the public authorities were so shortsighted as to acquire only the surface rights to build streets (and presumably pay less for them) they could not come before a court later and ask for rights of support without compensation.

The concluding paragraph of Justice Holmes' opinion is illuminating:

> We assume of course, that the statute was passed upon the conviction that an exigency existed that would warrant the exercise of eminent domain. But the question at bottom is upon whom the loss of the changes desired should fall. So far as private persons or communities have seen fit to take the risk of acquiring only surface rights, we cannot see that the fact that their risk has become a danger warrants the giving to them greater rights than they bought.[11]

The decision rests on Justice Holmes' conclusion that Mahon's predecessor had bought a property interest that carried with it certain risks. Having made that deal, he and his successors would not later be allowed to change it. Holmes' oft-quoted statement that "[t]he general rule at least is, that while property may be regulated to a certain extent, if regulation goes too far it will be recognized as a taking," does not appear

[9]260 U.S. 393 (1922).
[10]260 U.S. at 413.
[11]Id. at 416.

to be necessary to the holding in the case because there was a complete destruction of the property interest as he had characterized it, not a partial diminution in its value. In addition, the fact situation was, if not unique, certainly unusual in the there was a division of the fee interest and a specific assumption of the risk, which the plaintiffs later sought to avoid. Finally, the only individuals or municipalities protected by the Kohler Act were those who had specifically waived the right to support when they acquired the surface rights.

Justice Brandeis, on the other hand, began by characterizing mining that causes subsidence under public streets and the property of others as a public nuisance and therefore subject to legislative prohibition without compensation. "[R]estriction imposed to protect the public health, safety or morals from dangers threatened is not a taking. The restriction here in question is merely the prohibition of a noxious use."[13] "Restriction upon use does not become inappropriate as a means, *merely because it deprives the owner of the only use to which the property can then be profitably put.*"[14] He found that the Kohler Act was a reasonable exercise of the police power and would have granted the injunction.

In several other cases the Supreme Court has upheld police power regulations that significantly reduce the fair market value of specific properties.[15] Other than Mahon, the principal class of cases in which the Supreme Court has found that a taking occurred involved situations where the government had acquired property resources to facilitate uniquely public functions.[16] They can all be distinguished on that ground from efforts to preserve agricultural land by zoning.

Developments in the State Courts

In the years following the *Mahon* decision, taking doctrines were developed primarily in the state courts. The most commonly accepted line of analysis is well-exemplified by the New Jersey Supreme Court's reasoning in its 1963 decision, *Morris County Land Improvement Co. v. Township of Parsippany-Troy Hills.*[17] The court held that if a zoning ordinance so restricts the uses to which land can be put that it cannot be used for any reasonable profitable purpose, it constitutes a taking and therefore violates the fifth amendment's injunction that no property shall be taken for public use without just compensation. The *Morris* court examined the objective sought by the ordinance and balanced that objective against the harm to the owner's property rights. In this instance the court found that where the purpose and practical effect of the regulation is to appropriate private property the scales had been tipped. Here the detriment to the owner was found to outweigh the municipality's objective in regulation. It should be noted that the New Jersey Supreme Court subsequently suggested that this reasoning might require reexamination where vital ecological and environmental considerations are involved.[18]

---

[12]Id. at 415.

[13]Id. at 417 (dissenting opinion).

[14]Id. at 418 (dissenting opinion) (emphasis added).

[15]*See,* Goldblatt v. Hempstead, 369 U.S. 590 (1962); Miller v. Schoene, 276 U.S. 272 (1928); Gorieb v. Fox, 274 U.S. 603 (1927); Village of Euclid v. Ambler Realty Co., 272 U.S. 365 (1926); Hadacheck v. Sebastian, 239 U.S. 394 (1915); Reinman v. Little Rock, 237 U.S. 171 (1915); Welch v. Swasey, 214 U.S. 91 (1909).

[16]*See,* e.g., Griggs v. Allegheny Co., 369 U.S. 84 (1962); Causby v. United States, 328 U.S. 256 (1946); Portsmouth Co. v. United States, 260 U.S. 327 (1922).

[17]40 N.J. 539, 193 A.2d 232 (1963). N. Williams, 5 American Planning Law 436–42 (1975).

[18]AMG Assocs. v. Township of Springfield, 65 N.J. 101, 319 A.2d 705, 711 (1974).

A second approach was followed in the New York Court of Appeals' 1976 decision, *Fred F. French Investing Co. v. City of New York*.[19] The court focused on both the impact of the regulation and the legitimacy of the objective and balanced the two to determine the ordinance's validity. The court rested its analysis on a direct examination of the reasonableness of the police power. The court looked to the substantiality of the relationship of the ordinance to the protection of the public health, safety, morals, and general welfare, the relationship between the means used and the ends sought, and the extent to which the ordinance "renders the property unsuitable for any reasonable income productive or other private use for which it is adapted, and thus destroys its economic value, or all but a bare residue of its value."[20] In predominantly agricultural areas, where farming is an accepted, profitable way of life, a court following this analysis may be more likely to find that farming is still reasonably income productive and therefore that exclusive agricultural zoning is not an unreasonable mode of regulation. However, as development values of agricultural land climb because of approaching urbanization, the risk of judicial invalidation of agricultural zoning increases.

A third approach to the problem of highly restrictive regulation is found in the 1972 decision of the Wisconsin Supreme Court in *Just v. Marinette County*.[21] The court held that the owner of land within 1000 feet of a lake "has no absolute and unlimited right to change the essential natural character of his land so as to use it for a purpose for which it was unsuited in its natural state and which injures the rights of others."[22] This principle represents a significant departure from the traditional analysis of taking issue because it permits a severe restriction on the landowner's use of the land to be outweighed by the public's interest in the objective of ecological conservation. Although it may be explained in part by reference to the fact that the land involved was adjacent to a lake and therefore critical to the maintenance of the quality of the hydrological system and by the existence of the public trust doctrine in Wisconsin with respect to navigable water, it stands as a precedent that may be extended to embrace prime agricultural lands needed to produce our nation's food supply.

In the last 15 years over 200 county and local governments have adopted amendments to their zoning ordinances which were designed to keep land in agricultural use, either by zoning it exclusively agricultural, establishing area-based allocation of dwelling units, or imposing a number of eligibility conditions designed to prevent nonagricultural development on highly productive farmland. There have been only a few appellate court decisions that consider the constitutionality of exclusive agricultural use zoning in the face of a challenge that they constitute a taking. The majority of these cases come from California where the Supreme Court has sustained them uniformly, holding that an ordinance that on its face results in a mere diminution of property value is not improper,[23] and that a zoning ordinance is valid unless its effect is to

[19]39 N.Y. 2d 587, 350 N.E. 2d 381, 385 N.Y.S. 2d 5 *appeal dismissed*, 429 U.S. 990 (1976).

[20]350 N.E. 2d at 387.

[21]56 Wis. 2d 7, 201 N.W. 2d 761 (1972) (followed in Sibson v. State, 115 N.H. 124, 336 A.2d 239 (1975).

[22]201 N.W. 2d at 768.

[23]Sierra Terreno v. Tahoe Regional Planning Agency, 79 Cal. App. 3d 439, 144 Cal. Rptr. 776 (1978) (following HFH Ltd. v. Superior Ct., 15 Cal. 3d 508, 542 P. 2d 237, 126 Cal. Rptr. 365 (1975). This principle applies both when land had been zoned for agricultural use for 20 years so that the owner is being denied the opportunity to reap a speculative profit, see Brown v. Fremont, 75 Cal. App. 3d 141, 142 Cal. Rptr. 46 (1978), and when land had been rezoned from commercial and agricultural use to general forest use, thus preventing a previously permissible use.

deprive the landowner of substantially all reasonable use of his property. If land that is zoned exclusively for agricultural use is or could be productive, its owners will not be heard to complain.[24] In a 1979 case involving potentially highly restrictive regulations of a 5 acre (2.025 ha) lot overlooking San Francisco Bay, the California Supreme Court held that a landowner who was deprived of all reasonable use of his property could not recover damages for the destruction of his property value by way of inverse condemnation but was only entitled to a judicial declaration that the regulations were invalid, and that as long as some use of the property was allowed, the regulation was valid as a matter of law.[25] The court recognized the chilling effect that the potential liability for damages would have on municipal efforts to regulate land use and the need to impart flexibility in planning efforts.

In Oregon it was held in 1976 that a rezoning of 842 acres (341 ha) of land from low density residential to a farm and forest classification was not a taking because the land could be put to substantial, beneficial use for farming.[26] An intermediate court has also upheld the Oregon Land Conservation and Development Commission's power to adopt an agricultural goal specifying that soils in capability classifications I–IV of the United States Soil Conservation Service's classification system should be inventoried and preserved by exclusive farm use zones.[27] The commission's goal has been held applicable to decisions denying rezoning, partitioning (dividing into two or three lots), annexation, and subdivision requests. Thus, the developing Oregon case law strongly supports the legislature's program to preserve agricultural and forest land in the state.

In one case an Illinois intermediate court gave short shrift to a county's attempts to preserve farmland. The county had zoned 50 acres, 15 of which were submarginal farmland and 35 of which were covered with woods, for exclusive agricultural use. Even though the property was surrounded on three sides by farms, the court held that the regulation bore no "real or substantial relation to the public health, safety, morals, comfort, or general welfare" and was therefore unconstitutional.[28]

The paucity of cases dealing with exclusive agricultural zoning makes it difficult to predict how courts will rule in the many states whose municipalities have adopted such ordinances. It is certainly significant that the California and Oregon legislatures have both enacted strong state policies for the protection of agricultural and forest lands and open space

---

[24]*See also* Helix Land Co. v. City of San Diego, 82 Cal. App. 3d 932, 147 Cal. Rptr. 683 (1978); Pacific Properties, Inc. v. Santa Cruz, 81 Cal. App. 3d 244, 146 Cal. Rptr. 428 (1978); Gisler v. County of Madera, 38 Cal. App. 3d 303, 112 Cal. Rptr. 919 (1974).

[25]Agins v. City of Tiburon, 24 Cal. 3d 266, 598, P. 2d 25, (1979) aff'd 477 U.S. 255 (1980). See discussion at page 29 below.

[26]Joyce v. City of Portland, 24 Or. App. 689, 546 P. 2d 1100 (1976). See also Fifth Ave. Corp. v. Washington County, 282 Or. 591, 581 P. 2d 50 (1978).

[27]Meyer v. Lord, 37 Or. App. 59, 586 P. 2d 367 (1978).

[28]Smeja v. County of Boone, 34 Ill. App. 3d 628, 339 N.E. 2d 452, 454 (1975). *See* Pettee v. County of DeKalb, 60 Ill. App. 3d 304, 376 N.E. 2d 720 (1978); Continental Homes of Chicago, Inc. v. County of Lake, 37 Ill. App. 3d 727, 346 N.E. 2d 226 (1976). It should be noted that a leading commentator on American zoning law has described Illinois zoning law as unique in the United States in the strength of its pro-developer orientation and hostility to zoning. See N. Williams, 1 American Planning Law: Land Use and the Police Power, 143–48 (1974). In Pennsylvania, the Commonwealth Court sustained an agricultural zoning ordinance against a taking challenge [Snyder v. Railroad Borough, 59 Pa. Comwlth 385, 430 A. 2d 764 (1981)], while in another case the Supreme Court held that such an ordinance denied equal protection because the densities permitted discriminated against large land owners (Hopewell Township v. Golla 452 A. 2d 1337 (1982). *See also*, DuFour v. Montgomery County Council Circuit Court Mont. Co. Md. No. 56964 (1983), where the trial court upheld a 25 acre minimum lot use against a taking challenge.

generally.[29] The courts in other states that have not enacted such laws may be influenced by the most recent pronouncements on the taking issue by the United States Supreme Court.

Recent U.S. Supreme Court Decisions

In June 1978 the Supreme Court of the United States undertook a major review of the taking doctrine in *Penn Central Transportation Co. v. City of New York*.[30] The case involved the constitutionality of New York City's Landmarks Preservation Law. Under this law the Landmarks Preservation Commission may designate a building as a landmark, subject to modification or disapproval by the Board of Estimate. The owner of a landmark building must maintain the building's exterior and must secure the approval of the Commission before making exterior modifications. The owner may transfer unused development rights from a landmark parcel to nearby lots. The law provides for judicial relief if the owner is able to show that he cannot earn a reasonable return on the site. The Grand Central Terminal was designated as a landmark, a decision that Penn Central did not appeal. Penn Central then leased the air rights above the building to U.G.P. Properties so that U.G.P. could build an office building above the terminal. The Commission disapproved two designs for an office building over 50 stories high because of their adverse effects on the terminal's historic and aesthetic features.

Penn Central and U.G.P. brought suit alleging that the disapproval of these proposals constituted a taking of their property without just compensation in violation of the fifth and fourteenth amendments and deprived them of their property without due process of law in violation of the due process clause of the fourteenth amendment. The trial court sustained their claims but was reversed by the New York appellate courts, on the basis that there was neither a taking nor a denial of due process.

The Supreme Court affirmed, in an opinion by Justice Brennan with Justices Rehnquist, Burger, and Stevens dissenting. Justice Brennan postulated that the fifth amendment's guarantee is "designed to bar Government from forcing some people alone to bear public burdens which, in all fairness and justice, should be borne by the public as a whole."[31] He observed that the court has been unable to develop any set formula for determining when justice and fairness require compensation. In reaching his holding on the taking issue, Justice Brennan adopted a conceptual scheme composed of four steps. The first is to determine whether the interest at issue is one that is "sufficiently bound up with the reasonable expectation of the claimant to constitute property" for fifth amendment purposes.[32] If it is, the next step is to characterize the property interest involved. In Penn Central, for instance, the question was whether the interest was the full fee interest or merely the development rights. The third step involves an analysis of the character of the governmental

[29]Cal. Gov't Code 65560-65570 (West 1980); Or. Rev. Stat. 215.213, .243, .253 (Supp 1980). *See also* Oregon Land Conserv. & Dev. Comm'n, Statewide Planning Goals and Guidelines (Sept. 1978).

[30]438 U.S. 104 (1978). *See also*, Loretto v. Teleprompter Manhattan CATV Corp., 454 U.S. 938 (1982), where the Supreme Court seemed to assume without analysis that a person whose property has been "taken" is entitled to just compensation, and not simply to an invalidation of the law.

[31]438 U.S. at 123, 140 (citing Armstrong v. United States, 364 U.S. 40, 49 (1960).

[32]Id. at 125. If it is not, the inquiry stops at this stage. *See*, e.g., United States v. Willow River Power Co., 324 U.S. 499 (1945).

action. If it is pursuant to a "public program adjusting the benefits and burdens of economic life to promote the common good," such as an exercise of the taxing power, zoning laws, or other regulations designed to protect the public health, safety, morals, or general welfare, it will be sustained even though it destroys or adversely affects recognized real property interests, unless the impact is unduly harsh.[33] If the government action can be characterized as "acquisition of resources to permit or facilitate uniquely public functions," they may more readily be held to be taking.[34] The fourth step in Justice Brennan's analysis involves an examination of the nature and extent of the interference with the rights in the property, especially the extent to which the regulation affects investment-backed considerations. If the governmental action simply prohibited the most beneficial use of the land, it would not constitute a taking. Where, however, a regulation results in virtually complete destruction of a recognized property interest, it might.

Applying his conceptual scheme to the case at hand, Justice Brennan first determined that Penn Central's interest here was property for fifth amendment purposes. He then characterized it as the full fee interest, not simply the air rights. Third, he found that the Landmarks Law embodied a comprehensive plan to preserve a class of structures in New York City, namely, those of special historic or architectural interest, and that this objective was one that was a valid goal for the exercise of the police power. Fourth, he found that there was no interference with Penn Central's present use of the terminal as a major element in its transportation system, as it had been doing for 65 years. In fact, he regarded the Landmarks Law as permitting Penn Central to obtain a return from its investment. Next, he noted that Penn Central was not prohibited from all use of its air rights, only those contained in its two proposals for an office building of over 50 stories. He conjectured that the commission might approve a smaller, less obtrusive building, and observed that Penn Central could realize some economic return from its air rights by transferring them to other parcels it owned in the vicinity. He concluded that the interference with Penn Central's property rights was not of such a magnitude that it constituted a taking.[35]

Justice Rehnquist, in dissent, advocated a quite distinct, and perhaps novel, mode of analysis. He recognized as a general rule the principle that government is prohibited from destroying property interests without just compensation. Concluding that claimants' property, which he characterized as their air rights, had been destroyed by the Commission's action under the Landmark Law, he noted that there were two exceptions to the general rule. The first is the nuisance exception, which applies to situations when the regulation prohibits a noxious use of the property. Such a regulation would be valid against a taking claim even if it resulted in a virtually complete destruction of property value and even if the government singled out a particular property owner. The second exception, which applies even where the prohibition is of a noninjurious

[33]Id. at 124–27. *See*, e.g., Goldblatt v. Hempstead, 369 U.S. 590 (1962); Gorieb v. Fox, 274 U.S. 603 (1927); Village of Euclid v. Ambler Realty Co., 272 U.S. 365 (1926); Welch v. Swasey, 214 U.S. 91 (1909).

[34]Id. at 128 (citing United States v. Causby, 328 U.S. 256 (1946); Griggs v. Allegheny County, 369 U.S. 84 (1962); Portsmouth Harbor Land & Hotel Co. v. United States, 260 U.S. 327 (1922); United States v. Cress, 243 U.S. 316 (1917). *See also*, Kaiser Aetna v. U.S., 444 U.S. 164 (1979).

[35]438 U.S. at 129–38.

use, is when "the prohibition applies over a broad cross section of land and thereby secure(s) an 'average reciprocity of advantage.' It is for this reason that zoning does not constitute a 'taking.' "[36] He went on to state:

> Typical zoning restrictions may, it is true, so limit the prospective uses of a piece of property as to diminish the value of that property in the abstract because it may not be used for the forbidden purposes. But any such abstract decrease in value will more than likely be at least partially offset by an increase in value which flows from similar restrictions as to use on neighboring properties. All property owners in a designated area are placed under the same restrictions, not only for the benefit of the municipality as a whole but for the common benefit of one another.[37]

He emphasized that it is "the character of the invasion, not the amount of damage resulting from it, so long as the damage is substantial, that determines the question whether it is a taking."[38] Thus, his mode of analysis is starkly simple: any regulation of land use which destroys a property interest without just compensation is a taking unless it involves the prohibition of a nuisance or is imposed over a "broad cross section of land" to promote the general welfare. Restrictions that fall within one of these exceptions are valid even if they result in a substantial diminution of fair market value.

With this background it is appropriate to address the question of whether and under what circumstances exclusive agricultural use zoning would amount to a taking without just compensation using the conceptual schemes articulated by Justices Brennan and Rehnquist. Since factual circumstances are of critical importance in such a determination, let us hypothesize four typical counties. County A is located in the middle of a corn belt. Ninety-five percent of its land is in highly productive agricultural use, although there are two growing, small cities in the county. Farmers are the most politically powerful group. The fair market value of agricultural land approximates its farm use value in most of the county. County B is in the outer rural–urban fringe of a metropolitan area. Developers have bought portions of a farm and built small subdivisions. Farming is of considerable economic importance and occupies about 80% of the land area. Fair market values of undeveloped land are about one and one-half to three times farm use value. Speculators have begun to pick up farms as they come on the market and then lease them to neighboring farmers. Speculators continue to be active. County C is in the inner rural–urban fringe. About one-third of the county is developed, but farming is fairly widespread. Fair market values are three to about ten times farm use values, depending on accessibility to public water and sewer facilities, with the result that few farmers can afford to buy a farm or to add acreage to their present farm. Developers usually buy land under sales agreements that are conditioned on their being successful in obtaining rezoning at higher densities. County D is largely suburban and three-quarters of it is developed. Fair market values of land are about 15–20 times farm use value. A few farmers continue to farm but most of them are nearing retirement age. Here, developers also buy land under sales agreements that are conditioned on rezoning.

Assume that before adopting an exclusive agricultural zoning ordinance, each county completed a comprehensive planning program that included topographical studies that identified relatively steeply sloped

[36]438 U.S. at 141–47.
[37]Id. at 139–40.
[38]Id. at 149–50 (quoting United States v. Cress, 243 U.S. 316, 328 (1917).

areas, the hydrological system and areas of high erosion, soil maps showing prime and unique agricultural soils, and existing land-use maps. The planning process identified areas of logical growth especially those in which public water and sewer systems were available, and designated as development areas sufficient land to accommodate anticipated residential, commercial, and industrial development. The plans presented data showing the importance of agriculture to the counties' economic prosperity and noted relevant national and state policies with respect to preserving farming. Differential assessment is available to eligible agriculture land. The zoning ordinance creates exclusive agricultural use zones for those areas shown to have prime agricultural soil by the data developed in the planning analysis. Farmers are permitted to create one building lot of less than 1 acre (0.405 ha) for each 50 acres (20.25 ha) of qualified farmland they own and sell it to a family member or to one of their employees. Farms in these zones are excused from paying assessments for new roads and water and sewer facilities to the extent they do not serve the farm homestead. There are no provisions for transfer or purchase of development rights. The economic impact of the exclusive farm use zoning on the value of undeveloped farmland is negligible in County A and increases steadily through Counties B and C, and causes reductions in value of seventy-five to ninety-five percent in County D.

Under Justice Brennan's mode of analysis, it is clear that the interest involved here is property. Second, the relevant property interest is the full fee simple title, not the development rights alone as it was in Penn Central. Third, Justice Brennan would characterize exclusive agricultural use zoning as a general, communitywide exercise of the police power and not one whose impact falls impermissibly on a few landowners. Such zoning seeks to adjust "the benefits and burdens of economic life to promote the common good," regulates on an areawide basis and does not reduce current-use value by prohibiting existing uses. At least in Counties A and B, it does not appear to significantly frustrate "investment-backed expectations." Justice Brennan did not elaborate on this phrase, which embraces a multitude of complexities. His citation of previous cases that had sustained land-use regulations even though they prohibited potential future uses and therefore diminished fair market value supports the conclusion that "investment-backed expectations" is synonymous only with the expectation, made tangible by the commitment of resources, that the investor will be able to continue the current use to which the property is being put. This was precisely the kind of expectation that was frustrated by the Pennsylvania statute which was held to be a taking in Mahon where the use was extraction of coals from a seam. Thus, where there is a broad exercise of the police power, even a developer who has bought land outright for a premium over current-use value would be viewed as merely having assumed an investment risk. His hopes for profit does not constitute the kind of property interest which the fifth amendment was designed to protect. In County D, where the balance has shifted in favor of suburban development, it can be argued that it would be reasonable for a developer to expect that he would be allowed to develop of agricultural land. Under the circumstances hypothesized, the encroachment of suburbs with their attendant interferences with agricultural activities, the gradual disappearance of supportive services for farming, and aging farm population, and generally held values that are those of suburbanites, not agriculturists, make it more and more difficult to argue that agriculture is still a viable economic activity. Also, as the number of farmers decreases, the impact of the regulation becomes more individualized. As a result the likelihood of forcing a few to bear the burdens that should be borne by the whole (the evil that the fifth amendment seeks to prevent) becomes greater. Still Justice Brennan does not negate the possibility that he would find that a well-documented, well-conceived, and well-implemented exclusive agricultural zoning would not frustrate reasonable investment-backed expectations, especially if the areas so zoned were adjacent to similarly zoned areas in an adjoining county.

The fourth step in Justice Brennan's approach is to examine the nature and extent of the interference with rights in property. The landowner retains all the rights that he had before the enactment of the ordinance, except for the right to develop his land. Any diminution in value would be measured in terms of the fair market value of the fee interest. By hypothesis, the economic impact of exclusive agricultural use zoning, although often significant, is not as severe as that of the zoning ordinance sustained in *Euclid*, except in County D where the diminution in property values begins to approach this level. Thus, it would seem reasonable to conclude that if Justice Brennan found there was no taking in the *Penn Central* situation, then, *a fortiori*, he would not find a taking by an exclusive agricultural use zoning ordinance, at least in the first three of the counties hypothesized here.

In November 1979 the Supreme Court had another opportunity to examine the taking issue, in *Andrus v. Allard*.[39] The Eagle Protection Act[40] and the Migration Bird Act,[41] as interpreted by the secretary of the interior, prohibited commercial transactions in parts of birds that had been killed legally before the effective dates of the act (preexisting artifacts). A dealer of Indian artifacts sold artifacts containing feathers from protected birds that had been killed before the birds came under the protection of the Acts. After having been convicted and fined for violating the laws, he brought suit, alleging that the statutes did not cover the sale of preexisting artifacts and that if they did, they resulted in a taking without just compensation. A three judge court, harboring grave doubts about the constitutionality of the Acts as interpreted by the secretary of the interior, had held that they were not applicable to preexisting artifacts. The Supreme Court noted probable jurisdiction. Justice Brennan, writing for all of the justices except Chief Justice Burger who concurred in the judgment, first upheld the secretary's interpretation of the Acts as being applicable to preexisting parts.[42] Turning to the taking issue, he noted that *Penn Central* recognized that government regulation involves an adjustment of rights for the public good which often curtails some potential for the use or economic exploitation of rights. "The taking clause, therefore, preserves governmental power to regulate, subject only to the dictates of 'justice and fairness.'"[43]

Justice Brennan went on to state: "The regulations challenged here do not compel the surrender of the artifacts, and there is no physical invasion or restraint upon them. Rather, a significant restriction has been

[39]444 U.S. 51 (1979).
[40]16 U.S.C. § 668, and 703 (1980 Supp.).
[41]16 U.S.C. § 703 (1980 Supp.).
[42]444 U.S. at (1979).
[43]48 444 U.S. at (1979).

imposed on one means of disposing of the artifacts. But the denial of one traditional property right does not always amount to a taking. At least where an owner possesses a full "bundle" of property rights, the destruction of one "strand" (the right to sell) of the bundle is not a taking, because the aggregate must be viewed in its entirety. . . . In this case, it is crucial that appellees retain the rights to possess and transport their property, and to donate or devise the protected birds. "It is, to be sure, undeniable that the regulations here prevent the most profitable use of appellees' property. Again however, that is not dispositive. When we review regulation, a reduction in the value of property is not necessarily equated with a taking. . . . In the instant case, it is not clear that appellees will be unable to derive economic benefit from the artifacts; for example, they might exhibit the artifacts for an admissions charge. At any rate, loss of future profits—unaccompanied by any physical property restriction—provides a slender reed upon which to rest a taking claim. Prediction of profitability is essentially a matter of reasoned speculation that courts are not especially competent to perform. Further, perhaps because of its very uncertainty, the interest in anticipated gains has traditionally been viewed as less compelling than other property-related interests." He concluded by stating: "It is true that appellees must bear the costs of these regulations. But, within limits, that is a burden borne to secure 'the advantage of living and doing business in a civilized community' . . . We hold that the simple prohibition of the sale of lawfully acquired property in the case does not affect a taking in violation of the fifth amendment."[44]

Taken literally, *Allard* holds that Congress has the power to prevent the sale of property in order to achieve a desired public purpose, and that so long as the owner retains the right to possess, transport, donate, bequeath, or derive economic benefit from its use, there is no unconstitutional taking. Although it would be unwise to apply this doctrine woodenly to the regulation of the use of farmland, it certainly provides support for the central argument made here that a well-documented exclusive agricultural zoning ordinance that permits the farmer to possess, cultivate, sell, rent, donate, and bequeath his land but prevents him from developing it for urban uses would be sustained by the Supreme Court.

In 1979–1980, the U.S. Supreme Court decided two cases that dealt with government regulation of a property owner's right to exclude members of the public from his property. In *Kaiser Aetna v. U.S.*,[45] owners of a large private lagoon extending about 2 miles inland on the island of Oahu, Hawaii, dredged it, with the approval of the U.S. Army Corps of Engineers, cut a channel through the barrier reef, which barred boat access to it from the Pacific, and built an exclusive marina-based community around it. The United States brought suit to force the owners to grant the public free access to it. The Court of Appeals for the 9th Circuit held that the pond was now subject to a navigational servitude giving the public a right of access to what was a private pond. On appeal to the Supreme Court, Justice Rehnquist stated that when determining whether or not a taking has occurred, the court will examine the economic impact of the regulation, its interference with reasonable investment backed expectations, and the character of the governmental ac-

[44]Id.
[45]444 U.S. 164 (1979).

tion. He held that the lagoon was analogous to "fast lands" (lands above a flood plain) and that the right to exclude, "so universally held to be a fundamental element of property right, falls within the category of interests that the Government cannot take without compensation."[46] He noted that allowing public access would result in actual physical invasion of the property, and that preventing the owner from charging marina fees would significantly frustrate reasonable investment expectancies. Justices Blackman, Brennan, and Marshall dissented on several grounds. The one relevant to this discussion is that the lagoon was subject to a navigational servitude so that the owner had no right to compensation for being forced to allow free public access.

The second case is *Prune Yard Shopping Center v. Robins*.[47] Here the owners of a large shopping center sought to prevent students from distributing pamphlets and securing signatures opposing a U.N. resolution against Zionism. The students left and then filed suit claiming that the owners' attempt to exclude them interfered with their freedom of speech and petitioning under the California Constitution. The Supreme Court of California upheld this contention and rejected the owners' argument that their property rights were being infringed in violation of the just compensation and due process clauses of the Federal Constitution.

Justice Rehnquist followed the same line of reasoning here as he did in *Kaiser Aetna*. He noted that allowing a few students to distribute pamphlets at reasonable hours would not unreasonably impair the value of the large shopping center, and thus the fact that they "physically invaded" the property (along with 25,000 others each day) was not dispositive. Finding that the owners had failed to show that the right to exclude was essential to the use or economic value of their property, he held that this state-authorized regulation of the center did not amount to taking.[48] Several of the concurring justices emphasized that if this case had involved a small store, office, or hotel, they would have reached a different result.

Kaiser Aetna and *Prune Yard Shopping Center* demonstrate that when resolving taking issues, the Court will take a close look at the facts, especially the expectations of the owner and the impact on them of the regulations complained of and then engage in a balancing process in which it will weigh the character of the regulation, the extent of its interference with the owner's property, and the reasonableness of his expectations. The *Kaiser Aetna* decision also attests to Justice Rehnquist's independence of mind and influence over his brethren. Although he gave lip service to the general approach that Justice Brennan followed in *Penn Central*, he departed from it on the key issue of the characterization of the property interest involved. He identified it as the right to exclude the public from the lagoon, only one of the bundle of rights that constituted the owners' property, instead of the full fee interest in the development as a whole, including surrounding land. By declining to characterize as the full fee interest to the development, which is certainly how the developer would have viewed it, Justice Rehnquist was able to

---

[46]Id. at p. 4049.
[47]447 U.S. 74 (1980).
[48]Id. at p. 76.

convert an instance where government regulation merely reduced property value to one where it destroyed a property interest.

The final, recent Supreme Court decision is *Agins v. City of Tiburon*.[49]
Agins had bought 5 acres of open land on a ridge with a superb view over
San Francisco Bay. Thereafter, Tiburon rezoned the land, placing it in a
Residential Planned Development and Open Space Zone, whose density
restrictions would permit the owners to build between one and five
single family homes on the site. The owners had not applied for approval
to develop the land. They brought suit claiming that the zoning ordinance prevented its development and therefore constituted a taking
without just compensation. They sought either a declaration that the
ordinance was unconstitutional or damages by way of inverse condemnation. The California courts held there was no taking because the
ordinance allowed the construction of one to five homes and the owners
had not sought building permits.

The U.S. Supreme Court affirmed. Observing that there was not yet a
concrete controversy regarding the application of the regulations to
their property, Justice Powell framed the question before the Court as
whether the mere enactment of the ordinance constituted a taking. He
held that it did not because the ordinance (1) substantially advanced the
state's legitimate interest in limiting the loss of open space and the ill
effects of urbanization, and (2) did not deny the owners a commercially
viable use of their land. Since he reached this conclusion, he did not
reach the question of whether the owner could get damages for inverse
condemnation, had there been a taking.

The decision in the *Agins* case had been awaited with considerable
interest by the land-use lawyer fraternity. As it turned out, the decision
did not break any new ground nor did it demonstrate a particularly
sensitive application of the principles developed in *Penn Central*. Thus
the further refinement of "taking" doctrines and the answer to the
question of whether or not there is a right to damages for inverse
condemnation under federal constitutional law will have to wait for
another day.[50]

In summary, it is difficult to predict how a particular State Supreme
Court would view an exclusive agricultural use zoning ordinance, especially when the land subjected to it is located in a rural–urban fringe area
where fair market values are many times farm use values. Certainly a
court that adopts the *Just* approach would be much more likely to sustain
it as against a challenge based on the taking clause than one following the
traditional approach. More significantly, it is too early to assess the
impact the *Penn Central*, *Allard*, and other Supreme Court decisions will
have on state court interpretations of state's taking and due process
clauses. It is clear, however, that *Penn Central* and *Allard* provide strong
support for the position that a properly planned and implemented exclusive agricultural use zoning ordinance that is based on state policies for
saving farmland is safe from attack on taking clause grounds.

---

[49]447 U.S. 255 (1980) and San Diego Gas & Electric Co. v. City of San Diego, 440 U.S. 621 (1981) 101 S.
Ct. 1289 (1981), which discussed, without deciding, many of the issues not reached in *Agins*.
[50]It seems clear that a majority of the court believes that the "taking" doctrine is to be applied
literally, so that if a court holds that there has been a taking, the injured property owner is entitled
to just compensation. *See* opinion of Rehnquist and Brennan (dissent) in the San Diego Gas &
Electric case, *supra* n. 45.

As has already been suggested, the United States Supreme Court's articulation of the principles for determining when a state or municipal regulation becomes so restrictive that it is unconstitutional under the federal due process and taking clauses is significant both because it is the authoritative statement of federal constitutional doctrine and because of its potential impact on state courts' interpretations of analogous state constitutional provisions. Its importance is further magnified because many state courts have recognized a right of inverse condemnation which permits the owner of severely restricted property to damages from the government involved measured by the standards used in eminent domain proceedings.[51]

Liability of Local Governments under the U.S. Civil Rights Acts

The most far-reaching and profound implications of Supreme Court doctrines in this area of the law, however, arise because of the recent decision of *Monell v. Department of Social Services*,[52] in which the Supreme Court held that local governments are "persons" for the purpose of civil suits brought under section 1983 of the Civil Rights Acts. This section authorizes the recovery of damages by those who are deprived of their rights under the laws and Constitution of the United States by persons acting under color of any state law, ordinance, regulation, custom, or usage. The Monell decision overruled an earlier case,[53] which had held that while a person so injured could recover damages from state and local government officials under specified conditions, he could not recover them from the local government itself. In *Owen v. City of Independence*[54] the Supreme Court, answering some of the questions left open in *Monell*, held that local governments are liable for section 1983 violations by their employees even if the employees acted in good faith or violated a citizen's civil rights unintentionally, so long as the violation results from an official government policy. The Supreme Court has held that the deprivation of property without just compensation gives rise to a cause of action under section 1983.[55] In addition, in June 1980 the Court held first that section 1983 empowered persons injured by the failure of local government officials to adhere to their obligations under any federal law (such as the Housing Act or the Clear Water Act), not simply civil rights acts, could recover damages and second that they were entitled to attorney's fees.[56] An analysis of the developing principles concerning the requirements for establishing liability on the part of states, municipalities, and their officials, the defenses thereto, the limits on and measures of such liability, and the types of remedies available is

---

[51]*See* Kanner, The Consequences of Taking Property by Regulation, 24 Prac. Law. 65 (1978); Comment, Inverse *Condemnation: Its Availability in Challenging the Validity of a Zoning Ordinance*, 26 Stan. L. Rev. 1439 (1974). Note that two leading courts have refected the notion of inverse condemnation. Fred F. French Inv. Co. v. City of New York, 39 N.Y. 2d 587, 350 N.E. 2d 381, 385 N.Y.S. 2d 5, *cert. denied*, 429 U.S. 990 (1976); Agins v. City of Tiburon, 24 Cal. 3d 410, 598 p. 2d 25, 157 Cal. Rptr. 372 (1979), aff'd, 447 U.S. 255 (1980).

[52]436 U.S. 658 (1978).

[53]Monroe v. Pape, 365 U.S. 167 (1961).

[54]445 U.S. 622 (1980).

[55]Lake Country Estates, Inc. v. Tahoe Regional Planning Agency, 440 U.S. 391 (1979).

[56]Maine v. Thiboutot, U.S., 448 U.S. 1 (1980). *See* "The Supreme Court, 1979 Term," 94 Harv. L. Rev. 215–331 (1980).

beyond the scope of this chapter.[57] It is clear, however, that the Supreme Court's demarcation of the line between constitutional and unconstitutional regulation of property will determine the liability of state and local governments and officials in section 1983 actions. It therefore creates a federal cause of action analogous to a claim for inverse condemnation. If the Supreme Court interprets the federal constitution expansively so as to protect the rights of property owners, state and local governments will be severely restricted in their attempts to regulate land development. If the Court limits the area of unconstitutional regulation as this chapter suggests it has, property owners will often have to accept harsh regulation, but state and local governments will have a greater capacity to guide urban growth and protect critical agriculturally and environmentally significant areas, free of shackles of a federalized law of inverse condemnation.

Does the Program Expose the Municipality to Liability under Federal Antitrust Laws?

Another developing area of the law involves the liability of local governments for anticompetitive effects of local actions that violate the Sherman Antitrust Act and the Clayton Antitrust Act.[58] In a recent instance, for example, a developer, who was prevented from constructing a shopping center because the city refused to rezone his land from agricultural and mining to business, was held to have a cause of action if he could show that the city's refusal was motivated by an agreement to exclude competitive shopping center developments from the city.[59] This potential liability arises because of the recent Supreme Court decision in *City of Lafayette v. Louisiana Power & Light Co.*[60] In that case the Court held that municipalities may be held liable for antitrust violations unless countervailing policies are of such weight that they override the presumption against exclusions from coverage of the antitrust laws. The court had earlier recognized two instances where such policies arose: first, the objective of protecting citizens' right to petition lawmakers requires the exclusion of legislative lobbying from potential antitrust liability,[61] and, second, considerations of federalism arising out of a dual system of government in which the states are sovereign under the Constitution significantly protect a state's rights to control its officers and agents.[62] A plurality of the *Lafayette Court* articulated a third policy, holding that the *Parker* doctrine

exempts only anti-competitive conduct engaged in as an act of government by the State as sovereign, or, by its subdivisions, pursuant to state policy to displace competition with regulation or monopoly public service. . . . This does not mean, however, that a political sub-division necessarily must be able to point to a specific, detailed legislative authorization before it properly may assert a Parker defense to an antitrust suit. . . . [A]n adequate state mandate for anticompetitive activities of cities and other subordinate governmental units exists when it is found "from the authority given a

[57]*See* Freilich, Rushing & Noland, *1978–79 Annual Review of Local Government Law*, 11 Urban Law. 548 (1979); Schnapper, *Civil Rights Litigation After Monell*, 79 Colum. L. Rev. 213 (1979).
[58]15 U.S.C. § 17 and 1227 (1980 Supp.).
[59]Mason City Center Assoc. v. City of Mason City, 468 F. Supp. 737, 738 (N.D. Iowa 1979).
[60]435 U.S. 389 (1978).
[61]Eastern R.R. Presidents Conference v. Noerr Motor Freight, Inc., 365 U.S. 127 (1961).
[62]Parker v. Brown, 317 U.S. 341, 351 (1943).

governmental entity to operate in a particular area, that the legislature contemplated the kind of action complained of.[63]

The court ruled, then, that the state must impose the practices "as an act of government" for there to be an antitrust exemption.[64]

Three district courts have ruled on the availability of state immunity to local governments that sought to prevent land development projects. In *Cedar-Riverside Association v. United States*[65] the plaintiffs were developers who had been selected to develop 100 acres (40.5 ha) in the Cedar-Riverside Urban Renewal Area in Minneapolis, but were later prevented from doing so by the city and its redevelopment authority. Cedar-Riverside brought suit alleging among other claims that this action violated the federal antitrust laws. The court held that the relevant Minnesota statutes evidenced an intent by the legislature to permit the municipalities and the housing authorities to engage in anticompetitive activities in the area of urban redevelopment and renewal.

In *Miracle Mile Association v. City of Rochester*[66] the plaintiff-developers owned land in another municipality for which they alleged they had received zoning and site plan approval and were ready to proceed with construction. They alleged that the city had undertaken an extensive campaign to prevent or delay the development by instituting New York wetlands, state environmental assessment, federal water pollution control, and federal flood insurance proceedings against it. The court held that the city was immune from antitrust liability because its actions were "pursuant to a comprehensive regulatory scheme enacted by the State for the purposes of displacing competition with regulation. The court also held that the Noerr-Pennington exemption also applied to the city's attempts to secure action by other governmental entities."[67]

Finally, in *Mason City Center Association v. City of Mason City*,[68] the plaintiffs were developers who proposed to develop a regional shopping center on 35 acres of land in Mason City, Iowa, which was zoned A-Agriculture and Mining. The city refused to rezone it to G-Business which was necessary if the shopping center were to be built. The developers brought suit alleging that this refusal was pursuant to an agreement with another developer to prevent any firm from constructing a regional shopping center that would compete with the developer's proposed downtown center. The defendants moved to dismiss the complaint on the grounds that their refusal to rezone was protected as a matter of law by the state action exemption delineated in *Parker v. Brown* and its progeny, and by the *Noerr-Pennington* doctrine. The court rejected both of the defendants' claims. With respect to the state action exemption, the court held that Iowa's zoning enabling statute did not embody the kind of comprehensive regulatory system envisioned in *City of Lafayette* and that it did not reflect a clear state intent to displace competition with regulation or monopoly public service. The court made several observa-

[63]City of Lafayette v. Louisiana Power and Light Co., 435 U.S. 389, 413–15 (1978).
[64]Id. at 418. *See* Goldfarb v. Virginia State Bar, 421 U.S. 773, 79091 (1978); Cedar-Riverside Assocs., Inc., v. United States, 459 F. Supp. 1290, 1298 (D. Minn. 1978).
[65]459 F. Supp. 1290 (D. Minn. 1978).
[66](1979) Trade Cas. (CCH) 62, 735 W.D.N.Y. 1979).
[67]Id. at 78, 147, 78, 149 and 78, 151.
[68]468 F. Supp. 737 (N.D.) Iowa 1979).

tions. First, the Iowa enabling act did not require local governments to enact zoning ordinances. Second, the act did not require zoning decisions to be for the purpose of restraining competition. Third, the statute did not set up a state agency for supervising local zoning regulations as a sovereign policy maker. Finally, there was no evidence that the state legislature even contemplated that its municipalities would enter into anticompetitive agreements with developers.[69]

With respect to the *Noerr-Pennington* exemption, the court overruled the motion to dismiss because it concluded that it needed testimony on the question of whether or not the city entered into an agreement with a developer with the intent to exclude competition. If the testimony substantiated that fact, the city's actions would not be covered by the *Noerr-Pennington* exemption, which protects only efforts to influence the passage of enforcement of legislation.[70]

The small number of decisions involving the *City of Lafayette* exemption from antitrust liability for local governments requires that any conclusions drawn from them be viewed as tentative. Still they suggest that for a local government to qualify for this exemption, it must be acting pursuant to a comprehensive system of state regulation which requires it to engage in certain actions and reflects a state legislative intention to displace competition with regulation or monopoly public service. Thus, a county in Oregon acting pursuant of that state's comprehensive system for regulating land development and protecting key agricultural and environmentally significant areas would appear to be in much stronger position to claim the exemption than would a municipality in a state that has adopted a zoning enabling act patterned after the Standard State Zoning Enabling Act, and does not have to take an active role in supervising the regulation of land development. These cases demonstrate further the importance of comprehensive planning at both state and local levels for the preservation of agricultural land.

Does an Agricultural Land Preservation Program Constitute Exclusionary Zoning?

The courts in New Jersey,[71] Pennsylvania,[72] and New York[73] have responded to the widespread practice by municipalities of zoning so as to exclude low and moderate income housing by invalidating such regulations, on the basis of equal protection and due process doctrines. A municipality in those states which adopts comprehensive farmland preservation regulations may run afoul of these antiexclusionary zoning principles. Other state supreme courts may take similar positions, especially in the Northeast and Midwest where small, often parochial, municipalities have primary responsibility for land development regulations. The courts in these three states have held that municipalities must take the regional welfare into account in shaping their land development

[69]Id. at 740, 743.

[70]Id. at 744–46.

[71]*See* Oakwood at Madison, Inc. v. Township of Madison, 72 N.J. 481, 371 A.2d 1192 (1977); Southern Burlington County NAACP v. Township of Mt. Laurel, 67 N.J. 151, 336 A.2d 713, *cert. denied*, 423 U.S. 801 (1975) ("Mt. Laurel I"), 92 N.J. 158, 456 A.2d 158 (1983) ("Mt. Laurel II").

[72]Surrick v. Zoning Hearing Bd., 476 Pa. 182, 382 A.2d 105 (1977).

[73]*See* Berenson v. Town of New Castle, 38 N.Y. 2d 102, 341 N.E. 2d 236, 378 N.Y.S. 2d 672 (1975).

regulations and make provisions for accommodating their fair share of the regional demand for low and moderate income housing.[74]

More specifically, in its 1975 decision, *Southern Burlington County NAACP v. Township of Mount Laurel*, the New Jersey court held that a municipality with significant amount of undeveloped land near a metropolitan area

> must by (its) land-use regulations, make realistically possible the opportunity for an appropriate variety and choice of housing for all categories of people who may desire to live there, of course including those of low and moderate income. It must permit multi-family housing . . . as well as small dwellings on very small lots . . . and, in general, high density zoning, without artificial and unjustifiable minimum requirements as to lot size, building size and the like, to meet the full panoply of these needs.[75]

In *Oakwood at Madison, Inc. v. Township of Madison* the court amplified *Mt. Laurel* by holding that "it is incumbent on the governing body to adjust its zoning regulations so as to render possible and feasible the least cost housing, consistent with minimum standards of health and safety, which private industry will undertake. . . ."[76]

In 1977 the Pennsylvania Supreme Court articulated that state's anti-exclusionary zoning doctrines in *Surrick v. Zoning Hearing Board*.[77] The test set out in Surrick provided that a court will determine whether the municipality in question is "a logical area for development and population growth" and is "in the path of urban-suburban growth." In doing this, the court should consider factors such as proximity to a large metropolis and the projected population growth figures for the community and the region. The court should then ascertain the present level of development in the particular community by considering such factors as population density, percentage of undeveloped land within its borders, and the percentage of such land which is available for multifamily dwellings. Taken together, these factors determine whether a municipality is a developing municipality and therefore subject to the remaining principles.

Second, if a court finds that the municipality is a developing one, it must then examine the municipality's zoning ordinance to determine whether it contains exclusionary or unduly restrictive provisions which do not have the requisite substantial relationship to the public health, safety, moral, and general welfare. As Justice Nix stated, the court will determine "whether the zoning formulae fashioned by (the zoning hearing boards and the governing bodies) reflect a balanced and weighted consideration of the many factors which bear upon local and regional housing needs. . . ."[78] The court should evaluate the overall effects of challenged ordinances, not simply whether they exclude or severely

---

[74]The California Supreme Court has held that municipalities' land development regulations must serve the regional, as well as the local, welfare. Associated Homebuilders of Greater Eastbay, Inc. v. City of Livermore, 18 Cal. 3d 582, 60708, 557 p. 2d 473, 48788, 135 Cal. Rptr. 41, 55–56 (1976). In Save a Valuable Environment v. City of Bothell, 89 Wn. 2d 862, 871, 576 P.2d 401, 406 (1978), the Supreme Court of Washington adopted a regional welfare test in evaluating a city's zoning for commercial uses.

[75]Id. at, 336 A.2d at 731–32.

[76]371 A.2d. at 1207 (1977). In 1983 the New Jersey Supreme Court issued a broad-ranging opinion disposing of six exclusionary zoning cases. Southern Burlington Co., N.A.A.C.P. v. Township of Mount Laurel, 92 N.J. 158, 456 A.2d. 158 (1983). The opinion is a veritable treatise on the substantive, procedural, and implementative issues that arise when a court seeks to end exclusionary zoning.

[77]476 Pa. 182, 382 A.2d 105 (1977).

[78]Id. at, 382 A.2d at 10910.

restrict a particular use. Furthermore, these effects will be measured against the regional welfare as well as that of the locality.

The *Surrick* court confirmed, then, that it had adopted the "fair share" concept as a means of measuring whether a particular municipal ordinance has the requisite substantial relationship to the local and regional welfare. Justice Nix reasoned that municipalities must determine regional housing needs and then fashion their zoning regulations so as to make realistically possible the construction of the municipality's fair share of present and prospective regional housing needs of all categories of people who wish to live within its borders including those with low and moderate incomes. The court did not attempt to specify how a municipality's "fair share" would be ascertained.

Applying this analytical matrix to the controversy before him, Justice Nix found the ordinance exclusionary and directed the zoning hearing board to grant a variance and issue a building permit conditioned on Surrick's compliance with the administrative requirements of the zoning ordinance and other reasonable regulations consistent with the opinion.

The New York Court of Appeals, in *Berenson v. Town of New Castle*,[79] adopted a two-branched test with which to determine the validity of an allegedly exclusionary zoning ordinance. First, the court should look to see whether the municipality has provided for a properly balanced and well-ordered community. Second, consideration must be given to regional needs and requirements. "There must be a balancing of the local desire to maintain the status quo within the community and the greater public interest that regional needs be met."[80]

The policies supporting the preservation of farmland and the provision of low and moderate income housing intersect in the rural–urban fringes of our country's metropolitan areas. More and more states will follow the antiexclusionary zoning doctrines enunciated by the New Jersey, Pennsylvania, and New York courts, as they come to realize the impact of local exclusionary zoning practices on the availability of low and moderate income housing. Land development regulations adopted in the name of agricultural land preservation may run afoul of antiexclusionary zoning principles. A recent Pennsylvania case[81] involving West Nantmeal Township, a rural municipality about 20 miles west of Philadelphia, illustrates this point. Six percent of the township was in residential use, 61% in cropland, and 29% in woodland. The remaining 4% was in other uses. The township adopted a zoning ordinance that made no provision for apartments and zoned 37% of the land for single family residential use with a minimum lot size of 10 acres. Only 11% was zoned for single family homes on an acre or less of land. The Commonwealth Court, an intermediate court that is the state's court of last resort for most zoning cases, held that the township's zoning ordinance was unconstitutional under the principles of the *Surrick* decision. The court found that the township was a logical area for development and growth because of its proximity to Philadelphia and an interchange on the Pennsylvania Turnpike. The claimed justification for the ordinance by the township board of supervisors, that it would preserve the best farmland and limit development where there were inadequate transpor-

[79]38 N.Y. 2d 102, 341 N.E. 2d 236, 318 NY.S. 2d 672 (1975).
[80]Id. at, 341 N.E. 2d at 242, 378 N.Y.S. 2d at 681.
[81]*In re* Application of Wetherill, Pa. Commw. Ct., 406 A.2d 827 (1979).

tation and public water and sewer facilities, was held to be untenable. It does not appear from the court's brief opinion that the township provided an adequate planning basis for its large-lot zoning approach to preserving farmland. Thus, the case should not be read to establish a broad principle of invalidity for all efforts to preserve agricultural land on the rural–urban fringe. But it emphasizes the need for municipalities located there both to articulate clearly the basis for their agricultural zoning and to make adequate provision for projected growth with a full range of housing types.

Legal Problems Arising Out of the Use of the Taxing Power

Differential Assessment Programs

Forty-seven states have enacted legislation permitting land in agricultural or other eligible use to be assessed at its current or agricultural use value.[82] Here the focus will be on some of the legal problems that have arisen in connection with these programs.

The principal legal issue raised by differential assessment programs is whether they violate the uniformity clauses found in most state constitutions, which provide that taxes shall be levied on real property uniformly, based on fair market value. Differential assessment laws permit eligible land to be assessed at current-use value. In many cases agricultural land will have a lower value in its current use than it would if its development potential were taken into account, as would be done if its fair market value were the measure. Thus, differential assessment programs create two classes of real property and assess one at a lower rate with a resultant reduction in taxes. Most courts that have addressed the issue have held that the program violates the uniformity clause, whereas a few have sustained such laws.[83] At least half of the states with differential assessment laws have anticipated the potential inconsistency with uniformity clauses and have passed constitutional amendments expressly authorizing this technique.

The provisions of the various differential assessment laws vary widely from one state to the next and present a potentially rich but presently untapped mine for litigation. For instance, one recent case involved a challenge to the deferred taxation or rollback provisions of Illinois' differential assessment law on the ground that they denied equal protection. In *Hoffman v. Clark*[84] the landowners argued that these provisions created two classes of agricultural land, one consisting of land that was later converted on nonagricultural uses and subjected retroactively to higher taxes during the 3 years prior to conversion because of the rollback provisions. They asserted that there was no reasonable basis for this classification so that it denied the equal protection. Observing that

[82]See Keene, John C., et al., *The Protection of Farmland, supra* note 3, and Dunford, *A Survey of Property Tax Relief Programs for the Retention of Agricultural and Open Space Lands*, 15 Gonz. L. Rev. 675 (1980).

[83]See State Tax Comm'n v. Wakefield, 222 Md. 543, 161 A.2d 676 (1960); Boyne v. State, 80 New. 160, 390 P.2d 225 (1964); Switz v. Kingsley, 69 N.J. Super. 27, 173 A.2d 449 (1961), *modified*, 37 N.J. 566, 182 A.2d 841 (1962).

[84]69 Ill. 2d 402, 372 N.E. 2d 74 (1977).

the legislature had broad discretion in classifying the objects of legislation, the court held that the rollback taxes were designed to deter conversion of agricultural land to nonfarm uses and that this constituted a reasonable basis for treating the two classes of farmland differently.

Two recent decisions of the Florida Supreme Court illustrate some of the legal issues which may be involved in the determination of eligibility. The Florida preferential assessment law[85] provides that to be eligible land must be *"actually used for a bona fide agricultural purpose."* It lists several factors that may be considered in determining eligibility, one of which is that if land is sold for a price more than three times its agricultural assessment, a rebuttable presumption is created that the land is not being used in good faith for agricultural purposes. In *Roden v. K. & K. Land Management, Inc.*[86] the court held that even though part of the 350 acre tract which was sold for six times its agricultural assessment was used for an amusement park, the balance, which was in citrus groves was still eligible for preferential assessment because sufficient evidence had been submitted to rebut the presumption.

Another provision of the Florida preferential assessment law requires that whenever a subdivision plat is recorded for land receiving preferential assessment, the land must be reclassified as nonagricultural.[87] In *Bass v. General Development Corp.*[88] the court held that the conclusive presumption that an owner who files a subdivision plan is not using the land for agricultural purposes is unreasonable and a violation of the due process clauses of the Florida and U.S. Constitutions. The court found that since the actual present use of the land controls, not the intended future use, the conclusive presumption deprives the owner of due process by denying him the opportunity to prove otherwise. The statute was also held to be a denial of equal protection because there was no rational basis for dividing land in actual agricultural use into two classes and making those owners file subdivision plans ineligible for preferential assessment.

Connecticut's land-use change tax[89] was challenged on the grounds that the 10 year decreasing tax denied equal protection in that it bore no reasonable relationship to the goal of preserving open space. A state trial court found that deterrence of rapid turnover on conveyances of land held for progressively shorter terms of ownership constituted a reasonable basis for distinguishing between short-term and long-term ownership and sustained the law.[90]

In an effort to deter short-term speculation in undeveloped land, the Vermont legislature enacted a land gains tax,[91] which shares many of the characteristics of rollback taxes. The tax is imposed on gains from the sale of land and its rates are inversely proportional to the length of the holding period starting at less than 1 year and ending after 6 years, and proportional to the percentage of profit. The maximum rate of 60% applies to a gain of 200% or more on land held for less than 1 year, and the rate declines to a minimum of 5% for gains of 0–99% on land held

---

[85]Fla. Stat. Ann. 193.461 (West Supp. 1978).
[86]368 So. 2d 588 (Fla. 1978).
[87]Fla. Stat. Ann. 193.461 (4) (a) (4) (West Supp. 1978).
[88]374 So. 2d 479 (Fla. 1979).
[89]Conn. Gen. Stat. 12504a (Supp. 1979).
[90]Curry v. Planning & Zoning Bd., 34 Conn. Supp. 52, 376 A.2d 79 (1977).
[91]Vt. Stat. Ann. tit. 32., §§ 10001-10 (Supp. 1980).

between 5 and 6 years. The objective of the tax was to deter short-term speculation on land because it was viewed as particularly disruptive to the land market. Recent litigation attacked the tax on two grounds: first, that it denied equal protection because it discriminated unreasonably between land held for less than 6 years and land held for a longer period of time, and second, that it deprived landowners of property without due process of law because it amounted to double taxation since capital gains were also subject to federal capital gains taxes. The Vermont Supreme Court rejected both arguments, holding that deterring short-term land speculation was a legitimate public purpose, which provided a reasonable basis for treating land held for a shorter period differently from land held for a longer period and that cumulative taxation such as was found there was permissible.[92] The actual effects of this tax on land prices are difficult to ascertain.[93]

Estate Tax Benefits for Farmers

In addition to raising the threshold of taxability for federal estate tax purposes, the Tax Reform Act of 1976 (modified by the Tax Equity and Fiscal Reform Act of 1981) created two tax benefits designed to help farm estates that suffer from liquidity problems because a major portion of their assets is in the form of farm land, buildings, and equipment. Section 2032A allows qualified farmland to be valued at its agricultural use value, provided a complex set of requirements is satisfied. Section 6166 permits an executor of a farm estate, in certain circumstances, to defer paying the estate taxes for 5 years and then pay them in installments over the next 10 years. These provisions are quite technical and will not be discussed here. Many states have taken steps to ease death tax burdens for farmers. More than twenty use the federal estate tax law to define the taxable estate for state estate tax purposes and, in most cases, impose a state estate tax in the amount of the permissible state death tax credit. Seven states have incorporated the provisions of Section 2032A into their death tax laws and four more permit preferential valuation in some other manner (Table 3.1).

Table 3.1 State Death Tax Benefits for Farmers

States using federal definition of taxable estate thus incorporating Section 2032A		
Alabama	Georgia	New York
Alaska	Minnesota	North Dakota
Arizona	Missouri	Utah
Arkansas	Montana	Vermont
Colorado	New Mexico	Virginia
Florida		
States having provisions like Section 2032A in their death tax law		
Delaware	Kentucky	Tennessee
Illinois	Mississippi	Washington
Kansas		
States with other forms of farm use valuation		
Connecticut	Michigan	
Maryland	Oregon	

[92]Andrews v. Lathrop, 132 Vt. 256, 315 A.2d 860 (1974).
[93]Baker, Controlling Land Uses and Prices by Using Special Gain Taxation to Intervene in the Land Market: *The Vermont Experiment*, 4 Envt'l Aff. 427 (1975).

The only legal challenge to date has been in Oregon. Oregon's statute[94] states simply that interests in real property passing by reason of death that had received special assessment as farm use land shall be valued at farm use value for inheritance tax purposes if they are in exclusive farm use pursuant to Oregon's farmland preservation law. An earlier version of this statute, which accorded this preference only to land that was zoned for exclusive farm use, was challenged in *Winningham v. Department of Revenue*[95] by the executors of the estates of two decedents who had owned land which had received preferential assessment as unzoned farmland under Section 308.370(2) of the Oregon Revised Statutes, not as zoned farmland. The Department of Revenue disallowed current-use value appraisal because the land was not in an exclusive farm use zone as required by the then applicable provisions of section 118.155 of the Oregon Revised Statutes. The executors argued that distinguishing between zoned and unzoned farmland would violate the state's uniformity clause. The court sustained the statute on the grounds that the legislature's desire to save farmland by encouraging the creation of exclusive farm use zones sustained the nonuniform treatment.

Legal Problems Arising from Programs for Acquiring Interests in Land

Land Banking

Land banking has received considerable attention over the past several years as a means of providing for a more orderly process of urban growth and for controlling urban land prices.[96] Although the concept is a controversial one in a country that places a high value on private property and freedom from governmental regulation, it received a significant endorsement in 1975 when the American Law Institute included a land banking section in its Model Land Development Code.

There are two principal legal problems involved in land banking. The first is whether the agency undertaking it has adequate legislative enabling authority. Although there are many laws authorizing the acquisition of interests in real property for fairly specific purposes such as preservation of open space or scenic vistas, removal of urban blight, and development of housing and industrial parks, only Puerto Rico has enacted the kind of broad-based, comprehensive legislation necessary to support a land banking program. The enactment of such legislation is nevertheless a prerequisite before a state or local government can implement a general land banking program as a way to preserve prime agricultural land.

The second major legal challenge that a land banking program must face is whether the acquisition of land for unspecified uses satisfies the

[94]Or. Rev. State. § 118.115 (1975), *as amended by* ch. 553, § 12, 1979 Or. Laws. *See* (1980) 3 State Inheritance, Est. & Gift Tax Rep. (CCH) Paras. 1800, 1805.

[95](1979 Current Volume) State Inheritance, Est. & Gift Tax Rep. (CCH) para. 20, 999.

[96]*See,* e.g., H. Franklin, D. Falk & A. Levin, In-Zoning: A Guide for Policy Makers on Inclusionary Land use Programs (1974); A. Strong, Land Banking: European Reality, American Prospect (1979).

constitutional requirement that the power of eminent domain can be used only to acquire land for a public purpose. In the only decision considering this issue, *Commonwealth v. Rosso*,[97] the Supreme Court of Puerto Rico sustained the Land Administration Act and the constitutionality of land banking, at least under the conditions it found to exist in the Commonwealth. The case is not completely dispositive of the issue because the court's reliance on rapid inflation of land prices, the concentrated ownership of land, and the density of population on the island gives it limited precedential value for mainland jurisdictions where social and economic conditions are significantly different. At any rate, after reviewing related cases involving the use of eminent domain for fairly broad, loosely defined purposes, the commentators for the ALI Model Land Development Code concluded that "it seems likely that the important public benefits of land banking will prove persuasive against an attack by a condemnee or by a taxpayer challenging the expenditure of public funds."

Purchase of Development Rights Programs

Six states, New Jersey, Maryland, Massachusetts, Connecticut, Rhode Island, and New Hampshire, and four counties, Suffolk (NY), Burlington (NJ), King (WA), and Howard (MD), have enacted legislation authorizing state agencies or local governments to acquire less than fee interests in land for the purpose of preserving good agricultural land, and the approach is currently being considered in many parts of the country.[98] To date there have not been any legal decisions concerning the substance of these programs.

Legal Problems Arising from the Use of the Spending Power to Protect Agricultural Land

As already emphasized, the greatest pressures to convert agricultural land to incompatible nonagricultural uses occur in the rural-urban fringe of growing metropolitan areas. There, the picturesque, rolling, well-drained prime agricultural land is as well-suited for urban development as it is for farming. It is here that there are two markets for land: one for farmers who want to expand their holdings but who can afford to pay only agricultural use value, and one for developers who can afford to pay much higher fair market value. Because of this bifurcation in demand, there is a great differential in bidding prices which makes control by police power regulation so problematic, because of the taking issue. In the last 20 years many suburban municipalities have come to realize that the problems of guiding new development and protecting agriculturally and environmentally significant areas must be solved together using a comprehensive growth management program. This section will discuss some of the legal issues arising out of the use of the spending power of

[97]95 P.R.R. 488 (1967), *appeal dismissed*, 393 U.S. 14 (1968).
[98]*See, generally*, Keene, et al., The Protection of Farmland, note 3 and, Netherton, *Restrictive Agreements for Historic Preservation*, 12 Urban Law. 54, 58, 6265 (1980); Netherton, *Environmental Conservation and Historic Preservation through Recorded Land-Use Agreements*, 14 Real Ppty., Prob. and Tr. J. 540580 (1979); Hiemstra, H., Purchase of Development Rights Programs to Protect Farmland (NASDA Research Foundation, Washington D.C. 1983).

government to provide the water supply, sewerage, transportation, and other infrastructural systems so as to encourage development in some areas and deflect it from those where farming is an important economic activity.

Extension of Water and Sewer Service and Sewer Moratoria

One method of channeling development away from agricultural areas is for a municipality to require that new developments have public water and sewer services and then refuse to extend such facilities to areas that are to be kept undeveloped. This technique raises an interesting question concerning the legal duty of a municipality, acting as a public utility, to extend its services to all members of the public if it has the carrying and treatment capacity to do so. The issue is whether a municipality can use its powers as a public utility to provide or withhold water and sewer facilities as a tool for implementing its comprehensive growth management plan, when it has the technical capacity to provide the services. In *Robinson v. City of Boulder*,[99] the Colorado Supreme Court held that the city could not restrict development in this manner, at least not in the area outside its city limits where it was the sole purveyor of water and sewer services. Other states have generally held that local governments have a measure of discretion in deciding whether to extend utilities within their borders,[100] and *Robinson* can be read to imply that the court might have reached a different conclusion had the application for extension concerned an area within the city.

Faced with overburdened sewerage systems and more stringent federal water quality regulations, many suburban municipalities have imposed moratoria on the issuance of sewer hookup permits and the extension of sewerage systems. As would be expected, developers who were prevented from building new homes have challenged these moratoria in court with varying degrees of success. The New York Court of Appeals had held that while it is an unreasonable use of the police power for a municipality to bar indefinitely all multifamily construction on the basis that the sewer system is overloaded,[101] it is permissible for it to suspend temporarily the issuance of sewer permits while it takes bona fide steps to construct adequate sewerage facilities.[102] These decisions also highlighted the importance of the comprehensive plan in such situations when the court held the proposed multifamily unit invalid because it was not based on planning considerations. Several courts have emphasized the municipalities have a duty to construct necessary sewerage facilities to protect the public's health and cannot use sewer inadequacy as a pretext for exclusionary growth management regulations.[103] A federal district court in Maryland sustained a state moratorium on sewer hookups in Montgomery and Prince George's counties which had been in effect for 5 years, holding that the moratorium did not constitute a taking of property because of the serious public injury that would occur if it

[99]190 Colo. 357, 547 P. 2d 228 (1976).

[100]*Note*, Control of Timing and Location of Government Utility Extensions, 26 Stan. L. Rev. 945 (1974).

[101]Westwood Forest Estates, Inc. v. Village of South Nyack, 23 N.Y. 2d 424, 244 N.E. 2d 700, 297 N.Y.S. 2d 129 (1969).

[102]Belle Harbor Realty Corp. v. Kerr, 35 N.Y. 2d 507, 323 N.E. 2d 697, 364 N.Y.S. 2d 160 (1974).

[103]*Compare*, National Land Inv. Co. v. Kohn, 419 Pa. 504, 215 A.2d 597 (1965) *with* Charles v. Diamond, 41 N.Y. 2d 308, 360 N.E. 2d 1295 392 N.Y.S. 2d 594 (1977).

were not imposed, that it is not a deprivation of property without due process because it was a reasonable government policy to use sewer service restrictions to state development, and that 5 years was not an unreasonably long period of time because of the complexities of securing federal grants for the construction of new facilities.[104] These decisions indicate that well-planned community programs to preserve prime agricultural land, which rely on municipal powers to control the location and phasing of infrastructural facilities to encourage development in nonagricultural areas, will be generally favorably received by the courts.

Capital Improvements and Comprehensive Growth Management

A few communities have developed comprehensive growth management systems which seek to tie development approval into the availability of urban infrastructure.[105] The best known of these are the systems adopted in Ramapo, New York, a large town to the west of New York City,[106] and Petaluma, California, across the Golden Gate Bridge from San Francisco.[107] In brief, Ramapo's plan keyed subdivision approval to the availability of sewers, storm drainage systems, public parks and schools, major roads, and firehouses. The program was based on a comprehensive planning analysis, sewerage and drainage studies, and a capital program, and envisaged the possibility that development might be postponed as much as 18 years in some parts of the town. Two landowners challenged the plan on the grounds that it was not authorized by the New York Town Law and that, even if it were, it constituted a taking without just compensation because it imposed long-term restrictions on the development of land. The New York Court of Appeals sustained the Plan. The Court noted that "(t)he undisputed effect of these integrated efforts in land use planning and development is to provide an over-all program of orderly growth and adequate facilities through a sequential development policy commensurate with progressing availability and capacity of public facilities."[108] It analyzed the relevant provisions of the enabling act and, despite the fact that there was no specific authorization for controlling the timing or sequence, held that the words "restrict and regulate" conferred the power to control the rate of development as well as its location, type, bulk, and density. The court also rejected the taking challenge, finding that these restrictions did not constitute a permanent, blanket prohibition of development. Developers could often qualify for approval by installing their own infrastructure and, in any case, the regulations were accompanied by what appeared to be bona fide efforts by the town to provide the necessary capital improvements. In summary, the court held that a municipality may control the timing and location of development, if it has prepared the way by thorough comprehensive planning and has demonstrated its good faith in accommodating the

[104]Smoke Rise, Inc. v. Washington Suburban Sanitary Comm'n, 400 F. Supp. 1369 (D. Md. 1975).

[105]M. Gleeson, I. Ball, S. Chinn, R. Einsweiler, R. Freilich, & P. Meagher, Urban Growth Management Systems: An Evaluation of Policy Related Research (1975).

[106]See Golden v. Planning Bd., 30 N.Y. 2d 359, 285 N.E. 2d 291, 334 N.Y.S. 2d 138, appeal dismissed, 409 U.S. 1003 (1972). See also, "Ramapo," Planning, July 1972, at 10812.

[107]See Construction Indust. Ass'n v. City of Petaluma, 375 F. Supp. 574 (N.D. Cal. 1974), Rev'd, 522 F. 2d 897 (9th Cir. 1975), cert. denied, 424 U.S. 934 (1976).

[108]Golden v. Planning Bd., 30 N.Y. 2d 359, 369, 285 N.E. 2d 291, 296, 334 N.Y.S. 2d 138, 144, appeal dismissed, 409 U.S. 1003 (1972).

pressures of developing, including the need for low and moderate income housing.[109]

The Petaluma plan was premised on two growth management techniques. The first limited the number of building permits which would be issued to 500 per year (a significant reduction from the pre-existing rate of growth) and used a complex evaluation system to allocate these permits among the builders who submitted development proposals. The second established an urban extension line based on availability of water supply, sewerage, and other municipal services, and sought to limit growth beyond the line. The local homebuilders association challenged the plan, principally on the grounds that it impermissibly restricted the right to travel of families who would be prohibited from moving to the city and that it denied substantive due process because it was exclusionary in purpose and effect and therefore served no legitimate public purpose. The lower court sustained the right to travel argument,[110] but was reversed on appeal on the basis that the builders' association did not have standing to assert the rights of third parties to travel.[111] The court of appeals also rejected the substantive due process argument, holding that preserving the town's environment and managing its growth were legitimate public interests, which provided a valid basis for the program that Petaluma had adopted.

Although the comprehensive growth management plans considered in the Ramapo and Petaluma plans were not primarily concerned with the preservation of agricultural lands, they suggest, together with the exclusionary zoning decisions in New Jersey, Pennsylvania and New York, the basic principles by which farmland preservation programs will be judged: (1) the programs must be based on and consistent with thorough comprehensive data gathering and planning which takes into account state and local policies concerning agriculture, (2) they may be integrated with environmental protection programs, especially the provision of adequate sewerage and wastewater treatment facilities, but these programs must be undertaken in good faith and cannot be used as an excuse for exclusionary land development programs, and (3) counties and local governments must make adequate provision for low and moderate income, or at the minimum, "least cost" housing.

Conclusion

Government officials and citizens concerned with the preservation of agricultural land must remember that their primary objective must be to enable farmers to continue farming by making agriculture an economically and humanly attractive way of life. Land development regulations and incentives deal with only a part of the overall problem and must meet the various legal and constitutional requirements reviewed in this chapter. Farmland preservation programs must be set in the general context of growth management and resource development programs. To increase their chances of success, they should be based on sound enabling

[109]Id. at 380–83, 285 N.E. 2d at 303–05, 334 N.Y.S. 2d at 153–56.
[110]Construction Indust. Ass'n v. City of Petaluma, 375 F. Supp. 574 (N.D. Cal. 1974). *rev'd*, 522 F. 2d 897 (9th Cir. 1975), *cert. denied*, 424 U.S. 934 (1976).
[111]522 F. 2d 897 (9th Cir. 1975), *cert. denied*, 424 U.S. 934 (1976).

legislation, developed through comprehensive planning and policies that give appropriate recognition to low and moderate income housing, commmercial and industrial development, and environmental protection objectives. At the same time, they must not contravene the fundamental safeguards accorded to private property by the due process, equal protection, and taking clauses of the U.S. Constitution.

4

The Ethical Dimension of Farmlands Protection[1]

R. Neil Sampson

Problems Amid Plenty

> The United States food system's dependence on increasingly fewer farmers, who in turn are dependent on a series of factors beyond their control, raises a basic question of farm sector resiliency to withstand supply-demand fluctuations without increasing government assistance (GAO 1978).

Never before have American farmers produced so much, fed so many people per farmer, or talked so openly about an impending agricultural crisis. Crisis? Impossible! Maybe. Maybe not.

Can we have a farm *land* problem in the middle of a farm *production* boom? The evidence is that we not only can, we do. But that problem is not well recognized, and is masked by analyses that measure resource adequacy on the basis of annual, or average, production figures.

Americans must begin to think about land, land quality, and land adequacy in a way that will allow us to evaluate the land's needs irrespective of the current situation on agricultural commodity supplies and prices. To aid in that thinking process, we should start with a basic statement of the relationship of agriculture to land.

Agriculture is a man-made ecological system. Viewed through the eyes of an ecologist, agriculture can no more escape certain ecological laws than Newton's apple could ignore the law of gravity. Any ecosystem, whether man-made or natural, must in the long run achieve a steady state in regard to both energy and materials. Fertility, organic matter, energy, and water must flow into the system in relationship to outflow, or the system is depleting. The soil is a living resource reservoir of constantly shifting dimensions. If the size and capability of that soil reservoir is shrinking, it is certain that, if this trend continues, it will lead to problems.

Agriculture is, to that soil reservoir, like a pump on a well. The food produced can be increased, as can the water from the well, by speeding up or improving the pump. But that will only be profitable so long as the

[1]Earlier versions of this chapter appeared as The Ethical Dimension of Farmland Protection, in *Food, Farmland and the Future* (Soil Conservation Society of America) and "A New Land Ethic," in *Farmland or Wasteland: A Time to Choose* (Rodale Press). Rewritten material has been used with permission.

level in the reservoir is maintained. If we begin depleting the reservoir, improvements in the pump and ever-increasing energy inputs become essential in order to maintain current levels of production.

American agriculture is in precisely that position today. Past productivity increases have come through the adoption of new technology and a huge increase in the amount of capital used, during a period when climatic conditions may have been unusually favorable. This has enabled a steadily dwindling number of farmers in America to stay in business by growing larger in size, adopting the latest in techniques, and absorbing narrow (or non-existent) profit margins. But how much more of this trend are we able to absorb? Is the pump speeded up about as fast as it will go? All the evidence indicates that the water level in the well is continuing to drop.

Unless we turn to the land that makes up the "reservoir" from which agriculture "pumps" food, and find ways to reverse the damage and loss that is steadily depleting it, serious agricultural problems seem certain, and in the not too distant future. And those problems, because they will affect the nation's most basic economic industry, will reverberate throughout the entire economy, undermining every effort to slow inflation and imperilling our ability to produce enough export goods to pay for increasingly costly imported oil. The strength of the nation comes from the land, and the land is in trouble.

Stress on the Land Base

The amount of cropland that will be paved over, built on, strip-mined, or flooded by a dam by the end of this century is unknown. However, if world population projections materialize, 2.3 billion people will be added between 1975 and the year 2000, a far larger increase than the 1.5 billion added during the preceding 25 years. Given those population projections and the projected gains in income, every nonfarm claimant on cropland—urbanization, energy production, transportation— is certain to be greater during the last quarter of this century than during the third (Brown 1978).

The symptoms of today's problems are fairly well known. Despite some disagreement among researchers as to the acreage of agricultural land that is being converted to other uses, there is a consensus that it is more than the nation can afford, at least in the long run. The best data available indicate that we are converting something in the range of 1 million acres of prime farmland to other uses each year, with an additional 2 million acres of land with agricultural potential being converted as well. That means that we are losing land from our total agricultural resource reservoir at the rate of roughly 3 million acres (1,215,000 ha) each year (National Agricultural Lands Study 1979).

In addition, it appears that we are losing the productive equivalent of between 1 and 3 million acres each year due to the effects of soil erosion on the nation's cropland. This is a very difficult measurement to verify, since what is happening is the loss of a tiny fraction of the productivity from many millions of acres. But these tiny fractions add up. If we calculate the soil loss from croplands that is over and above what the SCS calculates as "allowable soil loss," we see that over 1 million acres (405,000 ha) would be stripped of 6 in. (152.4 mm) of soil if all the erosion were concentrated in one area (National Association of Conservation

Districts 1980). If we take the total sheet and rill erosion from cropland, we would have to strip over 3 million acres (1,215,000 ha) of a 4 in. (101.6 mm) topsoil layer (Sampson 1979).

If we add the land that is being damaged or lost due to gully or streambank erosion, as well as from wind erosion, the toll goes still higher. Add to that the loss of soil productivity from salinization, desertification, acid rain, and similar environmentally damaging processes, and you see why the 3 million acres (1,215,000 ha) per year figure has been proposed as the best estimate of the productive capacity being lost each year from soil damage. With another 3 million acres (1,215,000 ha) of land being taken out of commercial agriculture's total inventory, the loss to our total productivity runs to 6 million acres (2,430,000 ha), or the equivalent of roughly 1.5% of the 400 million acres (162 million ha) we currently use as cropland in this country.

Thus, it is clear that we are rapidly losing our nation's farmland produc-

Fig. 4.1.   (a) Typical sheet erosion on North Idaho burned-over lands. Unprotected soil washes rapidly following a heavy rain, revealing seams and fissure of underlying rock.

Fig. 4.1. (b) Gully in Monona County, Iowa. Photos courtesy of Soil Conservation Service.

tivity, and that is a concern. It adds to other concerns about land, such as the loss of wetland, the clearing of bottomland hardwoods, the deforestation of vast areas, and the increasing competition of energy-related production for land and water. For a running account of the emergence of the farmland issue, it is instructive to read the sections on "natural resources" in the Annual Reports of the President's Council on Environmental Quality, beginning in about 1975 and proceeding to 1980. The reports are for sale by the Superintendent of Documents, U.S. Government Printing Office, Washington, D.C. 20402.

In addition to these concerns about the physical capability of the land, we can point to other, metaphysical reasons why people are uneasy about what is happening to our land. Berry (1978, p. 22) put it eloquently:

we and our country create one another;. . . our land passes in and out of our bodies just as our bodies pass in and to our land;. . . therefore, our culture must be our response to our place, our culture and our place are images of each other and inseparable from each other, and so neither can be better than the other.

When we speak of the land in these terms, we are aware that land means more to us than just acres, or tons of topsoil, or dollars. It is inextricably woven into the fabric of our hopes, our aspirations, our very lives. Ownership and management of land is part of the American dream, part of our national common heritage, our culture. There are few families in this nation who have not, at some time, attempted to take part in the common vision of land ownership. We share the view that "as many as possible should share in the ownership of land and thus be bound to it by economic interest, by the investment of love and work, by family loyalty, by memory and tradition" (Berry 1978, p. 13).

But we are also aware that this goal of land ownership is merely a dream for more and more Americans. The price of land has been rising at about 14% per year lately, roughly 2.5 times as fast as the rate of inflation. It has become difficult, if not impossible, for new farmers to buy land, and the temptation to sell prime farmland for nonagricultural uses, at nonagricultural prices, is strong. As Charles Little has pointed out, "The capability of land to be sold for development *somewhere*, suggests to each and all that land can be sold for development *anywhere*. Therefore the prices go up *everywhere*, making the marketing of land for non-agricultural use almost mandatory" (Little 1979, p. 47).

When we measure the value of land solely by economic criteria, we find ourselves measuring the amount of profit, in dollar terms, that the land can return to its current tenant. If it is cheaper this year to import food from abroad than to grow it at home, or more profitable to build

Fig. 4.2. Newly constructed townhouse developments are taking prime farmland out of production in Richmond, Virginia area.

houses than plant corn, short-term economics tells us to convert or abandon farmland. But we are not even sure that is a good economic decision, if we are forced to face any kind of long-range economic analysis, and we are fairly certain it is a costly social decision, at least in most cases.

What *is* certain is that we cannot follow such a theory of land value to its logical conclusion. We cannot make the greatest profit by destroying all the land. We cannot ignore the needs for future people to harvest crops and enjoy a benign and productive environment by focusing entirely on this year's balance sheet.

The Value of the Land

> The real wealth of the planet is its natural resources. Our real wealth is our ability to use these resources without destroying their source. Money has no value unless it represents energy, food materials, or products. No amount of monetary manipulation can create natural resources (Peter 1976).

It is clear that farmland values are not measured simply by price, and that there is a fundamental difference between money and wealth. But economic analysis does not measure, or even recognize, these differences.

One noted economist, the late E. F. Schumacher, was fairly harsh in his assessment of the state of the economic theory in dealing with the value of land:

> Economics, as currently constituted and practiced, acts as a most effective barrier against the understanding of these problems, owing to its addiction to purely quantitative analysis and its timorous refusal to look into the real nature of things (Schumacher 1973, p 45).

A new ethic needs to overcome the idea that the rights and privileges of ownership include the right to destroy the land for immediate profit, or use it in such a way that its destruction is hastened or assured. Although farmers, in particular, are loath to think about it, we are in no short supply of social restrictions on the ability to maximize profit from land.

If one is a farmer, *Cannabis*, not corn, may be the most profitable crop to grow today, but one had better not try it. The potential profit notwithstanding, society still says we do not want people smoking marijuana, so we do not want farmers growing it. If society's views on pot were different, the land-use options open to farmers would change.

Do farmers rebel at such restrictions on their right to make a profit? No, not really. They, too, subscribe to the common morality that underlies the limitations. But where is the moral principle that tells us that no one has the right to rape the landscape for a fast buck? We know Wayne Davis is right when he says, "The destruction of the land for personal financial profit is a behaviour that is simply not ethical and cannot long be tolerated," but when will we get up the gumption to say so? (Davis 1973, p. 47).

A new ethic needs to kill the notion that we owe the speculator, or the entrepreneur, his profits. Not that profits are bad, not at all. We encourage them, but we do not guarantee them; and when the prevailing land use game has become clearly tilted so that some people are reaping windfall profits while others are effectively prevented from profiting at all, we need to change the rules of the game. "Scratch a farmer, and you'll find a speculator," says Hector McPherson, an Oregon farmer who knows the land-use game from all sides (Little 1979). The reason is simple: we have the game set up these days so that speculators make money; farmers do not.

A new ethic must contain some responsibilities for all of us, and the governments that represent us, as well as for the individuals who own land, and are thus able to exercise management control. Individuals use the land, and land-use decisions are essentially private decisions, but it is seldom that those private decisions are made in the absence of conditions imposed by the public.

Take the example of a farmer who knows that his land needs a year or two in clover or alfalfa to build up the soil and make it more resistant to erosion. He may forego that option, not because he is insensitive to the needs of the soil, but because the government may establish crop acreage limitations on his cash crops that are based on the cash crop history of his farm. If he happens to get "caught," as thousands of conservation-minded farmers have been, with a history based on years when a portion of his cropland was in soil-building crops, his ability to grow cash crops, and, perhaps, stay in business, will be limited so long as the government is in the business of controlling agricultural production.

So he makes a decision balanced between his desire to keep the land healthy and his need to avoid opening himself and his family up to economic penalties. His disinclination to make the proper decision, in terms of soil stewardship, is understandable; the governments's policy of penalizing him for the stewardship is unconscionable. The new land ethic must be clear enough, and bold enough, to move those who represent us in Washington to the action needed to eliminate such policies.

The new ethic must state, in clear terms, that antisocial conduct in relation to the land is becoming a very real, and serious, threat to the continued existence of our society. Whether that antisocial conduct stems from private greed or public stupidity makes little, if any, difference.

The capability to produce ample supplies of food, far more than enough to feed our own people, has long been assumed by most Americans. But is it only Americans that we must consider?

The loss of 6 million acres (2,430,000 ha) of productive capacity a year equates to over 115,000 acres (46,575 ha) each week; over 16,000 acres (6480 ha) every day! An acre of prime farmland in this country produces enough food to equal the caloric intake of 16 people at the accepted minimum of 2000 calories per day. [Calculated at 100 bushels of corn per acre, 60 lb per bushel, 2000 kcal per pound. This equals 12 million kcal per acre $\div$ 730,000 kcal per person per year (2000 kcal/day x 365) = 16.4.] If you multiply those numbers out, you get a truly alarming statistic. We may be losing enough potential productivity each day to produce a minimum diet for nearly a quarter of a million people. Many nations, where people starve when the weather turns bad, now look to us as a reliable source of food when they need one. That may be, in the near future, an unfounded hope.

But how much suffering around the world and economic stress at home will be needed before we move toward a new ethical basis for treating our land? How long will we, as Cahn (1978) has said, "take for granted that the waters, the soils, the trees, and the wildlife can be manipulated at will in the name of progress, even if that progress is short-lived and far outweighed by the loss of the land's long-term ability to benefit mankind?"

What is needed, clearly, is a new land ethic, an ethic forged of our twin concerns for the land's proper use and its proper care. We must begin to treasure the prime farmlands that have made us the world's richest nation, keep them available for agricultural use, help farmers survive economically and environmentally so that they can profitably produce from them, and insist that they be used in such a manner that soil depletion is minimized.

But the emergence of a land ethic strong enough to offset our current proclivity to measure in narrow economic terms will not come easily. As Collins (1976) has pointed out, "An ethic powerful enough to alter patterns of land use must necessarily challenge other accepted habits and vested interests." There are also important values that must be confronted, including individualism, liberty, property, the pursuit of happiness, and the proper role of government.

It may be, as Collins goes on to say, that "The land, because it is so intrinsically important as a source of nurture for life and pastoral values, as well as being the basis for deeply rooted Jeffersonian ideals of individualism and human freedom, is the battleground for the Nation's future."

If land and land use are to be a battleground, then facts, trends, and ideas must be the major weapons. The new land ethic must be a product of education and social evolution. It cannot be legislated, or imposed on people; human behavior, in the final analysis, is more effectively governed by ideas and attitudes than by rules and regulations. We must change first, the way Americans *think* about land. Only then will we successfully alter the ways in which we *use* this vital resource.

> An ethic, ecologically, is a limitation on freedom of action in the struggle for existence. An ethic, philosophically, is a differentiation of social from anti-social conduct (Leopold 1966).

References

Berry, W. 1978. "The Unsettling of America: Culture and Agriculture." Avon Books, New York.

Brown, L. R. 1978. The Worldwide Loss of Cropland. Worldwatch Paper No. 24. Worldwatch Institute, Washington, D.C.

Cahn, R. 1978. "Footprints on the Planet." Universe Books, New York.

Collins, R.C. 1976. Developing the Needed New Land Use Ethic, Land Issues and Problems, No. 18. Virginia Polytechnic Institute, Blacksburg, VA.

Davis, W.H. 1973. The land must live, *in* "The New Food Chain." Rodale Press, Inc., Emmaus, PA.

GAO. 1978. Changing Character and Structure of American Agriculture: An Overview, U. S. General Accounting Office, Washington, D.C.

Leopold, A. 1966. "A Sand County Almanac." Ballantine Books, New York.

Little, C.E. (Editor). 1979. Land & Food: The Preservation of U.S. Farmland, Rep. No. 1, American Land Forum, Washington, D.C.

National Agricultural Lands Study. 1979. Where Have the Farmlands Gone? Washington, D.C.

National Association of Conservation Districts. 1980. Soil Degradation: Impacts on Agricultural Productivity, Report presented to the National Agricultural Lands Study, Washington, D.C. (February).

Peter, L.J. 1976. "The Peter Plan: A Proposal for Survival." William Morrow & Co., New York.

Sampson, R.N. 1979. Protecting farmland: the ethical dimension, *in* "Food, Farmland and the Future." Soil Conservation Soc. of America, Ankeny, IA.

Schumacher, E.F. 1973. "Small Is Beautiful: Economics as Though People Mattered." Harper and Row, New York.

5

Farming on the Urban Fringe

Roger J. Blobaum

Efforts to preserve agricultural land on the urban fringe put little emphasis on making farms more profitable. Public programs designed to slow farmland losses focus, for the most part, on tax relief. Although this helps, its primary benefit is a modest reduction in production costs. It does little to assure the level of earnings needed to keep these farms economically viable.

The steady loss of farmland to urban development strongly suggests that traditional grain and livestock operations, which require substantial amounts of land, are not the best choice for urban fringe farming. It may make more sense to encourage farmers to phase out this kind of production and produce for local markets instead. A change to production of fruits and vegetables, for example, could increase gross income per acre several times over. It also would respond to growing consumer interest in local production of these and other high-value crops.

Public interest in locally produced food is high in places like the Northeast, where much of the good farmland has disappeared, and the Seattle area, where the connection between farmland preservation and local food production has been dramatized through referenda (see Chapter 8). In most cases, however, the connection among consumer interest in locally produced food, the economic viability of farmers on the urban fringe, and farmland preservation is not well established.

This may change as consumers become more aware of the growing vulnerability of the food system to energy shortages and price increases. In New England, for example, more than 90% of the food is shipped in and the supply lines reach to Florida and Texas and beyond. This level of dependence is not unusual for fruits and vegetables, even during the summer months, in many metropolitan areas.

The most significant factor in removing the need for farmer proximity to consumers in recent years has been the technology of transportation, including refrigerated trucks using the interstate highway system. Rapidly rising energy costs and the possibility of diesel fuel shortages, however, are certain to reduce the reliability of this important sector of the food industry and focus increasing attention on local production.

It appears that enough good farmland is left in urban fringe areas for production of high-value crops for local markets. While Standard Met-

ropolitan Statistical Areas contain only 16.7% of the nation's land, they
have more than 20% of its prime farmland (Vining and Strauss 1976). It
has been estimated that these metropolitan areas account for about 21%
of the value of all agricultural products sold.

Consumers have little direct input into the farmland preservation
discussion. Most of the literature deals with topics like cropland classification, preferential taxation, agricultural zoning, and land preservation
techniques. Much of it is written from the point of view of the outside
expert, often an agricultural economist or a planner, who is interested in
managing urban growth. Little is written from the point of view of urban
consumers who usually end up paying the bill for land preservation and
wondering what they are getting in return.

Approaches developed thus far for preserving farmland, with the
exception of the purchase of development rights, are little more than
holding actions (Blobaum 1974). Some cost more and some work better
than others. But none has been able to stop the conversion of prime
farmland on the urban fringe to nonfarm uses. They merely postpone it.

The purchase of development rights, on the other hand, is an extremely costly approach for any local unit of government and is difficult
to sell to most city dwellers. The development rights program passed by
King County, Washington, voters in 1979 had failed a year earlier to get
the required 60% approval. It provides $50 million for the purchase of
rights to about 10,000 acres (4050 ha). It is difficult to convince voters that
purchasing rights is a good way to save land for corn or wheat production, or even to maintain a good dairy herd, when they know grain, milk,
and meat will continue to be produced elsewhere.

Another reason for their skepticism is that few make the connection
between preserving close-in farmland and having locally grown food
available at reasonable prices. Farmland preservation policy is often
discussed in ways that suggest it has little to do with the production of
food or the urban people who consume it.

As long as farmland increases in value beyond the point where it pays
to farm it, farmers will continue to sell out to developers. That point is
reached fairly soon for grain, livestock, and dairy operations that normally require 200 acres (81 ha) or more. Reaching a decision to sell is
often helped along by the inconvenience of traveling long distances to
buy feed and fertilizer, competing with urban employers for labor,
putting up with vandalism, and dealing with nonfarm neighbors com-
plaining about noise and odors.

The challenge is to encourage farm operations that require much less
land, utilize intensive production methods, specialize in high-value crops,
and capitalize on opportunities to market locally. Farmers with operations of this kind can afford more expensive land, and the higher taxes
that go with it, and are much more likely to resist pressures to sell out to a
developer and move on.

These specialized farm operations also are more compatible with
conditions usually present in the urban fringe. They have less need to
move large machinery over public thoroughfares, avoid the odor problems associated with large livestock or poultry operations, and are less
likely to create noise and dust problems. They fit in better in the urban
fringe environment and are much more likely to survive there.

Regional Food Plans as Public Policy

These rural—urban connections suggest the need for cities to consider developing metropolitan area food plans in the same way they develop areawide plans for growth management or the delivery of public services. Regional plans are adopted routinely for public needs like transportation, housing, education, and recreation and normally include the urban fringe areas. An areawide food planning element would appear to be a much-needed addition.

A metropolitan area food plan would take into account the quality and availability of close-in farmland, the need to reduce dependence on food shipped from distant points, the need to deal with the lack of permanence and stability in nearby agricultural areas, the possibilities for extending the growing season with greenhouses, and the potential for recycling urban wastes on agricultural land.

As it is now, the only food plan most metropolitan areas have is the one developed informally for the region by food wholesalers and retailers. It does not provide for direct local citizen input, does not take the local farmland base into account, and is developed from an industry standpoint by Safeway, A&P, and other regional and national food chains. It provides shipped-in fruits and vegetables on a year-round basis in most areas, for example, whether local consumers want it that way or not.

Farmers on the urban fringe do not have anything to say about this food system either and their production, in most cases, is excluded. Schools and other public institutions that purchase large quantities of food do not have any input and neither do local units of government and other official bodies that set policy in metropolitan areas.

Most people in urban areas take their food supply for granted. They know their local supermarket is dependent on a nationwide food production and distribution system. They seem content to buy fruit that is picked green and wonder why vegetables, and tomatoes in particular, do not measure up to what they see grown in neighborhood gardens. They do not realize that they are in a position to upgrade the quality of the food they buy by influencing where it is grown.

Adoption of a food plan would focus the attention of urban consumers on urban fringe farmland, make them more aware of how important it is to preserve it, and help them make the connection between their own interest in food grown locally and the economic viability of the farmers who could provide it. It also would focus more attention on local efforts to preserve farmland and less on possible political solutions originating at the state capital or in Washington.

Putting Together a Metropolitan Food Plan

An areawide food plan should strengthen the connections between the economic viability of close-in farms, the preservation of farmland in the urban fringe, and the food needs of urban consumers. It should include components dealing with production capability, agricultural stability, off-season production, direct marketing, and waste recycling.

Production Capability

An initial step in preparing a food plan would be assessing the food production system already in place in the urban fringe area. Are the farms large or small? Are they conventional grain, livestock, or dairy operators or do they produce fruit, vegetables, and other labor-intensive crops? Are the operators of average age or do they tend to be older farmers nearing retirement? Do they own the land they farm or is it owned by investors or speculators?

Production capability also is determined by the quality of farmland left in the urban fringe. It is not enough, however, to protect only land classified as prime by the Soil Conservation Service (Fenton 1975). Less productive land this close to markets also should be entitled to a prime classification on the basis of location. Even poor land that will produce fruit, for example, should be preserved if this food production effort is to respond to the needs of urban consumers.

Agricultural Stability

Farmers in the urban fringe often succumb to what is called the "impermanence syndrome," a decreasing concern for the best production and conservation methods as the inevitable sale and conversion of the land approaches (Conklin and Dymsza 1972). This is accelerated when leapfrogging development surrounds individual farms or farm neighborhoods and large amounts of farmland are acquired by investors.

A Connecticut survey found, for example, that about half the dairy operations in the state were operating on rented land available on a year-to-year basis (Josephy 1976). The diarymen involved had no incentive to take care of the land or to spend money modernizing their operations.

Only when farmers are secure for a long period of time are they free to make long-term investments. These include barns, fences, and other capital improvements; soil-saving structures like terraces; and long-term investments like vineyards, orchards, and greenhouses. Young people often hesitate to start farming in these areas because they anticipate rising taxes, increased regulations, and other pressures associated with urbanization and assume they will eventually be forced to sell out. Farmers near retirement age tend to be the most likely to sell in urban fringe areas (Brown and Roberts 1978). Middle-aged farmers, who feel unable to start up a new farm and are not ready for retirement, tend to continue farming the longest as urban pressures mount.

Lack of permanence also threatens the viability of agriculture as an economic venture. A minimum amount of productive land is needed to provide the economic base for cooperatives, implement dealers, feed and fertilizer suppliers, and other small enterprises that serve farmers. A study prepared for the New Jersey Department of Agriculture found that the minimum needed to support dairying was at least 90,000 acres (36,450 ha) of cropland and pasture and 26,000 cows within a radius of 30–50 miles (48.27–80.45 km) (Rutgers University 1973). These requirements ranged down to 10,000 acres (4050 ha) in a 10 mile (16.09 km) radius for vegetable and potato production, which would appear to make enterprises of the kind much more appropriate for urban fringe areas.

The permanence problem would have to be addressed in any metropolitan food plan that called for local production. Solving this problem would be essential to maintaining the economic viability of the farmers involved.

Off-Season Production

One of the areas of greatest potential for improving the economic viability of farmers in the urban fringe is expansion of greenhouse production. Although this system requires a lot of labor and is capital intensive, it will produce 15–20 times as much per acre as can be grown under field conditions.

Before the interstate highway system was built, most of the tomatoes, lettuce, peppers, and cucumbers sold during the winter months in northern American cities came from greenhouses. The greenhouse industry has made considerable progress in finding ways to conserve fuel. In many areas, greenhouse production is now becoming competitive with shipped-in produce.

Locating greenhouses adjacent to industries that produce waste heat can help overcome this energy-related problem. It is estimated that sufficient industrial waste heat is available to warm enough greenhouse space to produce winter vegetables for the entire country.

Another option is construction of large solar greenhouses, a new approach that appears to be solving many of the industry's energy problems. A 5000 ft^2 (465 m^2) demonstration greenhouse in Cheyenne, Wyoming, for example, has produced vegetables through three winters without any backup heat (U.S. Office of Consumer Affairs 1980).

A food plan prepared for a metropolitan area could include a farmer-operated greenhouse component that would meet the need for much of the fresh produce sold during the winter months. It would be a major step in decreasing dependence on distant suppliers. Helping farmers produce on a year-round basis would go far in making them economically viable and in stabilizing the food production system in the urban fringe.

Direct Marketing

In places such as the Northeast, where most of the food is shipped in from other parts of the country, consumers pay about 15% more for it than the national average. Even though they have a price advantage, local farmers often have trouble developing a market for all they produce. That helps account for the "Buy Local" campaigns that have been launched in states like Vermont and Massachusetts. They use bumper stickers that urge urban consumers to "Support Your Local Farmer."

An innovative approach started four years ago in Nashville, Tennessee, by the Agricultural Marketing Project now provides fresh-picked produce during the growing season to consumers in more than 50 cities in the Southeast (Hiese *et al.* 1979). Small farmers on the urban fringe have organized into producer cooperatives and are linked to urban buyers through regularly scheduled "food fairs" conducted on church parking lots. Elimination of middlemen keeps prices of vegetables, fruit, honey, and other food items well under supermarket levels.

Another way close-in producers can cut costs is to invite urban consumers to pick their own. These pick-your-own operations, which provide significant savings in labor costs, are used for crops like strawberries. This approach also is used in some areas for apples, blueberries, and other fruit crops. In some cases members of food cooperatives pick produce as part of their monthly volunteer service.

It is not surprising that lower prices result. The U. S. Department of Agriculture reports that farmers received only 25% of each dollar consumers spent on fruit and vegetables in 1979. Nearly 30% of the cost of fruit and vegetables went for packaging, rail and truck transportation, and advertising.

Attempts also are being made to provide institutional markets for farmers selling locally. This was done in Massachusetts after it was noted that universities, hospitals, government cafeterias, correctional institutions, and schools accounted for 10% of the $3 billion spent in the state for food. A related approach is to have school districts contract with local farmers for fresh vegetables and fruit for school lunch programs. Some states use public funds to help bring local farmers and consumers together in farmers markets.

There clearly are many things that urban consumers can do to help make farming profitable on the urban fringe. An areawide food plan would identify them and suggest how they could be implemented.

Waste Recycling

Preserving sufficient close-in farmland to provide an option for urban waste recycling also is an important consideration for a city and the farmers in the urban fringe. Cities currently spend about $44 a ton (907.20 kg), or a total of $6.2 billion a year, to collect and dispose of waste (U.S. Environmental Protection Agency 1977). Most of it is dumped in landfills or oceans or burned in incinerators. Solid waste management costs more than doubled in the 1970s and are expected to more than double again by 1990.

An assessment of the potential for applying urban wastes to agricultural land in a three-county Midwest region showed that nearly all the fertilizer required on more than 80,000 acres (32,400 ha) of cropland could be provided by the year 2000 by applying all the sludge, paunch manure, and livestock manure available from urban sources in the region (Blobaum et al. 1979). This study, carried out in the Omaha-Council Bluffs SMSA, treated the entire region as a waste recycling system that included close-in, privately owned land as an essential component.

It was futurist in the sense that it attempted to show what would happen between now and the year 2000 if all suitable urban wastes in a region were applied at agronomic rates to close-in agricultural land. When urban wastes were composted and applied at the rate of 12 dry tons (10,886.4 kg) per acre (0.405 ha), for example, they provided all the nutrients needed in 5 of every 6 years under a 6 year rotation of corn, oats, alfalfa, and soybeans. Some nitrogen fertilizer would be required for the corn in the fifth year. By the year 2000, with increasing waste volumes and rising fertilizer prices, benefits to the region's farmers in terms of supplying nutrients for crop production could exceed $1 million annually.

Although the heavy metals content of sludge was not high enough to be a problem in the Omaha-Council Bluffs region, it would limit land application in many more industrialized areas. Farmers producing root crops would have to exercise considerable caution. What is needed, of course, is a ban on certain manufacturing and fabrication operations and pretreatment at the source for wastes released into public sewer systems.

Integration of an areawide land application system into a regional food plan would seem appropriate, both to make these organic wastes available to farmers in the urban fringe area and to make recycling possible. Preserving farmland on the urban fringe is one way to keep this option open.

Conclusions

There is a tendency for the experts to focus attention on government-sponsored programs for preserving farmland and for policy makers to commit public funds that support that approach. The urban input, for the most part, is strongly influenced by developers, builders, and financial institutions that view farmland in the urban fringe as an unrealized opportunity. The time has come to challenge urban consumers themselves to begin participating more fully and directly in the effort to preserve farmland and to develop a rationale for doing this. Preserving the farms on the urban fringe, and making them economically viable, is just as important as saving the farmland. Indeed it is part of the farmland preservation effort.

Preserving open space and the rural character of land in the urban fringe is not enough by itself to attract the public support needed to commit large amounts of funding. A connection must be made among urban consumers, the economic viability of farmers on the urban fringe, and farmland preservation. Developing and implementing a metropolitan area food plan is a good way to do this.

References

Blobaum, R. 1974. The Loss of Agricultural Land. A study report to the Citizens Advisory Committee on Environmental Quality, Washington, D.C.

Blobaum, R., Fast, S., Holcomb, L., and Swanson, L. 1979. An Assessment of the Potential for Applying Urban Wastes to Agricultural Lands. A report prepared for the National Science Foundation, Roger Blobaum & Associates, West Des Moines, IA.

Brown, H.J., and Roberts, N.A. 1978. Land Into Cities: The Land Market on the Urban Fringe. Department of City and Regional Planning, Harvard University, Cambridge, MA.

Conklin, H. and Dymsza, R. 1972. Maintaining Viable Agriculture in Areas of Urban Expansion. New York State Office of Planning Services, Albany, N.Y.

Fenton, T. E. 1975. Definitions and criteria for identifying prime and unique lands, in Perspectives on Prime Lands: Background Papers for a Seminar on Retention of Prime Lands. U.S. Department of Agriculture, Washington, D.C.

Hiese, L., Jones, L., and Vlcek, J. 1979. Everything You Ever Wanted to Know About Food Fairs. Agricultural Marketing Project, Nashville, TN.

Josephy, R. 1976. Farming in the Urban Northeast, presented at the annual meeting of the American Association for the Advancement of Science, Boston, MA.

Rutgers University. 1973. Issues in Agricultural Land Use Management in New Jersey, Spec. Rep. No. 17. New Brunswick, NJ. (February).

U.S. Environmental Protection Agency. 1977. Resource Recovery and Waste Reduction. Fourth Report to Congress, Washington, D.C.

U.S. Office of Consumer Affairs. 1980. Rural community greenhouses, in "People Power: What Communities Are Doing to Counter Inflation." Washington, D.C.

Vining, D.R., Jr., and Strauss, A. 1976. A Demonstration That Current Deconcentration Population Trends Are A Clean Break With Past Trends, Discussion Paper Ser. No. 90. Regional Science Research Institute, Philadelphia, PA.

Part II

Local Approaches for Farmlands Protection

6

Three Guidelines for Communities in Protecting Farming

William Toner

As part of the National Agricultural Lands Study, detailed investigations were made of ten communities using zoning and other powers to protect farming. In general, the investigation showed that communities were finding reasonable success in their farming protection efforts (Toner 1981a). It also showed that most communities relied on a package of tools, not just zoning, to protect farming and that the contents of the package varied from place to place.

Although the elements of protection program varied, many of the most successful programs evolved out of a fairly common set of planning guidelines (Toner 1981b). These planning guidelines were followed by the communities in developing and administering their programs. Of the guidelines, there were three which seemed especially important to the success of local efforts.

The Agricultural Community Should Play a Central Role in the Design, Development, and Application of Local Plans and Regulations to Save Farms and Farmland

Of all of the planning guidelines in maintaining farms and farmland, this is the most important. If a community is to be successful in saving farms and farmland, the agricultural community must be involved from the very start and on through the administration of the program. No matter how brilliant the planning technique or how exacting the administration, the program will not work without the support and participation of the agricultural community. For a good discussion, see Nellis (1980).

While farmers, ranchers, or growers are at the heart of the agricultural community, there are a number of other organizations and institutions to be considered. For an excellent discussion of the culture of agriculture, see Berry (1977). There are, for example, agricultural business such as feed stores or implement dealers, a soil and water conservation district, the Grange or Farm Bureau, soil scientists, extension agents as well as credit unions and other financial organizations serving the agricultural community. In designing local programs it is important to get a good cross section of this community to ensure that all key interests are represented.

There are a host of reasons for insuring the continued role of the agricultural community in any program to maintain farms and farmland. All of these reasons can be considered under the general rubric that planning is intended to serve. For the agricultural community this rubric takes on special meaning.

Consider, for example, that for most members of the agricultural community, public planning is a new and often objectionable task (Nellis 1981). For the most part, the history of public planning has a decidedly urban flavor. As a result, there is little planning or zoning history, no tradition of public planning, no anchor for farmland preservation efforts. This compounds the fears and suspicions of the agricultural community.

In order to overcome fears and misconceptions, a major education effort is required. This education must begin in the initial stages of the planning process. Failure to do so is likely to result in a program that will never have a chance to work since it is not understood or supported by the agricultural community. One Minnesota planner discovered this the hard way. Upon making a presentation of the agricultural preservation program to his planning commission, the chairman of the commission, also a farmer, stood up and commented, "You mean that you are going to tell me how I can use my land?" Clearly, in this case the preservation plan was in deep trouble long before it ever got to the planning commission. There was a failure in this case to work with the agricultural community from the beginning. For another example of difficulties see Heufner *et al.* (1975).

One must also consider the real experts on agriculture in the community are the members of the agricultural community. And since so many of the issues in the preservation plan and regulation are technical agricultural issues, it only makes good sense to go to the experts for the solutions.

For example, one of the more difficult questions in preparing a preservation plan is "What is prime agricultural land?" For planning purposes, this is more than a question of soil types or qualities of the soil. For local planning, prime land is considered on a parcel by parcel basis where the definition also includes size of parcel, access to parcel, shape of parcel, agricultural history of the parcel, and the like. These are technical questions, and the agricultural community, especially farmers, is best suited to answer them (Lapping 1979).

In developing land-use regulations similar questions must be resolved. For example, in the design of an effective minimum lot size for a large lot zoning ordinance governing agricultural land, one of the key criteria is, "What is the minimum land size necessary to operate a marginally profitable agricultural operation?" By virtue of education and experience, the farmers, growers, or ranchers should be the ones to answer this question.

In the administration of land-use regulations, there are also issues that demand the special expertise of the agricultural community. For example, in evaluating a proposed change that would take land out of agricultural use, one of the major considerations is "Is this parcel still suitable for agricultural use?" Or, "Will the proposed use interfere with neighboring farm operations?" Once more the agricultural community should be the experts in resolving such questions. A discussion of some of these needs is found in Kartez (1980).

A close working relationship between planners and the agricultural community also provides opportunity for local planners to ground themselves in the fundamentals of local agriculture. Since local planners will often be called on to explain, defend, critique, or comment on technical agricultural questions, working with the agricultural community allows the planner to understand at least the basics of local agriculture. By training, planners learn little of agriculture. They can overcome this deficiency by listening to what the community has to say.

The political virtues of working with the agricultural community are perhaps the most compelling reason for the relationship. To begin, in any community it is difficult to achieve instant consensus on the issue of agricultural land preservation. Instead, there may be some awareness of aspects of the problem: registered cattle harassed by suburban dogs; a township board swamped with snow removal requests from a new subdivision in an agricultural area; a rural suburbanite calling the county and demanding the removal of seven chickens roosting on his patio; or, complaints from rural suburbanites about odor, noise, or timing of farm operations. When these incidents are stacked one on the other, and when tales of harassment, vandalism, rising taxes, nuisance suits, and near traffic fatalities are told, there begins a process that leads to agricultural land preservation as the overriding issue.

But agricultural preservation as the issue only begins to surface once the agricultural community begins to share the information and experience. Further, in most communities there are a minority of farmers or ranchers who have direct experience with these problems and a majority who have not. In order to achieve consensus, it is important for those in the minority to share their experience with the majority. Farmers may not be convinced by a planner who tells them what can happen, but farmers will pay attention to other farmers who can tell them what has happened to them.

Once the agricultural community has achieved some consensus on land preservation and what to do about it, the agricultural community must then carry the message to citizens and elected officials. Citizens and elected officials are impressed by farmers or growers who talk about the need for land preservation. Similarly, if elected officials sense that the agricultural community is prepared to accept and work with land-use regulations, it becomes much easier for that official to approve the approach. Thus, in bringing proposals to the public, to elected officials, or to agricultural organizations, it is important to rely on the people who have the experience, interest, and commitment necessary to the task, that is, members of the agricultural community.

The agricultural community must play a central role in any program to maintain farms and farmland. There are a variety of methods (See Glass 1980). This includes direct participation in the definition of the issue, in the development of plans, and in the evolution of police powers or fiscal powers to put the plan into action. Finally, the agricultural community must be responsible for selling the program to the general public and, once adopted, should play a strong role in the administration of the program.

Rely on Conventional Planning Tools and Techniques, but Use All Tools at One's Disposal

The most successful programs to maintain farms and farmland rely on conventional planning tools and techniques. However, the distinguishing feature of these successful programs is that they put these tools and techniques into new combinations. It is the combination of these tools that make local programs work.

Initially, many communities attempted to maintain farms and farmland through a single method such as zoning ordinance. But when communities applied their single tool approach, it quickly became apparent that no one tool, in and of itself, was sufficient to do the job (Coughlin et al., 1977).

As a result, new programs evolved. In these efforts, emphasis was retained on conventional tools and techniques, but communities were beginning to use all of the tools at their disposal to maintain farm and farmland (Toner 1981a). Among these tools and techniques are the following.

Zoning

Communities have used agricultural zones with a large minimum lot size (from one unit per 35 acres to one unit per 640 acres), quarter/quarter density zoning, sliding scale zoning, and conditional zoning approaches. The zoning approach emphasizes the protection of land best suited for agricultural use while permitting nonagricultural uses on land least suited to agricultural use (Kartez 1980). Yet, within these zoning approaches, special attention is directed to these nonagricultural uses in order to ensure they are compatible with nearby agricultural use.

Community Plan

Most local approaches are anchored in a community plan. The community planning process is used to balance land use needs throughout the community, ensuring sufficient lands for nonagricultural use, while also protecting the best agricultural lands from nonagricultural development.

Capital Improvement Plan

At some point most nonagricultural uses require public expenditures for capital improvements: for roads, water lines, sewer lines, etc. (Lapping 1979). Communities use the capital improvement plan to guide the preponderance of nonagricultural uses into or around established population centers. In this way established population centers are built up to accept nonagricultural uses while the agricultural areas retain their dominant agricultural setting.

Annexation Agreements

Closely allied with both the plan for capital improvements and the community plan are annexation agreements. Commonly, municipalities and counties work together to reach understanding on the extent and timing of municipal annexation. This ensures that agricultural preservation plans will not be subverted by premature annexations and development.

Regional Planning Agencies

Regional planning agencies have served a variety of roles in local programs. This has included the use of regional land-use plans as surrogate local plans, the application of A-95 powers to protect farms and farmland, and the use of regional staff in preparing local programs. Many local programs are using regional planning agencies, their powers, their data, and their personnel to develop and administer local programs.

State Programs

As with the regional agencies, local programs also place heavy reliance on available state programs (Coughlin and Keene 1981). In some states, such as Wisconsin, Oregon, Michigan, and New York, there are unique state level programs. These programs give communities or farmers special authorities or powers in the protection of prime agricultural land. Nearly all states have special property tax relief programs that can also be integrated into local programs. Finally, state agencies have also been able to provide considerable technical support to local planning and regulatory efforts.

In the local planning process, communities rarely discover a one-time collection of tools or techniques. Instead, communities take a trial and error approach in which they are free to use some tools, attach new devices, discard unworkable methods, and work out problems. Slowly, the methods and techniques add up to a package that continues to be subject to the trial and error approach.

This makes it difficult to categorize or even inventory all of the local approaches in maintaining farms or farmland. In the course of the work on the National Agricultural Lands Study, a cursory inventory of local communities showed that at least 270 of them were using zoning to protect farmland. In addition to zoning, many communities used a host of other fiscal and police powers. Every program was unique in one way or another (Coughlin and Keene 1981).

About the best to be said is that communities are using all of the tools at their disposal to insure the protection of farms and farmland. These tools are being combined, one with the other, so that the result is a package of devices. This package includes regulatory powers, fiscal powers, planning methods, moral persuasion, as well as a long list of informal methods and agreements.

Keep in Mind That the Flip Side of Agricultural Preservation is Urban Development

To be successful, local programs must be structured around the notion that while land best suited to agriculture must be retained, sufficient lands should also be set aside for urban development needs. If communities fail to give attention to urban development needs, the effort to maintain farms and farmland would be placed in serious jeopardy.

The danger to agricultural preservation stems from two sources: economic and legal. On the economic side communities should consider that the dissolution of the agricultural community typically occurs because of urban development pressure. This pressure is translated into land value differences between land for agricultural use and land for urban use. When the differences become too great, the land is taken out of agricultural production.

In order to deal with this pressure, communities must ensure that they are able to meet urban development needs within or adjacent to established population centers. In almost all cases there is more than sufficient land capable of meeting urban needs, but unless the community evaluates the holding capacity within population centers, the question cannot be resolved with any degree of certainty. Moreover, if the community fails to provide land to meet urban needs, this would result in extreme pressure on the agricultural preservation program which could easily cause it to fail.

Legal attacks are also more likely where a community fails to account for urban development needs, especially for housing (Godschalk 1979). If, for example, a community relied on a large minimum lot size in the zoning ordinance to protect prime land but failed to consider its effects on housing, the program might easily fall to an exclusionary zoning attack. This is primarily due to the zoning history of large lot sizes which, in many cases, were used to exclude low and moderate income housing from the community. Thus, in considering the possibility of legal attack, communities are wise to deal carefully with urban land use requirements.

In planning for urban land-use needs, there are several ideas to keep in mind. First, the community must make an effort to ensure that lands are set aside to meet projected housing needs for varying family size and family income. But this raises the question of how much land should be made available for housing needs.

Regional projections can be very useful here. Where such projections have been made, it is fairly easy for a community to identify a fair share. In the case where no such projection exists, the community must rely on its own projections. In any event, the resultant estimates should reflect regional needs as well as local needs. So long as the community sets aside land to meet these needs, they have fulfilled their basic obligation in both protecting the agricultural area and in providing land for housing.

A second major consideration in planning for urban development is that the investments in urban development must be made in the established population centers. The capital improvement plan, for example, should be directed toward upgrading or renewing established centers. Urban investment dollars should be spent in preparing urban areas for urban development. Conversely, these same dollars should be kept out of agricultural areas.

For example, there is hardly a rural county road which could not stand some improvement: widening, painting lines, resurfacing, traffic control, etc. Yet these improvements in agricultural areas work more to the advantage of prospective urban developers than they do the agricultural uses. Thus, instead of upgrading the urban character of rural areas, this flow of investment dollars should serve as an important pull factor for urban development in population centers, and also work as a push factor in keeping urban development out of agriculture areas.

The more dollars spent by a community in improving or renewing population centers, the better the community will be able to guide new development into these areas. By preparing population centers to accept new development, communities will go a long way in maintaining their farms and farmland.

Conclusion

It would be foolhardy to conclude that communities following these guidelines would automatically develop a successful farming protection program. For if there was any single lesson to be drawn from the case studies, it was that each community was unique. The amount of development pressure on farming varied from place to place. There were sharp differences in the social, political, economic, and environmental contexts of the programs. The degree of consensus on the issue of protecting farming changed from community to community. As a result, in the ten communities there were ten different planning processes, methods, plans, and regulatory approaches. About the best that can be said about the guidelines is that they will help communities avoid some of the fundamental errors that have proved so disastrous in other places.

References

Berry, W. 1977. "The Unsettling of America: Culture and Agriculture." Sierra Club Books, San Francisco, CA.

Coughlin, R.E. et al. 1977. Saving the Garden: The Preservation of Other Environmentally Valuable Land. Regional Science Research Institute, Philadelphia, PA.

Coughlin, R.E. and Keene, J.C. (Editors). 1981. "The Protection of Farmland: A Reference Guidebook for State and Local Governments." National Agricultural Lands Study, U.S. Government Printing Office, Washington, D.C.

Godschalk, D.R. et al. 1979. "Constitutional Issues in Growth Management." American Planning Association, Planners Press, Chicago, IL.

Glass, J.E. 1980. Citizen participation in planning: The relationship between objectives and techniques, Journal of Soil and Water Conservation 35(5), 224–229.

Heufner, R.P. et al. 1975. Utah's support for land use planning: Fragile as the landscape, Journal of Soil and Water Conservation 30(3), 112–115.

Kartez, J. 1980. A zoning administrator's view of farmland zoning, Journal of Soil and Water Conservation 35(6), 265–266.

Lapping, M. 1979. Agricultural land retention strategies: Some underpinnings, Journal of Soil and Water Conservation 34(3), 124–126.

Nellis, L. 1981. Planning with rural values, Journal of Soil and Water Conservation 35(2), 67–71.

Toner, W. 1981a. Land use controls: Agricultural zoning, in "The Protection of Farmland: A Reference Guidebook for State and Local Governments," Robert E. Coughlin and John C. Keene (Editors). National Agricultural Lands Study, U.S. Government Printing Office, Washington, D.C.

Toner, W. 1981b. "Zoning to Protect Farming: A Citizen's Guidebook." National Agricultural Lands Study, U.S. Government Printing Office, Washington, D.C.

7

Local Approaches to Farmland Preservation: A Rural Renaissance for Zoning[1]

Jack Kartez

Agricultural Zoning

Planning literature often focuses on efforts to implement the purchase of development rights (PDR) and the transfer of development rights (TDR) as farmland preservation techniques in rapidly urbanizing jurisdictions such as King County, Washington; Howard County, Maryland; and Suffolk County, New York. Acquisition techniques entail high public costs per acre of farmland, but also provide the greatest certainty that participating lands will remain in agricultural use. PDR and TDR are better suited to the needs of metropolitan areas than predominantly rural counties, where "less-than-fee" acquisition techniques are financially unrealistic. In urban areas where farmland is a scarce open space amenity, the costs of PDR and TDR appear necessary and justifiable. Most rural counties, however, are limited to conventional exercise of the police power through zoning.

Reciting the flaws of zoning as an urban policy tool has been standard fare since the 1950s. As John Reps said in 1964:

> We have unnecessarily prolonged the existence of a land use control device conceived in another era when the true and frightening complexity of urban life was barely appreciated. We have, through heroic efforts and with massive doses of legislative remedies, managed to preserve what was once a lusty infant not only past the retirement age, but well into senility (Reps 1964).

Rural jurisdictions are now experiencing an equal frustration with zoning's inadequacies when applied to a rural environment. Planning consultant Scott Lefaver has argued that:

> public officials often attempt to solve rural problems with tools designed for urban areas. Zoning concepts are applied which are outdated, ineffective, and do not take into account the real dynamics of rural living (Lefaver 1978).

[1]This chapter was partially based on an article that appeared in the *Journal of Soil and Water Conservation* 35(6), 265-266.

The emergence of farmland preservation as a major objective of county planning as well as statewide legislation has spurred a renaissance of efforts to mold zoning into a workable tool for rural planning.

These efforts have generated numerous local variations on the traditional techniques of zoning. Localities and states scattered throughout the nation are facing common problems and adopting quite similar solutions in reworking conventional urban zoning concepts to fit rural needs. Three examples are briefly identified in this chapter: the development of new approaches to controlling density in agricultural zones; special use provisions needed in agricultural zoning districts; and similarities and differences in state-mandated provisions for locally adopted agricultural zoning districts. These are but a few examples indicating problems and workable solutions which jurisdictions considering adoption of strong agricultural zoning may expect to encounter.

Density Limits without Uniform Lot Size Provision

Traditional urban zoning controls density through requiring homogeneous minimum lot sizes throughout a use district. This approach has proved frustrating in rural areas where nonfarm residential uses on small lots may be mixed with large farm tracts at acceptably low densities over a large area. The approach to density suited to the city block is not always workable in rural areas where zoning districts cover thousands of acres for two reasons: First, provisions allowing small acreage lot sizes throughout such districts (say 1–5 acres, or 0.405–2.025 ha) ruin the effectiveness of zoning to protect farmlands from incompatible neighbors and urban conversion. However, large minimum lot sizes (20 or more acres, or 8.1 or more hectares) conflict with the commonly found local desire to allow limited numbers of small-acreage homesites at locations which do not interfere with farm neighbors.

Farm owners themselves can become bitterly opposed to inflexible zoning provisions, which prohibit selling isolated or unproductive portions of their land, or which frustrate their efforts to provide equity in homesites for younger family members. This inflexibility toward long-established social patterns only increases the rural citizen's belief that "zoning is a political ideology" instead of a rational method of community improvement (Getzels et al. 1980). However, the result of local attempts to squeeze flexibility out of conventional zoning codes is likely to be an unhappy experience with circumventing the code through "use variances," "family exemptions," "spot zoning," and other methods of dubious legality. This only undermines the credibility of zoning even further in a rural area. Many counties are approaching the problem through a fundamental restructuring of the density concept to fit rural (rather than urban) conditions. The common innovation in each case is that the definition of a limit on density changes has been changed from the minimum lot size to the total number of lots created.

A good example is "quarter/quarter zoning" first developed in Carver County, Minnesota (Toner 1978). Under this approach, each landowner is entitled to one nonfarm building site per 40 acres (16.2 ha) of land he owns. Lots separated from the farm must also meet several site-specific performance standards: a 1 acre (0.405 ha) minimum lot size; soils suitable for on-site sewage disposal and water supply; and access to a public road. A similar approach is "sliding scale zoning" entitling each landowner to a fixed number of buildable lots depending on the size of the original landholding.

A slightly different technique is to place a single limit on all land divisions within an agricultural zone. In Whitman County, Washington, for example, all landowners are limited to creating two new building lots regardless of the total size of the landholding. Lots must meet performance standards for sewage disposal and access, and in addition must be located on soils marginal for farming and in locations buffered from farm activities.

Special Agricultural Use Provision Problems

Zoning is a blunt instrument. Under the "equal protection" doctrine, identical restrictions must apply to each property within a use district. Counties grappling with zoning code provisions for agricultural areas soon discover that there are a variety of situations that arise that were never envisioned in code provisions designed for the strict separation of uses in a municipality.

Two examples of this problem are multiple farm dwellings and residual homesteads. The problem of multiple farm dwellings arises when a farmer wishes to place a second residence on the farm for a family member or hired help. Zoning administrators stuck with conventional use provisions in the zoning code have no choice but to follow the one lot/one use logic of urban zoning appeals or to send the matter on to the local planning commission or board of adjustment as a use variance request. Neither approach is a satisfactory solution to the problem. The extended family is an integral part of the farm life-style, and an additional dwelling unit on the large acreage of a farm is rarely a problem. Many rural counties eventually adopt specific provisions for the agricultural zone recognizing additional farm dwellings as a permitted or conditional use. This eliminates a drain on everybody's patience and avoids a great deal of adverse public sentiment in the farm community.

Residual homesteads are a problem caused by farm consolidations, which often leave the owner with one or more additional homes and out buildings on an acre of untillable land. Many farmers prefer to sell these as residential property rather than become landlords. However, in agricultural zones with large minimum acreages for single-family dwelling units, such unwanted homesteads become a problem of nonconforming use (again creating legal and procedural issues far out of proportion to the problem) or force the farmer to sell productive land. One benefit of rural density provisions such as sliding scale zoning is that they also provide solutions to specific problems such as the unwanted homestead. Such problems can often dominate the time and energy of tiny rural planning agencies and local officials to the detriment of the total farmland protection effort.

State-Mandated Agricultural Zoning

The states' earliest venture into land-use planning was the enabling of current use-value tax assessment for farmland from 1956 onward. Several states have also adopted statutory provisions for special or exclusive county agricultural zoning districts which incorporate provision of the tax incentive.

The earliest example of this was California's passage of two bills in 1957 enabling current use-value assessment and strengthening exclusive agricultural zoning at the local level (Kartez 1976). The zoning enabling law was limited to the provision that owners of land in such exclusive agricultural zones could not be annexed to a municipality without prior consent. Current use-value assessment was only to be available to lands in such zones, when "there was no reasonable probability of the removal or modification of the zoning restriction." Given the impermanence of local zoning, many California county assessors refused to extend tax benefits to farmlands until passage of the "Williamson Act" in 1965. However, the unprecedented action of a state legislature to intervene in writing local zoning ordinances established the concept of exclusive agricultural zoning in California. A study of more than 400 rural ordinances adopted before January 1965 found exclusive agricultural zoning in only 55 local ordinances among 15 states. Of these, fully 30 had been adopted by California counties (Hady and Sibold 1975).

Since then, the states of New York, Oregon, and Wisconsin have adopted legislation authorizing exclusive agricultural zoning and, tying local adoption of state-mandated use provisions to the availability of current use-value tax assessment for farmers. These enabling statutes also provide further protection for farmlands by widening the statutory authority of the local zoning code. For example, all three statutes prohibit the imposition of special service benefit assessments on land within state-mandated farm zones. Oregon's "exclusive farm use zone" and Wisconsin's "exclusive agricultural use district" are quite specific in defining requirements for the content of local zoning ordinances (see Chapters 13 and 14). Although implemented differently in each state, the Oregon and Wisconsin approaches to statewide standards for agricultural zoning are somewhat similar, as shown in Table 7.1.

Of interest is Wisconsin's specific provision for the residual homestead which states that "for purposes of farm consolidation, farm residences or structures may be separated from a larger farm parcel" caused by farm consolidation. Oregon's statute authorizes a special procedure for approval of nonfarm single-family dwellings which can be used to address the residual homestead situation. However, the lack of specific provisions for residual homesteads continues to generate some concern, judging from the 1979 Oregon Legislative Session. Three bills were introduced to specifically legitimize the creation of a nonfarm homesite in cases of farm consolidation within exclusive farm use zones. Local officials can face real difficulties when state-mandated agricultural zoning statutes do not anticipate local variations in the farm community and special use situations. Considerable uncertainty can be created.

For example, one Oregon county, which moved early to adopt exclusive farm use zoning, was faced with such a problem in 1976 when a request was made by a farm owner to place a mobile home for a family member (Kartez 1976). Oregon's statute does not directly address multiple farm dwellings. This left local officials in doubt as to how to comply with state law in good faith while finding a solution to a valid local need. The dilemma was finally resolved with some local fanfare when one of the law's original legislative sponsors reassured local officials that special provisions for farm community needs were consistent with state policy.

Table 7.1. Comparison of Selected Statutory Provisions for Local Agricultural Zoning in Oregon and Wisconsin

Statutory Provision	Oregon	Wisconsin
Authority	Oregon Revised Statutes Chapter 215.203	Wisconsin Statutes Annotated, Chapter 91.71
Permitted farm use defined	Yes	Yes
Other uses permitted outright	Schools; churches; forestry; accessory uses, utility facilities, excluding commercial power plants	Gas and electric utilities
Special or conditional uses permitted in local zoning ordinance	Commercial uses in conjunction with farm use; geothermal and aggregate mining; private/public parks, campgrounds and golf courses; public power plants	Agricultural-related, religious, utility, institutional or governmental uses that do not conflict with farm use
Nonfarm residential use provisions	Single-family permitted upon findings by local governing body that use will not conflict with farm practices and is located on land not suitable for farm use	Prohibited
Minimum lot size required	None (to be locally determined)	35 acres (14.175 ha)
Provision for multiple farm dwellings	None	None
Provisions for residual homesteads	Not defined separately from other single family dwelling units (see above)	For purposes of farm consolidation, farm residences or structures may be separated from larger farm parcel
Farms exempt from sewer and water benefit assessments	Yes	Yes
Restrictions on farm practices	State and local laws may not restrict accepted farm practices unless for health or safety purposes	Not defined

States that enter a partnership with local government in writing the zoning code should strive to anticipate the unexpected problems which zoning administrators and local officials know are a predictable burden of zoning.

A Rural Zoning Literature Needed

Municipal zoning has spawned considerable literature on problems and practices over the years. This is a valuable resource for those involved in land use planning implementation, administration, and enforcement. But this literature has focused on urban settings, and there is no less of a need to share experience with rural zoning as farmland protection goals become widespread. Rural zoning problems have their own unique characteristics and the applicable literature is limited.

It should be noted that there has recently been a flowering of literature on rural and small town planning in general, and furthermore, the United States Department of Agriculture has for many years published leaflets and handbooks on rural zoning. However, the USDA materials have tended to be summaries of general approaches to zoning ordinance drafting, and they have maintained a neutral, noncritical tone and have not dwelt on the frustrations of day-to-day administration. This is not surprising, given the purpose of these materials.

On the other hand, recent literature has boldly faced the issues of comprehensive planning in rural areas with great honesty and sensitivity to the problems involved. Two recent examples are the book "Rural and Small Town Planning" (Getzels et al. 1980) and an article by a Wyoming

Fig. 7.1. Farmland being turned into a housing development in Bucks County, Pennsylvania.

planner called "Planning With Rural Values" (Nellis 1980). However, these materials stop short of detailed analysis of techniques and administrative practices necessary to implement the plan fairly and efficiently through zoning.

A good example is Nellis' account of successful comprehensive plan adoption in Big Horn County, Wyoming. A planning process with attention to rural concerns and values in this farming area resulted in overcoming resistance to farmland protection through zoning. Nellis believes success was achieved because:

> Big Horn County's planning effort recognized . . . reasons for resistance to planning and dealt with them, not as obstacles or unfortunate realities, but as positive guidelines as to how the local planning process should and could develop.

Much the same could be said of the need to consider day-to-day administrative problems in zoning and subdivision regulation administration as opportunities rather than obstacles. And Nellis notes the problems of postplan regulation:

> The learning process that led to a plan's adoption in Big Horn County has continued . . . almost every development review raised unanswered questions. . . . Is the proper applicant the landowner or the builder? What is a fair way of evaluating lot sizes? . . . Persistent problems have arisen. The first and most vexing is record-keeping. The informal atmosphere of rural decision-making makes it difficult to keep precise records . . . The second problem is enforcement. The rural tendency to 'work things out' is pronounced in Big Horn County.

Again, these are problems that have received much attention in municipal and urban planning. For example, at a 1969 national short course on regulatory devices convened by the American Society of Planning Officials, Jack Noble admitted that

> A lot of us are muddling through, and not all that well. Norman Williams writes of towns where no one can find the zoning map. A lawyer friend described a town where there was no zoning map, although the town clerk had carefully filed—in chronological order and without an index—each of the hundreds of zoning amendments since 1929 (Bair, 1969).

Short course chairman Fred Bair summed up the prospects by saying "we need improvements in the manner and substance of regulation and in the way regulations are administered and enforced. And most of all—before we start tinkering with details—we need better understanding of what planning regulations should and should not be used for" (Bair 1969).

Those of us involved in farmland preservation and rural planning should pay heed to Bair's challenge because we are likely to be relying on zoning and other conventional controls. The examples of problems and solutions to rural and farmland zoning presented earlier in this chapter represent but a few considerations that rural counties have found important in developing workable agricultural zoning. Foreseeing problems can prevent them from dominating the time and energy of tiny rural planning agencies. Documenting and sharing what we have learned, and what problems we still seek solutions for, can aid us in that process.

Acknowledgment

The author wishes to acknowledge the contributions made to the subject of rural planning techniques by Mark Hinthorne, Principal Planner, Yakima County, Washington, Planning Department.

References

Bair, F.H. (Editor). 1969. Regulatory Devices, presented at the Regulatory Devices Short Course Held at the 1969 ASPO National Planning Conference, American Society of Planning Officials, Chicago, IL.

Getzels, J. and Thurow, C. (Editors). 1980. "Rural and Small Town Planning." American Planning Association, The Planners Press, Chicago, IL.

Hady, T.F. and Sibold, A.G. 1974. State Programs for the Differential Assessment of Farm and Open Space Land, Agricultural Economics Rep. No. 256, U. S. Department of Agriculture, Economic Research Service. U. S. Government Printing Office, Washington, D.C.

Kartez, J.D. 1976. Planning Preservation: Issues in Implementing Oregon's Statewide Agricultural Land Preservation Policy in the Willamette Valley. Department of Urban and Regional Planning, University of Oregon, Eugene, OR.

Lefaver, S. 1978. A new framework for rural planning, *Urban Land,* April. The Urban Land Institute, Washington, D.C.

Nellis, L. 1980. Planning with rural values, *Journal of Soil and Water Conservation* **35**(2), 67-71.

Reps, J.W. 1964. Requiem for Zoning, Pomeroy Memorial Lecture, 1966, *in* "Planning 1964." American Society of Planning Officials, Chicago, IL.

Toner, W. 1978. Saving Farms and Farmland: A Community Guide. American Society of Planning Officials, Chicago, IL.

Yakima County Planning Department. 1978. Methods of Guiding Rural Land Use: A Summary. Yakima, Washington.

8

King County's Purchase of Development Rights Program[1]

John Spellman

In November of 1979, the voters of King County, Washington, approved a $50 million bond issue to purchase the development rights on designated farmlands in the county. The purchase of development rights is the purchase of the right to develop from owners of specific parcels, leaving the owner all the other rights of ownership. The price of the rights is diminution in the market value of the land as a result of the removal of development rights. The remaining value of the land is the "farm use" value (Coughlin and Keene 1981). This was the first time that a purchase of development rights (PDR) program has been approved in a general election anywhere in the United States. The PDR proposition passed 63% to 37% despite the widespread tax-revolt sentiment in 1979. The purpose of this chapter is to present some background information on the county, the history of its PDR program, the rationale for choosing this approach, and why it was accepted by the farm and nonfarm communities in King County. A summary of events since November 1979 concludes this chapter.

Agriculture in King County[2]

King County is located in northwestern Washington. Puget Sound forms its western boundary and the Cascade Mountains define the eastern boundary (Fig. 8.1). The county covers 1.36 million acres (550,400 ha) but the Snoqualmie National Forest (in eastern King County) accounts for

[1]An earlier version of this chapter was the keynote presentation at the farmlands preservation conference held at Washington State University in November 1979. At that time John Spellman was serving his third term as King County executive. One year later he was elected governor of the state of Washington. The original chapter has been revised to include recent developments as of the fall of 1981. Governor Spellman was assisted in preparing and revising this paper by Patrick W. Dunn, formerly his administrative counsel in King County and currently special assistant to the governor and director of the Washington State Planning and Community Affairs Agency, and Richard W. Dunford, associate professor of agricultural economics at Washington State University.
[2]Much of information in this section was obtained from Sanger (1978, Sec. V, pp. 1–63).

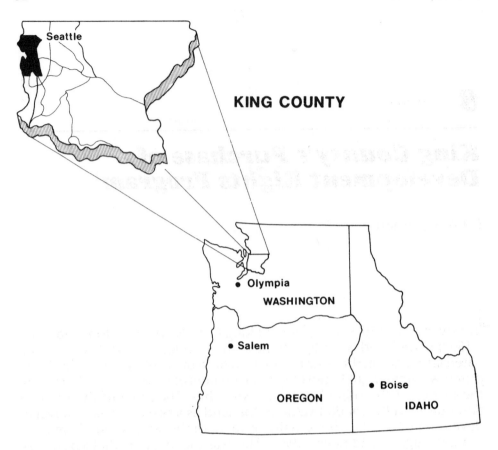

Fig. 8.1. Location of King County, Washington.

one-quarter of this land area. About 1.25 million people live in King County, which represents approximately one-third of the state's total population. Sixty percent of the people in King County reside in Seattle and other smaller cities. The population density of the county is approximately ten times the average population density for the entire state (Washington Office of Financial Management 1977, pp. 3, 190).

Urbanization since World War II has resulted in a precipitous decline in farm acreage and numbers. Between 1945 and 1975, land in farms dropped from 165,000 acres (66,775 ha) to 55,000 acres (22,258 ha). The rate of loss of farmland in recent years has averaged about 2000 acres (809 ha) annually. During the post-World War II period, the number of active farm operations has decreased from 6500 to only about 1200. Of these remaining farms, approximately 270 are commercial farms. These farm enterprises receive over 90% of the gross farm income in the county. About 70% of all farm operators also work off the farm, and over half of all farmers earn the majority of their income from nonfarm jobs.

The leading agricultural enterprises in King County are dairying, ornamental horticulture, egg production, beef cattle, and vegetable/berry enterprises. Dairy farms receive about half of the county's gross farm income and cover approximately 80% of the land in agricultural use. Much of the land on dairy farms is used for growing feed. Between 1964 and 1974, the majority of the decrease in acreage in agricultural use resulted from less pastured land on dairy farms. Greenhouse crops, outdoor nursery crops, and bulbs are the primary ornamental horticulture products produced in King County. Most of the acreage in these crops is planted in sweet corn, lettuce, rhubarb, cabbage, strawberries, and red raspberries. The vegetable/berry operations are particularly dependent on productive soils. The acreage devoted to these crops declined almost 50% between 1964 and 1974, primarily as a result of urbanization. Deteriorating markets for processed vegetables/berries and a shortage of seasonal harvest labor contributed to the decline in output of these agricultural products.

Farmland in King County has traditionally been found in its fertile river valleys, which contain about three-fourths of the county's class II and III soils. (There are no class I soils in King County.) Due to their proximity to Seattle and good transportation linkages, several of these valleys have experienced rapid urbanization. Most development has involved industrial and commercial land uses like warehouses and distribution centers. Drainage problems and high site-development costs have limited residential development in these river valleys. The more distant agricultural areas contain most of the dairy farms in King County. Large-lot residential developments, hobby farms, and ranchettes have absorbed a significant amount of farmland in these areas in recent years.

Most inputs needed for agricultural enterprises must be imported from outside King County and the local food processing industry is rather small. However, the dairy farms are very dependent on local feed suppliers, and a relatively high percentage of farm products are sold directly to consumers through farmers' markets, roadside stands and "u-pick" operations. About 1% of all jobs in King County are a result of agriculture. Two-thirds of these jobs are in the ornamental horticulture and vegetable/berry sectors. Dairying is less labor intensive and more mechanized. Consequently, only 25% of the agricultural jobs are associated with dairying in King County.

Why Save Farmland in King County?

Given the relatively urban/suburban nature of King County, some people have asked "why should we use public funds to retain farmland in King County when the land could be used for new housing and industry with the needed food brought in from other parts of the state or other states?" There are a number of reasons why the residents of King County have supported farmland retention efforts:

1. Farmland is a unique resource and irreplaceable once lost.
2. Farming is a valuable economic activity and industry.
3. The open space and urban separation created by farms are important to a developing area.
4. Locally grown produce is cheaper and fresher than produce coming from outside the region.
5. Cheaper local produce helps keep down the price of imported produce.
6. The energy costs of shipping food are getting more expensive all the time, and many people do not want to become completely dependent on growing conditions in other parts of the country.
7. There is an abundance of vacant, non-farmland that could be used for new housing and industry.

8.   Farming and farmland is our heritage in this country. Franklin Roosevelt said, "the history of every nation is essentially written in the way it cares for its soil." The ethic of the land is not one that is taken lightly.

History of the King County Program

The retention of farmlands has been a specific goal of King County's comprehensive plan since 1964. To achieve this goal, certain areas were established as "agriculture" zones. In spite of this policy, the agricultural land base in the county continued to decline as the area experienced significant population growth. After a series of fact finding meetings in 1976 involving the farm community, the county placed an 18-month moratorium on the development of designated farmlands. During this period, advisory committees of farmers in the affected communities were formed to examine various policy options for retaining farmland. These advisory committees recommended a voluntary purchase of development rights program to permanently protect these lands.

After studying all aspects of the PDR approach, a $35 million program was placed on the ballot and received approval from 59.7% of the voters in November 1978. This was just short of the 60% needed to pass a property tax bond issue in Washington. After that election, I asked the supporters and opponents of the program to join forces and study the problem of farmland conversion and to make recommendations. Ninety citizens drawn from all parts of the community (farmers, realtors, developers, bankers, environmentalists, businessmen, and elected officials) participated in this study. After considerably strengthening the basic plan,[3] this citizens study committee proposed a $50 million PDR program. A larger expenditure was required due to the price of land having risen substantially and anticipated federal funds for the acquisition of some land had not been appropriated. The voters overwhelmingly approved this proposal in September 1979 but there were not enough people voting to validate the election. To validate a special election in Washington, the total number of votes cast must be greater than or equal to 40% of the total number of votes cast in the last general election. In the general election on November 6, 1979, the PDR proposition was again on the ballot. It received an affirmative vote from 63% of the voters and the turnout was sufficient to validate the results.[4]

Provisions of the King County Program

The ordinance establishing the PDR program divided eligible farmlands into three purchase priorities. The first priority lands are those most

[3]The citizens study committee produced a very thorough and informative booklet entitled, "Saving Farmlands and Open Space," which can be obtained by writing to the Office of the King County Executive, King County Courthouse, Seattle, WA 98104 (206) 344-4040. The ordinance creating the purchase of development rights program is included in this booklet.
[4]The Save Our Local Farmlands Committee (Ellis and Golub 1979) compiled a very complete report about the campaign containing copies of all major campaign literature, letters, speeches, and documents. This publication, "King County, Washington, The Campaign for Farmlands, 1978-1979" can be obtained through the libraries of the University of Washington, Seattle, and King County.

threatened by development. The acquisition of development rights will occur in a series of purchase rounds. In the first two rounds only Priority 1 lands will be eligible to enter the program. In the third round Priority 1 and 2 lands will be eligible, and land in any of the three priorities will be eligible in succeeding rounds. The rounds will continue until the $50 million is expended or until 6 years have passed.

The value of the development right is determined by subtracting the appraised value of the property as farmland from its appraised value at what is called its "highest and best use." By law, the county cannot pay more than this difference in appraised values. The executive branch of the county decides which properties and bids meet the requirements of the ordinance and then submits them to an independent citizen selection committee. This committee makes the final recommendations to the county council for adoption. It has been estimated that the available funds will allow the purchase of development rights on at least 10,000 acres (4047 ha) of farmland. This is only about one-third of the eligible farmland but its protection should serve to stabilize the agricultural land base in King County.

Rationale for the PDR Approach

One of the most common questions is "Aren't there are other ways to retain farmland which are much less expensive than purchasing development rights?" Zoning and use-value (current use) taxation are two alternatives frequently suggested. Unfortunately, neither has proved to be *effective* against the intense pressures of growth and development experienced in King County.

Use-value taxation (also known as current-use taxation) encourages the retention of agricultural land in farm use by providing property tax relief to eligible farmland owners. This property tax relief is provided by assessing eligible farmland on the basis of its agricultural value rather than its market value, which may be inflated by various nonfarm influences.

Zoning is dependent on the particular officials in office and can often be changed relatively easily. Much of the agriculturally zoned land in King County was lost when it was annexed into a city or was part of an incorporation that created a city. Once in a city, the local council would change the zoning to allow the development on this land. Although use-value taxation effectively reduces the property tax burden on farmland, it cannot effectively counteract the development pressures on farmland near a growing urban area. For more information about property tax relief programs, see Dunford (1980).

The much greater value of farmland for nonfarm uses is the key factor contributing to the loss of farmland. As a farmer retires or wants to leave the area, he naturally wants to sell his farmland for the best price he can receive. Farmland that is relatively flat, well-drained, and in proximity to a large city is very valuable to developers and builders. This is particularly true when these individuals can receive a property tax break on the land (due to current-use taxation) until they are ready to develop it. Thus, the value of farmland for nonfarm uses may substantially exceed the agricultural value of the property. This large differential in values effectively eliminates the possibility of young people entering farming to keep the

Fig. 8.2. Urban sprawl, partially caused by "spot" zoning. Once a development occurs in an area previously used for farming, it forces the taxes on properties in the vicinity to escalate, making farming prohibitive. This development in King County, Washington, is on soil once considered to be prime agricultural land. USDA Soil Conservation Service photo.

industry alive, since young farmers cannot afford to buy farmland at the "highest and best use" value. Consequently, farmland is usually sold to nonfarmers.

The people of King County wanted a *permanent* solution that would stabilize the farm economy. By selling the development rights on farmland, the farmer receives the extra value associated with nonfarm uses of his property yet the land remains in farming. After selling these rights, the price of the land decreases considerably to its value in farm uses. Thus, when the farmer decides to sell his land, other farmers can afford to buy it. Furthermore, the farmland is still on the tax rolls and the public does not have to maintain the property as it would if the farmland were purchased outright.

Purchasing development rights is expensive, but it is a permanent way of securing the many benefits associated with retaining farmland: cheaper and fresher produce; less reliance on uncertain supplies of food from other regions; open space, urban separation, and other amenities; savings on the cost of providing public services to the developments that would have displaced the farmland; the retention of jobs in related agribusiness activities; and the intangible benefits of not destroying a unique and irreplaceable resource.

The Crucial Elements for Acceptance

In order to be successful, a farmland retention program must be supported by both farmers and the nonfarm residents who will pay the majority of its costs. The King County PDR program was supported by both of these groups. Several aspects of the PDR proposition and its presentation to the voters were crucial in gaining this support. First, participation in the program is *totally voluntary*. Farmers must petition the county to get in the program. Critics in the first campaign charged that the program was not voluntary. Strong emphasis was placed on its voluntary nature in the subsequent campaigns. The involvement of the farm communities in studying various options and ultimately choosing the PDR approach was also responsible for securing their support.

Although the concept of development rights is somewhat complicated, the electorate understood and accepted the concept after an intense educational effort. The broad-based citizens study committee played a crucial role in this educational effort. The citizens study committee educated the public about the need for the program as well as its provisions and anticipated impacts. There was only one comprehensive ordinance that created the program. The procedures were detailed and specific but readily understandable by the general public. Hence, the voters knew what they were being asked to support.

The cost of the program did not seem to be a major factor in any of the elections. The proposed 30-year maturity on the bonds allowed the cost to be borne by future residents as well as current residents. Consequently, the cost of the program to any individual would fall as the county continued to grow. It was estimated that the program would cost the owner of a $50,000 house approximately $9 a year. A citizen's selection committee was placed between the county executive and the county council giving assurances to the citizens that they would be able to keep a constant watch over the administration of the program and their funds. Furthermore, the program is strictly limited to 6 years and the overhead is minimal. No permanent or continuing bureaucracy is created by this program. Undoubtedly, all of these elements contributed to the successful passage of the King County PDR program.

Recent Events

Since the passage of the PDR proposition in November 1979, two very different types of activities have been pursued. Opponents have tried to stop the program via lawsuits, while the King County Office of Agriculture has been preparing to administer the program. The activities in each of these areas are summarized in this section.

In total, three lawsuits were undertaken in an attempt to stop the implementation of the King County PDR program. In the first lawsuit the constitutionality of the program was challenged on the grounds that the purchase of development rights to save farmland was not a public purpose and therefore public funds from the sale of bonds could not be used to finance the program. A lower court declared that preserving farmland was indeed a legitimate public purpose. This verdict was upheld by the state supreme court.[5]

A second lawsuit was undertaken once the county had accepted a low bid of about 8.44% interest on $30 million in bonds. There was an 8% interest rate ceiling on bonds when the PDR program was approved by the voters. This interest rate limit was subsequently raised to 12%. The lawsuit contended that the county could not finance the PDR program with bonds paying in excess of 8% interest since that was the interest rate limit in effect at the time of the election. A lower court disagreed with this contention but the state supreme court ruled that the bonds could not be sold for an interest rate greater than 8%. Hence, the bond sale to finance the PDR program was not finalized. Since that time, the interest rate on bonds has not dropped below 8%. Consequently, no bonds have yet been sold for the PDR program.

Another opponent of the PDR program filed a suit contending that the program should be overturned because a number of county officials improperly supported the bond issue and that other supporters who stood to gain financially from the program did not properly file their election financial statement. This lawsuit was withdrawn after the third day of the trial.

While these lawsuits were under way, the King County Office of Agriculture proceeded with preliminary implementation steps. [A more detailed description of the program administration can be found in the basic ordinance and other publications of the Office of Agriculture (See King County Farmlands Study Committee 1979).] As soon as the election was officially certified, letters were mailed to the property owners who were eligible in the first round of the program. The owners of over 60% of the acreage in this "most-threatened" category indicated that they were interested in proceeding with a title search on their property and a confirmation of their eligibility. About 80% of this acreage was found to be eligible for the first round of the program. In summary, the owners of slightly less than half of the farmland in the priority one area were interested and eligible for the PDR program.

The staff from the Office of Agriculture visited each eligible property owner to discuss the program. The staff included a director, two secretaries, an administrative assistant, an agricultural program support person, an accountant, two project managers, and a real estate specialist. Staff assistance was also received from the prosecuting attorney, the real estate section, and the comptroller. All of these farmland owners agreed to proceed to the next step of the program, namely, appraisals. (Appraisers were selected through the county's normal competitive bidding process.) Separate appraisals were done for the agricultural value and

[5]*Louthan v. King County*, 94 Wn. 2d 422, 617 P. 2d 977 (1980).

market value of the farmland. A third appraiser reviewed this work and made many necessary adjustments for consistency and completeness so that the properties would all be treated equally. Landowners were also allowed to get a review appraisal from an approved firm (Table 8.1).

The appraisals are a very important part of the PDR program since the county can only pay the landowner the difference between the appraised agricultural value and the appraised market value. The average appraised value of the development rights on the eligible farmland in the first priority area was $5000 per acre, ranging from $4000 to $6000 per acre.

While King County Office of Agriculture was proceeding with preliminary administrative steps, I appointed an agricultural task force of farmers, bankers, businessmen, and citizens to review the economics of agriculture and suggest ways to further increase the vitality of King County's agriculture. The task force formed a number of smaller groups to deal with particular issues such as credit, labor, marketing, and regulation. In their report, they suggested ways to simplify regulations currently constraining farmers, ways to expand marketing opportunities, new financial mechanisms for local farmers, and ways to provide additional labor for harvesting (King County Agricultural Task Force 1980). Their report also confirmed that agriculture could be a very viable economic activity in an urban county like King County if a land program was successful in keeping the price of agricultural land affordable for agricultural use.

Since 1982

In 1981, I began my term as Governor of the State of Washington. During most of 1981, the PDR program languished under the interim Executive appointed to complete my term. In 1982, King County elected a new executive who was also committed to the PDR program, Randy Revelle.

Under Executive Revelle, new funding mechanisms have been designed that satisfy the financial constraints placed on the PDR program by the Washington State Supreme Court. These mechanisms are being implemented to realize the full $50 million PDR program. The first two selection rounds are currently nearing completion using the $15 million that already has been secured with the new funding mechanisms. The

Table 8.1. King County Farmlands Preservation Program

Priority 1 Areas	Eligible landowners/ acreage (ha)	Applications received/ acreage (ha)	Applications/ acreage (ha) ineligible or withdrawn	Applications/ acreage (ha) to appraisers
Upper Green	80/1,962 (794.61)	40/1,295.54 (524.69)	11/538.77 (218.20)	32/756.77 (306.49)
Lower Green	81/1,804 (730.62)	29/992.80 (402.08)	5/41.58 (16.84)	25/951.22 (385.24)
Sammamish	53/1,475 (597.38)	31/1,397.14 (565.84)	6/60.36 (24.45)	28/1,336.78 (541.40)
Food-producing farmlands (1-B)	87/1,800 (729)	20/685.29 (297.54)	11/261.26 (105.81)	12/424.03 (171.73)
Total	301/7,041 (2,851.61)	120/4,370.77 (1,770.16)	33/901.97 (365.30)	97/3,468.80 (1,404.86)

remaining $35 million of program authority is expected to be utilized over 1984 and 1985. The first two selection rounds include parcels that have been pending since 1980. The average cost of development rights per acre in these rounds has now risen to approximately $8000.

The almost 3-year delay in the implementation of the program is largely the result of opposition by a few individuals who have tried to frustrate the objective of the majority of King County citizens. The delay likely will result in an acquisition of fewer development rights than would have been possible if the program had successfully begun in 1980. However, the need for the program has, if anything, increased over the last 3 years and it is rewarding to see it now being implemented.

A few years ago, I received a note from a woman in Seattle, and she included a quote of William Jennings Bryan, who over half a century ago declared:

> Burn down your cities and leave our farms . . . and your cities will spring up again as if by magic; but destroy our farms and the grass will grow in the streets of every city in the country.

No doubt in his time, Mr. Bryan was caught up with enthusiasm for his cause, but there remains no doubt in our time that this is a vital public business.

References

Coughlin, R.E. and Keene, J.C. (Editors). 1981. "The Protection of Farmland: A Reference Guidebook for State and Local Governments." U.S. Government Printing Office, Washington, D.C.

Dunford, R.W. 1980. A survey of property tax relief programs for the retention of agricultural and open space lands, *Gonzaga Law Review*, **15**(3), 675–99.

Ellis, J. and Golub, S. (Editors). 1979. King County, Washington, The Campaign for Farmlands, 1978-1979. Seattle, WA.

King County Agricultural Task Force. 1980. King County Agricultural Task Force Report on Local Agriculture. Seattle, WA.

King County Farmlands Study Committee. 1979. Saving Farmlands and Open Space. Citizens Study Committee Report to the Executive and Council of King County, Seattle, WA.

Sanger, J.M. 1978. Purchase of Development Rights to Retain Agricultural Lands: An Economic Study. Report to the Office of Agriculture, King County, Washington.

Washington Office of Financial Management. 1977. "Pocket Data Book 1977." Olympia, WA.

9

Agricultural Land Preservation in Whitman County, Washington

William R. Wagner

Impacts of Concern

Whitman County has experienced a relatively slow rate of growth over the last decade. Between 1970 and 1980, the population increased from 37,900 to 40,300. During this period, the most pressing land use issues have been scattered-site rural development and major public and private projects (e.g., dams, roads, and energy transmission facilities). Scattered-site development is directed away from commercial quality agricultural land through the combined application of exclusive agricultural zoning and a site specific land capability evaluation system. The county has encouraged state and federal legislation requiring local input into land-use decisions of other levels of government, to attack the problem of major developments.

The keystone to the present preservation strategy is the 1978 comprehensive plan. It states that commercial agriculture is the highest and best use of all lands capable of commercial production. Lands that can be cultivated successfully should remain in cultivation. Lands that can support commercial cattle herds should remain as pasture. All competing uses should be developed in or adjacent to urbanized areas or on land unsuited for a commercial level of production.[1]

Geological History

Because of the manner of formation and erosion of cultivatable soil in the Palouse region of eastern Washington State (see Fig. 9.1), the distinction between cultivatable land and noncultivatable land is fairly obvious. This allows for a simple system of detecting where nonfarm development should occur, if not on good farmland.

At one time the Palouse consisted of a mountain range of crystalline rock. The area was, over time, covered by lava flows to the extent that

[1]*Whitman County Comprehensive Plan*, pp. 25-38.

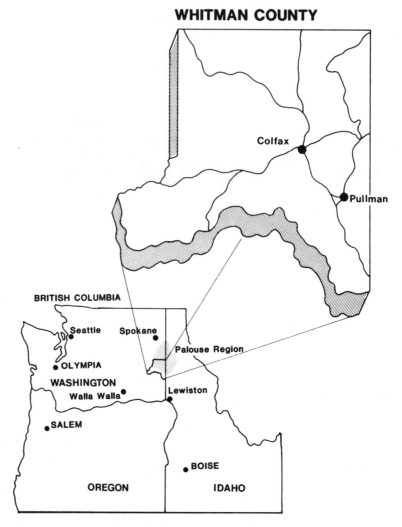

Fig. 9.1. Location of Whitman County, Washington.

only an occasional mountain peak is now exposed. Over this bed, soil was transported in by wind and deposited to a maximum depth of 200 ft (61 ms). The area now resembles a rolling sea of hills and ridges. Wind and rain erosion has exposed the underlying lava and cut valleys sometimes several hundred feet deep. It is on the sides and bottom lands of these valleys that land unsuitable for cultivation is found.

Land-Use Planning History

The Whitman County Planning Commission and Board of County Commissioners became concerned in 1960 with the impact of scattered development when several commercial businesses, including mobile home parks, were built under liberal zoning laws. To counter this trend, a 35 square mile area around the City of Pullman, the area of highest demand, was designated a "transitional zone" in 1962. Within this area residential development was permitted on 1 acre sites. This effectively stopped mobile home park and commercial development, but did nothing to stop rural residential development.

In the early 1970s scattered site residential development began to occur at a noticeable rate, following the nationwide trend of "back to the land." Farmers began getting complaints from nonfarming neighbors that weed spraying was killing plants, dust was coating houses, and equipment noise in the morning and evening was interfering with the nonfarmers' enjoyment of his home. It became apparent that even limited rural residential development was having a negative impact on farming. The U.S. Environmental Protection Agency and Washington State courts began to limit the types of farming operations around nonfarm housing and even suggested that a suit might be successful in recovering accidental and incidental damage.[2]

Concern mounted among the county's farmers about the existence of nonfarming operations in rural areas. This concern lead to the adoption of a 20 acre (8.1 ha) minimum lot size in 1975 for all new housing built outside incorporated towns or the Pullman area transitional zone.

In 1977 the transitional zone was eliminated, however residential subdivisions were possible if land could be rezoned to a 1 acre (0.405 ha) lot agricultural suburban zone. Although several small-scale developments were proposed, zone changes were rejected in each case. Typically, it was argued that a proposed development was too remote from a major town, and would be in conflict with surrounding farming operations; as well, urban services, such as snow removal, a higher level of road maintenance, police services, and fire services, would be economically difficult for the county to provide.

Current Land-Use Strategy

Recognizing their farmland protection policy could be criticized as exclusionary and of limited relationship to the potential use of the land, the Whitman County Planning Commission and Board of County Commissioners decided to significantly revise their development policies. A new comprehensive plan was adopted which had as a basic premise that all desired development can be accommodated with a minimum impact on agricultural land and agricultural practices if the agricultural potential of land is considered paramount in planning and zoning decisions.

If a site can be shown to have no commercial agricultural potential, then it can be put to another use. Or, when it is shown no appropriate commercial or industrial site for a proposed use exists in an urban area and/or the use is inappropriate for an urban area, then agricultural land adjacent or near an urban area can be converted to another use. The burden of proof is on the developer that a greater community good is being accomplished as a result of the conversion.

Density incentives and site location criteria are used to encourage development on lands unsuitable for commercial agricultural production. For example, only farm employees homes are allowed on good farmland. However, nonfarm homes are allowed on a small lot on less

[2]Langan v. Valicopters, Inc; 88 Wn. 2d 855, 567 P. 2d 218

productive soils close to existing roads and other man-made improvements.

An interagency staff review panel looks at each site proposed for nonfarmland development. The team consists of a regional planner, a U.S. Soil Conservation Service soil scientist, and a county health officer. Their review culminates in a decision allowing or disapproving the site.

Requirements Related to the Production Potential of the Land

1.   The very near surface geology must be rocky or wet alluvium to an extent that farming on a commercial scale is not practical.
2.   The site has not been used for at least 3 years for commercial agricultural purposes.
3.   A lot of 15 acres (6.075 ha) or less is so situated that it cannot be productively farmed even though it has good soil quality.

Note: Two of the above three characteristics would have to be met to get a development permit plus all of the following that would be applicable.

Site Characteristic Requirements

1.   The site must have at least 200 ft (61 m) frontage on an *existing county or state road with gravel surface or better,* or the Army Corps project boundary within the Snake River Canyon. Intervening public or private easements or rights-of-way for roads, railroads, or utilities shall be ignored.
2.   If on perennial surface water, a 200 ft (61 m) frontage would be required to keep impact on such surface water at as low a density as possible.
3.   Less than one-half of the site can be a flood plain area.
4.   Existing vegetation shall be preserved as wildlife habitat to the maximum extent feasible.
5.   The site must be designed to meet county and other health department standards for water production and sewage disposal.

Using the information gathered by this team, the regional planning director recommends to the county building official granting or denying permission to build on the proposed sites. If the decision is to allow development, the applicant is informed as well as neighboring property owners. The decision can be appealed within 20 days by the neighbors on the basis that the site does not, in fact, meet the adopted selection criteria. If permission to develop is denied, the applicant can appeal within 20 days. All appeals are submitted to a special hearings examiner committee, and then the state court system.

Land-Use Management Improvements Still Needed

The 1978 Whitman County Comprehensive Plan called for legislation in three areas:

1.   Protect farming from "nuisance suits."
2.   Seek better control over land division.

3. Seek cooperative arrangements or other means of maintaining harmony between local plans and those of the state and federal government.

Shortly after the adoption of the new plan, the state legislature did pass a "nuisance protection" law for farmers. It was proposed and adopted on behalf of dairy farmers. No one can speculate its effectiveness for wheat farming; only time will tell.[3]

Over the next several years the Board of County Commissioners and the County Planning Commission will seek to foster legislation to review large divisions of land and require the coordination of state and federal programs with local plans. Partial success has been made at both governmental levels to achieve this objective.

Summary

Whitman County is in control of development at its current pace. It utilizes a carrot-and-stick approach; in some places one cannot build; in others one can build on small lots if the land is not appropriate for commercial agriculture.

The county is also very concerned regarding the development plans of other layers of government. Legislation at the federal and state level is being sought to foster cooperation on the part of all parties involved.

Reference

Whitman County Board of Commissioners. 1978. Whitman County Comprehensive Plan. Whitman County Regional Planning Council, Colfax, WA. (July).

[3]Washington Laws of, 1979 Ch. 122 created RCW 7.48, which gives priority to preexisting safe agricultural practices, and defines "agricultural activity" and "farmland."

10

Techniques for Protecting Prime Agricultural Land: Zoning Applications in York County, Pennsylvania

William J. Conn

Introduction

York County is located in south central Pennsylvania just west of the Susquehanna River. The county is at the crossroads of U.S. Route 30 and Interstate 83 approximately 50 miles (80.45 km) north of Baltimore, 25 miles (40.225 km) south of Harrisburg, Pennsylvania, and 90 miles (144.81 km) to the west of Philadelphia (see Figure 10.1). The county has a current estimated population of just under 313,000 people (final count from 1980 U.S. Census of Population) living on 911 square miles (2358.58 km^2). The city of York, with a population of 45,000 is the central place. The county is composed of 72 local municipal governmental units (York City, 35 townships, and 36 boroughs). Each of these municipalities has the right under Pennsylvania law[1] to govern their own land development through application of subdivision and land development ordinances and zoning techniques. The county also has the power to adopt similar regulations; however, where local ordinances have been enacted they take precedence over any county ordinance in effect. Because of this situation the county has not adopted any zoning ordinance to date and although there have been county subdivision and land development regulations in effect since 1964 they are currently applicable in only a handful of boroughs. The following summarizes population data, indicates the amount of land and farms, average size of farms, gross farm income, value of farm land, and provides some characteristics of our farmers. It also provides information on the agricultural capability of soils in the county based on the Soil Conservation Service's standard class ratings.[2] As can be seen from reviewing these data, York County's agricultural land is indeed one of its prime resources.

[1]The Pennsylvania Municipalities Planning Code, Act 247, enacted 1968 and amended.
[2]From *Soil Survey of York County*, Series 1959, No. 23, U.S. Department of Agriculture Soil Conservation Service, issued May 1963.

	1970	1975 Est.	1980	
Population	272,600	288,100	312,963	(15% increase over 1970)
Total land		583,040 acres (235,131.2 ha) or 911 square miles (2,358.58 km²)
Land in farms		304,880 acres (123,476.4. ha) 52% of the county and decreasing; down 20,450 acres (8282.25 ha) or 6% between 1969 and 1978
Number of farms		2,349 (down 629 or 21% between 1969 and 1978; Rank #2 in the state behind Lancaster County)
Ave. size of farms		130 acres (52.65 ha). Up 21 acres (8.505 ha) or 19% between 1969 and 1978.
Gross farm income		Rank #5 in Pennsylvania behind Lancaster, Chester, Berks, and Franklin ($84 million cash receipts in 1978)
Value of farmland		$970/acre (0.405 ha) in 1974; $1700/acre (0.405 ha) in 1978; $1800−2200/acre (0.405 ha) in 1981
Farmers		63% are full owners, 10% are tenants; owners control 90% of farmland; the average age is 51

Agricultural capability of soils

	All townships (35)	12 townships with agriculture zoning
Classes I and II	149,603 acres (60,589.215 ha) (27% of the total county land)	51,757 acres (20,961.6 ha) (35%)
Class III	158,730 acres (64,285.65 ha) (28% of total county land	73,295 acres (29,684.5 ha) (46%)
	308,333 acres (124,874.86 ha) (55% of the total county land)	125,052 acres (50,646.1 ha) (41%)

Sources:
York County Planning Commission Compiled Data
Various Crop and Livestock Annual Summary Reports of the Pennsylvania Crop Reporting Services of the Pa. Dept. of Agriculture, Harrisburg, Pa.
1978 Census of Agriculture, Preliminary Report for York County, Pa., U.S. Dept. of Commerce Bureau of the Census, Washington, D.C. 1980.
Soil Survey of York County, Series 1959, No. 23, U.S. Dept. of Agric. Soil Conservation Service, Washington, D.C. 1963.
1974 Census of Agriculture, Vol. 1 Part 38, Pennsylvania, State and County Data, U.S. Dept. of Commerce Bureau of the Census, Washington, D.C., 1977.

The York County Planning Commission became involved with the problem of declining agricultural land in 1975 following a particularly heavy growth spurt in the county during the early 1970s. In researching the problem as the basis for a publication entitled *Agricultural Land Preservation, A Topical Study for York County*, which was produced in June 1975, it was found that the main threat to farmland in the county stems from speculative subdivision by outside interests. York County's soils, climate, and farmers are all conducive to excellent agricultural productivity. Given their druthers, the majority of York County farmers would rather stay on the farm and continue the long-standing tradition of small family farming. However, faced with the numerous problems currently associated with agriculture (inflation, spiraling energy costs, market uncertainties, and pressure from expanding suburbia) York's small family farms became prime targets for rich investors seeking to acquire the land, sit on it for a few years, subdivide it into as many building lots as possible, and reap a tremendous financial reward. Municipal officials in sections of the county where this phenomenon was centered began asking the York County Planning Commission for assistance and guid-

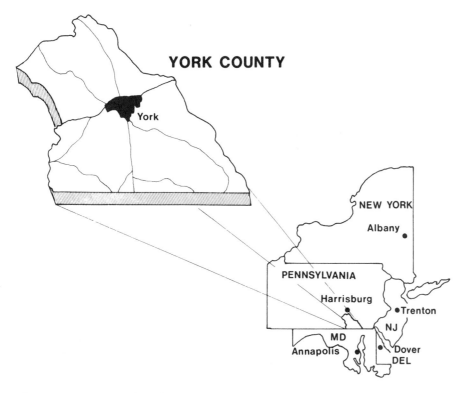

Fig. 10.1. Location of York County, Pennsylvania.

ance in this matter. The planning commission reviewed a wide variety of potential techniques prior to selecting a preservation method that was felt would work in this area. They considered but eliminated Transfer of Development Rights (TDR), Purchase of Development Rights (PDR), easements, and tax benefits as all being either too costly, too complicated, and/or too lengthy to establish. What was needed was a technique that was simple and quick that could be understood and put into operation by any of the muncipalities. They chose zoning regulation as the best approach to suit this purpose.

Evaluation of Agricultural Zoning Techniques

As part of the agricultural land preservation study, the planning commission's staff reviewed and categorized six possible techniques for agricultural zoning which are summarized in Table 10.1. The techniques reviewed included exclusive agricultural zoning, very low residential density control, large lot zoning, subdivision restrictions, prime agricultural land preservation, and lot frontage control. After thorough consideration of the advantages and disadvantages of each, a "hybrid" approach was selected involving a combination of three of the aforementioned techniques: low density control, subdivision restrictions, and prime land preservation. It was determined after numerous and lengthy conversations and meetings with the farm community, local municipal officials, Soil Conservation Service, and Cooperative Extension Service staffs in the

TABLE 10.1   Techniques for Agricultural Zoning

	Technique	Description	Advantages	Disadvantages
I.	Exclusive agricultural zoning	The use of land in agricultural zones would be limited to agricultural uses and related supporting uses. Activities of a residential (other than farmsteads), commercial, or industrial nature would be prohibited.	(1) Protect agricultural operations from conflicting land uses. (2) Stabilize agricultural land values. (3) Provide for orderly extension of public facilities and services. (4) Totally prevent scattered or sprawl development. (5) Would preserve prime agricultural lands for future food production. (6) Would completely prevent intensive residential subdividing.	(1) Deny rural landowners the speculative benefit from the sale of land. (2) May initially slow down the township tax base increase. (3) Would eliminate the opportunity for people to live on residential lots in the agricultural areas.
II.	Very low residential density control	All agricultural uses would be permitted. Residential uses would be permitted in the agricultural zones on a very low density basis (1 dwelling unit per 25–50 acres, 10.125–20.25 ha) however, dwelling units could be located on a minimum lot size of 1–2 acres (0.405–0.810 ha). No commercial or industrial uses would be permitted.	(1) Would help to stabilize agricultural land values. (2) Would provide for the preservation of some prime agricultural lands for future food production. (3) Would provide limited opportunity for people to live on residential lots in the agricultural areas. (4) Would generally prevent intensive residential subdividing.	(1) Would probably result in a pattern of scattered roadside development. (2) Would deny rural landowners of most of the speculative benefit from the sale of the land. (3) Would require limited public services and facilities to be provided throughout the rural area. (4) Would not guarantee preservation of prime agricultural lands. (5) Would not completely eliminate the conflict between agricultural and other land uses.
III.	Large lot zoning	All agricultural uses would be permitted. Residential uses would be permitted to take place only on lots of 5 acres (2.025 ha) or more in size. No commercial or industrial uses would be permitted.	(1) Would stabilize agricultural land values to a limited extent. (2) Would provide limited opportunity for people to live in the agricultural areas. (3) Would prevent intensive residential subdividing. (4) Would provide for the preservation of some prime agricultural lands. (5) Would slow down the rate of residential development in the agricultural areas.	(1) Would require limited public services and facilities to be provided throughout the rural areas. (2) Would result in large lots as isolated units or in subdivisions to be scattered throughout the rural areas. (3) Would provide the opportunity for only wealthy people to live in the agricultural areas. (4) Would partially reduce the speculative value of land for rural landowners. (5) Would not guarantee the preservation of prime agricultural lands. (6) Would not prevent the conflict between agricultural and other land uses. (7) Wastes land.

TABLE 10.1 *(Continued)*

	Technique	Description	Advantages	Disadvantages
IV.	Subdivision restrictions	All agricultural uses would be permitted. Residential subdivisions (other than minor subdivisions) would be prohibited in agricultural zones or permitted only when connected to public water and sewer facilities. No commercial and industrial uses would be permitted.	(1) Would provide opportunity for some residential lots in the agricultural areas. (2) Would prevent intensive residential development not served by public water or sewers or at least permit it only in conjunction with the orderly extension of public services. (3) Would provide for the preservation of some prime agricultural lands or at least assure more open, undeveloped land.	(1) Would result in isolated roadside development still being scattered throughout the agricultural areas. (2) Would not prevent the conflict between agricultural and other land uses. (3) Would not guarantee the preservation of prime agricultural lands. (4) Would only partially reduce the speculative value of land for rural landowners. (5) Would probably require the extension of some public services and facilities into the agricultural areas.
V.	Prime agricultural land preservation	All agricultural uses would be permitted. Residential uses would be permitted only on soils other than the prime agricultural soils (Classes I, II, and possibly III). Commercial and industrial uses would not be permitted.	(1) Would preserve all prime agricultural lands for future food production. (2) Would partially help to stabilize agricultural land values. (3) Would provide the opportunity for people to live on residential lots in the agricultural areas.	(1) Would not prevent intensive residential development. (2) Would encourage the haphazard scatteration of residential uses. (3) Would only partially prevent the conflict between agriculture and other land uses. (4) Would eventually require the provision of public services and facilities throughout the rural area. (5) Would only partially reduce the speculative value of land for rural landowners.
VI.	Lot frontage control	All agricultural uses would be permitted. Residential uses would be permitted with lot sizes of from 1 to 2 acres (0.405 to 0.81 ha) but extended frontage (250–300 ft, 76.25–91.5 m) would be required. Commercial and industrial uses would not be permitted.	(1) Would generally prevent intensive residential subdividing. (2) Would only slightly stabilize agricultural land values. (3) Would only partially preserve prime agricultural lands for future food production. (4) Would provide the opportunity for people to live on residential lots in the agricultural areas.	(1) Would tend to result in stripped roadside development along the existing improved roads. (2) Would not guarantee the preservation of prime agricultural lands. (3) Would require the provision of public services and and facilities throughout the agricultural lands. (4) Would only partially reduce the speculative value of land for rural owners. (5) Would not prevent the conflict between agricultural uses and other land uses.

Source: York County Planning Commission, 1975.

area that the county needed to control the number of new dwelling units being built in our rural agricultural areas; it needed to limit the amount of land being subdivided for speculative purposes; and it wanted to assure that any new construction that did take place would be relegated to nonprime agricultural land.

Application of Zoning Approach

Exactly when, where, and how was this technique applied? The county's best farmland lies roughly on its southern border in the area between York City and the Maryland State Line. Coincidently, because of the excellent access afforded by Interstate 83 in the north–south direction and the pressure of workers in a huge industrial complex developing north of Baltimore who were looking for homes but could not find them either available or at least reasonably priced in northern Baltimore County, most of the county's problems were centered in southern York County. Figure 10.2 indicates the 16 municipalities (12 townships and four boroughs) that currently have single family zoning restrictions in agricultural areas. The first to adopt these regulations was Hopewell Township in June of 1974. The bulk of the others went into effect between that time and 1977 with Newberry Township being the most recent (October 1982) municipality to put the technique into operation.

There are two main variations of the selected approach to zoning regulation being utilized. They are uniform restriction of single family

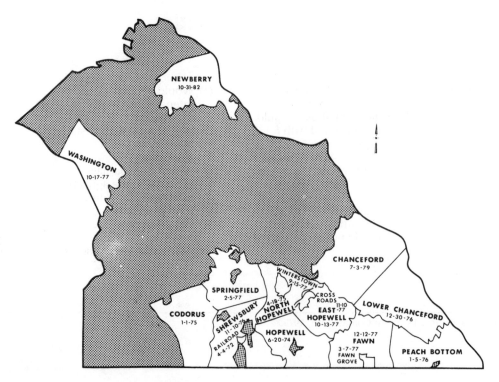

Fig. 10.2. Municipalities with single family zoning restrictions in agricultural areas of York County, Pennsylvania. Dates are effective dates of restrictions.

development lots as utilized in North Hopewell Township and the sliding scale restriction as exemplified by Peach Bottom Township.

As shown in the following excerpt from North Hopewell Township's zoning ordinance new single family dwellings in the rural agricultural zone are limited to minor residential land developments. As noted in the definition, this in effect limits the number of new single family dwellings permitted on an existing tract of ground to six in addition to the prime farmstead, providing, of course, that minimum lot area and minimum lot width requirements are met. Note that a maximum lot area provision is also established to prevent the wasting of good agricultural land for large building lots. The six lot restriction was arrived at through a process of compromise. Some (particularly young farmers) argued that no new dwelling units should be permitted in the agricultural zone. Others (including the older farmers) felt there should be few limitations as to the number of new permitted dwelling units. The end result was a figure of six which is uniformly applied to all tracts of ground in the agricultural zone regardless of initial tract size.

Excerpt from North Hopewell Twp. Zoning Ordinance (1975)

Section 203 RURAL AGRICULTURAL ZONE (RA)
s.203.1 *Purpose:* The primary purpose of this zone is to maintain and promote the rural-agricultural character of the land within this zone. This zone is composed of those areas in the township whose predominant land use is rural residential and agricultural. The regulations for this zone are designed to protect and stabilize the essential characteristics of these areas, to minimize conflicting land uses detrimental to agricultural enterprises and to limit development which requires highways and other public facilities in excess of those required by rural-oriented uses.
s.203.2 *Uses by Right:* The following principal uses are permitted by right in the RA zone:
1. Single-family dwelling on an approved lot in a minor residential land development (6 or fewer existing or proposed dwelling units excluding the prime farmstead; see definition on page 1-9) or on an individual lot the dimensions of which have not changed since April 18,1975.
2. Farm Buildings
3. Crops, Pasture
4. Dairy, Livestock, Poultry, Small Animals
s.203.4 *Lot Area and Width:* Lot area and lot width consistent with the following dimensions shall be provided for each principal use hereafter established in this zone:
Minimum Lot Area—1 acre, 0.81 ha
(43,560 ft.^{2} or 4051.08 m^2)
Minimum Lot Width—175 feet (53.375 m)
Maximum Lot Area—No maximum except for single-family dwellings as follows. A lot on which a new dwelling is to be located shall not contain more than one and one-half (1.5) acres (0.6075 ha)(65,340 ft.^{2} or 6,076.62 m^2), unless it is determined prior to subdivision or land development approval that the property owner has sufficient low quality land not suitable for agricultural purposes to justify using more than 1.5 acres for the location of the proposed dwelling unit; or unless the physical characteristics of the land (ex: topography, underlying rock structure, shape of existing lot boundaries) require a lot size in excess of 1.5 acres.
RESIDENTIAL LAND DEVELOPMENT (1) The improvement of one lot or two or more contiguous lots, tracts or parcels of land involving (a) a group of two or more buildings to be occupied as dwelling units, or (b) the division or allocation of land or space for dwelling purposes between or among two or more existing or prospective occupants; (2) A residential subdivision. In determining the number of lots in a residential land development all lots which on April 18, 1975 were a part of the same

parcel shall be included. A property owner submitting a subdivision plan will be required to specify on his plan which lot or lots shall carry with them the right to erect or place any unused quota of dwelling units his tract may have.

Minor Residential Land Development   Any residential land development consisting of six (6) or fewer existing or proposed dwelling units, excluding the prime farmstead.

Major *Residential Land Development*   Any residential land development involving seven (7) or more existing or proposed dwelling units (including dwelling units previously approved for minor residential land developments, but excluding the prime farmstead).

RESIDENTIAL SUBDIVISION   The division or redivision of a lot, tract or parcel of land by any means into two or more lots, tracts, parcels or other division of land including changes in existing lot lines for the purpose whether immediate or future of lease, transfer of ownership, or building or lot development where one or more of the lots, tracts, parcels or division will be used immediately or in the future as a place for a dwelling unit to be occupied by human beings. In determining the number of lots in a residential subdivision all lots which on April 18, 1975 were a part of the same parcel shall be included. A property owner submitting a subdivision plan will be required to specify on his plan which lot or lots shall carry with them the right to erect or place any unused quota of dwelling units his tract may have.

LOW QUALITY LAND   Includes land: (1) denoted in soil capability units III e-3 through VII s-2, as classified by the *Soil Survey of York County, Pennsylvania*. series 1959, No. 23, issued May, 1963; or (2) characterized by rock outcroppings, swamp or heavily wooded areas; or (3) having slopes exceeding fifteen percent, or (4) which is of such size or shape that is insufficient to permit efficient use of farm machinery.

Peach Bottom Township officials opted to go with what is considered the sliding scale approach. They felt that permitting a set number of dwelling units, such as North Hopewell Township's ordinance was unfair to larger land owners. They therefore established a system whereby the number of new single family dwellings permitted on a tract of land is regulated according to a sliding scale which increases the permitted number of units for larger farms. The following excerpt from Peach Bottom's Zoning Ordinance describes this process. Note that Peach Bottom regulates single family dwelling development in the agricultural zone via the conditional use procedure as opposed to North Hopewell Township's administration as a use by right. In Peach Bottom, a minimum lot size of one acre is permitted and a maximum of one acre is also established unless it is determined that the additional land desired is either on poor soil or it cannot feasibly be farmed because of size, shape or topographical considerations.

Excerpt from Peach Bottom Twp. Zoning Ordinance (1971)

G.   CONDITIONAL USES

s.493   All applications for approval of a conditional use shall be referred to the Township Planning Commission for recommendation.

s.494   Single family dwelling units in the agricultural zone shall be subject to following limitations:

a)   There shall be permitted on each tract of land the following number of single family dwelling units:

Size of Tract of Land		Number of Single Family Dwelling Units Permitted
0-7 acres	(0-2.835 ha)	1
7-30 acres	(2.835-12.15 ha)	2
30-80 acres	(12.15-32.4 ha)	3
80-130 acres	(32.4-52.65 ha)	4
130-180 acres	(52.65-72.9 ha)	5
180-230 acres	(72.9-93.15 ha)	6

Size of Tract of Land		Number of Single Family Dwelling Units Permitted
230-280 acres	(93.15-113.4 ha)	7
280-330 acres	(113.4-133.65 ha)	8
330-380 acres	(133.65-153.9 ha)	9
380-430 acres	(153.9-174.15 ha)	10
430-480 acres	(174.15-194.4 ha)	11
480-530 acres	(194.4-214.65 ha)	12
530-580 acres	(214.65-234.9 ha)	13
580-630 acres	(234.9-255.15 ha)	14
630-680 acres	(255.15-275.4 ha)	15
680-730 acres	(275.4-295.65 ha)	16
730-780 acres	(295.65-315.9 ha)	17
780-830 acres	(315.9-336.15 ha)	18
830 acres and over	(336.15 and over)	19

b) New single family dwelling units shall be located on lots in soil capability units III e-3 through VII s-2, as classified by the Soil Survey of York County, Pennsylvania, Series 1959, No. 23 issued May, 1963, or on lots on land which cannot feasibly be farmed, (1) due to existing features of the site such as rock outcroppings, swamps, the fact that the area is heavily wooded, or the fact that the slope of the area exceeds fifteen (15%) percent, or (2) due to the fact that the size or shape of the area suitable for farming is insufficient to permit efficient use of farm machinery. Where such location is not feasible, permits shall be issued to enable dwelling units to be located on lots containing higher quality soils. However, in all cases such residential lots shall be located on the least agriculturally productive land feasible, and so as to minimize interference with agricultural production.

c) A lot on which a new dwelling is to be located shall not contain more than one (1) acre (.405 ha), unless it is determined from the subdivision plan submitted by the property owner that the property owner has sufficient land of the type described in paragraph e of this section to justify using more than one (1) acre (.405 ha) for the location of the proposed dwelling unit, or that the physical characteristics of the land itself require a lot size in excess of one (1) acre (.405 ha).

d) A property owner submitting a subdivision plan will be required to specify on his plan which lot or lots shall carry with them the right to erect or place any unused quota of dwelling units his tract may have.

e) Lots for the location of single family dwelling units in addition to those authorized by subparagraph (a) may be permitted provided that all of the new dwelling units permitted by subparagraph (a) and all the additional new dwelling units are located on lots which are located:

1) On land in soil capability units IV e-5 through VII s-2 as classified by the Soil Survey of York County, Pennsylvania, Series 1959, No. 23, issued May, 1963; or

2) On lands which cannot feasibly be farmed:
    (a) Due to the existing features of the site such as rock outcroppings, rock too close to the surface to permit plowing, swamps, the fact that the area is heavily wooded, or the fact that the slope of the area exceeds fifteen (15%) percent; or
    (b) Due to the fact that the size or shape of the area suitable for farming is insufficient to permit efficient use of farm machinery.

f) The applicant shall have the burden of proving that the land he seeks to subdivide meets the criteria set forth in this section.

g) Any landowner who disagrees with the classification of his farm or any part of it by the Soil Survey of York County, Pennsylvania, Series 1959, No. 23, issued May, 1963, may submit an engineering analysis of the soils on the portion of the farm which he seeks to have reclassified, and if the Board of Township Supervisors finds his study correct, it shall alter the Township Soil Map to reflect the results of such analysis.

The majority of county municipalities utilizing the techniques described have opted for the sliding scale approach. Such an approach, however, does not necessarily mean that many more new dwelling units are being allowed to be created. The fact is that the average farm in York County is less than 200 acres (81 ha) in size; therefore, the number of dwelling units permitted per farm under the sliding scale approach is really no greater and in some cases may even be less than the set or fixed scale approach. The setting of the scales and final determination of the permitted number of dwelling units in all cases have been basically a subjective approach. It was the result of numerous meetings and much haggling between farmers, small residential property owners, developers, local officials, and planners.

Legal Tests of These Zoning Restrictions

There have been three cases argued in courts to date concerning the agricultural zoning restrictions used in York County. The result of these decisions has cast doubt on the validity of the uniform or set scale approach to dwelling unit limitation but the sliding scale approach has been affirmed.

The first case, *Stewart Snyder v. Railroad Borough*, challenged in part the borough's uniform limitation of one dwelling unit per tract in the agricultural zone. This challenge was unanimously dismissed by the Court of Common Pleas of York County on January 29, 1980. A subsequent appeal to the Commonwealth Court of Pennsylvania resulted in a unanimous order of June 2, 1981 affirming the decision of the lower court concerning the agricultural zone. Therefore the uniform approach, upon first test, seemed reasonable.

The second case, *Edward Golla v. Hopewell Township*, challenged in part that township's uniform limitation of five dwelling units per tract in the agricultural zone. In split decisions the County Court on November 30, 1979, The Commonwealth Court on April 21, 1981, and the Supreme Court of Pennsylvania, Middle District, on November 5, 1982 declared the uniform limitation approach to be unreasonably severe and invalidated it. The Supreme Court decision however took an extra step and alluded to that court's belief that a sliding scale approach ". . .would have a more equitable effect and would avoid impacting landowners on an arbitrary basis" (p. J-176-16 of the *Golla* case decision).

The third case, *Corstiaan Van Vugt v. Zoning Hearing Board of Springfield Township*, challenged in part the township's sliding scale restrictions in the agricultural zone. The Court of Common Pleas of York County in a unanimous opinion on January 24, 1983 dismissed the challenge with the following affirmation. "The Springfield Township Ordinance. . .sets a sliding scale on the number of lots that can be subdivided depending upon the size of the tract of land. We are satisfied that this distinction is significant, and that it bears a rational relationship to the avowed purpose of preserving prime agricultural land within the township" (p.4 of the *Van Vugt* decision).

Evaluation of This Zoning Approach

The success of the sliding scale is largely dependent on how long the limitations can be maintained. Agricultural zones are much more stable than they were 8 or 9 years ago in York County. County officials are satisfied that with the ordinances municipalities have slowed premature subdivision considerably and have reduced land speculation.One reason for the success of the sliding scale can be traced to its acceptance by farmers and other large landholders. The support of the agricultural community stems from the flexibility of the scale and the farmer's direct participation in setting the dimensions of it. While most young farmers wanted very little new development activity infringing on their farming activity, older farmers were a little more reluctant to close the door on lucrative financial offers. As it turned out, all of the farmers involved wanted to have at least a little disability and retirement insurance and thus opted to permit at least some new dwelling activity to continue in the rural areas.

Real estate interests failed to show the same enthusiasm as did the farmers but in most cases the communities went out of their way to demonstrate that there was more than sufficient land in the urban areas to accommodate all land-use needs at least to the year 2000. In several of the York County townships the land set aside in their residential areas to accommodate expected population growth would be able to account for three or four times the projected figure, all in addition to the families who choose to live in the agricultural zone. Furthermore, each of the townships was careful to provide for a variety of housing types and a variety of densities. This settled any questions of exclusionary zoning.

These techniques suffer from the traditional problem with zoning, that is, they can be changed. Any ordinance enthusiastically adopted by one set of municipal officials can just as enthusiastically be taken off the books by the next board of elected officials. Another long-term threat to the zoning techniques may surface when land owners have used up their development allotments. Will landowners then begin to pressure for more and more lots? The answer will come partly in response to long-term trends in the farmer's market and partly in response to cost differentials between land reserved for development in urban areas and land in the agricultural zone. As long as land remains undeveloped in the urban areas, there will be less pressure to develop land in the rural hinterland. If agricultural land prices continue to rise relative to other land prices, that too will reduce the pressure. One thing is certain though, based on the experience of the last 9 years: the sliding scale is indeed protecting farm land and eliminating speculation.

Before concluding, a couple of important points regarding administration should be made. The sliding scale zoning technique requires continuous monitoring from the first day the ordinance is passed. When the ordinance is passed the community must have a tax parcel map or any map that indicates the existing pattern of land ownership. On the day the ordinance is passed development allotments should be made to each of the parcels based on the ordinance scale. As the allotments are used up the parcel map must be changed to show remaining allotments. Most municipalities use a single map, usually a tax parcel map. Since the maps are one of a kind and in continuous use, it is important to keep them in excellent condition and to keep them safe. If the map becomes defaced, blurred, or lost, the entire process of development regulation could be placed in jeopardy. Recreating such maps is an expensive, time consuming, and very frustrating job.

The administration of sliding scale, however, really is a comparatively simple task. Since most of the municipalities in York County have no planning staff, administration is placed in the hands of the local planning commissions or local zoning hearing boards. Decisions on the number of lots permitted are fairly straightforward. Most of these will be indicated on the tax parcel map, but administrators must ensure that changes are posted on the allocation map to guarantee a continuing up-to-date development record.

References

North Hopewell Township. 1975. North Hopewell Township Zoning Ordinance, York County, PA. (amended).

Pennsylvania Department of Agriculture, Crop and Livestock Annual Summary, Pennsylvania Crop Reporting Service, Harrisburg, PA. Various years.

Peach Bottom Township. 1971. Peach Bottom Township Zoning Ordinance, York County, PA. (amended).

U.S. Department of Agriculture. 1963. Soil Survey for York County, Pennsylvania., Ser. 1959, No. 23. Soil Conservation Service, Washington, D.C.

U.S. Department of Commerce, 1977. 1974 Census of Agriculture, Vol 1. Part 38, Pennsylvania State and County Data: Bureau of the Census, Washington, D.C.

U.S. Department of Commerce. 1980. 1978 Census of Agriculture, Preliminary Report for York County, PA. Bureau of the Census, Washington, D.C.

U.S. Department of Commerce. 1980. 1980 Census of Population, Preliminary Figures for York County, PA. Bureau of the Census, Washington, D.C.

York County Planning Commission. 1975. Agricultural Land Preservation, A Topical Study for York County, PA. York, PA.

11

Corn Suitability Ratings: A Method of Rating Soils for Identifying and Preserving Prime Agricultural Lands in Black Hawk County, Iowa

Sonia A. Johannsen and Larry C. Larsen

Introduction

Black Hawk County, Iowa, is located 80 miles (128.72 km) south of the Iowa–Minnesota border and 90 miles (144.81 km) west of the Mississippi River (Fig. 11.1). The county contains a land area of 570 square miles (1475.73 km^2) and is bisected from the northwest to the southeast by the Cedar River. The county is a Standard Metropolitan Statistical Area (SMSA) with a population of 135,000 persons, of whom approximately 112,000 inhabit the urbanized area of the adjacent cities of Waterloo and Cedar Falls which is located on 10% of the land, slightly north and west of the geographic center of the county. A relatively steady growth rate has been established over the past years, which is expected to continue. The urban area is an industrial and commercial center serving most of northeast Iowa.

The two major cities of the county, Waterloo and Cedar Falls, adjoin each other and support the area's largest places of employment. John Deere and Company has established four major production sites within the metro area employing about 18,000 persons. Waterloo is also the home of The Rath Packing Company, a nationwide distributor of processed pork. The University of Northern Iowa is located in Cedar Falls, and the Hawkeye Institute of Technology, a nationally recognized vocational-technical school, is located in Waterloo.

Physical Characteristics

The county is located on a glacial till plain known as the "Iowan Surface" that gently slopes to the southeast. The topography of the area can be

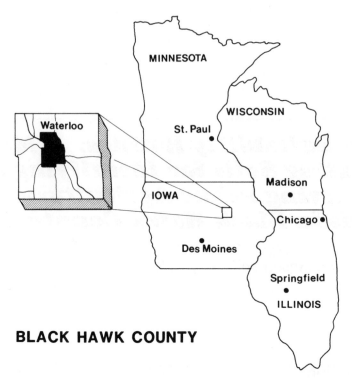

BLACK HAWK COUNTY

Fig. 11.1.   Location of Black Hawk County, Iowa.

characterized by gently undulated uplands of low relief and flat horizon. The major geologic process that formed the landscape was the continental glaciers of the Nebraskan and Kansan stages of the Pleistocene Epoch. Some modification was experienced due to wind-carried loess soils and glacial melt waters of the latest glacial state, the Wisconsin, which covered the land 40 miles west and north of Black Hawk County.

The plain is cut by the valleys of the Cedar and Wapsipinicon Rivers and their tributaries, where the local relief is the greatest. The rivers are wide meandering streams, dendritic in pattern. They formed a broad flood plain bordered by wide, distinct second and third alluvial terraces, which are slightly higher in elevation than the immediate plain. Above the bedrock of the county lies a layer of soil and subsoil, which is almost entirely glacial till or drift. At the surface and above the glacial drift, some areas of the county and particularly the southwest are covered with loess, but usually to a depth of only a few inches. The soils that later formed under the native prairie vegetation have proved to be some of the most fertile in the world.

The county's climate is ideal for grain crop production with the average growing season about 160 days, and the majority of the yearly precipitation occurring during the early summer months.

The combination of relatively level topography, extremely fertile soils, and ideal climate has helped this area develop into one of the world's richest agricultural regions. The forces of nature have been very kind to Black Hawk County and her surrounding neighbors. The major crops produced in the region are corn and soybeans with some oats and sorghum.

History

The land in Black Hawk County was acquired by the United States as part of the Louisiana Purchase in 1803. It was not until after the Sauk and Fox Indian cession for 1842 that the county was open for settlement by the early pioneers. The county was surveyed during the years 1845—1848. The first settlements congregated along the major river of the county, the Cedar, and later developed into the present day cities of Waterloo and Cedar Falls. The population continued to grow rapidly during the first decade, providing services to the settlers within the county and the many westbound pioneers.

The two most significant factors in the development and urbanization of the county were the railroads and industrialization. During the 1860s, the construction of the railroads had provided the farmers a means to transport their crops to the east and south. By the turn of the century, the Industrial Revolution had helped the county to establish the industrial employment base and the supporting retail and service industries that would pave the way for development of the metropolitan area that exists today. Many of the early settlers found the land highly fertile in the production of grain crops and continued to farm.

The cities found themselves in the heart of a prospering agricultural area, an ideal place to develop agriculture related industries. A major meat packing industry and tractor manufacturer began to operate, continuing to be the major employers of the area even today. Many other farm machinery companies located in the county and supplemented the tractor works in supplying farmers with machinery.

Between 1890 and 1895, Black Hawk County became urban with better than 50% of the population living in urban areas. While agriculture would still remain a major industry in the county, a smaller percentage of the people would be involved in rural farm operations. This trend continued until after World War II, when a major shift in the population began. Commercial and industrial workers began to look for their place in the "country." Automobiles and inexpensive fuels provided a major catalyst in encouraging the outward flight from the urban center usually described as "urban sprawl."

Urbanization and the County's Attempt to Control It

Urban sprawl developed in Black Hawk County much like that of other areas of the United States: the growth of smaller cities surrounding the urban "core" area, the development of small "bedroom" communities, and the proliferation of rural individual acreages or country estates.

The need for land-use planning became evident by many concerned citizens. In 1951, Black Hawk County adopted its first zoning ordinance. The Iowa State Zoning Enabling Act, at this time, enabled county zoning only after separate township approval of 60% of the landowners. Needless to say, this provided inconsistent and almost totally unadministrative controls. After the state zoning enabling act was modified, countywide zoning was established in 1960. The ordinance was now centralized and administered equally throughout the unincorporated areas of the county. Still, the county zoning laws were relatively liberal; rural residential development could take place on a 3 acre or larger lot anywhere in the unincorporated areas of the county, with the development of 0.5 acre (0.2025 ha) lots permitted in residentially zoned areas. This law had the net effect of encouraging development, not discouraging it.

During the 1960s, evidence clearly demonstrated that new long-range planning was needed to provide orderly and environmentally sound direction to the new rural growth. Land-use problems, such as strip development along the major highways, began to occur. It became evident that if the trend was allowed to continue, the county would find its entire road system lined with residential and commercial areas and the use of some of the county's best agricultural land would be lost forever. Members of the Black Hawk County Board of Supervisors, farmers, farm organizations, and interested individuals began to push for remedial action to change the course in which the community found itself.

In 1971, planners began to seek methods to better control and direct future residential growth, culminating in a new zoning ordinance adopted in October of 1973. During the period between 1971 and 1973, the county contracted with the Iowa Northland Regional Council of Governments (INRCOG) to provide staff for developing and for the administration of the proposed ordinance. It was during this time that an INRCOG staff member, Kenneth Lind, attended a planning and zoning seminar sponsored by the University of Wisconsin Extension College at Madison. Mr. Lind returned from the conference with information about the Walworth County, Wisconsin, ordinance which identified and preserved prime agricultural lands by using USDA Land Capability Classifications and restricted residential development on those lands with the higher classifications. The staff began working with the district USDA soil conservationist, Bart McAninch, to look into such a program for Black Hawk County. Mr. McAninch informed the county that field work was complete for a new soil survey and the advance report copy would soon be available for their use. It became apparent that the county was not only concerned about controlled and directed growth but with the preservation of the region's most important natural resource, namely, prime agricultural soils.

What is "prime agricultural land?" Black Hawk County turned to the United States Department of Agriculture Soil Conservation Service's "Soil Survey for Black Hawk County, Iowa." In addition to identifying and mapping the types of soils within an area, the soil survey provides information that contains characteristics of the soil, drainage, erosion factors, suitability of the soil for various uses including building site development and septic disposal fields, plus a rating for crop production known in Iowa as the "corn suitability ratings" (Table 11.1).

Development of Corn Suitability Ratings as a Tool in County Zoning

Corn suitability rating (CSR) is a system of rating soils, on a scale of 5 to 100, to aid in the valuation and assessment of agricultural land that is now

Table 11.1. Soil Potentials of Black Hawk County

Map Symbol	Soil	Agricultural					Residential		Environmental			
		Slope (%)	Acres	%	CSR	USDA Capability Class	Building site: Dwelling with basement	Sanitary facilities: Septic tank absorption fields	Landscape position	Natural internal drainage	Erosion hazard	Flooding frequency
7	Wiota	0–2	4,010	1.1	95	I	Severe: Floods	Moderate:[a] Floods	Terrace	Good	None	Rare
11B	Colo-Ely complex	2–5	3,625	1.0	75	II	Severe: Wetness, shrink–swell	Severe: Wetness	Upland	Poor	Slight	Common
41	Sparta loamy fine sand	0–2	4,055	1.1	45	IV	Slight	Slight[b]	Terrace	Excessive	Severe	None
41B	Sparta loamy fine sand	2–5	14,345	4.0	40	IV	Slight	Slight[b]	Upland	Excessive	Severe	None
41C	Sparta loamy fine sand	5–9	2,090	0.6	25	IV	Slight	Slight[b]	Upland	Excessive	Severe	None
41D	Sparta loamy fine sand	9–18	300	0.1	13	VI	Moderate: Slope	Moderate:[a] Slope	Upland	Excessive	Quite severe	None
43	Bremer silty clay loam	0–2	5,015	1.4	85	II	Severe: Wetness, shrink–swell, low strength	Severe:[a] Percs slowly	Terrace	Poor	Slight	Occasional
54	Zook silty clay loam	0–2	680	0.2	70	II	Severe: Floods, shrink–swell, low strength	Severe: Percs slowly, floods, wetness	Bottomland	Poor	Slight	Common
63B	Chelsea loamy fine sand	2–5	1,310	0.4	36	IV	Slight	Slight[b]	Terrace	Excessive	Severe	None
63C	Chelsea loamy fine sand	5–9	505	0.1	21	IV	Slight	Slight[b]	Upland	Excessive	Severe	None
63D	Chelsea loamy fine sand	9–18	240	0.1	11	VI	Moderate: Slope	Moderate:[b] Slope	Upland	Excessive	Quite severe	None
83B	Kenyon loam	2–5	46,570	12.8	86	II	Moderate: Wetness	Severe:[c] Percs slowly	Upland	Good	Slight	None
83C	Kenyon loam	5–9	4,610	1.3	71	III	Moderate: Wetness	Severe:[c] Percs slowly	Upland	Good	Moderate	None
83C2	Kenyon loam	5–9	4,705	1.3	69	III	Moderate: Wetness	Severe:[c] Percs slowly	Upland	Good	Moderate	None
83D2	Kenyon loam	9–14	245	0.1	59	III	Moderate: Wetness, slope	Severe: Percs slowly, slope	Upland	Good	Moderate	None
84	Clyde clay loam	0–3	17,180	4.7	76	II	Severe: Floods, wetness	Severe:[c] Floods, wetness	Upland	Poor	Slight	Frequent
88	Nevin silty clay loam	0–2	3,430	0.9	90	I	Severe: Floods	Severe:[a] Wetness	Terrace	Poor	None	Rare
110B	Lamont fine sandy loam	2–7	650	0.2	45	III	Slight	Slight[b]	Terrace	Excessive	Moderate	None
118	Garwin silty clay loam	0–2	2,280	0.6	95	II	Severe: Wetness, shrink–swell, low strength	Severe: Wetness, percs slowly	Upland	Poor	Slight	None
119	Muscatine silty clay loam	0–2	1,225	0.3	100	I	Severe: Wetness	Severe: Wetness, percs slowly	Upland	Poor	None	None
119B	Muscatine silty clay loam	2–5	2,210	0.6	95	II	Severe: Wetness	Severe: Wetness, percs slowly	Upland	Poor	Slight	None
120B	Tama silty clay loam	2–5	3,170	0.9	95	II	Moderate: Low strength, shrink–swell	Slight	Upland	Good	Slight	None
T120	Tama silty clay loam	0–2	325	0.1	100	I	Moderate: Low strength, shrink–swell	Slight	Upland	Good	None	None
133	Colo silty clay loam	0–2	2,930	0.8	80	II	Severe: Floods, frost action, wetness	Severe: Percs slowly, wetness, floods	Upland	Poor	Slight	Common
C133	Colo silty clay loam, channeled	0–2	250	0.1	—	V	Severe: Floods, frost action, wetness	Severe: Percs slowly, wetness, floods	Bottomland	Poor	Slight	Common
135	Coland clay loam	0–2	1,730	0.5	80	II	Severe: Floods, frost action, wetness	Severe: Wetness, floods	Bottomland	Poor	Slight	Common
151	Marshan clay loam	0–2	2,305	0.6	64	II	Severe: Floods, cutbanks cave, wetness	Severe:[b] Wetness, floods	Terrace	Poor	Slight	Occasional
152	Marshan clay loam	0–2	6,745	1.9	72	II	Severe: Floods, cutbanks cave, wetness	Severe:[b] Wetness, floods	Terrace	Poor	Slight	Occasional
154F	Loamy escarpments	14–40	250	0.1	5	VII	Severe: Slope	Severe: Slope	Bottomland/terrace	—	Quite severe	None
159	Finchford loamy sand	0–2	4,465	1.2	30	IV	Slight	Slight[b]	Terrace	Excessive	Severe	Rare
159C	Finchford loamy sand	2–9	820	0.2	5	IV	Slight	Slight[b]	Terrace	Excessive	Severe	Rare
166	Bremer silty clay loam	0–2	180	<0.1	64	II	Severe: Wetness, shrink–swell	Severe: Percs slowly, wetness	Terrace	Poor	Slight	Rare
171B	Bassett loam	2–5	1,025	0.3	81	II	Moderate: Wetness	Severe:[c] Percs slowly, wetness	Upland	Good	Slight	None
171C2	Bassett loam	5–9	215	0.1	64	III	Moderate: Wetness	Severe:[c] Percs slowly, wetness	Upland	Good	Moderate	None
175	Dickinson fine sandy loam	0–2	1,870	0.5	60	III	Slight	Slight[b]	Upland/terrace	Excessive	Moderate	None
175B	Dickinson fine sandy loam	2–5	3,600	1.0	55	III	Slight	Slight[b]	Upland/terrace	Excessive	Moderate	None
177	Saude loam	0–2	8,545	2.4	63	II	Slight	Slight[b]	Terrace	Good	Slight	None
177B	Saude loam	2–5	4,775	1.3	58	II	Slight	Slight[b]	Terrace	Good	Slight	None
178	Waukee loam	0–2	3,910	1.1	79	I	Slight	Slight[b]	Terrace	Good	None	None
178B	Waukee loam	2–5	2,285	0.6	74	II	Slight	Slight[b]	Terrace	Good	Slight	None
184	Klinger silty clay loam	1–3	13,605	3.7	90	I	Severe: Wetness	Severe: Percs slowly, wetness	Upland	Poor	None	None

(Continued)

Table 11.1 (Continued)

Map Symbol	Soil	Slope (%)	Agricultural				Residential		Environmental			
			Acres	%	CSR	USDA Capability Class	Building site: Dwelling with basement	Sanitary facilities: Septic tank absorption fields	Landscape position	Natural internal drainage	Erosion hazard	Flooding frequency
198B	Floyd loam	1–4	5,400	1.5	80	II	Severe: Wetness	Severe: Wetness	Upland	Poor	Slight	None
213B	Rockton loam	2–5	610	0.2	71	II	Severe: Depth to bedrock (20–40″)	Severe: Depth to bedrock (20–40″)	Upland	Good	Slight	None
221	Palms muck	1–4	185	0.1	50	III	Severe: Wetness, floods	Severe:[b] Wetness, floods	Upland	Very poor	Moderate	Frequent
225	Lawler loam	0–2	1,870	0.5	66	II	Severe: Wetness, floods	Severe:[b] Wetness	Terrace	Poor	Slight	None
226	Lawler loam	0–2	2,230	0.6	78	I	Severe: Wetness, floods	Severe:[b] Wetness	Terrace	Poor	None	None
284	Flagler sandy loam	0–2	4,510	1.2	50	III	Slight	Slight[b]	Terrace	Excessive	Moderate	Rare
284B	Flagler sandy loam	2–5	1,490	0.4	45	III	Slight	Slight[b]	Terrace	Excessive	Moderate	Rare
290	Dells silt loam	0–2	560	0.2	74	II	Severe: Wetness	Severe: Wetness	Terrace	Poor	Slight	Rare
C315	Loamy alluvial land, channeled	—	17,665	4.9	5	V	Severe: Floods	Severe: Floods	Bottomland	Varies	Moderate	Frequent
354	Marsh	—	175	<0.1	5	VII	Severe: Wetness	Severe: Wetness	—	Very poor	Slight	Frequent
377B	Dinsdale silty clay loam	2–5	22,800	6.3	90	III	Slight	Slight	Upland	Good	Slight	None
377C	Dinsdale silty clay loam	5–9	1,055	0.3	75	III	Slight	Slight	Upland	Good	Moderate	None
377C2	Dinsdale silty clay loam	5–9	595	0.2	73	III	Slight	Slight	Upland	Good	Moderate	None
382	Maxfield silty clay loam	0–2	7,080	1.9	90	II	Severe: Wetness, shrink–swell	Severe: Wetness, percs slowly	Upland	Poor	Slight	None
391B	Clyde-Floyd complex	1–4	31,025	8.5	72	II	Severe: Wetness, floods	Severe: Wetness, floods	Upland	Poor	Slight	Frequent
398	Tripoli clay loam	0–2	9,695	2.7	81	II	Severe: Wetness	Severe: Wetness	Upland	Poor	Slight	None
399	Readlyn loam	1–3	20,805	5.7	91	I	Severe: Wetness	Severe: Wetness, percs slowly	Upland	Poor	None	None
408B	Olin fine sandy loam	2–5	7,225	2.0	66	II	Slight	Severe: Percs slowly	Upland	Good	Slight	None
408C	Olin fine sandy loam	5–9	540	0.1	51	III	Slight	Severe: Percs slowly	Upland	Good	Moderate	None
412C	Sogn loam	2–9	200	0.1	13	IV	Severe: Depth to bedrock (4–20″)	Severe: Depth to bedrock (4–20″)	Upland	Excessive	Severe	None
426B	Aredale loam	2–5	5,520	1.5	85	II	Slight	Slight	Upland	Good	Slight	None
426C	Aredale loam	5–9	2,545	0.7	70	III	Slight	Slight	Upland	Good	Moderate	None
426C2	Aredale loam	5–9	1,460	0.4	68	III	Slight	Slight	Upland	Good	Moderate	None
471	Oran loam	1–3	950	0.3	86	I	Moderate: Wetness	Severe: Wetness, percs slowly	Upland	Poor	None	None
485	Spillville loam	0–2	1,920	0.5	92	I	Severe: Floods	Severe: Wetness, percs slowly	Bottomland	Poor to good	None	Common
585	Spillville-Alluvial land complex	0–2	3,550	1.0	60	II	Severe: Floods	Severe: Wetness, floods	Bottomland	Poor to good	Slight	Common
688	Koszta silt loam	0–2	470	0.1	85	I	Severe: Floods, wetness	Severe:[a] Wetness	Terrace	Poor	None	Rare
725	Hayfield loam	0–2	1,945	0.5	61	I	Moderate: Wetness	Severe:[b] Wetness	Upland	Poor	Slight	None
726	Hayfield loam	0–2	500	0.1	73	II	Moderate: Wetness	Severe:[b] Wetness	Upland	Poor	Slight	None
761	Franklin silt loam	1–3	830	0.2	90	I	Severe: Wetness	Severe: Wetness, percs slowly	Upland	Poor	None	None
771B	Waubeek silt loam	2–5	440	0.1	87	II	Moderate: Low strength	Slight	Upland	Good	Slight	None
776C	Lilah sandy loam	2–9	395	0.1	7	IV	Slight	Slight[b]	Upland	Excessive	Severe	None
777	Wapsi loam	1–3	890	0.2	58	III	Slight	Slight[b]	Terrace	Good	Slight	None
782B	Donnan loam	2–5	985	0.3	50	II	Severe: Wetness, shrink–swell, frost action	Severe: Percs slowly	Upland	Poor to good	Slight	None
782C	Donnan loam	5–9	180	<0.1	35	III	Severe: Wetness, shrink–swell, frost action	Severe: Percs slowly	Upland	Poor to good	Moderate	None
798	Protivin loam	1–3	845	0.2	60	II	Severe: Wetness, shrink–swell, frost action	Severe: Percs slowly, wetness	Upland	Poor	Slight	None
809B	Bertram fine sandy loam	2–7	385	0.1	25	IV	Severe: Depth to bedrock (20–40″)	Severe:[b] Depth to bedrock (20–40″)	Upland	Excessive	Severe	None
933	Sawmill silty clay loam	0–2	6,145	1.7	80	II	Severe: Wetness, floods	Severe: Floods, wetness	Upland	Poor	Slight	Common
—	Borrow area	—	495	0.1	—	—						
—	Limestone quarries	—	225	0.1	—	—						
—	Madeland	—	1,970	0.5	—	—						
—	Sand and gravel pits	—	110	0.1	—	—						
	Total[d]		363,520	100.0								

[a] Some areas are underlaid by sand and gravel at depths below 5 ft.
[b] Excessive permeability rate may cause pollution of groundwater.
[c] The water table is generally perched for a short time during extended wet periods.
[d] Totals include urban land complex soils not contained in table.

provided in Iowa with the completion of each county soil survey. Soil productivity indexes or ratings are widely used in several Midwest states. These ratings reflect the physical and chemical properties of the soil in terms of soil productivity for commonly grown crops such as corn and soybeans. After the survey is complete, each soil mapping unit is assigned a CSR. These ratings provide a relative ranking to compare all other mapped soils in the state. An individual CSR for a soil mapping unit reflects the integrated effect of numerous factors that influence the potential yields and frequency that the soil could be used for row-crop production at a specified management level. The properties of the soil and the climatological conditions are the dominant factors that affect the soils yield potential, whereas the slope gradient and length affect the frequency of use.

The corn suitability ratings are developed in the following way: benchmark soils (soil comprising large acreages with considerable data available) are first rated in terms of their suitability for producing corn. Next, ratings are developed for soils with limited data and yield information. Benchmark soils, a knowledge of soil characteristics and their effect on yield potential, and available data provide the basis for these ratings. The guidelines used in establishing corn suitability ratings are given here. The assumptions in the guidelines are used by the soil scientists of the Iowa State Agricultural and Home Economics Station and the Soil Conservation Service in establishing individual CSRS for each soil type. Additional technical information can be found in Fenton *et al.* (1971).

Guidelines Used in Establishing Corn Suitability Ratings

The information concerning factors affecting corn suitability ratings represents an initial effort in establishing criteria applicable on a statewide basis.

A. Slopes (Values listed are subtracted from CSR of same soil on A slope.)

Soil Group I

well, moderately well, or somewhat poorly drained; uneroded; <45% clay; friable or firm; >48″ solum.

	Slope Group						
	A	B	C	D	E	F	G
Index soil		−5	−20	−30	−40	−60	−70

Soil Group II

Well, moderately well, or somewhat poorly drained; uneroded; >45% clay with >48″ solum; firm; very firm <45% clay; or 20 to 40″ to bedrock, sands, or gravels.

	Slope Group						
	A	B	C	D	E	F	G
Index soil		−5	−25	−40	−55	−75	−85

B. Erosion

	Erosion groups		
	1	2	3
1. AC profiles <35% clay and loamy sand or sand	Index soil	Index soil	−5 index
2. Solum >48″, <35% clay in B	Index soil	−2	−5
3. Solum >48″, 35−42% clay in B or very firm soils <35% clay	Index soil	−5	−10
4. Solum >48″, 42% clay in B	Index soil	−5	−15
5. Solum 20 to 40″, 18−45% clay in B	Index soil	−5	−15
6. Solum <20″, 18−45% clay in B	Index soil	−10	−20

(Continued)

Guidelines Used in Establishing Corn Suitability Ratings *(Continued)*

C. Biosequence (Prairie soils have higher CSRs than Gray—Brown Podzolic soils. Values listed are subtracted from P index soil for P/F and for F soils.)

		P	P/F	F
1.	Medium and moderately fine textured soils	Index soil	−5	−10
2.	Fine textured soils	Index soil	−10	−20
3.	Sandy loam soils	Index soil	−4	−8
4.	Loamy sand soils	Index soil	−2	−4

D. Wetness (Landscapes that contribute to wetness conditions and wet, poorly drained soils have lower CSR ratings than do somewhat poorly drained soils in a hydrosequence.)

	Soils	*Drainage*		*CSR*
1.	Moderately permeable; solum >48″; <35% clay in B	Poor	somewhat poor	−5
2.	Slowly permeable; solum >48″; 35−42% clay in B	Poor	somewhat poor	−7
3.	Very slowly permeable; solum >48″; >42% clay in B except Edina is −5 < Seymour	Poor	somewhat poor	−10
4.	All depressions and Planosols except Edina, Belinda, and Beckwith soils	Depressions	poor	−25
5. a.	All concave positions versus associated upland soils (concave level uplands)	Well and moderately well / Somewhat poor / Poor		−3 / −5 / −10
b.	Somewhat poor; very firm B with 30−35% clay in B and >42% clay in B	Poor	somewhat poor	−10
6.	Moderately well or well vs. somewhat poorly drained for moderately well or well < somewhat poor			
a.	Sharpsburg < Macksburg Marshall < Minden Clarion < Nicollet	Add for somewhat poor		+3
b.	Galva < Primghar	Add for somewhat poor		+5
c.	All other moderately well or well versus somewhat poor	Somewhat poor, moderately well, or well		0
7.	Upland drainageway areas: CSR av. of soils in complex minus approximately 15 CSRs.			

E. Calcareous soils (Calcareous soils have a lower CSR than associated noncalcareous soils.)

1.	Poorly drained noncalcareous soils versus poorly drained calcareous	−5 for calc.
2.	Highly calcareous poorly drained versus noncalcareous poorly drained.	−20 for highly calc.
3.	Calcareous upland versus noncalcareous upland	
a.	Calcareous soils: deduct 5 CSRs from comparable upland that is not calcareous	
b.	Loamy sand, sand, or gravels: calcareous versus noncalcareous, subtract 10 CSRs for calcareous soil	

F. Depth phases (Soils with thin solums have a lower CSR than comparable soils with thick solums.)

1. Well or moderately well drained (medium and moderately fine textured)

Soil depth	*CSR*
>48″ thick	Index (upland soil)
Deep	−16 less than index soil

Guidelines Used in Establishing Corn Suitability Ratings *(Continued)*

Moderately deep   −16 less than deep
<20" to sand, gravel or bedrock   −25 less than moderately deep

2. Somewhat poorly drained (medium and moderately fine textured)

Soil depth	*CSR*
>48" thick	Index (upland soil)
Deep	−12 less than index soil
Moderately deep	−12 less than deep
<20" to sand, gravel or bedrock	−20 less than moderately deep

3. Poorly drained

Soil depth	*CSR*
>48" thick	Index (upland soil)
Deep	−8 less than index soil
Moderately deep	−8 less than deep
<20" to sand, gravel or bedrock	−16 less than moderately deep

4. Sandy loam over sand, gravel, or bedrock (well or moderately well drained)

Solums	*CSR*
>48" thick	Index soil
Deep	−10 less than index soil
Moderately deep	−10 less than deep
<20"	−15 less than moderately deep

5. Loamy sands over gravels or bedrock

Solums	*CSR*
>48" thick	Index soil
Deep	−5 less than index soil
Moderately deep	−5 less than deep
<20"	−10 less than moderately deep

G. Sandy or gravelly soils

    1. Sandy loam profiles versus loamy uplands   −35 for sandy loam
        >48" thick

    2. Loamy sand and sand profiles versus   −50 for loamy sand and sand
        loamy uplands >48" thick

H. Precipitation factors for Iowa (Index soil is Tama; well-drained soils in northwestern and western Iowa have lower CSRs than Tama soils.)

    1. Southern Iowa loess soils versus Tama soils (CSRs less than Tama)

−15	−10	−8	Index
Monona	Marshall	Sharpsburg	Tama

    2. Galva versus Tama   Galva = 0.75 × Tama
    3. Tama versus Moody   Moody = 0.70 × Tama
    4. Loamy sand and sandy loam: eastern Iowa versus western Iowa
                 western Iowa 0.70 × eastern Iowa soil
    5. Well and moderately well drained bottom lands
                 western Iowa 0.96 × eastern Iowa soil

I. Deposition and special soil modifiers
    1. Deposition on units 133, 53, 134, 248, 172, add 5 CSRs for deposition.
    2. All overscore (i.e., 133), channeled (133c), or gullied (5 erosion) are rated at 25 CSRs.
    3. T units are the same as uplands except that alluvial benches are   2 CSRs less than uplands.

J. Parent materials

    1. Deoxidized loess: 3 CSRs less than oxidized

2.	loess	loess/till	till
	Index soil	5 less than loess	10 less than loess

    3. Loamy versus silty bottom lands
        loamy: 3 CSRs less than silty

(Continued)

Guidelines Used in Establishing Corn Suitability Ratings *(Continued)*

K. Muck and peaty soils

1. Muck

<20″ over mineral soil	15 CSRs less than poorly drained landscape associate
20 to 40″ over mineral soil	30 CSRs less than poorly drained landscape associate
>40″	25 CSRs less than 20–40″ depth

2. Peat

Peaty muck and peat	10 CSRs less than comparable depth phase of muck (20″ 10 CSRs less than poorly drained associate)

Soil productivity indexes assume an adequate level of management. In Iowa, the CSR system assumes an average level of management and, in addition, the following conditions are specified: (1) natural weather conditions (not irrigated), (2) artificial drainage has been provided where required, (3) soils on lower landscapes are not subject to frequent damaging floods, and (4) no land leveling or terracing has been done. These conditions help formulate the improved ratings. The other category, unimproved ratings, are provided for poorly drained soils that require aritificial drainage and have not been drained and/or are subject to frequent flooding.

The CSR ratings range from 5, for soils with severe limitations, to 100 which is reserved for those soils (1) located in areas of most favorable weather conditions for Iowa, (2) that have high yield potential, and (3) that can be continuously used for row crop production with little soil erosion. The ratings developed are for soil and weather conditions near the geographic center of a particular soil association area. Ratings are prepared on an individual county basis as part of the soil survey program by soils scientists of the Iowa State Agriculture and Home Economics Experiment Station in Ames, and by the Soil Conservation Service.

After 2 years of hard work, the County Planning and Zoning Commission recommended to the County Board of Supervisors that they accept and approve the new ordinance. The ordinance that was adopted in October 1973 left no doubt that the agricultural lands and socioeconomic base of the unincorporated areas of the county held a high priority and many provisions and regulations were established to maintain that status quo. The county, at this time, agreed on several land-use policies, one of which stated "that prime agricultural lands (defined as soils with a Corn Suitability Rating of 85 or above) shall be retained for agricultural purposes only." Thus, Black Hawk County began its commitment to preserve agricultural lands.

The Planning and Zoning Commission simply would not approve any request for other uses, other than agricultural, on those soils rated above 85 unless there were extenuating circumstances. The policy statements were revised in 1976 lowering the CSR scale to include all soils rated as having a CSR of 70 or above as prime. The CSR of 70 or above, in effect, preserved about 69% of the total area of the county. The county zoning ordinance and comprehensive plan has undergone major revisions in 1980 and 1982. Included in the current ordinance is the defining of agricultural soils of those soils having a CSR of 50 or above. It is apparent that the CSR scale is quite flexible and can be adjusted to meet individual community goals.

The Application of the Corn Suitability Ratings and Land Use

Naturally, the soil variation indicates each individual farm's productivity in terms of crop-producing ability. Every parcel of land is identified as to soil type. Every soil type has its own set of characteristics or properties, and we know how many acres of each soil type exist in the county.

To explain how the CSR is applied to county zoning we should look at the procedures for rezoning land in Black Hawk County. The request for rezoning is first made by an application to the county zoning office. If the application is presented in person, the zoning administrator advises the applicant concerning the county's zoning regulations and land-use policies. If the applicant desires to continue, the following procedures are followed: First, an information packet is developed for the parcel. As part of this packet an on-site visit is made by the commission's technical review committee, which drafts a written report describing the parcel's characteristics. The technical review committee is composed of local technical personnel educated and trained in various fields related to land use; the committee membership includes the county zoning administrator, the council of governments' assistant director and environmental planner, the county environmental health department supervisor, the county engineer, the county conservation board's planner, and the district Soil Conservation Service conservationist. The report addresses the parcel's physical characteristics, site characteristics, wildlife habitat, socioeconomic factors, suitability, availability of public services, and other matters deemed important (Table 11.1). In addition to the report, other information is also included with the packet: a soil map (as found in the Soil Survey) with important soil properties including the CSR, the building site characteristics, and the suitability for the operation of sanitary facilities (Fig. 11.2); a U.S. Geological Survey topographic map of the area; a map showing flood prone areas, if necessary; and a township map showing existing dwellings and zoned districts.

This report and photographic slides are presented to the commission at their regular monthly meeting. The applicant at this time presents his/her reasons for the request. The commission also receives comments from the public and adjacent property owners, who are notified of the request per written information. Consider the example found in Fig. 11.3, the 13.24 acre (5.3622 ha) parcel consists of five soil types as identified in the soil survey. Four soils within the site have CSR of 50 or above: the Wiota Silt Loam (CSR 95) comprising 42.7% of the area, the Waukee Loam (CSR 79) 2.4% of the area, the Spillville Loam (CSR 92) 14.7% of the area, and the Flager Sandy Loam (CSR 50) 1.2% of the area. Approximately 61.0% of the area has soils defined by the zoning ordinance and the county comprehensive land-use plan as "prime." It is now the responsibility of the applicant to prove to the commission that because of size, slope, surrounding residential development, vegetation cover, or other extenuating circumstances the parcel is not suitable for agricultural production. The commission will then do one of three things: (1) recommend approval, (2) recommend denial of the request, or (3) table the request pending further information. If the request is either recommended for approval or denial, the application and the information packet is sent to the Black Hawk County Board of Supervisors who, after an advertised public hearing, make the final decision.

Name of Request: Belfield   **Date:** November 4, 1980

Location: Part of the NW¼ of Section 12, Township 90 North, Range 14 West.

Reason for Rezoning: Development of an eight lot subdivision.

I. PHYSICAL FEATURES:

A. Eco-System: Row crops, road ditch grasses, and scattered trees along fence line.

B. Soils: 7(95) Wiota Silt Loam – 42.7% of area.
41B(40) Sparta Loamy Fine Sand – 39.0% of area.
178(79) Waukee Loam – 2.4% of area.
284(50) Flagler Sandy Loam – 1.2% of area.
485(92) Spillville Loam – 14.7% of area.

C. Slope: Moderately level – 61% of area.
Moderately sloping (2 to 5%) – 39% of area.

D. Drainage Basin: Site drains west approximately one mile to the Cedar River.

E. Landscape: Terrace.

F. Surface Geology/Bedrock: Stratified Loamy and sandy alluvial sediment/ either Devonian Wapsipinicon or Silurian Niagaran.

G. Aquifer/Aquifer Recharge Zone: The bedrock formation or alluvial aquifers available. Area may be considered a minor aquifer recharge zone.

H. Flood Prone: Not in the identified flood plain.

I. Vegetation: Row crops, grasses, and scattered trees along fence line.

J. Unique Features: None.

II. SITE CHARACTERISTICS:

A. Agricultural Suitability: High.

B. Urban Suitability: Moderate.

C. Surface Drainage: Adequate on majority of parcel, some ponding may occur on southern most area of the parcel.

D. Soil Erosion: Silting of road ditch, some sheet erosion evident in open field.

E. Soil Drainage: Majority of the parcel is classified as good to excessive. The Spillville soil is poorly drained.

Fig. 11.2. Black Hawk County Planning and Zoning Commission Technical Committee Review Sample.

F. **Energy Potential:** No existing windbreak, level topography does not lend itself to passive earth sheltered dwellings.

G. **Sewer and Water Systems:** Required engineering analysis of proposed sub-division sewer and water systems per Black Hawk County Health Department criteria for subdivision developments. Recommend shared water system. Possible septic field problems associated with the Wiota and Spillville soils. Sparta soils excessive permeability may pollute the groundwater.

III. WILDLIFE HABITAT:

A. **Open Land:** Road ditch, minimal due to proximity of U.S. Highway 218.

B. **Woodland:** NA

C. **Wetland:** NA

IV. PUBLIC SERVICES:

A. **Sewer:** Individual.

B. **Water:** Individual.

C. **School:** Janesville Community School District.

D. **Utilities:** Iowa Public Service. Janesville Telephone Exchange District.

E. **Fire Protection:** Janesville Fire Department.

F. **Police:** County Sheriff.

G. **Transportation:** Access onto U.S. Highway 218 (Waverly Road). Eight separate driveways would probably not be approved by the Iowa Department of Transportation. Access road would be recommended, but would need additional land rezoned to meet "R-5" district requirements. Moderate increase in traffic.

V. SOCIOECONOMIC:

A. **Economic Activities:** Agricultural; trapshooting range, seed plant, and engineering firm one-half mile south.

B. **Land-Value:** Not available.

C. **Population Distribution:** Moderately sparse.

D. **Historical Significance:** None.

E. **Cost/Revenue Flow:** No available data to project flow.

Fig. 11.2 *(Continued)*

VI. LAND USE:

A. Existing: Agricultural.

B. Adjacent: Agricultural, non-farm residential strip development to the south, private recreation site trapshooting range to the southwest, ag-related industry to the south (seed processing), and an engineering firm to the south.

VII. ADDITIONAL INFORMATION:

- Compliance with Black Hawk County Comprehensive Land Use Plan:

  A. Conflicts with Policy #1 - agricultural uses only on prime agricultural land.

  B. Conflicts with Policy #6 - encouraging residential development in the incorporated areas, the previously rezoned residential areas, and upon buildable soils of the county.

- No apparent livestock feedlots within quarter mile limit.

- Approximately 12 road miles to economic center of county.

- Preliminary and final platting required before construction may begin.

- 1980 growing season - corn.

Fig. 11.2 *(Continued)*

NW¼ of Section 12, T 90N, R 14W

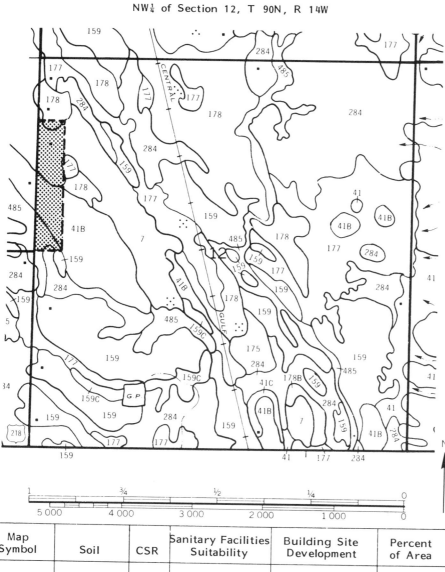

Map Symbol	Soil	CSR	Sanitary Facilities Suitability	Building Site Development	Percent of Area
7	Wiota	95	Moderate: Wetness	Severe: Wetness	42.7
41B	Sparta	40	Slight	Slight	39.0
178	Waukee	79	Slight	Slight	2.4
284	Flagler	50	Slight	Slight	1.2
485	Spillville	92	Severe: Wetness	Severe: Wetness	14.7

Fig. 11.3. Soil information, Belfield request.

Experience and Impact of Using Corn Suitability Ratings

The county has found that the use of the CSR system has lived up to expectations. It should be emphasized that CSR is just that, a tool. As with any tool, one must exercise skill and training in its use and understand its limitation.

The system relieves the zoning commission from the chance of making error in evaluating a parcel of land. The need for local control should be emphasized here. The amount of prime agricultural land will vary from county to county. A determination must be made as to the amount of development which is desirable and permissible. Even more importantly these questions must be answered: "What do we want our countryside to look like 25-50 or 100 years from now?" "Will it have been essentially urbanized?" "Will it have maintained its integrity as an efficient producer of food and fiber?"

Since 1979 to the end of 1981, the county considered over 680 acres requested to be rezoned from "A-1" Agricultural District to another district. Only 72 acres were approved and of that total 42 acres were on lands that had a majority of its soils rated as "prime." A 25 acre parcel was rezoned on land in which a subdivision was already platted. The land was already lost for agricultural purposes; the rezoning thus encouraged a more productive use of the land. Other requests on prime soils were approved only after careful consideration that because of limited size, excessive slope, vegetation cover, or the presence of glacial erratics the sites were not suitable for row crops production. Many potential requests for rezoning of farmland have been discouraged by the county's reputation for preserving these lands.

Two conditions have a significant impact in undermining the county's policies for preserving farmland: (1) the taking of land by other governmental agencies for the construction of freeways and supportive roads: two new major highways have begun construction that will take over 500 acres (202.5 ha) of land out of production; and (2) the annexation of farmland by the municipalities of the county. During the 1960s, the three largest cities engaged in a land rush to gain control of land where future industrial sites were proposed by John Deere and Company, and several hundred acres were lost.

According to the report "Field Research on the Policies of Black Hawk County, Iowa, for Protecting Farmland," by J. Dixon Esseks of Northern Illinois University for the National Agricultural Lands Study, the productivity of the soil (CSR) is the major criterion considered by the commission and the board in hearing requests for rezoning. This created a secondary problem: several members of the community have expressed the philosophy that if the land is not rated as prime agricultural, then it is prime for development. This philosophy, if allowed to prevail, would lead to haphazard spot developments, degradation of "natural" areas of the county, and unfair burden on the taxpayers to support these unplanned, energy consuming rural residences. These issues hastened the development of a new comprehensive plan, completed during the summer of 1980. Policies included in the plan specifically address those issues of protecting "natural" areas and encouraging development in the incorporated areas, the previously rezoned residential areas, and on buildable soils of the county.

Another major consideration of the Black Hawk County agricultural land preservation policies, as pointed out by Professor Esseks, is the diversion of development to neighboring jurisdictions. Professor Esseks states

If such diversion took place, there would be no net saving of prime land. Some development which may otherwise have been located in the county has occurred in Waterloo and Cedar Falls and in some cases on prime land, but much or most of that development had the advantage of being closer to schools and other public services and, hence, less expensive to serve. The six Iowa counties adjoining Black Hawk may have also received more diverted development, but as of 1983, four of the six had adopted zoning ordinances patterned after Black Hawk's and, therefore, faced developers with basically the same restrictions. This harmonization of zoning policies, so critical to successful preservation of good farmland, was largely the result of efforts of the Iowa Northland Regional Council of Governments, the agency located in Waterloo, which provided most of the staff support for the adoption and implementation of Black Hawk's policies.

During the 10 years since the implementation of the zoning ordinance, Black Hawk County and its four surrounding rural counties with similar ordinances have experienced a major redirection of land utilization. The rate of residential development within the unincorporated areas has remained relatively steady, but this development is now occurring on soils deemed suitable for such land use, while the prime land remains in agricultural production.

The Present Status of the CSR in Zoning in Black Hawk County

On November 18, 1982, a new zoning ordinance became effective. As part of the comprehensive plan this ordinance is basically the same as the October 1973 ordinance; however, a major new section was added. This section entitled "Natural Resource Protection and Preservation" specifically addresses what is prime agricultural land and how it is identified. That portion of the section is as follows:

Natural Resource Protection and Preservation

Significant Lands
    Significant lands are agricultural lands of highly productive soils, renewable resource lands, which promote the long-term productivity of an area by contributing to water, soil, or vegetation cover conservation, and fragile lands.
Identification
    Agricultural Lands of Highly Productive Soils: Shall be defined as a parcel of land where more than twenty-five (25) percent of its area consists of agricultural lands of productive soils (having a corn suitability rating that has been rated at fifty (50) or above). Determination regarding corn suitability ratings and other soil characteristics shall be referenced from the official *Soil Survey of Black Hawk County, Iowa*, published by the United States Department of Agriculture Soil Conservation Service, December 1978.
Soil boundaries shall be determined from the soil maps found in the official *Soil Survey of Black Hawk County, Iowa*, or from a soil map upon an aerial photograph compiled and attested by a certified soil scientist or technician.
It shall be noted that it is the policy of Black Hawk County, Iowa, rich in fertile productive soils to maintain this nonrenewable resource for future generations to employ in the production of food and fiber; therefore, such lands shall be preserved as "A" Agricultural District, unless there are extenuating circumstances.
    Other Significant Lands: Shall be identified by reference from the *Black Hawk County Conservation Resource Inventory*. These lands shall include wetlands, recre-

ational lakes, forest covers, forest reservations, rivers and streams, river and stream banks, open and native prairies and wildlife habitats, as designated upon the established priority list approved by the County Board of Supervisors, as amended.

The citizens of Black Hawk County are fully aware of the CSR system and are proud of its effects on preserving agricultural land. The media has played an important role in presenting the land use policies in a favorable light. The two major farm organizations, the Farm Bureau and the National Farmers Organization (NFO), have members sitting on the planning and zoning commission and view the policies as important in maintaining the rural economy of the unincorporated areas of the county.

In addition to the four adjacent counties that have adopted similar ordinances, other counties in Iowa have begun to develop preservation programs utilizing CSR. For an example, Story County (Ames) in central Iowa has found that growth needs could be handled without developing any land with a rating of over 62, thus preserving 93% of that county for agricultural uses. Scott and Johnson Counties have begun research into the system for their agricultural lands.

Black Hawk County has received nationwide attention in many publications as a leader in preserving prime land, Articles in *Successful Farming*, the National Association of Counties' *County News*, *Saturday Review*, *U.S. News and World Report*, *Ways and Means*, *Soil Conservation*, and *National Wildlife* have appeared in recent years applauding the county's efforts. In July 1979, the *Des Moines Register* ran a series called "Vanishing Acres," which explored the dimensions of the problem of loss of prime lands and how the situation could affect the production of food. That article explained Black Hawk County's success in the use of soil information and zoning in restricting development of prime farmland. Black Hawk County was one of five areas selected in *Disappearing Farmlands—A Citizen's Guide to Agricultural Land Preservation*, highlighted as a local government that has adopted measures to combat the loss of farmland.

Edward Thompson, Jr., of the National Association of Counties Agricultural Lands Project, concludes in his article "Soil Used to Protect Ag Lands in Black Hawk":

Black Hawk's farmland preservation program is attracting the attention of other counties because of its thoughtful, direct approach that is based upon the soil itself. Soil classification as a policy tool has the potential to work just about everywhere that farmland remains, but is flexible enough to be modified to suit regions where crops other than corn predominate, and where a different mix of agriculture and development is desired by county officials and their constituents.

References

Anthan, G. and Parker, K. 1979. Vanishing Acres, *Des Moines Register*, July 8–15, 1979.

Clark, J. 1977. Agricultural Zoning in Black Hawk County, Iowa. Iowa Northland Regional Council of Governments, Waterloo, IA.

Clark, J. 1978. Developing and Contents of a Zoning Ordinance—The Rural View. Iowa Northland Regional Council of Governments, Waterloo, IA.

Clark, J., Lind, K.E., and Sieglaff, R. 1978. Developing An Organized Community Growth Plan Through Effective Planning and Zoning. Iowa Northland Regional Council of Governments, Waterloo, IA.

Esseks, J. 1979. National Agricultural Lands Study: Preliminary Report on Field Research on the Policies of Black Hawk County, Iowa, for Protecting Farmland. Northern Illinois University, De Kalb, IL.

Fenton, T.E. 1975. Use of soil productivity ratings in evaluating Iowa agricultural land, *Journal of Soil and Water Conservation* **30**(5), (September-October).

Fenton, T.E., Duncan, E.R., Shrader, W.D., and Dumenil, T.C. 1971. Productivity Level of Some Iowa Soils, Spec. Rep. 66, Agriculture and Home Economics Experiment Station and Cooperative Extension Service, Iowa State University, Ames, IA.

Iowa Northland Regional Council of Governments. 1975. A Natural Resource Inventory of Black Hawk County. Waterloo, IA (August).

Iowa Northland Regional Council of Governments. 1975. Land Use Element: Region Seven. Waterloo, IA (November).

Johannsen, S. and Larsen, L.C. 1979. How Black Hawk County, Iowa, Identifies and Preserves Prime Agricultural Lands by Using Corn Suitability Ratings. Iowa Northland Regional Council of Governments, Waterloo, IA.

Metropolitan Planning Commission of Black Hawk County. 1967. Land Use Plan. Waterloo, IA (December).

Scholted, W.H. and Riecken, F.F. 1952. Use of soil survey informa-tion for tax assessment in Taylor County, Iowa, *Soil Science Society of American Proceedings* **16**(3), 270–273.

Sieglaff, R.L. and Larsen, L.C. 1980. The Role of the Soil Survey and CSR in Black Hawk County, Iowa, Zoning to Preserve Prime Agricultural Lands. Iowa Northland Regional Council of Governments, Waterloo, IA (July).

Thompson, E., Jr. 1980. Soil Used to Protect Ag Land in Black Hawk, *NACo County News*. (January 21).

U.S. Department of Agriculture. 1979. Soil Survey of Black Hawk County, Iowa. Soil Conservation Service, Waterloo, IA.

Part III

Middleground and State Approaches for Farmlands Protection

12

Farmland Conservancies: A Middleground Approach[1]

Charles E. Little

In the effort to come to grips with the problem of how to preserve farmland permanently and affordably, analysts have been casting about for new approaches for the direct control of farmland. The idea is to find something that can be added to standard techniques to increase the options for farm communities to protect their land.

What has been sought, in short, is a kind of middleground between zoning (mutable, but cheap) and development rights purchase (permanent, but expensive) that has the best features of both. There are no perfect examples of such a middleground, but there are enough bits and pieces to fit together a passable concept. And while the bits and pieces are quite variable, there is one feature that seems to be central—the purchase of land as a last resort, when its sale would result in an inappropriate change of use, and its resale with restrictions insuring continued agricultural use.

Various expressions of this idea exist in Pennsylvania, California, Canada, France, and among private land conservancies in the United States that have used purchase and resale extensively for natural areas preservation and now are seeking to adapt the activity for farmland.

Deed Restrictions in Pennsylvania

It started out naturally enough. Amish and Mennonite farmers in southeastern Pennsylvania did not want to see land going out of farming, so they cooperatively bought land so threatened and resold it to people interested in retaining the land in agriculture. Subsequently, since 1973, Amos Funk, a vegetable farmer and conservation leader in Lancaster County, Pennsylvania (the most productive nonirrigated county in the United States), has sought to codify such a notion in his county and in the laws of Pennsylvania. The result is called the "deed restriction" proposal.

[1]A somewhat longer version of this chapter appeared in *American Land Forum* Magazine, Vol. II, No. 1, under the title "On Saving Farmlands." The current version first appeared in the *Journal of Soil and Water Conservation*, **35**, 204-211 and is reprinted here with permission.

The idea is to place a covenant in the deeds over farmland within a duly established agricultural preserve district. The deed restriction is to last 25 years and preclude inappropriate conversion of the land to other uses. Landowners would pay lower taxes. They would also be protected from condemnation, nuisance ordinances, and the like.

The effort to secure covenants would take place in three "tiers." First, donated covenants would be sought. Where donations are not made over land thought to be significant in the district, the agriculture preserve board would seek to purchase such covenants based on a percentage of the overall land value or for a flat fee per acre. The price offered would be significantly less than a "development right" permanently deeded as a negative easement running with the land. For Lancaster County, the figure of $200 per acre (0.405 ha) was agreed upon.

Assuming that not all landowners within the district would think the compensation offered for a 25-year deed restriction sufficient, a third tier could come into play. If and when unrestricted farmland were sold, the board could insert itself into the transaction if it wished by exercising a presumptive option on the land at a purchase price at or exceeding the selling price, then reselling the land itself, with the 25-year restriction, to the buyer or to someone else. This transaction is voluntary on both sides—the agricultural preserve board does not have to buy the land, nor does the new owner have to sell it. Moreover, the board cannot keep title to the land; but if it cannot resell it with a restriction, it may sell the land without one.

All of this is complicated, but important as an example of a purchase and resale approach. Following is a summary prepared for an early draft of the agricultural preserve district bill by the chief counsel of the Pennsylvania House of Representatives.

> It [a preliminary draft of the bill] would authorize counties to adopt agricultural preserve ordinances. The ordinances could enable counties to create special agricultural preserve districts. Any time land is sold within a special district, a copy of the contract must be submitted to a newly created agricultural preserve board. The sale of land would have no binding legal effect and could not be recorded for a period of 30 days after the filing of such a contract with the board. The board would be authorized to acquire the purchaser's interest in the land, within this 30-day period, by making a binding, written offer to the seller at a price which exceeds the original contract price. Such an acquisition must be approved by a majority of the county commissioners. If the board fails to take any action within this 30-day period, the initial land sale takes effect and cannot be set aside. The board must impose a restrictive covenant upon any land it acquires under this act, limiting it to agricultural [use]. The board must resell the land as restricted. The county is authorized to lease the land until it is resold. The board must first offer the land, at cost, to the initial purchaser, and if rejected, to any person leasing the land. If neither offer is accepted, the board must sell the land at a public sale. The draft [bill] will also enable persons owning land within an agricultural preserve district to voluntarily subject their land to such a restrictive covenant [presumably by either donation or with compensation]. Land voluntarily restricted would be entitled to the same benefits [tax abatement, e.g.] and protections [against condemnation, nuisance ordinances, etc.] as land acquired and resold by the county.

In November 1979 a bill generally conforming to this description was introduced in the Pennsylvania legislature. The bill, H.B. 1983, failed to be reported out of the Agriculture and Rural Affairs Committee.

While state-level legislation did not succeed, Lancaster County did establish a first-step deed restriction program. On April 2, 1980, the county commissioners unanimously passed a measure establishing an agriculture preserve board, and a voluntary program can now begin in most townships. The board's mandate includes the following (Harler 1980):

- Development of sample deed restrictions.
- Delineation of agricultural preserves, initially and on a continuing basis, in cooperation with the Lancaster County Planning Commission and similar groups.
- Education of the general public and potential participants about the deed restriction program.
- Provision of assistance to those farmland owners who wish to apply deed restrictions.
- Administration of necessary procedures for obtaining restrictions.
- Preparing recommendations for legislation for a more effective deed restriction program.
- Expansion of the deed restriction program when and if new legislation is passed.

The last two points, of course, are crucial if the central element of the idea (purchase and resale) is to be realized. But even though this element is missing, most believe that the county's action to establish a board is an important step and should not be thought of merely as a compromise.

"It is very affordable," says Amos Funk (1979), "and offers, by providing large contiguous areas designated as preserved, the only real assurance farmers have to provide for themselves 'the right to farm.' We certainly have not given up on bill [H.B.] 1983. We will push for its passage as hard as we can. However, we can wait."

California Coastal Conservancy

Possibly the most ambitious land-use regulatory effort in the United States is the California Coastal Commission program, enacted under a citizen-led ballot initiative known as Proposition 20. Proposition 20 was approved by 55% of those voting in the general election of the fall of 1972, and it was by all accounts an amazing demonstration of a shared sense of the value of an important resource (Duddleson 1978).

The regulatory aspects of the commission's program have received most of the attention since—both good and bad. This involves permit and planning authority over lands within the coastal zone, in some cases severely limiting its use. Less well known is a state-level agency called the State Coastal Conservancy that was established by the legislature in 1976 to augment the planning and regulatory work of the commission (Environmental Protection Agency 1980).

Beginning operations in 1977 with a $7 million budget, the California Coastal Conservancy has undertaken 39 projects through one or another of its five program areas: (a) to preserve coastal "resource" lands, such as wetlands and habitat areas; (b) to redesign unacceptably planned developments, such as the many 40-by-60 foot (12.2-by-18.3 meter) seaside subdivisions of the 1930s still uncompleted but still "legal" by lot consolidation and resale; (c) to provide public accessways to the shore; (d) to reserve coastal resource sites, that is, advance acquisition of land for later development as recreation areas by municipalities or state agencies; and (e) to preserve agricultural land by acquisition of fee or lesser interest if necessary to restore such lands to productivitiy (California Coastal Conservancy 1980).

What distinguishes the California Coastal Conservancy is its conscious effort to come up with innovative solutions to land preservation challenges, using all forms of acquisition and resale or leaseback to achieve its purposes. Most spectacular are the projects consolidating lots in badly platted subdivisions by purchasing the unbuilt-upon lots, replatting, and then offering better planned homesites for sale. In the Santa Monica Mountains, one subdivision, El Nido, was reduced from 202 lots to 16 this way. In Seal Beach, the conservancy developed a public/private investment scheme in which 7% of the site will pay for 80% of the public cost on the remainder of the site. Working with a private land trust in Humboldt, the conservancy saved the state as much as 34% in land costs by judicious, advance purchase of lands slated for park use by means of creatively using tax laws to negotiate so-called "bargain sales" from landowners (California Coastal Conservancy 1980).

Despite these successes, the most "monumental" of the conservancy's mandates, as agency officials describe it, is the preservation of agricultural land; and this mandate seems also to be the most elusive. Under the state coastal conservancy statute, "The conservancy may acquire fee title, development rights, easements, or other interests in land located in the coastal zone in order to prevent loss of agricultural land to other uses and to assemble agricultural lands into parcels of adequate size permitting continued agricultural production.

"The conservancy shall take all feasible action to return to private use or ownership, with appropriate use restrictions, all lands acquired for agricultural preservation under this division" (Section 31150, Ch. 1441, California Statutes, 1976).

Though the instructions are clear, the conservancy has been unable to get started on the purchase and resale, or lease, of any of the 3.5 million acres (1,417,500 ha) of the state's coastal agricultural lands (California Coastal Conservancy 1980).

A model agricultural land preservation project was to be undertaken in the Morro Valley in San Luis Obispo County. The idea was to purchase, in fee, some 46 acres (18.63 ha), record an agricultural preservation easement over the land, and transfer the land to an adjoining farmer who would, in turn place an easement over his own 192 acre (77.76 ha) property. The scheme would have permanently preserved 238 acres (96.39 ha) as agricultural land. The difficulty was that the conservancy's appraisal of the value of the land did not meet the owner's expectations and the deal fell through (California Coastal Conservancy 1980).

Though the agency has indirect powers of eminent domain (through the State Public Works Board), condemning the property in order to carry out the plan apparently was not appropriate. Among other things, the conservancy must get approval from the California Coastal Commission before any effort to condemn land; and the commission must, in turn, assure itself that there is "no other reasonable means, including the use of police power, of assuring continuous use of such lands for agricultural purposes" (Section 31152).

Subsequently, four other efforts were made to bring about an agricultural purchase and resale. Though one of these remains a possibility, no project has yet been completed.

The conservancy blames its lack of success on the relatively short time it has been in operation and extreme budget constraints. Based on its research and field experience, the conservancy estimates that, because of dramatic increases in the development value of coastal land, the resale of purchased land would recoup only $0.50 for each acquisition dollar after imposition of a restrictive easement on the land. Therefore, a fund for purchase and resale would have to be substantial in order to sustain such losses on each transaction. At present only $1 million is allocated for the farmland program; and according to the conservancy, the acquisition budget for most single projects would be about $1.5 million each. "Nevertheless," says the conservancy's report, "because this program is so vitally important, the conservancy (will) try to demonstrate the efficacy of the program's techniques and potential, given adequate funding" (California Coastal Conservancy 1980).

Canadian Examples

Seeking precedents abroad for domestic policy concepts is usually of more interest to researchers than to policy-makers. Nevertheless it may be important to know something about conservancy techniques in two countries, Canada and France. In Canada, three provinces—British Columbia, Saskatchewan, and Prince Edward Island—seem to have lessons for the United States.

Agricultural Districting in British Columbia

British Columbia's experience demonstrates well the concept of agricultural districting by means of governmental edict. In 1972, when the New Democratic Party (NDP) was elected to form a government for the province, one policy priority was the protection of farmland from urban encroachment. Accordingly, the NDP government ordered a "freeze" on the subdivision of farmland, except as ordered to the contrary by the government. Under the 1973 Environment and Land Use Act, the freeze was redefined as pertaining to any parcel of land two acres or more that had been designated as agricultural for property taxation or was in Canadian soil class 1, 2, 3, or 4, meaning good to excellent in terms of soil capability.

A land commission was empowered to establish permanent agricultural land reserves wherein nonagricultural use of land is prohibited. Such reserves now represent about 5% of the total land area in the province. Appeals for exclusion from the reserves are possible; and as of 1978, about 25,000 acres (10,125 ha) have been exempted out of the 11.6 million acres (4,698,000 ha) in reserve status. In dealing with amendments to reserve zoning, the basic criterion is agricultural land capability, which indicates how seriously British Columbia takes the preservation of its prime farmland (Manning and Eddy 1978).

Germane to the conservancy idea, the province also takes seriously the nature of farmland ownership. Preservation of family farms is second only to land preservation in terms of commission priorities. One way the commission helps to encourage small proprietorships is to purchase farms that come on the market and resell them to young farm families unable to afford the high capital costs of entering the industry as an owner. Fifteen such purchases had been made by the commission as of 1976. Total acres, just over 6000; the cost, $4.3 million, including improvements. The commission will also permit young farm families to sign a long-term lease that provides a sense of ownership "just short of outright title" (Ward 1976).

Saskatchewan's Land Bank

It is Saskatchewan, though, that is best known for its land purchase program to enable young farmers to enter agriculture. The Saskatchewan Land Bank Act of 1972 has been widely reported in the United States and has served as inspiration for a "Young Farmers" program in Minnesota and for a 1978 proposal introduced in the U.S. House of Representatives as part of the Family Farm Development Act (H.R. 10716).

The land bank program was established to help solve a number of interrelated farmland ownership and use problems. In rural Saskatchewan, farm areas needed economic revitalization; farmers wishing to sell land could not find qualified buyers; and young or new farmers were unable or unwilling to make the large capital investments required to enter agriculture. As a result, farm ownerships were getting larger and small farms were disappearing. Land was being lost to agriculture, and rural economies were becoming depressed.

The objective of the land bank program was to help owners of farmland dispose of their land at a fair price and to help new or young farmers get established in the industry. This was accomplished by purchasing land, then leasing it to qualified applicants on a long-term basis with an option to buy after 5 years if conventional financing could be secured (Ward 1978).

As of 1978, some 350 of the program's 2300 participants had completed 5 years of leasing and were eligible to purchase their land. During that year, the province changed the policy to reduce the amount paid by the buyer. According to a Lands Directorate report (Ward 1978), "The land will be sold at average market price, with 20 percent of the market price, to a maximum of $5,000, refunded to the purchaser at a rate of 20 percent of that amount for the next five years so long as the purchaser continues to farm and live in Saskatchewan during those five years." Hence, those persons exercising the purchase option would be the most likely to keep the land in productive agriculture over a long period of time.

Prince Edward Island's Land Development Corporation

Of all the provincial agricultural land programs, perhaps the most interesting is one of the least well known—the Prince Edward Island Land Development Corporation, established in 1969. In part, the corporation's job is, like that of the California Coastal Conservancy, to augment the regulatory provisions of the province's development plan by means of judiciously buying and selling properties to advance the purposes of the plan.

A major problem in Prince Edward Island, as in British Columbia and Saskatchewan, was the abandonment of small farm holdings, many on first-rate agricultural land. The corporation can purchase such lands, improve them by repairing structures, installing drain tiles, undertaking erosion control measures, and the like, then resell them on favorable terms to adjoining or other bona fide farmers. In acquiring land, the corporation may buy land outright from an owner; but if the owner is a farmer of retirement age, the corporation will set up an annuity program for him, if he chooses, providing him with a pension. Also, the farm owner can be eligible for a lifetime lease of his house, plus 1 acre and guaranteed access (Crammel 1974).

Another element in the province's program is the Rural Development Council, a now-inactive citizen organization that in the early stages worked closely with the Land Development Corporation and the Land Use Service Center. The latter agency prepared local plans throughout the province. The Rural Development Council organized meetings to discuss these local plans, obtain feedback, and generally involve citizens in the planning effort. In connection with land acquisition and resale by the Development Corporation, a council staff person is located in the Land Use Service Center to determine those farmers who might be interested in expanding their holdings by purchasing corporation land and those farmers who might be interested in retiring (Crammer 1974).

The Land Development Corporation also purchases land proffered to nonresident or alien buyers but not approved for sale by the lieutenant-governor-in-council, who under a 1972 provincial law, must approve all such transactions involving 10 acres (4.05 ha) or more than 330 feet (100.65 m) of shoreline. In a 1976 update, the lieutenant-governor-in-council may require a nonresident purchaser whose petition to buy more than 10 acres (4.05 ha) or 330 feet (100.65 m) of shore frontage has been approved to enter into an agreement with the provincial Land Use Commission to guarantee satisfactory use of that land as a condition of the approval (Prince Edward Island Land Use Service Centre and Maritime Resource Management Service Council of Maritime Premiers 1978).

Taken together, the activities of the Prince Edward Island Land Development Corporation, the early work of the Rural Development Council, and the provision in provincial law regulating land sales to nonresidents suggest a means by which many interrelated agricultural land-use problems can be dealt with creatively, sensitively, and comprehensively at the local level.

French SAFERs

Despite the proximity of Canada and similarities in settlement patterns and historical land use, the foreign program most significant to a study of conservancy techniques may be the SAFERs of France. As described by Professor Strong of the University of Pennsylvania Department of City and Regional Planning, the work of local, nonprofit *Sociétés d'Amènagement Foncier et d'Établissement Rural,* which are statutorily empowered with the right to preempt any sale of farmland in their district, is effective "both to assist those who wish to remain in farming to obtain suitable land, and to keep prime land from being subdivided" (Strong 1976).

The basic operation of a SAFER is relatively straightforward. Authorized in 1960 as nonprofit corporations empowered to buy and sell farmland, a SAFER could be established for a single *departement* (county) or for several together. SAFERs now extend to virtually all *departements* in France. The largest covers five *departements*.

Most capital for their operation, primarily for a revolving fund, comes from local farm organizations and farm lending institutions. The average start-up capital subscription is $200,000.

SAFERs can buy farmland either through voluntary sale or by right of preemption in previously designated areas. Preemption, which is used in 16% of the cases, is considered essential to the effective operation of the SAFER. Professor Strong (1976) describes the process as follows:

> The SAFER requests the prefect to designate a given area as subject to the right of preemption for farm use. No land in a development district and no land shown in an adopted plan as intended for urban uses may be included. The prefect must seek the advice of farm organizations concerning the proposed designation and then submit a recommendation to the minister of agriculture. If the recommendation is favorable, the minister publishes a decree designating the area [as subject to preemption]. The decree is published among the legal notices in newspapers, posted at municipal offices, and mailed to notaries. People selling farm land are deemed to have notice of it, and any sale without prior notice to the SAFER is void. The right of preemption is granted for a three to five year term and may be renewed. About 60 percent of agricultural land is subject of a SAFER right of preemption.

Under a voluntary sale of land to a SAFER, the price paid is negotiable. When preemption takes place, the price is set by a public appraisal. Farm organizations in France insisted on the right of preemption coupled with a public appraisal to assure that the SAFER could keep good land in agriculture and avoid a hit-or-miss performance that might vitiate a preservation program if these authorities were not available.

After acquiring land, the SAFER may make conservation and other improvements before resale. The land may be held up to 5 years (10 years under special circumstances) so that a tract-assembly project can be carried out. In France the tradition has been to divide land among heirs rather than passing it on wholly to the eldest son. The result is that in some areas farmland holdings are in inappropriately small acreages.

The SAFER resells most of its land to farmers. "The objective is to sell the land not to the highest bidder," writes Strong (1976), "but to the person who will benefit most as a farmer by its acquisition. Favored by the law are farmers with too little land, farmers willing to change their present tracts for more efficient holdings, farmers whose land had been condemned for a public purpose, and young farmers anxious to establish themselves." Significantly, the purchaser must farm the land for a minimum of 15 years. The land may not be sold or subdivided during that period, except in extraordinary circumstances approved by the SAFER.

Altogether, from 1964 to 1975, SAFERs purchased 2.1 million acres (850,500 ha) of land and sold 1.7 million. They buy an average of only 12% of the agricultural land up for sale each year, but most people believe the SAFERs influence is much greater than this figure suggests. The key feature is the right of preemption. Even when not used, the possibility of its use can have an important effect on market behavior, an aspect of the device that might be overlooked by those concerned that preemptive purchase is too expensive or too controversial for effective use in the United States. According to Strong (1976), "Preemption is a power compatible with the American legal system and with American values. There is ample precedent for it in the private market's use of the right of first refusal. Preemption is an approach which, with minor modifications, could be adopted in the U.S. for the purpose of preserving farmland."

Nongovernmental Programs

Real estate activity has become a common land preservation technique for both national and local private conservation organizations in recent years. During the 1960s, the Nature Conservancy, with a substantial line of credit guaranteed by the Ford Foundation, began the advance purchase of natural areas for later resale to public agencies, such as the National Park Service. Other organizations have used this technique also, including the Western Pennsylvania Conservancy and the Trust for Public Land. What such institutions can provide is an opportunistic and efficient way to acquire needed land for public use quickly and cheaply— two qualities tending to elude public agencies, which must move slowly and carefully in the sensitive matter of land acquisition.

By and large, such private acquisitions for resale to public agencies have been limited to recreational sites, natural areas, and historic places. But since the emergence of national concern about the loss of farmland, many organizations have sought to adapt their expertise on behalf of farmland preservation.

One model for such an effort is the Lincoln, Massachusetts, Rural Land Foundation. Though Lincoln is a Boston suburb and not a farm community, the foundation, in effect a consortium of public-spirited investors, has been able to purchase land and "repackage" it, selling off some areas for development and protecting others as open space (Lemire 1979).

Possibly the first private conservancy established solely for the preservation of farmland in association with a state-level program is the Massachusetts Farmlands Trust. In Massachusetts, a statewide governmental program to purchase "agricultural preservation restrictions," called APRs, was established in 1977, with an initial $5 million budget to acquire APRs on 19 farm properties in the state, plus another $5 million available from a recent bond issue. Aware that the effectiveness of this state-managed program might be significantly augmented by a parallel private organization, officials of the Nature Conservancy, along with state agency executives and other conservation leaders, helped bring the Massachusetts Farmlands Trust into being. It began operations in 1980.

According to Davis Cherington, director of the trust, the organization is prepared to undertake the following five functions.

1. The trust will acquire farm property that comes on the market, using established bank lines of credit. The trust will then hold the property in its own name, ultimately placing ownership of the development rights (APRs) with the state of Massachusetts, the municipality, the local land trust, or a combination of these. The farm can then be resold to a qualified buyer at a price that will permit operations as an economically viable farm.

2. At the request of the (Massachusetts) Department of Food and Agriculture, the trust will buy an APR on a specific farm in those instances where the owner cannot afford to wait for the department approval process to be completed. Later, the trust will resell the APR to the department.

3. In cooperation with professional capital management specialists, the trust will organize tightly controlled private partnerships to acquire key farm properties for which the state lacks a preservation solution.

4. The trust will serve as an interstate clearinghouse for information on methods to protect agricultural land.

5. The trust can assist local conservation commissions and (local land) trusts with farmland acquisition and protection projects. The trust can provide real estate negotiation expertise, financial loans, and fund-raising assistance.

At the national level, private farmland preservation programs have been mounted by the Trust for Public Land and the American Farmland Trust. Moreover, a great many new regional and local conservancies have come into being, showing that nongovernmental conservancy techniques might provide a significant capability in certain areas, especially if activities are designed to complement governmental programs.

Defining the Middle Ground

The foregoing case histories are surely not the only examples of creative new techniques to preserve farmlands, but they provide a basis for discussion. The new middle ground approaches have been described as "conservancy techniques," and so long as the term is not thought to represent any specific kind of organization, public or private, or an overly narrow set of purposes, "conservancy" may be a helpful term to use in conceptualizing a middle ground land-saving program. What kind of activities, then, would a farmland conservancy undertake?

Sources for a Definition

The best of all possible farmland conservancies should draw on the best parts of predecessor programs and leave aside irrelevant aspects. Thus, the conservancy might be a local body with close ties to its constituency, such as the Lancaster County Agricultural Preserve Board, but draw its authority from a nonlocal level of government, as does the Coastal Conservancy in California (or as envisioned in the Pennsylvania Agricultural Preserve Act). Its area of operation should be specific, based in part at least on the quality of the land, as in the British Columbia Agricultural preserves, but also correlate with political boundaries, as do the French SAFERs. Like the SAFERs, too, the conservancy should be able to undertake a range of imaginative real estate operations, with the fast-moving, opportunistic quality of private land trusts, such as the Lincoln Rural Land Foundation or the Massachusetts Farmland Trust.

Like these private organizations and the Rural Land Council, the citizen group in Price Edward Island, the conservancy should have a civic group ambiance, not a bureaucratic one. In terms of its particular powers, though, the conservancy should part company with the civic-group model. It should possess preemptive power, like the SAFERs, or at least have this power available as a backup, such as the ability of the Coastal Conservancy to "borrow" eminent domain powers from the California Public Service Board.

The conservancy should be well-financed, of course, an attribute difficult to locate in any of the cases examined. But like most of them, the bulk of the financing should consist of separate, "up front" money to establish a revolving fund, replenished from time to time, to carry out a core program of purchase and resale.

Institutional Possibilities

Another way to assess the potentials for adapting conservancy techniques is to evaluate them in the context of possible institutions charged with carrying out a program. This way, the farmland conservancy concept begins to lose its ivory tower quality. For the sake of argument, a description of the duties of a conservancy might be summarized as follows.

A farmland conservancy is a local organization operating within a conservancy district coterminous with county or multicounty lines. The conservancy is empowered by state law to buy and sell land or rights in land for the purpose of maintaining prime, unique, and locally important farmland in farm use, to use its lands to retain or increase the numbers of farms in appropriately sized family proprietorships; and on its properties (and others as appropriate) to undertake needed soil and water conservation improvement projects. The conservancy may acquire land when offered for sale when it believes that the sale will result in a use inimical to farming, farmland, and conservation values in its area. It may resell the land with restrictions on use to an appropriate buyer. If there is a dispute over the price of land, the price offered shall be based on independent appraisals, or determined by a court in a condemnation proceeding. The conservancy has the right to intervene in any sale of land previously designated by the conservancy as prime, unique, or locally important farmland. The conservancy may use a wide variety of real estate transactions to pursue its purposes, including trades of land or rights in land, payment through pensions or annuities, and the like. It may assemble tracts of land for efficient farm use, or subdivide large tracts into smaller units appropriate to family farming or for young farmers. If the conservancy has undertaken extensive conservation projects on land it has acquired, it may stipulate in the deed upon resale that the conservation improvements be maintained, enforceable by right of reverter. In the area of its operations, the conservancy will cooperate with other government authorities, encouraging them to plan, regulate, tax and otherwise control land use in the agricultural area in such a way as to stabilize and enhance farming as an enterprise and way of life.

For a concept such as the foregoing, any number of different institutions might be able to carry out the program, including agencies of local government, agencies of state government, special districts (especially conservation districts), or private organizations with public charter.

The Lancaster Agricultural Preserve Board is an example of an agency of general-purpose local government. It was created by the county commissioners as, in effect, a committee. This status gives the board access to the powers of the local government, and vice versa. The board does not yet have its sought-after deed restriction authority, but if this element is added to the program, the work of the board can be coordinated with other authorities held by local government, including zoning, taxation, and eminent domain.

There are some who believe that it might be improper for the same government that depresses the value of land through regulation to turn around and buy the land at the reduced price to accomplish the same general purposes as the regulation. This would be especially improper, some think, if condemnation is used, or even if condemnation is threatened. This is one of the reasons why the Coastal Conservancy in California was set up as a separate organization from the Coastal Commission.

While the Coastal Conservancy does not have the problem of zoning land and acquiring it too, there are other difficulties with it as a model. The main problem is that the conservancy is not local and does not operate within any kind of predetermined area in which farmland values are specifically identified. This should not be interpreted as a criticism of the conservancy, for its program is comprehensive and not limited to agricultural land. Still, there are probably better models for state level agencies taking on the role of a farmland conservancy. Localized state park authoritites possibly could be looked to for guidance. Conceivably, there could be a state-level farmland conservancy operated on a farm-district basis with local operations in each cooperating district. This would effectively separate the program from general purpose local government, but it could become a bit more bureaucratic than necessary.

Special districts are a traditional means to provide for special programs. School districts are the most prevalent case in point, but in many areas, special districts provide most services, and farmland conservancy activities need not be an exception. It is entirely conceivable that state-enabling legislation could be enacted that would provide sufficient statutory authority for a local conservancy district to be established, drawing funds and its general powers from the state level of government.

In this connection, there already exists a special district program associated with agricultural land nationwide. Conservation districts were set up under a model state-enabling act sent to state governments in 1937 by President Franklin Delano Roosevelt. Such districts duly established under suitable state law are eligible for soil and water conservation grants and technical assistance from the U.S. Department of Agriculture and other agencies. The standard state law provides a procedure, including a local petition and referendum, for the organization of conservation districts as governmental subdivisions of the state, but governed by a local board of supervisors. A state-level committee administers the procedures establishing the districts and provides administrative assistance and coordination of programs.

What is significant about the nation's nearly 3000 conservation districts is that some might be able to undertake most farmland conservancy techniques, as described, with little if any change in their charters. Some 775 districts, or 41% of those responding to a 1979 survey, expressed concern about the loss of agricultural land to urban development. In some areas, conservation districts have led the way in urging local farmland protection ordinances. In others, they are not so effective.

Lastly, it is possible that private organizations might have a direct as well as a complementary role in conservancy-type activities. State governments could charter existing private organizations, such as land trusts in New England towns, to undertake expanded programs for land-saving and be empowered to use or "borrow" authorities necessary to carry out such programs. Without the authority to preempt land sales or to protect against profiteering by private landsellers, however, private groups would be limited to a kind of "augmenting" role, such as that described for the Massachusetts Farmlands Trust.

Issues and Options

There are, without question, serious issues to be resolved concerning any possible farmland conservancy program. Five issues stand out: the problem of money, the problem of equity, the problem of sufficiency, the problem of unintended effects, and the problem of politics.

The money issue has several parts, the most important being the amount of money needed up front for a revolving fund. Also important is the amount of money needed to replenish the fund, assuming that stripping development rights from land titles would lower the price considerably in some areas. With farmland prices averaging $1500 per acre (0.405 ha) in the Northeast and the Corn Belt, the acquisition of a single 250 acre (101.25 ha) farm in these areas would run $375,000.

According to Coastal Conservancy calculations, one should expect to lose 50% on a turnaround transaction after taking out development value. The net cost for "processing" a 250 acre (101.25 ha) farm thus would be $187,000, not counting overhead or cost of improvements on the property. Using SAFER figures, where *departement* capitalization averaged $200,000 (much higher today), one farm turnover would be enough to break the budget.

But this manner of figuring may be excessively negative. To begin with, only 3% of farm properties turn over in a given year. And not all of these would necessarily relate to preservation of prime land. Therefore, only a small percentage of farms in any given conservancy district would be up for sale, and only a fraction of those would require intervention. Moreover, if the French experience is any guide, inappropriate sales will probably be suppressed by the very existence of conservancy-type institution.

One last observation: With the cost of land escalating at present rates, chances are that many conservancies might well recoup their investment, even after stripping development rights from the title. Given this rough arithmetic, money would be a problem, but possibly not across the board.

Equity issues concern "fairness." On the one hand, is it fair to the farm owner in a conservancy district to subject his property to special rules and regulations, inhibiting his freedom to sell his property to whomever he wishes? On the other hand, is it fair to the taxpayer to be asked to subsidize, in effect, the farm sector by having to insure that land is not misused? While these are serious questions, and not the only ones bearing on equity issues, the fact remains that conservancy techniques may well have less difficulty in this regard than either the use of police power without compensation or the use of tax revenues for the large-scale purchase of development rights, the perpetuity of which is open to question.

The problem of operational sufficiency has several aspects. First, can a local body be expected to undertake sophisticated land transactions? Will not the problems of loopholes, favoritism, or just plain administration stupidity creep in? The SAFERs of France are heavily criticized for various operational failures. At the same time, the program is still in effect; and while not perfect, most believe that the French agricultural land base has benefited enormously from the program, possibly in ways that are difficult to measure. Moreover, the U.S. agricultural community is well organized. By virtue of the institutional and agency programs in operation, much administrative capability is already in place.

These days, official Washington, as well as many state capitals, are concerned about the unintended effects of new governmental programs. Indeed, it is almost mandatory to mention in any analysis of land-use policy that governmental programs are more a part of the problem than a part of the solution. Could this be true of an organized farmland conservancy program?

The fact is that an aggressive operation could, by intervening vigorously in the land market, distort prices. Worse, it might be that a future generation will find that the wrong land has been preserved. Areas that might have been best used for urban expansion, say, might be those protected as farmland.

There are some technical problems too. What, for example, should a conservancy program imply for agricultural zoning? Would such zoning be superfluous in an area where farmland is subject to preemptive purchase and resale with deeded restrictions? And if this is true, could conservancies ultimately be subversive of the long and difficult efforts many farm counties have made to achieve farm-use zoning?

There is hardly any way to answer these questions, except possibly to place the issue of potential unintended effects stemming from farmland conservancies against the effects stemming from zoning and/or development rights purchase, or simple tax abatement for that matter. In every case, government intervention into the market mechanism has and will have the possibility of producing an unhelpful result. Still, this possibility may well be less pronounced for conservancy techniques than for more traditional, routine approaches.

This last point leads into the problem of politics. Any kind of intervention in land use is difficult to sell in the United States, and most difficult in rural areas where a *laissez-faire* attitude about land use has been a long tradition. Conservancy techniques, while perhaps more in "the American grain" than some kinds of zoning or even purchase of development rights, are easily misunderstood, especially when coupled with the right of preemption and back-up powers of eminent domain to settle problems of compensation. A new idea is always hard to introduce. It is harder usually in rural areas than in urban ones. And if the idea has something to do with "land use," there are those who would not even consider trying.

One would hope, though, that the farmland conservancy concept will continue to attract interest. What is so different about this approach to farmland preservation—in contrast to zoning and development rights acquisition—is that a single mechanism can deal with and integrate the primary issues of farmland ownership and use: the family farm issue, the resource stewardship issue, and the farmland conversion (urbanization) issue. These problems are not all that are awry with farming these days, but they go to the very foundation of U.S. agriculture.

References

California Coastal Conservancy. 1980. Report to the Governor and Legislature. Oakland, CA.

Calif. Statutes, Section 31150, Ch. 1441, 1976.

Calif. Statutes, Section 31152, Ch. 1441, 1976.

Crammer, V. 1974. Land Use Programs in Canada: Prince Edward Island. Lands Directorate, Environment Canada, Ottawa, Ontario, Canada.

Duddleson, W. J. 1978. How the citizens of California secured their coastal management program, *in* "Protecting the Golden Shore," Robert G. Healy. (Editor). The Conservation Foundation, Washington, D.C. pp. 10-15.

Environmental Protection Agency. 1980. California Coastal Management, *EPA Journal* 25, (May).

Funk, A.H. 1979. A Deed Restriction Program (mimeo). (May 1).

Harler, C. 1980. Lancaster County establishes agricultural preserve board, *Lancaster Farming* 1, 21, (April 5).

Lemire, R.A. 1979. "Creative Land Development." Houghton Mifflin, Boston, MA.

Manning, E.W., and Eddy, S.S. 1978. The Agricultural Land Reserves of British Columbia: An Impact Analysis. Lands Directorate, Environment Canada, Ottawa, Ontario, Canada.

Prince Edward Island Land Use Service Center and Maritime Resource Management
    Service Council of Maritime Premiers. 1978. Non-resident Land Ownership Legisla-
    tion and Administration in Prince Edward Island. Lands Directorate, Environment
    Canada, Ottawa, Ontario, Canada.
Strong, A.L. 1976. Preemption and Farmland Preservation: The French Experience.
    Regional Science Research Institute, Philadelphia, PA.
Ward, E.N. 1976. Land Use Programs in Canada: British Columbia. Lands Directorate,
    Environment Canada, Ottawa, Ontario, Canada.
Ward, E.N. 1978. Land Use Programs in Canada: Saskatchewan. Lands Directorate,
    Environment Canada, Ottawa, Ontario, Canada.

13

Wisconsin's Farmland Preservation Program

James A. Johnson

Introduction

Wisconsin has not escaped the national problem of losing productive farmland to urban uses. Farmers have been increasingly concerned with restrictions placed on farm operations and rising property taxes as the cities continue to move into the countryside. Nonfarm people are also becoming alarmed over the increasing cost of servicing urban sprawl and the loss of open space. Both groups recognize the importance of farming to the state and local economies. A legislative study committee considered these dual concerns of urban and rural people and reviewed the experience of many other states in dealing with these issues. The Wisconsin Farmland Preservation Law is therefore a program that is responsive to both urban and rural interests, and is based on some of the most effective features of other states' programs.

Although the Wisconsin Farmland Preservation Program has been in effect for only 5 years, early participation already indicates that it may become a very effective program to protect important farmland in Wisconsin.

The Wisconsin Farmland Preservation Act went into effect in December of 1977. At this time, approximately 4.5 million acres (1,821,150 ha) of farmland are protected with farmland preservation contracts or exclusive agricultural zoning, and more than 20,000 farm owners are qualified to receive tax credits for participating in the program (Table 13.1). In addition, 70 counties have completed or are preparing agricultural preservation plans under the program, many of which are also developing exclusive agricultural zoning districts for farmland they designate as preservation areas. The planning and zoning programs already encompass 99% of the total farmland in the state. Total tax credit payments were $17 million in 1983. The average credit payment in 1983 was $1400 per farm, which is about one-half of the property tax.

This favorable response can be attributed to some rather simple but unique concepts. The Wisconsin Farmland Preservation Law is innovative because it combines tax relief for farmers with incentives for local

147

Table 13.1   Farms and Areas Protected by the Farmland Preservation Program as of December 31, 1982 (Approximate)

	No. of Farms Protected	Acres Protected
Contracts	2,428	558,123
Zoning	18,030	3,576,100
Total	20,458	4,134,223

governments to adopt agricultural preservation plans and exclusive agricultural zoning ordinances. It is unique because preservation is achieved with traditional land-use tools, and implementation is at the local level.

These concepts and tools are available to most governmental units, yet to date they have not been widely used in farmland preservation efforts. In addition to describing basic provisions of the law, this chapter will suggest some of the reasons for the favorable early response to the program and will look at its potential for effective, long-term preservation of farmland in Wisconsin.

How the Law Works

Basic Concepts

The following underlying concepts, which are inherent in the law, seem to be most responsible for favorable response and participation:

1. *Tax relief is in the form of a "circuit-breaker" credit against state income tax.* The "circuit-breaker" tax relief concept is progressive; it directs tax credits to younger farmers and others whose income is low compared to their property tax, and eliminates many high-income, non-farm investors.

2. *There is an initial "startup" phase and a second "permanent" stage to the program.* The initial stage generates interest and participation by individuals and encourages local governments to take necessary steps to qualify landowners for the second stage of the program.

3. *Areas of greater development pressure (urban counties) are required to have stronger preservation programs.* Lands under the greatest development pressure require stronger protection. Urban counties require zoning. Rural counties have the option of zoning or using a plan with individual contracts.

4. *Tax incentives increase as the method of preservation becomes stronger.* Zoning, based on a plan, is the strongest method of preservation, and is consequently given the highest tax incentive—100%. Zoning without a plan, or individual contracts under a plan, are adequate preservation measures, and qualify for 70% level of credit. Initial contracts are short term and affect only lands under contract, and therefore receive only 50% credit.

5. *Implementation is at the local level. The state's primary rule is to assist local units of government.* Individual farmers decide if they should enter into contracts. Town (township) and county boards decide if they should adopt local plans and zoning ordinances. Each county identifies preservation areas on the basis of local needs and conditions.

6. *Traditional land-use tools are used to preserve land.* Traditional land-use plans (Ag preservation plans) are used to identify preservation and development areas. Zoning ordinances are used to implement plans.

A sound planning *process* provides the proper foundation for effective zoning.

7. *The state provides grants to counties to assist in the county planning and mapping projects.* Many counties do not have adequate staff to prepare agricultural plans. State funding provides timely assistance to start the process.

Program Provisions

In general, land is preserved under the program by farmers entering into contracts, or by local governments adopting agricultural plans and/or zoning. The contracts or zoning require that the land remain in agricultural use and qualify the owner for tax relief.

Initial Program

In the first 5 years of the program (1977–1982) any qualified farm owner could obtain a contract. The contract restricts the land to agricultural use and makes the owner eligible for an income tax credit. To qualify, the land must be 35 acres in size, and must have produced $6000 in gross farm sales in the last year. Also, a soil conservation farm plan must be in effect or under preparation. Each application is approved by the county. The tax credit available under the initial contract was 50% of the maximum available under the credit formula.

Second Stage

No county is required to participate, but after 1982, counties or town must have taken some action if individuals were to remain eligible for tax credits. The options differ for urban and rural counties.

Rural Counties

Counties with a population density of less than 100 persons per square mile are defined as rural counties. These counties have a choice of (1) adopting an agricultural preservation plan, which would allow individual farmers in preservation areas to take out long-term contracts and obtain 70% level tax credit; (2) adopting exclusive agricultural zoning, which allows tax credits on zoned farms at the 70% level without a contract; or (3) adopting both planning and zoning, thereby enabling 100% level tax credits without individual contracts. A long-term contract under the permanent program runs from 10 to 25 years, and requires that an SCS farm plan be in effect on the land.

Urban Counties

Counties are urban when their population density reaches or exceeds 100 persons per square mile. In these counties exclusive agricultural zoning must be in effect for owners to remain eligible for tax credits. The zoning can be a county ordinance (which also requires town approval), or a separate town (township) ordinance.

Planning

After 1982, in rural counties a county agricultural preservation plan must be adopted for individuals to obtain a long-term contract. Approval of contracts are then based on whether or not the farm is located in a preservation area as delineated in the plan. Also, if the county subsequently adopts agricultural zoning, the plan is the foundation for the zoning districts. Plans are certified by a land conservation board for conformance to state planning standards in the law. A county agricultural plan is a very important element of a successful preservation program and will be described in more detail later.

Zoning

Exclusive agricultural zoning must also be certified by the Land Conservation Board for zoning requirements according to the law. These requirements prohibit nonagricultural uses on the land. Development for a nonagricultural use requires a full rezone procedure, including a public hearing.

Tax Credits

Tax credits are based on a "circuit-breaker" concept that provides a credit against state income tax for property taxes deemed "excessive" in

Fig. 13.1. Farmland preservation planning projects as of December 31, 1982. Open areas: Plans in effect and certified; striped areas: planning/mapping projects in process; boxed areas: nonparticipants. *Plan completed but not adopted by County Board of Supervisors.

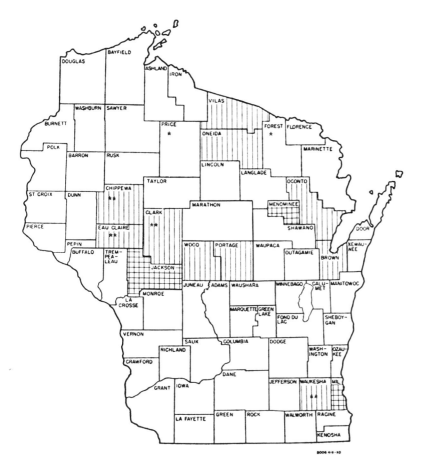

Fig. 13.2. Status of planning/mapping projects as of June 30, 1983. Open areas: Plans in effect and certified; striped areas: planning/mapping projects in process; boxed areas: nonparticipants. *Will be considered for certification by ALPB on June 29, 1983. **Plan completed but not adopted by County Board of Supervisors.

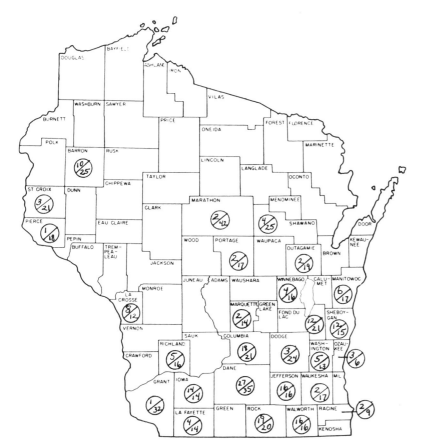

Fig. 13.3. Exclusive agricultural zoning in effect as of December 31, 1982. The top number is the number of towns that have adopted exclusive agricultural zoning. The bottom number is the total number of towns in the county.

relation to the farm household's income. Under the formula for calculating credits, as income rises, tax credits increase; but as property taxes rise, credits also rise (Table 13.2). As property taxes increase to an excessive level (when compared to income), the tax credit acts as a "circuit breaker" by relieving the overloaded property tax burden. Tax credits are paid out of the state's general fund, and do not affect property taxes. The following table shows the relationship between income and property tax to the credit payment.

Rollback

When land remains in the program by renewing of contracts or by maintaining agricultural zoning, no payback of tax credits is required. However, if land is removed from the program (by failure to renew a contract, or by rezoning) a rollback payment is required of up to 10 years of tax credits received. Therefore, the tax relief may be a combination of tax deferral and tax break depending on the length of participation in the program.

Planning Grants

The Wisconsin legislature allocated $2 million in grant funds to aid counties in planning and mapping of preservation areas in their respective counties. These funds are administered by the Department of Agriculture, Trade and Consumer Protection (DATCP) and the Department of Development, and are allocated by a Conservation Board. To date, 67 counties have received a total of $1.7 million, for an average of $25,000 as the state's contribution to county agricultural preservation plans. There is no requirement for counties to match state funding, but many counties add financial support to the projects.

Land Conservation Board (LCB)

The program is supervised by the LCB, whose membership consists of the secretaries of the DATCP, the Department of Natural Resources, the Department of Administration, and five public members. In addition to

Table 13.2 Maximum Tax Credit Schedule[a]

| Income | Property Taxes | | | | | |
	$1,000	$2,000	$3,000	$4,000	$5,000	$6,000
$ 0	$900	$1,800	$2,500	$3,200	$3,700	$4,200
5,000	900	1,800	2,500	3,200	3,700	4,200
10,000	585	1,485	2,255	2,955	3,525	4,025
15,000	180	1,080	1,940	2,640	3,300	3,800
20,000	100[b]	585	1,485	2,255	2,955	3,525
25,000	100[b]	200[b]	720	1,620	2,360	3,060
30,000	100[b]	200[b]	300[b]	405	1,305	2,115
37,500 & over	100[b]	200[b]	300[b]	400[b]	500[b]	600[b]

[a]Except for the categories marked by [b], the actual credit received by farmers is Initial contract=50% of these amounts; exclusive agricultural zoning=70% of these amounts; agricultural preservation plan plus 10-25 year contract=70% of these amounts; zoning plus an agricultural preservation plan= 100% of these amounts.

[b]Applies only to land in an exclusive agricultural zone under a certified county, town, village or city ordinance. For land under a farmland preservation agreement (and *not* zoned), the tax credit in these categories is zero. Households whose land is in an exclusive agricultural zone and whose income is above $37,500 receive a minimum tax credit of 10% of the eligible property tax.

allocating funds and establishing administrative policy, the Board certifies county agricultural plans and zoning ordinances, and acts on appeals and relinquishments of farmland preservation contracts. This Board also has responsibilities for the state's soil and water conservation program.

The Role of the Farmland Preservation Staff

The staff of the Farmland Preservation Unit consists of four persons who carry out the administrative functions of the program. This includes the issuing of farmland preservation contracts, record keeping on all individuals participating through contracts and zoning, assisting in the preparation of agricultural plans and zoning ordinances, and informing people of the law and the program.

Much time has been devoted to providing information on program details to individual participants and planning and zoning information to county and town officials. A rather complete set of informational pamphlets and guidelines have been developed to assist in this critical function. Most counties have, in turn, conducted their own educational programs.

Several other state agencies also have important roles in the program: the Department of Revenue with tax credit payments, the Department of Development with grants and Land Conservation Board Member, the Department of Administration with another Board member, and the university extension service with education. These functions have been effectively coordinated at the state level.

What Have We Learned? How Has Local Government Responded?

It is obvious that part of the reason for early interest and participation is the tax credit incentive. But it is more than that. Farmland preservation is an idea "whose time has come." There is much local concern over the loss of farmland and its counterpart of urban sprawl. The Wisconsin approach offers *timely* help to *local people* and *local governments* that already have a *commitment* to preserve land and manage growth in their communities.

Because implementation occurs at the local level, it is essential that local people are informed and involved. It is their program. Therefore, it is essential that the planning *process* include local input and decision-making. This kind of process insures that the plans are responsive to those being planned for, and certainly enhances the likelihood of the plan being implemented.

Our experience in working with counties and towns has confirmed our faith in the basic concepts of the law, and has taught us some new lessons.

General Lessons (Conceptual)

1. *The use of traditional land-use tools of planning and zoning can be effective if applied properly and carefully.* There are many facets to "proper application" but the core of the formula is as follows: a good planning process = a good plan = effective implementation, usually

through zoning. The key then begins with the planning process; a process that involves local people developing their plan to meet their needs. Most of the other lessons deal with techniques to strengthen and support local planning.

2.   *State funds for county planning provide essential support.* Counties that have a planning staff often have limited and usually committed budgets. Many rural counties have no planning staff. Yet, counties in Wisconsin are being increasingly besieged with new state-directed program responsibilities, usually without accompanying monetary support. These new responsibilities are overwhelming even the most dedicated counties.

3.   *Incentives vary for urban and rural counties, but remain strong for both.* Early expectations were that rural counties would be the first to zone because adoption would be easier where development pressure was light, and it would be an easy avenue to the tax credits. But the opposite has occurred. Most zoning is occurring in urban areas where there is general public awareness of development problems. The main incentive has been to correct urban sprawl with growth management programs, which usually include zoning. In these situations the tax credit has been a secondary incentive.

In rural counties the main incentive to plan appears to be the tax credits. Exclusive agricultural zoning is not well established in many rural areas. Here the tax credit provides an adequate incentive to begin the less threatening planning process. This should lead to a stronger land-use program, and protection of farmland through individual contracts (as well as some zoning).

The most interesting reaction is occurring in the "second tier" counties that are located between truly urban and rural areas. Here the land-use problems and tax credit incentives seem to combine most effectively to encourage all types of participation: planning, zoning, and individual contracts. Being one step removed from the most severe development pressure allows zoning to occur before development forces become too strong a deterrent. Tax credits are equally effective because they act as an added preservation incentive to the rather stable farming communities that still exist in these areas.

There is also a general incentive for county and town officials to take some action to insure that they are not responsible for excluding farmers from maintaining eligibility for tax credits.

4.   *Town (township) government is strong in Wisconsin, and provides a good base for grass roots planning.* Any small, homogeneous unit is an effective area for planning. It is close enough to the people to be responsive to their needs, and they can be a part of the process. In addition to proper size, the town in Wisconsin has implementation authority. County plans are often coordinated compilations of town plans. Implementation through zoning can be achieved with a county ordinance which requires town adoption, or with a separate town ordinance.

5.   *Local leadership is a necessary ingredient.* Every successful planning or zoning program seems to be headed by one or two key individuals that have leadership abilities. These qualities include a commitment to the program, understanding of the process, ability and inclination to communicate and work with people, and some time to devote to the project. The best combination is to have leadership at both the county board (committee) and staff level.

6. *Adequate time is needed for the process to work.* A plan is effective if it addresses local needs and can be implemented. Local needs, values, problems, and solutions form the basis of the plan. But local involvement requires time. Time to raise issues, set goals, prepare and analyze studies, and design solutions. Any short-cutting of this process, and particularly the excluding of citizen input, compromises the plan and its potential adoption and implementation. Nothing turns the public off faster than a "railroad job," even if it is a good railroad. The informational and educational process takes time to gel. It is a mistake to expect interest and reaction to occur too quickly. Let the planning process work, and the end result will be both a better plan and one that is used.

7. *Formal planning is not always effective.* It has been interesting to observe that the most successful county projects are not always in counties with planning departments. Planners have prepared some of the best plans, but other excellent projects have been developed in counties with no professional planning staff. In fact, in some cases it almost seems that professional planners have obstructed the process.

Why has this occurred? Perhaps it is because most planners are trained in rather sophisticated planning techniques that are most appropriate in metropolitan settings. The process of developing an agricultural plan requires someone to collect good data, to analyze what the data means, and to suggest what to do about it. A local team of nonplanners almost always works effectively because it applies a common-sense, group analysis to the problems. The key here is to step back and think. It does not usually require the preparation of sophisticated, computerized plans. Instead, a straightforward thought process that produces logical objectives and studies, and develops policies to carry out objectives, will result in a workable plan.

More Specific Lessons (Technical and Procedural)

1. *Local flexibility is necessary.* Every county has unique physical characteristics and land-use needs. It also has a unique political environment, based on traditions, values, and attitudes. No one knows better than local elected officials and staff how to proceed in their county. Staff can identify what data are available, and what resources are needed. Local officials can then set appropriate objectives and policies, and a practical course of action that will meet the objectives.

State support in the form of standards, funding, and expertise is helpful, and the tax credit is a real incentive. Also, uniform statewide classifications of productive farmland, such as the SCS classification system, is a good place to start in identifying preservation areas. But local definitions, based on local perceptions and needs, make county plans realistic and workable. For example, in mapping preservation areas, the importance of certain types of farms to the local economy is an important preservation criteria, and usually results in a more meaningful map of preservation areas.

2. *Local options allow choices of planners.* Flexibility is also needed in the area of who does the planning. Several options are available: the "local team" approach, city-county planning, the regional planning option, and the use of a consultant. Most counties use a combination, depending on what is most appropriate for the particular phase in progress. Allowing counties this option of planning staffs helps insure that the best quality planning is available to each planning situation.

3. *The local team approach is almost always successful.* The local team is formally called a technical advisory committee (TAC). Each county has a number of people with special knowledge of agriculture and planning. Commonly, the TAC includes staff representatives of the county extension office, SCS offices, county planning and zoning departments, county Agricultural Stabilization and Conservation Service office, the regional planning commission and local Department of Natural Resources offices of forestry, game and fish management. In addition, other farmers are usually represented.

The TAC is often headed by a county board member and supervised by a county committee (usually the agriculture or planning and zoning committee, or both). This is a technically oriented group whose function is to prepare maps, write the plan, and to steer the project. Its purpose is *not* to obtain citizen input.

4. *Citizen participation is a requirement.* The LCB has directed that there be substantial citizen involvement in the preparation of agricultural plans. Most counties have appointed citizen committees representing a wide range of interests. In addition, some counties are using other techniques, such as the use of opinion surveys or small group meetings. These small group sessions lend themselves very well to town meetings. Some counties have conducted a series of public informational meetings at the beginning of the planning process, to inform people of the law and what is to be done; and then another series at the completion of the plan to explain what has been done.

5. *Counties have already done much of their homework.* One outline of the planning process consists of the following steps: set goals; compile information; analyze data; develop policies; design plan; and implement plan. Most counties already have a fair idea of their general goals, a relatively complete data base, and some existing land-use policy. Most counties also have a strong public commitment to the preservation of farmlands and natural resources. The process of preparing an agricultural plan allows the county to focus on what lands they want to preserve, what land should be developed, and how to make these objectives happen on the land.

Most counties, for instance, have a rather complete set of maps and studies. By pulling together this existing data, a good part of the planning work may already be done and the remaining steps will be more clearly understood and accomplished.

6. *Town by town mapping aids the planning process.* Previous comments have noted that the rural township is a proper size for effective planning. Preparation of township resource maps is an excellent way to present the land use issues to the people in each town, and to obtain local reaction. By applying defined criteria for lands to be preserved, excluded lands, development areas, and transitional areas, a local town plan emerges. The maps do two things: they present information clearly; and they show how goals and policies actually apply to the land, allowing better decision-making at the local level.

Some of the counties have turned much of the planning job over to the towns, usually after resource maps have been prepared. Town residents provide information on types of farm operations, ownership patterns, and other information used to map preservation areas. When these decisions are made by local landowners it becomes "their plan"—to support and sell to the neighbors.

7. *Growth management is the rule.* Most counties wish to preserve farmland, but do not want to stifle growth. These need not be conflicting goals. In most counties there is adequate land available to accommodate growth without serious encroachment into prime farming areas. Growth management policies can be adopted that meet both preservation and growth objectives at the same time, by channeling development in the right direction, according to the plan. This brief statement is an oversimplification, but accurately portrays what every county thus far has been able to accomplish in specific ways in their agricultural plans, both in rural and in urban counties.

8. *A local educational program is needed.* Some individual, group, or agency must take on the responsibility of a well-directed, countywide effort to inform people of the state law and the county program. In Wisconsin this function is usually carried out by the county extension office, and often by one individual who "takes up the cause." The numbers of farmland preservation contracts received thus far have been directly related to the number of educational meetings held in various counties. Educational programs can be directed to individuals, interest groups, elected officials, and the general public, all at the same time. It is a necessary ingredient to the planning process. The key here is a commitment to public information and education by the county board, thereby enabling staff to devote time in this direction. It should be an ongoing effort.

What Are the Major Problems?

Planning and Zoning Problems

1. The problems are mostly technical in nature. It takes a certain amount of time for the planning process to work, but program deadlines for tax credits sometimes push counties into moving too fast. For example, if plans or zoning ordinances are certified by December 31 of any year, more farmers can claim higher tax credits against the current year's property tax. This tax incentive is causing a rush of certifications at the end of each year. Sometimes the plans would be of better quality and zoning ordinances better accepted if additional time were given to their preparation and adoption.

2. Another problem with some plans is that planning analysis is weak. After many data are collected and resource maps are prepared, there is a tendency to move directly into mapping of preservation areas without carefully studying the data. Plans prepared in this way use preconceived ideas for criteria of planning districts. It would be much better if the persons preparing the plan would take a close look at the data and determine what this information really means for their county. When the data are not analyzed carefully, it is a lost opportunity to design the most effective plan.

3. Also, problems occur when the county board formally endorses a project, but does not support the work by allowing staff time to be devoted to the planning process. This happens when the motive to plan is to avoid excluding individuals from eligibility for tax credits, rather than the motive of preserving land.

4. A fourth problem is related to jurisdictional arguments between

cities and rural towns. Most development action occurs at the urban–rural fringe. It is common for local governments to put as much effort into protecting territorial rights as they devote to land use issues.

Program Problems

1. *Tax credit formula excludes some large farms.* The tax credit payments decrease as household income rises. "Household income" under the law is net farm income plus other miscellaneous income of the farm household. Some larger farms, however, produce net farm incomes too high to receive an attractive credit, or any at all. But these operations are on productive lands that should be preserved. It is assumed that the larger, productive farms are the least likely to convert out of agricultural use, but this may not always be the case. In 1980, an amendment to the law provided for a minimum credit of 10% of property tax to any farm located in a certified exclusive agricultural zoning district. The purpose was to make every restricted farm eligible for at least some credit, and helped to mitigate the concern of high income farmers that were initially ineligible for benefits. Some farmers would still prefer a program that related tax credit incentives more to the land and less to the farm owner, but it is unlikely that further changes in this direction would result in more land being protected.

2. *Farmers lack adequate information.* The provisions of the law are necessarily quite complex (to effectively meet tax relief and land preservation objectives). Before a farmer will commit his land to participation, he must have access to factual and detailed information on the program. The new legislation has been subject to considerable public controversy and political rhetoric, making it difficult for individuals to evaluate accurately the benefits and restrictions for their farm operations. A statewide blitz of news releases, educational materials, and meetings failed to reach many farmers with the necessary details. Time and continued education are curing the problem. Also, farm organizations have been very helpful in getting out the word. But a problem remains with the informing of the 90,000 individual farmers of the ways the program can affect their particular farming situations.

3. *Urban counties may need more help.* As development pressures grow in urban areas it will be increasingly difficult to establish and maintain exclusive agricultural zoning ordinances. Our early experience is encouraging in that many close-in townships have been able to adopt effective ordinances because of their strong planning programs. However, when these areas become thoroughly spotted with subdivisions, and the "farming community" has moved on to greener pastures, additional incentives may be needed in the form of direct compensation for loss of development potential. The experience of other states with purchase or transfer of development rights programs should be very helpful to these local situations.

Conclusion

At this endpoint of the initial phase, it is apparent that the program objectives are being met faster than originally expected. *Land preservation* is widespread and growing. *Tax relief* is also increasing rapidly. And this combination preservation and tax relief effort promises to be one of the most effective and cost effective programs in the nation.

Wisconsin is experiencing excellent participation in the program to date. If participation continues to grow, this acceptance of the program must be attributed to program provisions and incentives that are particularly appropriate to the current land use environment and development pressures in Wisconsin. The Wisconsin approach to preserving farmland could have wide application in other states that are experiencing the loss of farmlands under similar circumstances. The focus on implementation at the local level, and the creative use of the traditional tools, are concepts that have gained acceptance by landowners as well as state and local governments, thereby becoming a far-reaching program of land reform: "An idea whose time has come."

References

Amato, P. (Coordinator). 1978. Farmland Preservation Planning: State of the Art, Wisconsin. Univ. of Wisconsin-Extension, Madison, WI, 224 p.

Amato, P., Barrows, R., Fodroczi, D., Johnson, J., and Wiley, P. 1978. Planning to Preserve Agricultural Land. Wisconsin Dept. of Agriculture, Trade and Consumer Protection, Madison, WI, 86 p.

Barrows, R. 1979. Testimony before the U.S. Senate, Select Committee on Small Business. Univ. of Wisconsin-Extension, Madison, WI, 33p.

Barrows, R. 1982. Wisconsin's Farmland Preservation Program. Univ. of Wisconsin-Extension, Madison, WI, 4 p.

Barrows, R., Klingelhoets, A. J., Krauskopf, T., and Yanggen, D. No date. Mapping to Preserve Agricultural Land; Alternatives for Local Officials and Citizens. Wisconsin Dept. of Agriculture, Trade and Consumer Protection, Madison, WI, 27 p.

14

Oregon's Agricultural Land Protection Program

Ronald Eber

Introduction

The preservation of agricultural land is one of the primary objectives of Oregon's statewide planning program. Oregon has determined that it is in the state's interest to protect the resource foundation of its largest industry, agriculture, which according to the Oregon Extension Service in 1982 recorded gross sales of $1.68 billion and contributed $5 billion to the state's economy.

The purpose of this chapter is to explain briefly Oregon's land-use program, to set forth the seven major components essential to protect agricultural lands and how Oregon's program addresses these, and finally to make some general comments and observations on Oregon's experience in implementing its program.

Oregon's Land-Use Program

Oregon's planning program came of age with the passage of Senate Bill 100 (SB 100) in 1973. This law created the Land Conservation and Development Commission (LCDC) and gave it the responsibility to oversee and direct the preparation of comprehensive plans in Oregon. The commission is comprised of seven members appointed by the governor. SB 100 requires every city and county to prepare and adopt a comprehensive plan and implementing measures.

LCDC was empowered to set mandatory planning standards (goals) with which each city and county plan, zoning, and subdivision ordinance must comply. There are 19 statewide planning goals. The first 14 were adopted in December 1974, and set the standards in part for citizen involvement; the protection of agricultural, forest and other natural resource lands; natural hazards; housing; the provision of public facilities and services and for urban growth. In December 1975, a fifteenth goal was adopted to protect and manage the Willamette River Greenway. Four coastal resource goals were adopted in December 1976. This state-

161

wide land-use program serves as the basis of Oregon's federally approved coastal zone management program.

SB 100 originally required that all local plans comply with the statewide goals within 1 year of their adoption. This expectation proved to be optimistic. The commission then required that all plans be completed by July 1, 1980. To carry out this task, there are seven field representatives and staff, who review local plans for compliance with the goals. Oregon has provided about $25 million to local governments to develop or update plans. Out of 280 jurisdictions, 206 had been acknowledged to be in compliance as of January 1984 including 18 of Oregon's 36 counties. The remaining jurisdictions' plans will be reviewed by July 1, 1984.

The 1981 Oregon legislature extended the scope of SB 100 to define the responsibilities of LCDC to review amendments to completed plans and ordinances to ensure continued compliance with the statewide planning goals.

Another important part of the Oregon program is the appeals process. Local governments, state agencies, and affected citizens can appeal a local or state government action affecting land use to the Land Use Board of Appeals (LUBA). This three member panel, appointed, by the governor, is akin to a land-use court although it is in the executive branch. The Board of Appeals will hear all land-use cases previously heard by the circuit courts and LCDC. LCDC has statutory authority to bring appeals of local land use decisions to LUBA. The board's decisions are reviewable by the Court of Appeals.

Through the appeals process, the LCDC has been able to interpret the statewide planning goals, particularly, Goal 3, "Agricultural Lands." Commission decisions have been instrumental in clarifying policy questions and have advanced the actual application of the goal on the ground.

The Agricultural Lands Protection Program

Oregon's agricultural lands protection program is based on statutory and administrative rule provisions, the agricultural lands goal, and commission appeals decisions and policies. What has brought these together into a program is statewide planning Goal 3, "Agricultural Lands." This goal requires the identification of agricultural lands, defined by the goal, and their preservation by the use of an exclusive farm use (EFU) zone established by the Oregon legislature. The EFU zone sets forth the farm and nonfarm uses allowed and provides tax and other benefits to the property owner. The goal also establishes a standard for land divisions and minimum lot sizes.

Although the effort to protect agricultural lands is part of a broader statewide program, it includes seven basic elements that are essential to any effort to protect agricultural lands. Whether a program is at the county, regional or state level, the following seven basic elements must be included.

1.   Policy statements on the economic and environmental value of agricultural lands.

2.   A clear, measurable definition of the agricultural lands to be inventoried and protected.

3.   The specific farm and nonfarm uses that can or cannot take place on these lands.

4. Standards for review of land divisions and minimum lot sizes.
5. Standards for the conversion of agricultural lands to nonfarm uses.
6. The provision of tax and other benefits to the protected lands.
7. The encouragement of urban development in urban areas and the limitation of rural residential development.

Policy Statements

Everyone favors the protection of agricultural lands but usually someone else's. The economic and environmental importance of agricultural land must be clearly set forth as explicit public policy. Too many people believe that the motivation to preserve agricultural land is only to increase open space, and maintain a pleasant pastoral setting for city folks to enjoy. That impression must be changed.

In 1973, the Oregon legislature completed a major revision of the farm use tax deferral system and adopted an "Agricultural Land Use Policy" (ORS 215.243). There are four basic elements to this policy:

1. Agricultural land is a vital natural and economic asset for all the people of this state,

2. Preservation of a maximum amount of agricultural land, in large blocks, is necessary to maintain the agricultural economy of the state,

3. Expansion of urban development in rural areas is a public concern because of conflicts between farm and urban activities,

4. Incentives and privileges are justified to owners of land in Exclusive Farm Use zones because such zoning substantially limits alternatives to the use of rural lands.

Goal 3 adds to this policy. It states:

Agriculture lands shall be preserved and maintained for farm use, consistent with existing and future needs for agricultural products, forest and open space. These lands shall be inventoried and preserved by adopting Exclusive Farm Use zones pursuant to ORS Chapter 215.

These policy statements clearly set forth the state's interest in the preservation of agricultural lands, the means for their protection (EFU zoning) and establish that incentives and privileges (i.e., tax benefits) are justified because of the limits placed upon the use of the land.

Defining Agricultural Lands

Any effort to protect agricultural lands must begin with a clear definition of the lands to be preserved. One of the most controversial parts of Oregon's program has been its definition of agricultural land. It is not limited to just "prime farmlands" but covers essentially all suitable agricultural land.

Goal 3 defines agricultural lands as those lands of predominately SCS Class I–IV soils in western Oregon and I–VI soils in eastern Oregon and "other lands suitable for farm use." More detailed soils data can also be used by local government. These are the lands to be inventoried and preserved.

The significance of this definition is that it is based on objective, scientific field data, not on current trends in agricultural economics or the individual management skills of the farmer. It does not distinguish between "prime" or so called "marginal" farmland. It is an attempt to minimize the endless debate over whether it is good land or marginal land or if an individual can make a living on a particular parcel.

Local agricultural economies are not only dependent on the best or prime farmlands but on the not-so-prime as well. A successful program must inventory all farmlands based on the *land's* resource capability, not the *farmer's* management ability.

Only after the completion of an objective resource inventory, can it be decided whether the land is *actually available for farm use or has been committed to nonfarm uses* based on surrounding development, parcelization, available services, etc.

It is time to stop making long-term resource decisions based on short-term economics. Commercial property is not rezoned for industrial use everytime a business goes under and it should not be for agricultural lands. As one farmer recently stated at a local land-use hearing, "These lands aren't marginal, they're just owned by marginal landowners."

Allowed Farm and Nonfarm Uses

It is important to limit incompatible nonfarm uses on agricultural lands. In Oregon, agricultural lands are to be preserved by an EFU zone. This zone is in actuality not a traditional Euclidian zone but more like the agricultural districts used in New York. At present, about one-half of the private land or 16 million acres (6,480,000 ha) in Oregon are included in the EFU zone.

The EFU zone was developed by the Oregon legislature in 1961 along with the farm tax deferral program. Farm use is encouraged and protected within the zone and it also allows a variety of nonfarm uses. The legislature recognized that some nonfarm uses are compatible with farm operations such as schools, churches, farm related commercial activities, and home occupations.

Nonfarm single-family dwellings are permitted only upon a finding that each dwelling is compatible with farm uses, does not seriously interfere with adjacent farm practices, and is situated on land generally unsuitable for farm use. Allowing some nonfarm dwellings is a safety valve that recognizes that within farm zones there are small areas that can accommodate a rural dwelling on a small lot without affecting an area's overall farm character. Small lots with such nonfarm dwellings also cannot qualify for farm use tax deferral. The importance of this process is that the nonfarm development is sited in a way that minimizes its impact on agriculture and thus protects the primary use within the zone.

Land Divisions and Minimum Lot Sizes

Clearly, one of the most difficult problems faced in protecting agricultural lands is how to control the constant parcelization of farmland into smaller and smaller lots. What standards should be applied to land divisions and on what basis should a minimum lot size be established? Nothing is achieved if after zoning the land for EFU it can be cut up into 5-acre tracts.

Oregon's approach has been to require that divisions of land or minimum lot sizes be "appropriate for the continuation of the existing commercial agricultural enterprise" in the area. LCDC realized, when developing Goal 3, that a statewide minimum lot size could not be established where farm acreage needs vary from large dryland wheat ranches to small intensive farm operations. Therefore, a standard was established in Goal 3, to be applied to the creation of new lots to prevent agricultural land from being divided into parcels that will not contribute to the local commercial agricultural enterprise.

The importance of this standard is that it requires a distinction between farm and nonfarm development and thus the application of different and more appropriate standards to each. Agricultural land is being preserved to protect Oregon's largest industry, commercial agriculture, and not to allow hobby farms and ranchettes.

Conversion Standards

Once land is identified as agricultural then some very specific procedures and findings are required before that land can be designated for nonfarm residential, commercial, or industrial development. In Oregon, this is called the "exceptions process." About 750,000 acres are now designated for rural residential uses with 200,000 acres designated in the highly productive Willamette Valley as of June 1983.

If agricultural land is already *built on or committed* to nonfarm uses, it need not be zoned EFU. If the uncommitted agricultural land is *needed* for nonfarm uses a detailed justification is required. Four criteria must be considered before conversion: (1) need, (2) alternative locations, (3) impacts, and (4) compatibility.

In order to allow residential development outside an urban growth boundary, an exception must set forth the facts and assumptions used as the basis for determining that the proposed use should be provided for, including the amount of land for which the use is being planned and why the use requires a location on resource land.

The reasons cannot be based on market demand for housing, assumed continuation of past urban and rural population distributions, or housing types and cost characteristics. A county must show why, based on the economic analysis in the plan, there are reasons for the type and density of housing planned which requires this particular location on resource lands. A jurisdiction could justify an exception to allow residential development on resource land outside an urban growth boundary, by determining that the rural location of the proposed residential development is necessary to satisfy the need for housing generated by existing or planned rural industrial, commercial, or other economic activity in the area.

This approach was affirmed by the Oregon Court of Appeals. The court stated:

> A market demand for rural residential development, however, does not constitute a "need" for it, . . . Goal 3 was enacted to preserve agricultural land from encroachment by urban and suburban sprawl by subordinating the free play of the marketplace to broader public policy objectives. Land is not excepted from the agricultural goal merely because somebody wants to buy it for a house (*Still v. Marion County*, 42 OR App 15 1979).

Lands zoned EFU under Goal 3 and later proposed for conversion require the same "exceptions process" findings. Oregon's 1983 legislature enacted a "Marginal Lands" bill (Chapter 826, Oregon Laws 1983). The Act is entirely voluntary. Counties may or may not choose to identify and designate marginal lands. However, if a county so chooses it must also adopt some tighter restrictions within its Exclusive Farm Use zones for the review of farm and nonfarm dwellings.

Marginal lands can be identified either on the basis of parcelization or productivity with the added consideration in both cases that the proposed marginal land was not managed as part of a commercial farm or forest operation. Uses allowed are those now allowed within an EFU zone and a single family dwelling on all existing lots created prior to July 1, 1983. The minimum lot size is 10 acres unless the parcel is adjacent to land zoned EFU in which case it is 20 acres.

Tax and Other Benefits

There are two other important aspects of Oregon's EFU zone and agricultural lands protection program. The first is a legal prohibition on any state agency or local government from adopting a rule or ordinance that unreasonably restricts or regulates "accepted farming practices" that cause noise, dust, or odors outside an urban growth boundary. This restriction does not limit the lawful exercise of any governing body's power to protect the health, safety, and welfare of its citizens. This provision establishes the principle that in farm areas restrictions should not unduly get in the way of the farmer by not allowing tractors to run before 8 AM or to create noise or dust. After all, they are farm areas, not residential zones.

The second is the provision of certain tax benefits to property owners. Land zoned EFU *and farmed* is appraised at its farm-use value for property and inheritance tax purposes. In addition, these lands are also exempt from certain special district and rural service assessments (i.e., sewer, water, solid waste, etc.).

This is a significant difference between Oregon's agricultural land protection program and those of other states. Although most states have voluntary farm-use tax assessment programs, Oregon is one of the few states to directly link comprehensive planning and zoning with its farm-use tax assessment program.

This link between zoning and special tax treatment is essential. It provides a balance between the public and private interests in the use of agricultural lands. The preferential tax treatment is extended in order to aid the farmer and help keep the agricultural land in production. The zoning restrictions on the nonfarm use of the farmer's land assures the balance of the taxpaying public that the program's objective is being met: protection of agricultural lands.

It is now realized in Oregon that these benefits are not enough. Zoning land for farm use no more creates farms than zoning land for industry creates a factory. The objective is to protect commercial agriculture. The protection of agricultural land is one way to do this; however, also needed are special loans for equipment and land improvements, new crop research and marketing studies, and some limitation on a farmer's nuisance liability for regular farming practices. The 1981 Oregon Legislature passed a "right to farm" law to provide some limitation on a farmer's nuisance liability for regular farming practices. This protection is not limited, however, to only those farms zoned EFU.

Encouragement for Growth in Alternative Areas

There is one final element for a viable program that is essential in the long run. If we limit development on agricultural land, it must be provided for and even encouraged somewhere else. Oregon's planning program puts a great deal of emphasis on meeting future housing and development needs in urban areas or on nonresource lands. Every city is required to establish an urban growth boundary that includes enough land to satisfy the community's housing, commercial, and industrial needs.

The state's housing goal requires communities to meet all their housing needs, particularly those for low cost and multifamily housing types and that local ordinances eliminate vague and discretionary approval standards.

The home builders and development community support these policies. They, too, see the need to protect agricultural lands and will build in other areas if provided the opportunity.

Summary

Overall, Oregon has a viable program to protect agricultural lands, although there is much that needs to be completed. It does cover the seven basic elements just discussed. It is not perfect, but it is workable and working. It still can be improved and is continually evolving.

The protection of agricultural lands is both a technical and political process. Although the standards in Goal 3 are specific, there still remains a great deal of flexibility in their application. The actual implementation is done at the local level where the ultimate success or failure of the program relies on the political will of local officials and citizens to carry it out. The statewide interest, as expressed in the goals, should help local officials carry out the program in the face of sometimes strong opposition.

One of the major problems faced by Oregon has been to try to save agricultural lands by using the traditional planning process. Traditional planning has a built-in bias against protecting resource lands in general and agricultural lands in particular. Planning started in the cities. Planners are always planning *for* something (i.e., housing, industry and shopping centers). The leftover lands were and maybe still are colored green on the maps and labeled "Agriculture-Open Space" but it never really means it. What it really means is that it is unused space available for development.

It is time the planning community and the general public change their attitude on this issue. Agricultural land is not unused, undeveloped open space. It has been developed for agriculture; it is being used. It is the nonreplaceable foundation for crops and livestock and is a primary resource in its own right. Plans for the protection of agricultural land must achieve the same status and credibility that plans for industrial parks and single family neighborhoods receive. Public education and understanding of these issues are absolutely essential if any program is to be successful.

Finally, there is another value that Oregon continues to grapple with: America's love affair with land. The history of this country is founded on the ideal that the small landowner is precious and that country living is somehow better or healthier than city life. Yet, the farm community has been systematically replaced by urban folks who have no economic or cultural ties to the land.

Berry (1977) discusses society's desire to escape to a few acres in the country where one can watch "kids and crops grow on a handful of acres someone can call their own," and then asks:

> Why I wonder does this feeling assert itself when the handful of acres is owned by an urban immigrant but not when they are owned by a farmer. How can we continue to hold the small farm in contempt as the living of a farm family and then sentimentalize over it as the "country place" or hobby farm of an executive?

The answer to Mr. Berry's question will be necessary if Oregon or any place is to succeed in its efforts to protect agricultural lands.

Author's Note

The 1983 Oregon legislature enacted a number of important amendments to Oregon's statewide land-use program as well as changes to the agricultural lands protection program. These include speeding up the review of local plans, a definition of "marginal lands" separate from agricultural lands and the uses allowed on these lands, and new review standards for farm and nonfarm dwellings in EFU zones.

For a current description of Oregon's program contact the Department of Land Conservation and Development, 1175 Court Street N.E., Salem, Oregon 97310.

Appendix 1: Goal No. 3—Agricultural Lands

To preserve and maintain agricultural lands.

Agriculture lands shall be preserved and maintained for farm use, consistent with existing and future needs for agricultural products, forest and open space. These lands shall be inventoried and preserved by adopting exclusive farm use zones pursuant to ORS Chapter 215. Such minimum lot sizes as are utilized for any farm use zones shall be appropriate for the continuation of the existing commercial agricultural enterprise within the area.

Conversion of rural agricultural land to urbanizable land shall be based upon consideration of the following factors: (1) environmental, energy, social and economic consequences; (2) demonstrated need consistent with LCDC goals; (3) unavailability of an alternative suitable location for the requested use; (4) compatibility of the proposed use with related agricultural land; and (5) the retention Class I, II, III and IV soils in farm use. A governing body proposing to convert rural agricultural land to urbanizable land shall follow the procedures and requirements set forth in the Land Use Planning goal (Goal 2) for goal exceptions.

AGRICULTURAL LAND—in western Oregon is land of predominantly Class I, II, III and IV soils and in eastern Oregon is land of predominantly Class I, II, III, IV, V and VI soils as identified in the Soil Capability Classification System of the United States Soil Conservation Service, and other lands which are suitable for farm use taking into consideration soil fertility, suitability for grazing, climatic conditions, existing and future availability of water for farm irrigation purposes, existing land use patterns, technological and energy inputs required, or accepted farming practices. Lands in other classes which are necessary to permit farm practices to be undertaken on adjacent or nearby lands shall be included as agricultural land in any event.

More detailed soil data to define agricultural land may be utilized by local governments if such data permits achievement of this goal.

FARM USE—is set forth in ORS 215.203 and includes the nonfarm uses authorized by ORS 215.213.

Appendix 2: Incentives and Privileges to the Property Owner within an Exclusive Farm Use Zone[1]

The legislative "Agricultural Land Use Policy" (ORS 215.243) states that since EFU zoning substantially limits alternative uses of agricultural land, incentives and privileges are justified in order to hold such land in EFU zones. Below is a summary of the "incentives and privileges" provided by the Exclusive Farm Use zone.

• Assurance that only compatible nonfarm uses will be allowed within the EFU zone (215.213).

• Assurance that all divisions of land will be reviewed and not approved unless the parcel is appropriate for the continuation of the existing commercial agricultural enterprise within the area.

• Prohibition against restrictive local ordinances which would unreasonably restrict or regulate farm structures or accepted farming practices because of noise, dust, odor or other materials carried in the air if such conditions do not extend into an urban growth boundary. This section does not restrict any governmental unit from lawfully exercising its power to protect the public's health, safety and welfare. (ORS 215.253).

• Automatic review by assessor of land to determine if qualified for special farm use assessment. No application required. (ORS 308.370(1) and 308.397).

• No minimum income must be earned in three out of the five preceding calendar years in order to qualify for special farm use assessment. (308.372).

• No requirement that farmland be used exclusively for farm use in the two years immediately preceding qualification for special farm use assessment. (ORS 308.370(2)).

• No requirement that the farm unit produce over one-half of the owners adjusted gross income during the previous year in order to qualify for special farm use assessment for wasteland which in part is a farm unit or for the land under dwellings customarily provided in conjunction with farm use. (ORS 215.203(2)(b) and 308.372(4)).

• No tax penalty when land qualified for special farm use assessment is removed from an EFU zone following an action by the governing body that was not requested or initiated by the owner of the land. (ORS 308.397(2) and 308.399(3)(b)).

• Exemption for land qualified for special farm use assessment within an EFU zone, from certain special district assessments (sewer, water, solid waste, vector control). The exemption does not apply to the farm dwellings and up to one acre around it. (ORS 308.401).

• Farm use valuation for inheritance tax purposes for land qualified for special farm use assessment. (ORS 118.155).

Appendix 3: Statutory Provisions Related to the Exclusive Farm Use Zone and Special Farm Use Assessment

Subject	ORS
A. *Land Use/Zoning*	
Agricultural Land Use Policy	215.243
Establishment of exclusive farm use zone permitted	215.203 (1)
Definition of "Farm Use"	215.203 (2)
Nonfarm uses allowed	
• Permitted	215.213 (1)
• Conditional	215.213 (2)
single family nonfarm residences and required findings	215.213 (3)

[1]This information is a general description of some provisions of the exclusive farm use (EFU) zone and is not intended as a technical explanation of the zone or its related taxation statutes.

Subject	ORS
• Replacement of nonconforming uses allowed within EFU zone	215.215 (1)
• Spot zones allowed for nonfarm uses in the interior of an EFU zone consistent with 215.243	215.215 (2)
Prohibition against restrictive local ordinances of accepted farm practices in EFU zone	215.253 (1)
• Exemption for ordinances needed for the public health, safety and welfare	215.253 (2)
Public review of land divisions in EFU zone	215.263 (1)
• Exemptions	215.263 (4)

B. *Taxing*

Subject	ORS
Farm use valuation	308.345 (1)
• Comparable sales	308.345 (2)
• Income approach	308.345 (3)
Special farm use assessment	
• Zoned for exclusive farm use	308.370 (1)
• Not zoned for exclusive farm use	308.370 (2)
Minimum income required (unzoned)	308.372
Over 50% of adjusted gross income required to qualify wasteland and land under farm dwellings (unzoned)	308.373 (4)
Application for special assessment (unzoned)	308.375
"Farm Use" to be further defined by Department of Revenue (unzoned)	308.380
Disqualification from special assessment (unzoned)	308.390
Payment of deferred taxes (unzoned)	308.395
No deferred taxes paid when land taken by use of eminent domain (unzoned)	308.396
Disqualification from special assessment (EFU zone)	308.397
Tax penalty when land disqualified for special assessment (EFU zone)	308.399
• Exemptions	308.399 (3)
• Acquired by eminent domain	308.399 (3) (a)
• Removal from EFU zone when not requested by property owner	308.399 (3) (b)
Limit of special district assessment while land zoned EFU is qualified for special assessment	308.401
District attorneys to review and certify exclusive farm use zone	308.403
No tax penalty when farm use assessment changed to forest land assessment	321.960
Farm use valuation for inheritance tax purposes (EFU zone and unzoned)	118.155

References

Berry, W. 1977. "The Unsettling of America: Culture and Agriculture." Sierra Club Books, San Francisco, CA.

Henke, J. 1974. Preferential property tax treatment for farmland, *53 Oregon L.R.2*, (Winter) (general overview of Oregon system).

Roberts, O. 1967. The taxation of farm land in Oregon, *4 Willamette Law Journal* **431**, (history of farm taxation in Oregon).

Sullivan, E. 1973. The greening of the tax payer, *9 Willamette Law Journal* **1**, (March) (history of EFU zoning in Oregon).

Court Cases

Rutherford v. *Armstrong* (Yamhill County), 31 Or App 1319, 572 P2d.1331 (1977) *review denied* (1978).

1000 Friends v. *Benton County*, 32 Or App 413, 575 P2d.651 (1978) *review denied* 284 Or 41, (October 1978).

Meyer v. *Lord*, 37 Or App 59, 586 P2d.367 (1978)

Still v. *Marion County*, 42 Or App 115, (1979).

Jurgenson v. *Union County*, 42 Or App 505, 600 P2d.1241 (1979).

Hillcrest Vineyards v. *Douglas County*, 45 Or App 285, 608 P2d.201 (1980).

Miles v. *Clackamas County*, 48 Or App 951, 618 P2d.986 (1980).

Alexanderson v. *Polk County*, 289 Or 427, 619 P2d.212 (1980).

Columbia Hills Development Co. v. *LCDC*, 50 Or App 483, 624 P2d.157 (1981)

1000 Friends v. *LCDC*, 292 Or 735, 642 P2d.1158 (1982)

J.R. Golf Services, Inc. v. *Linn County*, 62 Or App 630, 661 P2d.91 (1983)

Statutes

Oregon Revised Statutes Chapter 197 and 215.
Chapter 826, Oregon Laws 1983 (SB 237)
Chapter 827, Oregon Laws 1983 (HB 2295)

Miscellaneous Sources

Property Tax Abstracts, Oregon Department of Revenue (published yearly, cumulatively). Abstracts of tax court and Revenue Department opinions on laws relating to assessment and taxation of property: referenced by ORS numbers.

Oregon Land Use Board of Appeals (LUBA). Decisions of the Board cover all land use issues in Oregon including many on agricultural lands. Butterworth Legal Publishers.

15

Protection Efforts in the Northeastern States

Mark B. Lapping

Among the oldest agricultural regions in the country, the Northeast's policies to protect farmland have largely been shaped by the need to control and limit the urbanization of agricultural land. Yet the story of the region's loss of farms and the erosion of its farmland base is a long-standing one with roots which predate urbanization within the region. As Tables 15.1–15.3 illustrate, the Northeastern states have witnessed a decline in the number of farms, land in farms and percent of total land in agriculture for over a century.

Over time, market specialization in a few commodities, such as fluid milk, replaced the food self-sufficiency of the region's farms. Other centers of production, such as the Middle West, overtook the Northeast in the production of many key commodities such as wheat, corn, and fruits. Much of the farming population abandoned rural areas and migrated to the emerging cities to work in the rapidly expanding industrial and commercial sectors; the "hill farm" towns were the first to depopulate. As the farms were abandoned, the forests reclaimed the land.

Since the conclusion of the Second World War, a new phase of farm decline and farmland loss has emerged. The construction of highway systems, subsidies and tax deductions for new housing units, utility rate structures, which promoted service extensions, and cheap and available energy resources, together with suburbanization, all conspired to bring hundreds of thousands of acres of the region's farmland under the bulldozer and pavement.

Policy Responses: The First Generation

The first type of policy response was the promulgation of differential tax programs, of various varieties, to aid the farming community. Differential assessment approaches are of three basic types: preferential assessments, deferred taxations, and restrictive agreements. Under a preferential assessment law, land in agriculture is assessed on the basis of its value as farmland as opposed to its market value in some other use. No

Table 15.1.   Thousands of Farms in Ten Northeastern States, 1850–1974

State	Census year					
	1850	1880	1910	1940	1970	1974
Maine	46.8	64.3	60.0	39.0	8.0	6.4
New Hampshire	29.2	32.2	27.1	16.6	2.9	2.4
Vermont	29.8	35.5	32.7	23.6	6.9	5.9
Massachusetts	34.1	38.4	36.9	31.9	5.7	4.5
Rhode Island	5.4	6.2	5.3	3.0	0.7	0.6
Connecticut	22.4	30.6	26.8	21.2	4.5	3.4
New York	170.6	241.1	215.6	153.2	51.9	43.7
New Jersey	23.9	34.3	33.5	25.8	8.5	7.4
Pennsylvania	127.6	213.5	219.3	169.0	62.8	53.2
Delaware	6.1	8.7	10.8	9.0	3.7	3.4
10 Northeastern States	495.8	704.9	668.0	492.3	155.6	130.9

Source: U.S. Censuses of Agriculture.

Table. 15.2   Total Land (millions of acres) in Farms in Ten Northeastern States, 1850–1974

State	Census year					
	1850	1880	1910	1940	1970	1974
Maine	4.5	6.5	6.3	4.2	1.8	1.5
New Hampshire	3.4	3.7	3.3	1.8	0.6	0.5
Vermont	4.1	4.9	4.7	3.7	1.9	1.7
Massachusetts	3.4	3.4	2.9	1.9	0.7	0.6
Rhode Island	0.6	0.3	0.4	0.2	0.1	0.1
Connecticut	2.4	2.5	2.2	1.5	0.5	0.4
New York	19.1	23.8	22.0	17.2	10.2	9.4
New Jersey	2.7	2.9	2.6	1.9	1.0	1.0
Pennsylvania	14.9	19.8	18.6	14.6	8.9	8.2
Delaware	1.0	1.1	1.0	0.9	0.7	0.6
10 Northeastern States	56.1	69.1	64.0	47.9	26.4	24.0

Source: U.S. Censuses of Agriculture.

Table 15.3   Percentage of Total Land Area in Farms in Ten Northeastern States, 1850–1974

State	Census year					
	1850	1880	1910	1940	1970	1974
Maine	23	33	32	21	9	8
New Hampshire	59	64	56	31	11	9
Vermont	70	82	79	62	32	28
Massachusetts	57	57	58	39	14	12
Rhode Island	82	78	66	33	10	9
Connecticut	77	79	70	49	17	14
New York	63	78	72	56	33	31
New Jersey	57	61	53	39	22	20
Pennsylvania	52	69	65	51	31	29
Delaware	76	86	82	71	53	50
10 Northeastern States	53	65	61	45	25	23

Source: U.S. Censuses of Agriculture.

penalty is imposed on landowners if the land is put into another use at a later date. The Connecticut and Delaware legislatures have adopted such policies. Under the deferred taxation scheme, land is assessed according to its value as farmland. If the landowner changes the use of the property receiving such an assessment, a deferred tax, or a rollback, is levied. Generally, the amount of the rollback is the equivalent to the tax savings received by the owner during the time the use-value assessment was in force. Maine, Massachusetts, New Jersey, New York, Pennsylvania, Rhode Island, and Vermont governments have promulgated such laws. Finally, a state or local government may make a restrictive agreement with landowners by which farmers agree to restrict the use of their land in exchange for use value assessments for only specific periods of time. Once the time period has elapsed, farmers are free to alter the use of their land without penalty. Within the region only authorities in New Hampshire and Pennsylvania have implemented restrictive programs.

All differential assessment programs operating in the Northeast share one basic characteristic: lands in agricultural use are assessed for their use value as opposed to market value. Assuming that use value is lower than market value in changing land markets, land assessments and taxes are lower. The expectation is that lower property taxes will encourage farmers to keep their lands in agriculture use, even in the face of development pressures.

For a number of reasons differential assessment programs in the region have not been fully effective. The most obvious reason appears to be that owners of land near population centers, who are most susceptible to conversion pressures, are generally unwilling to participate in such programs. Moreover, such tax concessions are largely overshadowed by the opportunities associated with development. This is the result of two factors operating within the land market. Penalities imposed by rollbacks are usually quite small relative to development opportunities. The size of the penalty depends on the divergence of market value from use value, and the larger the potential rollback penalty, the larger the potential capital gain associated with land-use conversion. Additionally, rollback taxes or other deferred taxes are deductible for federal income tax purposes.

There are additional concerns with differential assessment techniques. For example, lower assessments could reduce the property tax base of jurisdiction and thereby local government revenues typically used for schools, roads, and other services. The ability of a county or town to supply certain services might be sharply curtailed if a significant amount of land were brought into the program and taxes on nonparticipating land could not be increased to compensate for such losses. In an effort to address this problem Vermont reimburses local taxing jurisdictions for revenues lost from use value assessment.

It has also been argued that it is one thing to help farmers but another to aid speculators. Since many differential assessment programs in the region do not distinguish between bona fide farmers and speculators, they are sometimes described as a subsidized license to speculators. Such participants in the land market might benefit and be encouraged to hold out for greater future returns at the cost of those who have to absorb property tax shifts.

Differential assessment laws can be justified on the basis of promoting tax equity if the laws are written so that only those intended to receive benefits do so. When applied judiciously, as in New Jersey, a differential assessment system can be of some aid.

Another variant of tax policy fashioned to aid in the retention of farmland is the capital gains tax implemented in Vermont in 1973. Under the Vermont program, still the only one of its type in the nation, variations in the tax rate depend on both the degree of gain from a land transaction and the length of time the land is held prior to sale. Tax assessment rates rise as the percentage of gain from a sale increases, but decrease over time. Long-time owners are taxed far less than short-term owners. As each year passes after the initial purchase, the rate drops in each gain class, until the sixth year when the tax is eliminated totally. The purpose of the law is to tax the capital gains on land so heavily that speculation loses much of its profitability. Several evaluations of the program suggest that the results are mixed at best.

The "first generation" of Northeastern farmland protection policies, then, are largely driven by the belief that alterations in tax policy can aid farmers. In all cases, manipulation of tax policy vis-à-vis land has been the central feature of policy. Although such programs have not in themselves been totally effective, they have been pragmatic responses to the problem of farmland loss. The sponsors of such programs have seen the problem in terms of the economic viability of agriculture in a changing society.

Policy Responses: The Second Generation

If the first phase of farmland retention strategies was essentially taxation programs, this second phase has been land based. The pioneering effort of this type has been the agricultural district approach adopted in New York State in the 1970s.

Participation in the program is strictly voluntary. A proposed district must include at least 500 acres, and the farmers making the proposal must each own at least 10% of the land to be included. After a district is formed it is affected by the following provisions.

1. Farmers can apply for use value assessments. Later conversion to a noncomplying use subjects the landowner to a rollback levy on tax savings in the prior 5-year period.

2. Except for health and safety regulations, local government cannot regulate either farm practices or structures within the districts. This prevents even the regulation of farm odors, a favorite target of suburban residents who reside in transitional areas.

3. State agencies are directed to modify their policies and programs so as to encourage commercial agriculture.

4. Though it does not preclude the state's exercise of eminent domain, the agricultural district law makes it more difficult. Public agencies which might utilize such powers have to examine alternative areas for their projects.

5. The power of local agencies to fund community facilities which might encourage nonfarm development is modified. This is the least appreciated aspect of the New York program, though its control over public investments, such as sewage treatment facilities, water systems, highways, and other utilities, is fundamental to the success of the entire system.

6.   Where special service districts are created to tax land for sewage, water, and nonfarm drainage programs, this power is limited to assure low taxes on farmlands.

7.   Eight years after a formation, each district has to be re-examined by the county and the state. District boundaries might be modified but only at these 8 year intervals and not before the initial 8 year enrollment period has expired. The state and county have the authority to continue any district indefinitely, regardless of local wishes to the contrary.

The agricultural district program in New York won wide-based support because it emphasizes initiation of control at the local level. The impetus to create such a district must come from local farmers. The process of creating a district is a long one, and many local bases of power and authority in rural areas have to be consulted. A proposal has to be approved by the county legislature, the agricultural advisory committee, town and county planning bodies, and the State of New York.

By the middle of 1980, over 300 districts had been formed controlling approximately six million acres, or well over one-third of all farmland in New York. Districting was most popular in rural and semirural areas where the probability of selling farmland at greater than farm values in the foreseeable future was not great. Conversely, in suburban areas the program has met with resistance, and few districts were formed within a 25 mile radius of major cities. The reason, of course, is that farmland owners in the urban fringe areas anticipate an imminent conversion of their land to other more intensive uses.

At approximately the same time the state of New York was introducing agricultural districts, which are now in existence in Pennsylvania and Maryland, among other places, Suffolk County, New York, was the first place to implement a development rights purchase program.

Operating under state enabling legislation, and in response to concern about potential overpopulation, the loss of prime agricultural lands, and the diminution of open space resources, the county started to buy farmland development rights. The program attracted consistent support from county residents. Some perceived it as a way to guarantee open space; some saw it as a means to control growth; and still others thought it would assure locally produced fresh vegetables and fruits. The greatest support came from the farming community. This was not surprising, since farmers received upwards of $6000 per acre for their development rights while still keeping title to their property. By 1980, development rights to some 3883 acres of farmland had been transferred to Suffolk County at a cost of approximately $21 million. At the time of writing, it was anticipated that the program would expand to a total of 15,000 acres (just under a quarter of all farmlands in the county) at a total cost of $90 million.

Under this method a farmer sells to government his right to develop his land. The farmer keeps the fee interest except for this one right, retaining all of his other rights, including the right of possession. The encumbrance runs with the land and thus binds all subsequent purchasers as well. This method is very much like the sale of mineral rights by a farmer who retains fee simple to the surface.

The public acquisition of development rights presents several clear advantages over other methods. Buying development rights is likely to be cheaper than fee simple purchase, and the landowner still retains ownership and control of his farmland. Landowners receive a cash payment for giving up their right to develop, and this capital could be utilized further to enhance the farm operation. Farmers who sell their development rights still have to keep their lands on the tax rolls, but when the development rights are transferred to government, the farm can be taxed only on its agricultural use value. Moreover, the expense of maintaining the property is not transferred to a governmental agency, and the farmer can continue to keep his property in a productive, though limited, use. A more subtle, though very important, attribute of the program is that it addresses in a direct way some of the equity issues related to farmland retention.

All too often a farmer's land is at once his hospitalization plan, insurance policy, child's college tuition, and personal retirement fund. Consequently, farmers are clearly concerned about the issue of compensation when land use controls are established that they perceive as limiting their options. When compensation is provided, as in the development rights purchase, members of the agricultural community are more likely to participate. The point is that techniques to keep farmland in agricultural use often require that the development potential for agricultural lands will no longer be available to farmers. For a program to succeed, it clearly has to have the endorsement of the farming community. One element in obtaining such support and cooperation is dealing with the issues of justice and equity openly and directly.

The big problem of buying development rights is cost: the purchase of such rights can be expensive. In rural areas, where development pressures are less intense, the cost of buying development rights is lower. But in areas under conversion pressure, the cost of acquisition would be high, and the reduction in the local tax base is significant as lands have to be assessed at use value.

Programs to purchase farmland development rights were implemented in Connecticut, Massachusetts, and New Hampshire by 1980. In these three New England states farmland had been lost at staggering rates. Financing for these programs comes from state bonds. These three state strategies are in their infancy and hence cannot be fully evaluated. It appears that there is wide-scale support for them. In Massachusetts, for example, the number of farmers requesting development rights purchase has steadily increased. Moreover, the state's legislature, with the backing of the governor, has increased financial support for the program and this at a time of substantial fiscal constraint.

A possible way around the expense of purchasing development rights is outlined in a related concept known as the transfer of development rights (TDR). Under this type of program, a given area is designated as a *preservation* district that is to be kept in agriculture. Other lands deemed developable are placed in districts that may be developed at densities greater than permitted under existing zoning so as to absorb the growth that is deflected from the preservation zone.

Growth within the development district can continue along the lines and at the densities established in the zoning ordinance. Development can, however, exceed that permitted by the ordinance if development rights are purchased from landowners in a preservation zone who have exchanged development rights in the development area in return for the loss of development rights on their land in the preservation area.

Under any TDR proposal, the development rights are freely transferable among private parties or between a private party and a public agency at market prices. The use of these rights, however, is limited only by the comprehensive land use plan for that particular area. Ultimately, a landowner in a preservation district finds himself owning land with fewer use alternatives and owning development rights which relate to lands he does not own.

The TDR system does not fit precisely into the definition of either the police power or the power of eminent domain. Such programs have been utilized effectively in Britain for over 25 years, but experience in the United States is limited largely to efforts at historic preservation.

TDRs seem to present several advantages over other land-use control devices. The timing and pattern of development can be controlled, in part, through zoning and manipulation of the availability of public utility services. Moreover, TDR systems correct a serious flaw of the land development process by charging the costs of such growth to private sector participants rather than to the community.

The most serious obstacle to the implementation of a TDR program is the very real possibility that there will be insufficient demand in the private sector for the development rights. Unless owners of land in the preservation zone can find willing buyers for the development rights at a fair price, the value of the rights to the landowner will be severely limited. In a poorly organized or noncompetitive market, the developer is likely to reap large benefits from the development rights at a lower price. Furthermore, the developer can pass on his/her costs to consumers in higher purchase prices or rents. The presence of a public intermediary agency, acting as something of a broker for a development rights bank, could resolve this problem by controlling the available supply of development rights and by making market information available to prospective sellers. Yet the inability to guarantee justice and equity remains the greatest single drawback to this technique.

To date local programs to transfer development rights have been implemented in Connecticut, Maryland, Massachusetts, New Jersey (where the pioneering theoretical work on the technique was carried out at Rutgers University), New York, and Pennsylvania.

Policy Responses: The Third Generation

As the states of the Northeast grow in both experience and sophistication with farmland retention, still other modes of land protection are being articulated. Pennsylvania and Massachusetts are both encouraging land banking by local communities and municipalities. Within the private sector, land trusts are also growing both in size and number.

Some of the states, notably Delaware, Maryland, New York, Pennsylvania, and Vermont, have most recently promulgated "right to farm" laws. These laws attempt to respond to a growing rural-based problem.

At root underlying much of the farmland retention controversy have been local land-use conflicts between farmers and rural and suburban residential residents. The irony of the situation is obvious. While farming creates the atmosphere and bucolic landscape so many homeowners wish to be part of, it is the business of farming, which mandates certain practices and functions, that these same residents often find offensive. The result is a conflict wherein nonfarming neighbors try to restrict or eliminate agricultural practices. In the Northeastern context this has translated itself into a nonfarming majority which utilizes land-use controls to regulate farming, or nuisance lawsuits, which attempt to enjoin or severely restrict certain practices. What many seek, really, is a farmland without farmers!

Though not usually seen as a farmland preservation strategy, the newly promulgated "right to farm" laws and programs go right to the heart of the matter. The "right to farm" laws, in one way or another, try to arrest the growing number of restrictive ordinances and regulations and attempt to make void nuisance lawsuits, which unduly harass farmers and thereby reduce the inherent viability of agriculture.

The genesis of the "right to farm" laws can be found in New York State's pioneering agricultural district law (1971). While initially providing a mechanism whereby local farmers could voluntarily create a district to protect farmlands, the law also deals with the issue of potential restrictive land-use controls and nuisance lawsuits. The appropriate section of the law thus reads:

> No local government shall exercise any of its powers to enact local laws or ordinances within an agricultural district in a manner which would unreasonably restrict farm structures or farming practices in contravention of the purposes of the act unless such restrictions or regulations bear a direct relationship to the public health or safety.

The Maryland statute (1977) is more specific when it notes that the "operation at *any time of any machinery* used in farm production or the primary processing of agricultural products" is acceptable so long as farm practices do not "cause bodily injury or directly endanger human health. . . ."

The effectiveness of these sections of the state agricultural districts laws cannot be easily ascertained. Farmers perceive them to be of real benefit since the issue of conflicts between neighbors is a specific and long-term concern of the farming community. A review of the New York program indicates that this element in the law has been seldom invoked. Its existence, however, may be enough to deter governments and individuals from pressing claims or from promulgating restrictive ordinances (Hexem *et al.*, 1980).

Since 1979 five of the region's states have enacted specific "right to farm" laws. Though they differ on a number of points, the laws all attempt to do two things. First, right to farm laws seek to supersede the common law of nuisance. Second, they favor agricultural uses of the land above all others. Thus, the laws try to establish a "first in right" logic wherein preexisting agricultural uses have primacy against all others. The presumption is made that if a farm constitutes a nuisance, all users are coming to it and thus are themselves responsible for any liabilities against their property or person.

Because these laws are relatively new, constitutionality has not been established although a recent case in Connecticut has upheld that state's law. Until such time as that occurs, the laws remain untested. Suffice it to say that a number of problems suggest themselves, not the least of which is the basic vagueness of such terms as "improper" and "negligence," which raise "due process" problems.

Conclusion

Finally, the entire issue of farm economic viability is beginning to get addressed through state-level policy. The most encouraging sign in this regard is a substantial shift in the posture of the region's state agriculture departments: they have ceased to be solely regulatory in nature and are moving to become aggressive "boosters" of the region's agriculture. A saying that reflects much conventional wisdom goes something like this: there is nothing wrong with Vermont agriculture which a few more dollars in the farmer's pocket would not solve. Although this is surely an oversimplification, it must be noted that methods to retain a farmland base will be successful only to the extent that they are part of a larger effort to enhance the viability of the Northeast's agriculture. The melding of policy, to join land concerns with economic imperatives, is just beginning in the Northeast.

References

Baker, L. and Anderson, S. 1980. Taxing Speculative Land Gains: The Vermont Experience. The Environmental Law Institute, Washington, D.C.

Bryant, W.R. and Conklin, H.E. 1975. New farmland preservation programs in New York, *Journal of the American Institute of Planners* **41,** 390-396.

Conklin, H.E. and Bryant, W.R. 1974. Agricultural districts: A compromise approach to agricultural preservation, *American Journal of Agricultural Economics* **56,** 607-613.

Conklin, H.E. (Editor). 1980. Preserving Agriculture in an Urban Region. Northeast Regional Research Project No. 90 Rep. Cornell University, Ithaca, NY.

Coughlin, R.E. and Keene, J.C. (Editors). 1981. "The Protection of Farmland: A Reference Guidebook for State and Local Governments." National Agricultural Lands Study, U.S. Government Printing Office, Washington, D.C.

Dhillon, P.S. and Derr, D.A. 1974. Critical mass of agriculture and the maintenance of productive open space, *Northeast Agricultural Economics Council Journal* **3,** 23-24.

Hady, T.F., and Sibold, A.G. 1974. State Programs for the Differential Assessment of Farm and Open Space Lands. Econ. Res. Service Rep. No. 256, U.S. Department of Agriculture, Washington, D.C.

Lapping, M.B. 1980. Agricultural Land Retention: Responses, American and Foreign *in* "The Farm and the City." A.M. Woodruff (Editor). Prentice-Hall, Publishers, Englewood Cliffs, NJ.

Lapping, M.B. 1979. Agricultural land retention strategies: Some underpinnings, *Journal of Soil and Water Conservation* **34,** 124-126.

Lapping, M.B. 1982. Towards a Working Rural Landscape *in* "New England Prospects: Critical Choices in a Time of Change." C.H. Reidel (Editor). University Press of New England, Hanover, NH.

Lapping, M.B. and FitzSimmons, J. 1982. Beyond the land question: The viability of agriculture, *GeoJournal* **6,** 519-524.

Lesher, W.G. 1975. Land-Use Legislation in the Northeast, Reps. 75-12-75-23. Department of Agricultural Economics, Cornell University, Ithaca, NY.

Lesher, W.G. and Conklin, H.E. 1976. Legislation to Permit Agricultural Districts in New York, Rep. 76-41, Department of Agricultural Economics, Cornell University, Ithaca, NY.

Raup, P. 1975. Urban threats to rural lands: Background and beginnings, *Journal of the American Institute of Planners* **41,** 371-378.

Small, L. and Derr, D.A. 1976. Controlling development rights: The alternatives, *Journal of Soil and Water Conservation* **31,** 190-194.

Small, L. *et al.* 1978. Transfer of Development Rights: Marketability, Bull. No. 848. Rutgers University Agricultural Experiment Station, New Brunswick, NJ.

16

Property Tax Relief Programs to Preserve Farmlands

Richard W. Dunford

Since World War II population growth has been concentrated in or near urban areas (Gloudemans 1974). Most growing urban areas have expanded onto land previously applied to agricultural or other open space uses. New and improved transportation corridors have taken significant amounts of rural land and have also contributed to extensive land subdivisions around urban centers (Dunford 1979a). Hence urban growth has resulted in urban "sprawl" and the conversion of agricultural and open space lands into more intensive uses. In addition to the rural land actually converted to urban uses, a significant amount of agricultural land is often idled prematurely in anticipation of conversion (Gustafson 1977).

The idling or loss of agricultural and open space lands to urbanization, transportation corridors, and rural homesteads has concerned many individuals. Some have been concerned with the effect of rural–urban land conversions on our ability to produce food and fiber (Anderson *et al.* 1975). Even if the agricultural land base is adequate to meet projected food and fiber demands, other food-related concerns about the loss of agricultural and open space lands are often associated with increasing demands for local produce, a desire to mitigate foreign food shortages, and the future cost and availability of the water and energy needed to bring poorer quality farmland into production (Anderson *et al.* 1975; Dunford 1979a). Since many farmland conversions are essentially irreversible, some people have advocated the retention of farmland as insurance against unexpected economic, environmental, or technological problems (Ciriacy-Wantrup 1964).

Apart from food needs and costs, there is concern about the loss of agricultural and open space lands for many other reasons. For example, in a specific geographic context the widespread conversion of farmland to urban uses could adversely affect the agricultural service and supply firms in an area. If these agricultural firms go out of business, continuing farm operations may also be adversely affected, possibly leading to a further loss of farmland. Another concern involves the high public service costs associated with discontiguous, unplanned urban expansion.

Programs to retain agricultural and open space lands are viewed by some as a way to manage urban growth and reduce public service costs (Gustafson 1977). Others favor farmland retention programs for environmental reasons (Gustafson 1977). These individuals are interested in preserving the amenities provided by open space in an urban area. And finally, since rural–urban land conversions could significantly decrease our agricultural exports, some have favored farmland retention programs from a balance of trade perspective (Raup 1974). Thus, a variety of concerns have been expressed regarding the conversion of agricultural and open space lands to more intensive uses.

As a response to these concerns, 48 states have enacted some kind of property tax relief program to keep farmland in farm uses. The rationale for using these programs as a farmland retention policy is discussed in the next section of this chapter. The four principal types of property tax relief programs are then surveyed. This is followed with a general summary of the effectiveness of these programs. A discussion of the necessary elements for an effective farmland preservation program concludes this chapter.

Rationale for Property Tax Relief Programs

Property taxes are levied primarily to raise revenues for state and local governments. It has been recognized, however, that property taxes affect the economic incentives facing landowners and therefore indirectly influence the ownership and allocation of land among competing uses. Specifically, it has been argued that the property tax system encourages the conversion of agricultural and open space lands to more developed uses (Gloudemans 1974). As cities grow and expand, agricultural and open space land near these cities appreciates in value. This increase in property value is primarily due to places of employment and urban amenities such as shopping facilities, medical services, and entertainment complexes becoming closer and more accessible. In general, people are willing to pay more to live near their place of work and urban amenities. Therefore, as urban areas expand, the value of nearby farm and open space land begins to rise above its value in agricultural use.

Most states assess real estate for property taxation on the basis of "highest and best" use. Thus, the higher market values on agricultural and open space lands near urban areas lead to higher assessments on this rural land. For a given tax rate, these higher assessments increase the rural landowners' property taxes. Additionally, new residents may desire more and/or better public services like police and fire protection. Consequently, local governments may have to increase tax rates to accommodate the new residents. Higher tax rates further increase the property tax burden on nearby agricultural and open space lands.

Although farmland near an urban area may be increasing in value, higher property taxes must be paid out of current income. Typically, proximity to an urban area does not significantly increase the current incomes of farm and open space landowners. Thus, landowners on the urban fringe may experience a tax "squeeze" as property taxes rise faster than the income from the current use of the land (Gloudemans 1974).

This tax squeeze, which decreases the profitability of farming on the urban fringe, may contribute to further sprawl. Specifically, some farmers may not be able to meet continual increases in their property taxes. Consequently, they may sell their land to individuals willing to pay relatively high prices for developable land. To the extent that these parcels are scattered throughout the rural–urban fringe, urban sprawl will be encouraged. This phenomenon pushes the market value of near-by agricultural land higher, eventually generating more urban sprawl. In summary, urban sprawl tends to produce more sprawl in a type of vicious circle (Fig. 16.1).

As discussed later in this chapter, this is a simplistic and incomplete characterization of the rural land conversion process. However, this characterization has been an important rationale for the adoption of property tax relief programs in an effort to preserve farmland. Apart from this objective many states have enacted property tax relief programs with an objective of improving property tax equity. It is argued that the property tax burden on farmers is too large relative to their income. For a discussion of the rationale for farmland property tax relief programs based on the objective of improving tax equity, see Hady and Sibold (1974).

The influence of urbanization on the property tax burdens of agricultural land can be illustrated with the following data. Property taxes averaged about 7.5% of net farm income nationwide in 1974. But in some urbanizing states like Massachusetts, New Jersey, and New York, property taxes as a proportion of net farm income approached 20% (Gustafson 1977). Even in states where overall property tax burdens are a small proportion of net farm income, this proportion may be quite high near urban areas (Gloudemans 1974).

In an effort to counteract the tax squeeze just discussed, 46 states have adopted some type of use-value assessment (also known as differential assessment) program. Although there are many differences in these programs from state to state, they share one common characteristic: eligible lands are taxed on their current-use value rather than market value. Differential assessment is intended to break the urban sprawl cycle (see Fig. 16.1) by not allowing relatively high market values to increase the assessed value of agricultural or open space lands.

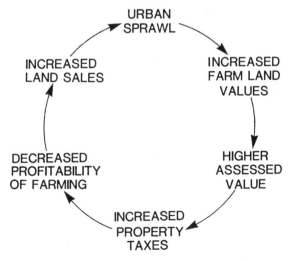

Fig. 16.1. Diagram of the urban sprawl cycle. From Dunford (1979a).

Two states, Wisconsin and Michigan, use circuit-breaker tax credits instead of use-value assessments to provide property tax relief. In these states, property taxes over a specified percentage of household income are rebated directly to the landowner. This approach is intended to break the urban sprawl cycle (Fig. 16.1) by not allowing "excessive" property tax burdens to decrease the profitability of farming. For a comparison of use-value assessments and circuit-breaker tax credits as alternative farm-land tax relief approaches, see Dunford (1979a).

Types of Property Tax Relief Programs

Maryland adopted the first differential assessment program to preserve farmland in 1956 (Hady and Sibold 1974, p. 37). As of 1981, 48 states have property tax relief programs (Coughlin and Keene, 1981). Only Georgia and Kansas, do not have property tax relief programs to preserve farmland. A constitutional amendment that allows for a differential assessment program has been adopted in Kansas but no implementing legislation has been enacted. These property tax relief programs can be divided into four categories:

1. Preferential assessment programs
2. Deferred taxation programs
3. Voluntary restrictive agreement programs
4. Mandatory zoning and planning programs

The classification of 48 state programs by type of program is shown in Table 16.1. Hawaii, New Hampshire, Oregon, and Wisconsin are listed as having two types of programs because under certain circumstances one type of program is applicable but under another set of circumstances another type of program is used. See Chapters 13 and 14 for more detailed reviews of the Wisconsin and Oregon programs.

Within each of the four types of programs many differences are found. Some programs limit eligible property to agricultural land. Other programs include open space lands, forest lands, and/or lands of historical, scenic, or ecological importance. Other differences in individual laws pertain to the following:

1. Size of eligible tracts
2. Prior use requirements
3. Productivity requirements (in output or value terms)
4. Permitted uses
5. Systems for determining use values
6. Term of classification
7. Withdrawal from the program
8. Rollback provisions
9. Application to partial sales or conversions
10. Application to buildings or improvements

Not all of the 48 property tax relief programs will be reviewed. The provisions of all of these programs are presented in a publication from the National Conference of State Legislatures (Davies and Belden 1979) and a recent report from the National Agricultural Lands Study (Coughlin and Keene 1981). A brief summary of one or two state programs within each of the four categories of programs will be presented.

Table 16.1. State Property Tax Relief Programs to Preserve Farmlands by Type of Program

State	Preferential assessment	Deferred taxation	Voluntary restrictive agreements	Mandatory zoning or planning
Alabama		X		
Alaska		X		
Arizona	X			
Arkansas	X			
California			X	
Colorado	X			
Connecticut		X		
Delaware		X		
Florida	X			
Georgia				
Hawaii		X		X
Idaho	X			
Illinois		X		
Indiana	X			
Iowa	X			
Kansas				
Kentucky		X		
Louisiana	X			
Maine		X		
Maryland		X		
Massachusetts		X		
Michigan[a]			X	
Minnesota		X		
Mississippi	X			
Missouri	X			
Montana		X		
Nebraska		X		
Nevada		X		
New Hampshire		X	X	
New Jersey		X		
New Mexico	X			
New York[b]		X		
North Carolina		X		
North Dakota	X			
Ohio		X		
Oklahoma	X			
Oregon		X		X
Pennsylvania		X		
Rhode Island		X		
South Carolina		X		
South Dakota	X			
Tennessee		X		
Texas		X		
Utah		X		
Vermont		X		
Virginia[b]		X		
Washington		X		
West Virginia	X			
Wisconsin[a]			X	X
Wyoming	X			

Source: Adapted from Davies and Belden (1979) and Coughlin and Keene (1981).
[a]Property tax relief is achieved using circuit-breaker tax credits instead of use-value assessments.
[b]Land within agricultural districts is automatically eligible, while other land must meet certain eligibility criteria.

Preferential Assessment Programs

Preferential assessment programs provide use-value assessment for eligible lands with no penalty imposed if the land is converted to non-permitted uses. Thus, a pure preferential assessment program is essentially a tax abatement program. Sixteen states have this type of program. The program in Idaho is an example. The "market" value of agricultural properties is based on "actual and functional" value. Agricultural lands which are eligible for farm use assessment must (1) consist of more than 5 contiguous acres (2.025 ha) used during the last year (a) to produce field crops, (b) for grazing, or (c) as part of retirement or crop rotation program; or (2) produce regardless of acreage agricultural commodities for sale or home use equal to 15% of the owner's annual gross income (Davies and Belden 1979).

Deferred Taxation Programs

Deferred taxation programs provide for the preferential assessment of eligible lands, but some or all of the property tax relief must be paid back when the land is withdrawn from the program. Rather than requiring repayment of past property tax relief, several states in the Northeast have recently changed their laws to make the deferred tax simply a specified percentage of market value or the difference between market value and use value. This has been done to simplify administration. For more information on this approach, see Coughlin and Keene (1981). Some states charge interest on the back taxes that are repaid and some states levy an additional penalty if certain withdrawal procedures are not followed. A few states require participating landowners to sign restrictive agreements, but allow for the automatic cancellation or termination of these agreements upon landowner request. This effectively eliminates the "restrictive" aspects of these programs. Thus, I have classified them as deferred taxation programs. In total, there are 29 deferred taxation programs. I will briefly review the Washington and New York programs.

The deferred taxation program in Washington is known as the Open Space Taxation Act (Dunford 1979b). The eligibility for agricultural land in the Washington program is based on parcel size and/or a minimum agricultural income. Forest land and open space land eligibility is based solely on historical use. Current-use assessments are determined by capitalizing the annual net income from growing "typical" crops averaged over the last 5 years. Advisory committees in each county assist assessors in determining current-use values.

Rural land must be enrolled in the program for at least 10 years. A 2 year notice must be given prior to withdrawal from the program. Upon withdrawal a rollback tax equal to the taxes saved over the last 7 years (plus interest) is levied. If a landowner withdraws from the program before the 10 year minimum and/or without the necessary 2 year notification, the rollback tax plus a penalty equal to 20% of the rollback tax is collected (Dunford 1979b).

In New York any owner or owners of at least 500 acres (202.5 ha) may request the formation of an agricultural district (Conklin and Bryant 1974). After a series of public hearings, county and state approval is needed for the proposed agricultural districts. Termination, modification, and continuation options are examined every 8 years. Only at this time may any changes in agricultural districts be made.

Within agricultural districts, state and local governments are limited in their ability to (1) restrict farming practices; (2) take farmland by eminent domain; and (3) levy special assessments for water, sewer, and other development activities. Owners of at least 10 acres (4.05 ha) used for agricultural production for a minimum of 2 years are eligible for use-value assessment. Development of land within an agricultural district is not forbidden. If land receiving preferential assessment is shifted to a more intensive use, a 5 year rollback tax is collected (Davies and Belden 1979).

Apart from land within an agricultural district other farmland in New York can be taxed on the basis of its use value. Eligible lands must be at least 10 acres (4.05 ha) in size and used for agricultural production for at least the 2 previous years. The landowner must enter into an 8 year agreement with the local government to restrict their property to agricultural uses. Each year this agreement must be renewed. If the agreement is not renewed or if a portion of the land is developed, a penalty equal to twice the following year's property taxes on the entire parcel is levied.

Voluntary Restrictive Agreement Programs

With voluntary restrictive agreement programs, eligible landowners agree through contracts or covenants to restrict the use of their land for a period of years. In exchange for this restriction, their property taxes are based on current-use assessments. Rollback provisions are specified to recapture part or all of the past tax relief if landowners are allowed to withdraw from the program. The principal difference between deferred taxation programs and voluntary restrictive agreement programs is that withdrawal from the latter programs is not automatic. Withdrawals must be approved by the local and/or state governments.

Voluntary restrictive agreement programs are found in only four states: California, Michigan, New Hampshire, and Wisconsin. The California program, popularly known as the Williamson Act, was initiated in 1965 (Gustafson 1977). Local governments were required to set boundaries for agricultural preserves, areas within which cities and counties could agree to contracts with owners. Agricultural lands are defined using a variety of criteria, including soil quality and a minimum agricultural income per acre. Landowners may voluntarily enter into contracts restricting the use of their land for an initial period of at least 10 years. Property taxes for participating lands are based on agricultural use value, which is derived from the capitalization of agricultural income.

The contract is automatically renewed annually unless written notice is given of a decision not to renew a contract. In the event of nonrenewal, the remaining 9 years of the contract must be honored prior to conversion to a nonpermitted use. Property tax relief is gradually eliminated over this 9 year runout.

To cancel a contract, the landowner must petition the county or city for release. Cancellations are granted only if it is in the public interest.

> Opportunity for an alternative land use will justify cancellation only if there is no other proximate, non-restricted land suitable for the alternative use. Similarly, the uneconomic character of agricultural use may be a reason for cancellation only if the land cannot be used for any other reasonable or comparable agricultural use (Davies and Belden 1979, p. 28).

If a cancellation is approved, a cancellation penalty up to a maximum of 12.5% of the market value of the property may be levied.

Mandatory Zoning or Planning Programs

Although their programs are quite dissimilar, Hawaii, Oregon, and Wisconsin have adopted programs that link exclusive agricultural zoning or farmland preservation plans to preferential assessment. Rather than discuss all three programs, I will briefly describe the Wisconsin program to illustrate the mandatory zoning or planning approach (Barrows and Yanggen 1978). The Wisconsin program distinguishes urban and rural counties on the basis of total population. Within these two groups of counties, the property tax relief received by landowners depends on the land use policies adopted by the local governments. An urban county must have exclusive agricultural use zones in order for landowners to be eligible for some property tax relief. Conversion to a nonagricultural use requires a full rezoning with public hearings. Local rezoning decisions must consider the availability of public services and environmental protection. If an urban county also has a farmland preservation plan (similar to a county land-use plan), eligible landowners can receive additional tax relief.

In rural counties, either exclusive agricultural zoning or an agricultural preservation plan must be adopted. If the latter approach is taken farmers must sign 10- to 25-year contracts agreeing not to develop their land in order to receive property tax relief. As in the urban counties, no contracts are necessary if an exclusive agricultural zoning policy is adopted. The maximum tax credits are available to eligible landowners when both exclusive agricultural zoning and a farmland preservation plan are adopted (Barrows and Yanggen 1978).

In all cases, Wisconsin counties are not required to have agricultural zoning or planning. However, eligible landowners cannot receive any property tax relief unless countywide zoning or planning occurs. If land is allowed to be removed from an exclusive agricultural zone or a farmland preservation contract, the tax relief for the last 20 years plus interest must be repaid (see Chapter 13).

Effectiveness of Property Tax Relief Programs

Many state property tax relief programs have been operational for such a short period of time that no analysis of their effectiveness is possible. However, some detailed analyses have been conducted on several of the older programs (Regional Science Research Institute 1976). Consequently, some generalizations regarding the effectiveness of the different types of property tax relief programs can be made (Coughlin and Keene 1981). But before discussing the effectiveness of these programs, I want to briefly examine the role of property tax burdens in the land conversion process.

The Land Conversion Process

The rationale for enacting a property tax relief program as a farmland retention policy rests on the assumption that increasing property tax burdens are a major factor in the conversion of agricultural and open space lands to more intensive uses. In general, there are, however, many factors that influence land conversions in a particular area (Regional Science Research Institute 1976; Coughlin 1977). These factors include

1. Profitability of farming
   a. Prices of products
   b. Costs of production
   c. Income taxes
   d. Property tax burdens

2. Urban conversion demand
   a. Population growth
   b. Investments in urban infrastructures like highways, sewage treatment facilities, and other public utilities
   c. Construction activity

3. Economic factors
   a. Rate of appreciation of land
   b. General price inflation
   c. Interest rates
   d. Availability of mortgages

4. Demographic factors
   a. Age structure of farmers
   b. Availability of heirs to operate farms
   c. Attitudes toward farming as a lifestyle

5. Land-specific factors
   a. Location
   b. Slope and drainage characteristics
   c. Availability of developable sites
   d. Value of farmland for alternative uses

The point to be made here is that property tax burdens are only one aspect of the profitability of farming, which in turn is only one factor which is considered by a farmer facing an opportunity to sell. In summary,

> Tax incentives will be effective in reducing sales only in those instances where rising taxes are the principle motivation for placing a farm property on the market (Coughlin and Keene 1981, p. 62).

As stated in another study,

> If an owner wants to keep his land in open-space uses, but finds this is financially difficult, the savings from differential taxation may prove critical in enabling him to attain his goal. But if the owner is indifferent, is influenced by non-economic factors, or is actively looking for an opportunity to sell to a developer, the tax savings from differential assessment will not have much effect in deterring him from selling (Regional Science Research Institute 1976, p. 115).

Even in those cases where differential assessment enables a farmer to keep farming, it often only postpones a sale until other considerations (like retirement) result in a sale.

Effectiveness of Alternative Types of Programs

In light of the limited role of property tax burdens in the land conversion process, it is not surprising that preferential assessment programs have been ineffective with respect to farmland preservation. The effectiveness of differential assessment programs vis-à-vis the improvement of property tax equity is examined in Regional Science Research Institute (1976). Except in strongly rural areas or extremely productive agricultural areas, the capital gains from selling farmland to a developer will almost always outweigh the use-value assessment incentive. Since there are no sanctions against participants who withdraw from preferential assessment programs, landowners can enjoy the financial advantages of the tax reduction while retaining the flexibility of withdrawing when it is economically advantageous.

Deferred taxation programs require the repayment of part or all of the property tax relief received in previous years if the land is converted to a nonpermitted use. Many states do not charge interest on these deferred taxes. This is equivalent to an interest-free loan to the landowner. The requirement of an interest charge on the rollback constitutes more of a penalty for withdrawal but most studies have concluded that a rollback plus interest "cannot offset the increased capital gain which is usually realized when land is converted to urban uses" (Keene 1977, p. 48). Since the amount of these rollback taxes is frequently less than the amount of property taxes the owner has saved, he will not pay more than he would have had he never participated in the program. Hence, even deferred taxation provisions will not prevent most landowners from selling their property, although they do provide more of a deterrent to changing use than pure preferential assessment programs.

Voluntary restrictive agreement programs prohibit participating landowners from developing their land for a period of years. In return, these landowners realize a decrease in their property taxes through use value assessments. This approach has "considerable potential as a means of maintaining current use, at least over the term of the contract" (Keene 1977, p. 44) provided that landowners participate in them. Studies of the California program have shown, however, few landowners participating in urbanizing areas (Gustafson 1977; Coughlin and Keene 1981). Most of the land enrolled under the Williamson Act is located in rural areas where there are no expectations of development in the near future. Thus, in the areas where most future land conversions will occur, rural land is not enrolled.

The mandatory zoning or planning programs which require the adoption of countywide exclusive agricultural zoning and/or farmland preservation plans for property tax relief appear to be the most effective farmland retention strategy. They combine relatively strict land-use policies with some compensation for the restrictions associated with these controls.

Elements of an Effective Farmland Preservation Program

The many studies of state tax relief programs (e.g., Barlowe *et al.* 1973; Barlowe and Alter 1976; Barrows 1974) and other programs (Steiner 1979) designed to preserve farmland suggest several common elements needed for an effective program:

Land-Use Planning

Sound land-use planning is essential for an effective farmland preservation program. Soil Conservation Service data and professional planning assistance are necessary to identify and designate high-quality agricultural areas and marginal lands more suitable for nonfarm uses.

Incentives

Farmland preservation programs will not be effective if the incentives offered are not sufficient to alter private land-use decisions. Landowners will participate in farmland preservation programs if they find that these programs offer them benefits. In general, the largest incentives should be available in the urbanizing areas.

Mandatory Land-Use Restrictions

The analysis of existing state programs suggests that voluntary land-use restrictions are not effective for preserving farmland. Exclusive agricultural zoning and/or farmland preservation plans as a requirement for tax incentives appear to be the most effective approach to farmland retention. Designated agricultural zones or districts should be functionally and economically viable. Urban infrastructure investments that encourage farmland conversion should be limited in these areas.

Supralocal Control

Since farmland retention is of greater than local concern and local governments generally have been ineffective in their efforts to preserve farmland, there is a need for some (but certainly not all) administrative authority at the regional or state level. For example, a regional governing body like the Metropolitan Council of the Twin Cities Area in Minnesota (See Coughlin and Keene 1981) may be needed.

Flexibility

Economic growth and land-use changes are dynamic processes. Policy instruments must be flexible enough so that modifications can be made when necessary without jeopardizing the continuity and strength of the program.

Coordination among Public Policies

Policies among and within various levels of government must be coordinated. For example, state highways should not be planned to cross an area designated as an exclusive agricultural zone by a county agency.

Citizen Support and Cooperation

Ultimately, the success of all farmland preservation programs depends on citizen support and cooperation. Educational programs have been used with the most successful programs to increase citizen awareness of the issues and concerns regarding farmland preservation.

References

Anderson, W. D., Gustafson, G. C. and Boxley, R. F. 1975. Perspectives on agricultural land policy, *Journal of Soil and Water Conservation* **30**(1), 36–43.
Barlowe, R., Ahl, J. G., and Bachman, G. 1973. Use-value assessment legislation in the United States, *Land Economics* **49**(2), 202–12.

Barlowe, R. and Alter, T. R. 1976. Use Value Assessment of Farm and Open Space Lands. Michigan State University, Agricultural Experiment Station, East Lansing, MI.(September).

Barrows, R. L. 1974. Use-Value Taxation: The Experience of Other States, Staff Paper No. 73. Department of Agricultural Economics, University of Wisconsin, Madison, WI.

Barrows, R. and Yanggen, D. 1978. The Wisconsin farmland preservation program. *Journal of Soil and Water Conservation* **33**(5), 209–12.

Ciriacy-Wantrup, S. V. 1964. The 'new' competition for land and some implications for public policy, *Natural Resources Journal* **4**(2), 252–67.

Conklin, H. E. and Bryant, W. R. 1974. Agricultural districts: A compromise approach to agricultural preservation, *American Journal of Agricultural Economics* **56**(3), 607–13.

Coughlin, R. E. and Keene, J. C. (Editors). 1981. "The Protection of Farmland: A Reference Guidebook for State and Local Governments." National Agricultural Lands Study from the Regional Science Research Institute, U.S. Government Printing Office, Washington, D.C.

Coughlin, R. E. et al. 1977. Saving the Garden: The Preservation of Farmland and Other Environmentally Valuable Lands. Regional Science Research Institute, Philadelphia, PA. (August).

Davies, B. and Belden, J. 1979. A Survey of State Programs to Preserve Farmland. National Conference of State Legislatures, Washington, D.C. (April).

Dunford, R. W. 1979a. Farmland Tax Relief Alternatives: Use Value Assessment vs. Circuit-Breaker Rebates, Circ. 617. College of Agriculture Research Center, Washington State University, Pullman, WA. (September).

Dunford, R. W. 1979b. An Overview of the Open Space Taxation Act in Washington, Bull. No. 879. College of Agriculture Research Center, Washington State University, Pullman, WA. (August).

Gloudemans, R. J. 1974. Use-Value Farmland Assessments: Theory, Practice and Impact. International Association of Assessing Officers, Chicago, IL.

Gustafson, G. C. 1977. Land-Use Policy and Farmland Retention: The United States' Experience, Working Paper No. 28. Natural Resource Economics Division, Economics Research Service, U.S. Department of Agriculture, Corvallis, Oregon.

Hady, T. F. and Sibold, A. G. 1974. State Programs for the Differential Assessment of Farm and Open Space Land, Agricultural Economics Rep. No. 256. Economic Research Service, United States Department of Agriculture, Washington D.C. (April).

Johnson, J. A. 1979. Wisconsin's Farmland Preservation Program. Paper presented at the Farmlands Preservation: The State of the Art conference held at Washington State University, Pullman, November 12–14.

Keene, J. C. 1977. Differential assessment and the preservation of open space, *Urban Law Annual* **14**, 11–56.

Raup, P. M. 1974. Policies for the Protection of Prime Agricultural Lands, Staff Paper No. P74-18, Department of Agricultural and Applied Economics, University of Minnesota, St. Paul, MN. (August).

Regional Science Research Institute. 1976. Untaxing Open Space: An Evaluation of the Effectiveness of Differential Assessment of Farms and Open Space, Prepared for the Council on Environmental Quality, Washington, D.C. (April).

Steiner, F. 1979. Agricultural Land Preservation: Alternatives for Whitman County, Report prepared for the Whitman County Agricultural Preservation Technical Advisory Committee, Washington State University, Pullman, WA. (October 1).

Part IV

Federal Involvement in Farmlands Protection

17

The Changing Role of the Federal Government in Farmland Retention

W. Wendell Fletcher

Conversion of high quality agricultural land into highways, housing subdivisions, water reservoirs,and other uses is increasingly viewed as a nationally significant problem. This is departure from the view that has prevailed in recent decades, a view holding that the loss of farmland is a local, or at most, a regional problem, about which the federal government need not, or should not, concern itself.

In fact, few federal agencies have concerned themselves with the loss of farmland to any great extent, even when their projects and activities have inadvertently forced the conversion of high quality farmland. Those state and local governments with farmland protection programs have not received much federal assistance or encouragement over the years. Until recently at least, it would not have been a great exaggeration to use the terms "benign neglect" and *laissez faire* to characterize the federal government's posture toward the loss of farmland. This does not mean the federal government has been unconcerned about other farmland resource problems, however. The U.S. Department of Agriculture (USDA) administers many programs designed to encourage use of conservation management practices on farmland to reduce soil erosion and related land degradation problems.

This traditional posture has been challenged from both inside and outside the federal government. Recently, policy changes have been made at the federal level to encourage the protection of high quality farmland, especially where federal activities might otherwise promote farmland conversion. Farmland protection issues are now addressed seriously in both the U.S. Congress and the executive branch of the federal government, something that could not have been said a few years ago.

Agricultural Land: A Significant National Resource

Unplanned development of land on the urban fringe has long concerned regional planners anxious to curb urban sprawl and preserve open space. Conversion of farmland to urban uses often affects local farm economies adversely as well.

Only recently, however, has widespread concern been expressed about the potential impact of cropland conversion on the overall, long-term productive capacity of American agriculture. This concern has grown out of a conviction that the nation's prime agricultural lands constitute an irreplaceable but finite national resource. USDA's Soil Conservation Service (SCS) estimates that 384 million acres (155,520,000 ha) of land across the country have the proper soil quality, growing season, and moisture supply to produce sustained crop yields using modern methods. Only 65% of this land, 250 million acres (101,250,000 ha), is currently cropped, however. The rest is used for pasture, range, forest, or other purposes (Council on Environmental Quality 1977).

During the 1950s and 1960s, an era of unprecedented advances in agriculture, there seemed little reason for such concern. At the time, it was widely held that any declines in production resulting from cropland conversion could be offset through advances in agricultural technology or by bringing irrigated land into production.

During the 1970s, however, a combination of factors, including escalating world demand for food, unfavorable weather, evidence of farmland's increasing vulnerability to development pressures, soil erosion and other "limiting" factors, as well as more conservative estimates of land that could be easily and inexpensively brought into production, elicited closer scrutiny of the cropland base and its relationship to national agricultural production goals.

Perceptions of this relationship changed significantly as a result of escalating world demand for food produced in the United States. Figures 17.1–17.3, published by USDA for the 1970–1977 period, show the significant increase in both the quantity and prices paid for agricultural exports during the period, and the growing importance of agricultural exports in partially offsetting the enormous trade deficits the nation is experiencing. Although agricultural exports are difficult to anticipate, there is every reason to believe that they will remain high. For example, former Secretary of Agriculture Bob Bergland noted on several occasions the potential for expansion of trade with the People's Republic of China.

Not surprisingly, therefore, recent projections suggest that more cropland must be harvested in the future than was anticipated in the 1960s and early 1970s. A 1978 USDA report, for example, compared two projections of cropland needs (Lee 1978). One, based on conditions in the 1950–1972 period, projected a need for 346 million acres (140,130,000 ha) of harvested cropland in 1985 and 354 million acres (143,370,000 ha) of harvested cropland in the year 2000, assuming moderate export demand. The other, assuming high export demand, estimated a need for 407 million acres (164,835,000 ha) of harvested cropland by 1985, 81 million acres (32,805,000 ha) more than was harvested in 1974. Some of this 81 million acres (32,805,000 ha) could come from pasture and unused cropland, but new cropland would have to be developed to reach the 407 million acre (164,835,000 ha) level.

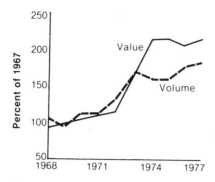

Fig. 17.1. Value and volume of U.S. agricultural exports.

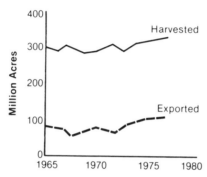

Fig. 17.2. U.S. Exports from harvested acres. Exported includes feed required to produce livestock products exported.

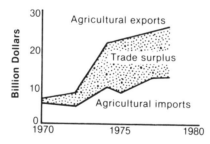

Fig. 17.3. U.S. Agricultural trade balance. October-September years. 1977/1978 was partially estimated.

Yet, we may have less land in ready reserve for this purpose than we had once thought. USDA has substantially reduced its estimate of the nation's reserves of high and medium potential cropland. Based on physical capability, USDA initially estimated that 266 million acres (107,730,000 ha) of noncropland was suitable for cultivation (Soil Conservation Service 1977b). This estimate, based on soil capability, was more than halved when other considerations, such as location and ownership, were assessed. The revised estimate (Lee 1978) identified only 135 million acres (54,675,000 ha) of land nationwide with a high or medium potential for conversion to cropland. About one-third (40 million acres or 16.2 million ha) could be converted without application of conservation practices. Much of the potential cropland is likely to be less suited for crop production than land already used for this purpose.

As for the actual loss of land to other uses, USDA estimated that about 24 million acres (9,720,000 ha) of rural land, not just farmland, were converted to urban uses or inundated with water during the 1967–1975 period (Soil Conservation Service 1977a). Roughly 13 million acres (5,265,000 ha) of this land were in soil capability classes I, II, and III, land with high or medium value for crop production. USDA's 1977 estimate was that slightly under 1 million acres (405,000 ha) of cropland were converted annually to other uses during the period (Soil Conservation Service 1977b).

But not all agricultural experts are convinced that the availability of land for crop production will become a significant problem. The present situation, and that of most of the post-World War II period, is one of agricultural surpluses. Furthermore, technological breakthroughs, a system of international grain reserves, and improvements in agricultural production by other countries could reduce future pressures on the land.

Given limited cropland reserves and high export demand, however, it appears that concern about the cumulative, long-range impact of continuing conversion of high quality lands is increasingly justified.

The Objectives of Change

Those who believe the federal government should assume a greater role in protecting high quality farmland have focused their energies on two separate but related objectives: adoption of policies by federal agencies to govern their own programs and activities that might inadvertently encourage the conversion of high quality farmland and provision of assistance to state and local governments that wish to carry out their own farmland protection programs.

Federal Activities and Farmland Conversion

Federal projects and federally assisted projects for highways, water resource development, sewage treatment facilities, and assorted other public works often are implicated as contributing to indiscriminate conversion of farmland, not only because of the farmland used for such projects, but because of the additional development that may be stimulated by major public works programs. Although the loss of some high quality farmland because of such projects is inevitable, few agencies have factored farmland protection considerations into their planning processes.

Other federal objectives can at times interfere with farmland protection needs also. Federal tax policies, for example, are thought to affect the pattern of rural land development (U.S. General Accounting Service 1978). A federal commitment to increasing domestic energy production could also result in adverse consequences for high quality agricultural lands unless special care is taken to accommodate agricultural needs, something that was ignored in federal energy development scenarios prepared after the Arab oil embargo in 1973.

The Federal Energy Administration (FEA), now part of the Department of Energy, estimated in 1974 that between 37.1 and 38.5 million acres (15,025,500 and 15,592,500 ha) of land could be used for energy production purposes by 1985 if the proposed Project Independence were fully carried out. This was more than double the 15.8 million acres (6,399,000 ha) of land that FEA estimated was dedicated to energy-related purposes in 1972. The following year, FEA, as part of its environmental assessment of President Gerald Ford's proposed Energy Independence Act, upped its estimate of energy-related land needs to 45 million acres (18,225,000 ha). Neither assessment specifically addressed impacts on farmland. Although these estimates were not reliable indicators of what actually happened, the absence of analysis of the potential for conflict with agriculture heightened concern about inadvertent impacts of federal activities for the land. In addition to conventional energy development, the federal government has at times encouraged biomass energy production, which could place a new overlay of demands on a limited land base.

It is not surprising, then, that many people feel a major priority in any national effort to conserve farmland should be to put the federal house in order first, or, if not first, at least concurrently with other efforts.

Federal Assistance to State and Local Governments

The second objective of those who seek a greater federal role in the effort to protect farmland is to encourage state and local governments to adopt their own farmland protection programs, or to incorporate farmland protection objectives into more comprehensive land-use planning and regulatory programs. State and local governments are also looking to the federal government for better information about high quality agricultural land.

A more direct federal role, while perhaps feasible, is considered politically unrealistic by many or unnecessary, mainly because, under our system of government, state and local governments are generally thought to be responsible for the regulation of private land use.

Over 40 states have adopted differential property tax programs. Although the efficacy of these programs in providing property tax relief to farmers and other landowners is uncontested, the programs have not been particularly successful in curbing farmland conversion. For an analysis of these programs, see *Untaxing Open Space*, a 1976 report prepared for the Council on Environmental Quality by the Regional Science Research Institute (Regional Science Research Institute 1976). With the exception of differential property tax programs, however, only a few state and local governments have put into effect farmland protection programs that specifically attempt to reduce the conversion of high quality agricultural lands. With few exceptions, most of the programs in effect are intended as pilot programs or are otherwise limited in effect. Nonetheless, these programs, which differ from earlier efforts to preserve open space or curb urban sprawl because they focus upon the land's value for agricultural production as well as environmental or aesthetic concerns, indicate an increasing recognition of the need for state and local governments to provide greater protection for farmland.

Wisconsin, New Jersey, Massachusetts, Maryland, Connecticut, and New York are among the states that have adopted farmland protection programs. Other states, most notably California, are considering legislation. A number of local governments, including Suffolk County, Long Island, and Black Hawk County, Iowa, also have adopted programs. Both the scope of these programs and the degree of implementation varies greatly from case to case. Other states, including Oregon, Vermont, Florida, and Hawaii, have adopted more comprehensive land-use programs, some of which factor agricultural land concerns into the overall planning process. In addition, all but one coastal and Great Lakes states are in the process of developing planning programs for their coastal areas. Although only a fraction of farmland is on the coast, some coastal programs address farmland issues.

The Federal Role in Transition

Recent actions by the U.S. Congress and certain agencies of the executive branch of the government indicate increased interest in farmland protection.

The Farmland Protection Policy Act of 1981

The Farmland Protection Policy Act was enacted as a separate sub-title of the Agriculture and Food Act of 1981 (P.L. 97-98). The purpose of the act is to "minimize the extent to which federal programs contribute to unnecessary and irreversible conversion of farmland to nonagricultural uses," and to assure where practicable that federal programs are administered compatibly with state, local, and private programs to protect farmland.

The law establishes the Department of Agriculture as the lead federal agency with respect to farmland protection, and calls on USDA (in cooperation with other federal agencies) to develop "criteria for identifying effects of federal programs on the conversion of farmland to nonagricultural uses." In addition, the law calls on each department, agency, independent commission, or other unit of the federal government "to develop proposals for action to bring its programs, authorities and administrative activities into conformity with the purpose and policy" of the Farmland Protection Policy Act. Each federal entity is also to assess its existing mandate to determine whether any existing laws, rules or regulations prevent full compliance with the Act. USDA is to report to the House and Senate Agriculture Committees on implementation progress.

In addition, the Act authorizes the USDA to provide states, local governments, and private parties with information "useful in restoring, maintaining, and improving the quantity and quality of farmland." It also directs the secretary of agriculture to design and implement farmland education programs and materials through existing agencies (such as cooperative extension). A final information provision in the Act calls on the secretary to designate one or more "farmland information centers," which would serve as depositories or information distribution points on farmland policies and programs.

The Farmland Protection Policy Act also encourages the secretary to provide technical assistance to any state or local government or (as determined by the secretary) nonprofit organizations that desire to develop programs or policies to limit farmland conversion.

Another law passed by the 97th Congress, the Omnibus Budget Reconciliation Act of 1981 (P.L. 97-35) contains a provision [section 160(a)(4)] pertaining to Farmers Home Administration loans involving activities on prime or unique farmlands. Interest rates on FmHA loans will be 2% higher if such lands are involved and if alternative sites not involving prime lands are available. The provision does not apply to guaranteed loans.

Restrictions on Surface Mining

Concern that the nation's effort to develop its coal resources could jeopardize high quality farmland prompted the U.S. Congress to place special restrictions on the surface mining of high quality agricultural lands. This limitation, part of the 1977 Surface Mining Control and Reclamation Act, is the most restrictive congressional commitment to the protection of prime farmlands to date.

The decision to restrict surface mining of prime farmland was, in part, a reaction to plans to expand coal mining activities in the West and Midwest and to the increase in surface mining that has occurred in recent years. By July 1, 1977, according to SCS, 1.7 million acres (688,500 ha) of land, not just farmland, had been surface mined for coal. About 570,000 of these acres (230,850 ha) were under legal reclamation requirements.

Although the SCS figures did not provide a breakdown of surface mining activities on high quality agricultural lands, a significant amount of coal surface mining has occurred in the Corn Belt: 158,000 acres (63,990 ha) in Illinois, 79,000 acres (31,995 ha) in Missouri, 42,000 acres (17,010 ha) in Kansas, and 14,000 acres (5670 ha) in Iowa.

Although the federal surface mining law does not ban surface mining on high quality agricultural lands, the act does have several significant provisions that will likely limit surface mining on prime agricultural lands in the future. Among other things, the act specifies that surface mining can only proceed where there is a technological capacity to restore the mined area so it is able to produce yields equivalent to or higher than those on nonmined prime farmland in the vicinity.

Agricultural Land Retention Proposals
in the 95th Congress

While Congress has adopted a policy of encouraging USDA to provide information and technical assistance for state and local farmland protection programs, it has so far rejected proposals to fund such programs directly.

Legislation was proposed, but not enacted, in the 95th Congress that would have established a commission to study the farmland conversion issue and set up a demonstration program to fund innovative state and local approaches for protecting farmland from indiscriminate development. (Among the bills introduced in the 95th Congress were H.R. 11122, S. 2757, and S. 1616. For a discussion of H.R. 11122 and the issues involved, see House of Representatives Report 95-1400. Hearing on the legislation, held by the House Agriculture Committee's Family Farms, Rural Development, and Special Studies Subcommittee in 1977, are reproduced in House Serial No. 95-L.) The House Agriculture Committee in July 1978 reported a version of this legislation that would have established an Agricultural Land Review Commission but not the grant program. Congress ultimately adjourned without considering the issue further.

Although it could be argued that such legislation, by encouraging state and local action, could reduce the likelihood of a more direct federal role in the future, the proposal proved controversial because of concern about federal influence over private land-use decision making. Opponents believed that even modest federal support of this kind would constitute an erosion of deeply held traditions of local autonomy over land-use decision making.

A number of federal programs involve far more direct influence over land-use decision making processes than this proposal. Examples are the National Flood Insurance Program, which prescribes flood-plain management guidelines for local governments participating in the program; dredge and fill permit requirements under the Federal Water Pollution Control Act; and approval processes associated with the siting of major air polluting facilities in "clean air" areas under the Clean Air Act. Nonetheless, there is little doubt that an effective federal support role would have to be fully sensitive to state and local authorities and traditional American attitudes about land ownership.

The Carter administration also opposed the $220 million demonstration grant program in the original legislative proposal on budgetary grounds. It argued that it was premature to provide federal funds for such a program until the farmland study commission proposed in the bill had completed its study. The administration supported the concept of the study commission.

Proposed Legislation in the 96th Congress

Support for the concept of farmland retention legislation carried over into the 96th Congress. Two major bills were introduced, H.R. 2551, sponsored by Congressman James M. Jeffords and over 40 colleagues in the House, and S.B. 795, introduced by Senator Warren G. Magnuson and 17 colleagues in the Senate. On February 6, 1980, the House defeated H.R. 2551 by a vote of 177 to 210.

Federal Executive Actions

Even before enactment of the specific congressional directive in P.L. 97-98, some agencies of the executive branch began to reexamine the farmland protection issue.

National Agricultural Lands Study (NALS)

In June 1979, USDA and the President's Council on Environmental Quality (CEQ) agreed to cosponsor a "study of the availability of the nation's agricultural lands, the extent and causes of their conversion to other uses, and the ways in which these lands might be retained for agricultural purposes." Eight other federal agencies also participated in NALS. The 18 month $2.1 million study resulted in a report to the president on January 1981. NALS assessed, among other things, the impact of federal programs and policies on farmland availability (see Chapter 19).

Council on Environmental Quality

CEQ provides guidance to federal agencies in their preparation of environmental impact statements required by the National Environmental

Policy Act. In 1976, the impact of federal agency activities on prime farmland was identified by CEQ as a consideration that should be included in environmental impact statements. CEQ's suggestion, set forth in an August 30, 1976, memorandum to heads of federal agencies (Council on Environmental Quality 1976) was nonbinding in nature, and federal agencies had considerable discretion whether to include prime farmland in their statements.

U.S. Department of Agriculture

As the department in charge of the federal farm programs, USDA has an interest in the protection of high quality agricultural lands. USDA also has major responsibilities for rural development, housing, and rural electrification which may have, at times, conflicted with farmland protection objectives.

During the 1970s, USDA began to assert a leadership role among federal agencies concerned about the loss of prime agricultural lands. In 1976, then Secretary of Agriculture Earl L. Butz announced a departmental land-use policy. That policy urged all federal agencies to use prime agricultural lands only when no suitable alternative site existed and when the use met an overriding public need.

On October 30, 1978, former Secretary of Agriculture Bob Bergland issued a revised version of this land-use policy (USDA 1978), under which USDA agencies were to avoid proposing or assisting activities that are likely to force the conversion of high quality agricultural lands. Bergland also indicated that he expected USDA agencies to increase their efforts to assist private citizens and state or local governments in efforts to retain important farmlands, as well as forestlands, rangelands, and wetlands.

Among other things, the secretary's memorandum directed agencies within USDA that administer grants, loans, regulations, or technical assistance programs to review their activities and to make necessary changes to minimize the impacts of their programs on farmland. These changes were to be made within 1 year.

The policy statement also indicated that USDA would "intercede" in "decision-making by other federal agencies where conversions of important farmlands and forestlands, prime rangelands and wetlands are caused or enabled by an agency of the federal government, or where conversions require federal licensing or approval." This intercession apparently would involve "participation in the planning of projects where invited" and review and comment on environmental impact statements, or other authorized review processes associated with federal and federally assisted projects. As has been discussed, USDA is the lead agency in overseeing implementation of the Farmland Protection Policy Act of 1981.

Environmental Protection Agency (EPA)

Like USDA, some programs managed by EPA exert growth-stimulating effects. This stems from the fact that EPA is not just the nation's chief pollution control authority, but also administers the federal government's largest public work program, the sewage treatment facility construction grant program set up the Federal Water Pollution Control Act in 1972. Under this program, and subsequent amendments, Congress has authorized $42 billion for local sewage treatment facilities through 1982.

Since sewage treatment facilities are major inducers of growth and often a precondition for new development, the way in which these facilities are planned has significant implications for farmland.

On September 8, 1978, former EPA Administrator Douglas M. Costle approved a new EPA policy "to protect, through the administration and implementation of its programs and regulations, the nation's environmentally significant agricultural land from irreversible conversion to uses which could result in its loss as an environmental or essential food production resource" (U.S. Environmental Protection Agency 1978).

As defined in the memorandum, "environmentally significant" farmland includes prime farmland, unique farmland, farmland identified by state or local agencies as being of state or local importance, farmland contiguous to environmentally sensitive areas, farmland of waste utilization importance, and farmland with significant capital investments to achieve soil erosion, nonpoint pollution best management practices.

The memorandum indicated that EPA would "apply the policy to the full extent of its authorities in implementing agency actions." Each agency office and regional office was to modify its operations accordingly, and staff were to be designated by EPA to assure that the requirements are carried out. The implementation effort would be monitored by EPA's Office of Federal Activities.

Assistant administrators and regional administrators for EPA were to ensure that their actions and the actions of staff "clearly advocate protection of agricultural lands." Specific agency actions stated in the memorandum included, among other things, consideration of agricultural land concerns in developing agency regulations, standards, and guidelines, and in planning specific projects.

The policy memorandum stated that, in the future, EPA-funded sewage interceptors and collection systems "should be" located on agricultural land only if necessary to eliminate existing discharges and serve existing habitation.

Other provisions of the policy specified that EPA permit actions requiring an environmental impact statement "shall ensure that the proposed activitiy will not cause conversion of environmentally significant agricultural land" and that primary and secondary impacts on prime agricultural land shall be considered in EPA impact statements, or in EPA's review of the impact statements of other agencies.

Finally, the policy called for a public awareness program that recognizes the environmental value of prime agricultural land, future research and study of the environmental roles of agricultural lands, and encouragement of state and local farmland protection programs.

Related Federal Measures

In addition to federal laws and programs that specifically provide for the protection of farmland, there are a number of other programs that could foster farmland protection in certain circumstances.

Federal Coastal Zone Management Act

Most coastal state governments are developing land-use planning and regulatory programs for their coastal areas. A major impetus for this state coastal planning effort has been the Coastal Zone Management Act, first passed in 1972 (P.L. 92-583) and significantly amended in 1976 (P.L.

94-370). The program is administered by the National Oceanic and Atmospheric Administration in the U.S. Department of Commerce.

Participation in this federal planning assistance program is voluntary. However, all but one coastal and Great Lake states are participating in the program.

Protection of high quality coastal agricultural lands may be a component of some state programs, but it is not a specific requirement of the act. Furthermore, since the coastal zone only covers a small proportion of a state's total land area, the impact of even a strong farmland protection component would have only modest impact on the overall loss of farmland.

Nonetheless, the experience gained from these state coastal planning efforts could have application elsewhere.

National Flood Insurance Program

The National Flood Insurance Program, administered by the Federal Insurance Administration in the U.S. Department of Housing and Urban Development (HUD), may, in some circumstances, have the effect of protecting farmland through its goal of limiting new development in flood-prone areas. Under the program, most of the nation's flood-prone communities are adopting flood-plain management guidelines developed by HUD. With restrictions on new development in high hazard areas, some farmland in flood plains that might otherwise be developed could be retained in farm use.

Programs Affecting the Quality of Farmland Resources

In addition to planning assistance programs, the federal government conducts a number of programs that provide farmers with assistance in managing their farmland or in maintaining or improving its quality. Examples are programs to reduce soil erosion and prevent water pollution. Because these programs can affect the productive quality of the land, they may indirectly affect land needs.

Soil and Water Resource Conservation Act of 1978

This law, a version similar to a proposal that was pocket-vetoed by President Ford at the end of the 94th Congress, is not a farmland protection measure. Nonetheless, the information this act requires could result in a better information base for defining farmland resource issues and problems.

The law calls on USDA to conduct a "continuing appraisal" of the "soil, water, and related resources of the nation." This appraisal is to include, among other things, data on the quality and quantity of these resources; data on the resource capabilities and limitations, given current and projected needs; and data on federal and state laws, programs, and policies that affect the "use, development and conservation" of these resources. The act also calls for the implementation of a national soil and water conservation program.

Current Status and Future Policy Options

The evolution of the debate over the federal government's role in agricultural land retention suggests that several issues may continue to be of concern in the future.

Information and Technical Assistance

Of all the roles the federal government could play in assisting state and local efforts to protect farmland, this may be the least controversial. By providing, upon request, useful information and technical assistance to communities that are developing their own farmland protection programs, the federal government could be of considerable assistance without infringing on traditional state and local prerogatives concerning the use of land. USDA and EPA significantly upgraded their efforts in this regard in the late 1970s. Explicit congressional encouragement for USDA assistance of this sort was provided in the Farmland Protection Policy Act of 1981, but only through "existing facilities and funds otherwise available."

Federal and Federally Assisted or Approved Activities

The impact of federal public works programs, tax policies, and other direct federal activities on farmland is, by most accounts, substantial. As agencies move to implement the provisions of the Farmland Protection Policy Act, continuing monitoring of their progress will be needed to determine whether the objectives of the Act are being met. While a basic legislature framework has been provided by the Congress, executive branch commitment will be central to effective implementation.

Of a more controversial nature, the federal government could also broaden policies that would require the consideration of impacts on prime agricultural lands when reviewing applications for federal grants, loans, and other financial assistance, or when approving activities that require federal permits, licenses, or other approvals. As has been discussed, Congress, in 1981, required that certain loans provided by the USDA Farmers Home Administration will have a 2% higher interest rate if the activity involved prime farmland or unique land (assuming alternative sites are not available). More far-reaching approaches are not without precedent. The National Flood Insurance Program, for example, prohibits the issuance of Veterans Administration and Federal Home Administration mortgage loans in flood-prone areas of communities that are not participating in the flood insurance program. Not surprisingly, however, the program provoked considerable antagonism in some local communities, and the Congress in 1977 toned down even more draconian sanctions that applied to nonparticipating communities.

Although few would find such a strong assertion of federal policy desirable or politically feasible in the case of prime agricultural land, it may well be that a targeted approach toward federally assisted projects will become acceptable. In any event, the impact of federal programs on farmland has become an important consideration in both the executive branch of the federal government and congress. Finding an appropriate balance between national concerns about agriculture applied to land and federally assisted activities will be a major challenge.

Federal Assistance for State and Local Planning

The question here is whether the federal government should provide planning and implementation grants to states and localities for their own farmland protection programs and, if so, at what cost and under what conditions?

There is ample precedent for federal planning assistance. The Coastal Zone Management Act, as noted, provides coastal states with planning and implementation grants for coastal area land-use planning and regulation. This program, which is voluntary, also has a provision for consistency of federal activities affecting the coastal zone in states with an approved coastal program. Although the Act identifies a number of components that a state coastal plan must include to receive approval, actual decisions are made by the state or local governments. Other federal programs, including EPA's 208 areawide water quality management planning program, also have provided planning assistance for land-use planning.

Although the precedents are there, such planning assistance has been controversial. So-called land-use planning assistance legislation, which would have provided statewide planning assistance grants similar to those in the coastal zone program, was passed by the Senate in 1972 and again in 1974, but the proposal never received House approval. Also, as mentioned, agricultural land retention legislation, which would have provided grants for state and local demonstration projects, did not pass the 96th Congress.

There are other planning assistance options, of course. One possibility is an effort to modify existing federal planning assistance programs to encourage state and local farmland retention planning.

Regardless of the approach, however, controversy is likely to arise. Those who advocate such assistance are not likely to succeed unless an approach is devised that is sensitive to the concerns of landowners and to this nation's preference for locally oriented control over the use of land.

References

Council on Environmental Quality. 1976. Analysis of Impacts of Prime and Unique Farmland in Environmental Impact Statements. (Memorandum for heads of agencies). Washington, D.C.

Council on Environmental Quality. 1977. Environmental Quality, 8th Annual Report of the Council on Environmental Quality. Washington, D.C.

Lee, Linda K. 1978. A Perspective on Cropland Availability, Agricultural Economics Rep. No. 406. Economics, Statistics and Cooperatives Service, U.S. Department of Agriculture, Washington, D.C.

Regional Science Research Institute. 1976. Untaxing Open Space. Council on Environmental Quality, Washington, D.C.

Soil Conservation Service. 1977a. Potential Cropland Study, Statistical Bull. No. 578. U. S. Department of Agriculture. Washington, D.C.

Soil Conservation Service. 1977b. Resource Inventories, 1977: Final estimates. U.S. Department of Agriculture. Washington, D.C.

USDA. 1978. Secretary's Memo. No. 1827, revised. Washington, D.C.

U.S. Environmental Protection Agency. 1978. Memorandum on Environmentally Significant Agricultural Lands. Washington, D.C.

U.S. General Accounting Office. 1978. Effects of Tax Policies on Land Use. CED 78-97. Washington, D.C.

18

Evolution of Land-Use Policy in the U.S. Department of Agriculture

Norman A. Berg and Warren T. Zitzmann

The U.S. Department of Agriculture (USDA) has had a long and distinguished record in land-use matters. A USDA poster issued in 1941 is titled "The Land Use Planning Process." It shows a brawny young man stripped to the waist and working with blacksmith's tools. Two statements appear, first "LOCAL COMMITTEES shape and temper ideas into plans—as a blacksmith shapes and tempers metal into tools." Second, "Ideas subjected to the HEAT of discussion, HAMMERED into shape by facts, TEMPERED by deliberation—are shaped into usable plans for developing—BETTER RURAL COMMUNITIES." This is rather flamboyant rhetoric, much more colorful than the plain statistics we use today to convince people of the necessity of doing an effective job of land-use planning in rural America.

The fact that we are still viewing the situation with concern in the 1980s is an indication that the florid prose of 1941 did not generate very effective action.

Some Early Activities

The USDA Agricultural Yearbook, 1923, contained a strong report by Lewis C. Gray calling for a national land utilization policy to replace the sectional policy of the past (USDA 1923).

USDA convened the first National Conference on Land Utilization in 1931. The conference established a National Land Use Planning Committee, the predecessor of the renowned National Resources Planning Board.

The 1938 USDA Yearbook, "Soils and Man," discussed the nation and the soil (USDA 1938). Articles on policies for public and private lands dealt with rural zoning and land-use regulations.

The 1940 USDA yearbook, "Farmers in a Changing World," included a section by Milton S. Eisenhower, who was land-use coordinator in USDA's Office of Land Use Coordination. That office was established in

1937, following the appointment in 1935 of a land policy committee and later a coordinating committee.

The need for this action stemmed from difficulties arising when the several new services of USDA, set up to deal with depression and drought, led to actions that produced land-use conflicts. Questions were raised about how far planning should go in a democracy. How much territory should the planning take in, and what is the proper balance between central authority and decisions by the mass of our citizens?

It was obvious that many of the problems of farmers were expressed in terms of land use and that land use was one of the common denominators of the federal and state programs for farm readjustment. For example, the program for income stability and conservation called for individual farm changes in land use, such as shifts from soil-depleting crops to soil-conserving crops. The heart of the rehabilitation program was the farm and home management plan on which loans were based. Erosion control and flood control programs were essentially land-use programs, based on the physical and economic requirements of the land and the people who used the land. Therefore, if consistency could be attained in the land-use phases of all public agricultural efforts, a major step would have been taken in overall program coordination.

The Office of Land Use Coordination brought together for the first time all USDA agencies dealing with land-use problems. These agencies agreed on a nationwide program for systematic coordination, with a view of achieving agreement on needs, aims, methods, and results. This systematic effort included these steps:

1. All basic fact-finding work essential to the action program, such as soil conservation and land-use surveys, would be coordinated by the appropriate agencies so as to avoid duplication and, more important, to achieve agreement on the relevant facts.

2. Both general planning, involving farmer-cooperation, and detailed planning by experts would be coordinated by the agencies so as to get agreements on general and specific objectives.

3. Current policies and programs would be scrutinized regularly so as to iron out conflicts.

4. Shortcomings in organization, which hampered unification of programs, would be studied, and appropriate changes would be instituted, such as a gradual shift to common regional headquarters to encourage regional coordination.

5. Uniform methods and policies in decentralization and in working with state and local agencies would be developed.

6. All existing and proposed legislation would be carefully studied so the secretary could advise Congress of any inconsistencies in basic policy.

7. The work of USDA would be coordinated with that of other federal agencies, and, especially, USDA would participate actively in the work of the National Resources Planning Board.

The land-use coordinator became a liaison officer with other departments of the government concerned about land use, such as the Department of Interior, the U.S. Army Corps of Engineers, and the National Resource Planning Board, whose committees dealt in a broad way with the nation's land and water resources. The need for agreement of facts, aims, and methods among these agencies was both obvious and urgent.

Concurrent with these early steps toward coordination and among federal agencies, progress was made toward decentralizing some major land-use activities of USDA. This was a response to the feeling that local communities were having plans and programs thrust on them, rather than initiating and carrying out what they themselves wanted to do.

The formation of soil conservation districts began in 1937, operating under state laws and state and local auspices. Under these laws, the planning and action required to solve major conservation problems in many areas were, and still are, squarely up to the local farmers. They could act or not act as they saw fit, and they worked out programs to satisfy their local needs. Federal and state agencies served in an advisory capacity, furnishing technical information on request.

In the meantime, for a period of about 3 years, committees of USDA and land-grant colleges were meeting and trying to iron out their conflicts and difficulties. The USDA committee, headed by the under secretary, worked constantly with the state committees for a solution to what had come to be called the federal–state relations problem. Finally, in July 1938, at a remote, unused Weather Bureau station called Mount Weather, in Virginia, the groups gathered to address the problem. After 2 days of intensive discussion, they emerged with a far-reaching agreement.

This agreement declared that the traditional federal–state relationship in research and extension was satisfactory and should continue. But it recognized that the action programs for agriculture, if they were to be correlated and localized effectively, required a new function that should parallel the functions of research and education. This new function was planning, planning that pooled the experience and judgment of farmers, specialists, and administrators.

It was agreed that planning, with first emphasis on land-use planning, was to begin in local communities with local committees. Local plans were then to be coordinated for an entire county by a county committee. County plans were to be coordinated statewide by a state committee, of which the state agricultural extension director was to be chairman. State programs were to be integrated for the entire United States by USDA.

Community committees were to consist of farm men and women only. County committees, however, were not only to be composed of farmer members but also the county representatives of state and federal land-use programs. The county agent usually served as the executive officer. State committees also were to have farmer members, but the number of federal and state representatives was to increase at this level.

Not all community plans, of course, would need to be considered by the county, nor all county plans by the state, nor state plans by the federal government. Many phases of county plans could be carried out by farmers, or by county commissioners, or by a local soil conservation district, or by a state agreement. There was considerable latitude for decentralized action in federal programs.

As a result of the Mount Weather agreement, committees worked in a large number of communities and counties, classifying land and developing plans to meet their own needs. A unified program, based on detailed study, was begun in 1940 in at least one county in each state. Forty-five states appointed state land-use planning committees.

The net results of this early venture into national land-use planning, especially the agricultural phases of land use, were mixed. It became apparent that water and land use were inseparable. The attitude of heedless and unplanned land exploitation was partially reversed. The point of view emerged that public policy should aim at effecting such ownership and use of land that would best serve general welfare rather than private advantage only. Knowledge of good land-use practices was the key.

However, when the idea that land-use policy and public decisions resulting from a careful planning process were viewed as a threat to private property rights, the whole scheme was terminated during World War II throughout rural America.

After World War II, Renewed Interest in the Land-Use Issue

The secretary of the Department of Agriculture wrote in the foreword of *Land—the 1958 Yearbook of Agriculture*, "this book will stimulate thought about our land and its use. This is as it should be, for discussion often strikes the spark to ignite inspired thoughts that guide us into a better future" (USDA 1958).

In January 1962, the secretary of agriculture called a National Conference on Land and People to obtain assistance in shaping USDA's land and water policies and programs. A preliminary report, "A Land and Water Policy for the United States Department of Agriculture," was prepared by the USDA's Land and Water Policy Committee.

The conference summary was given by John F. Timmons, professor of economics at Iowa State University, who said in part:

> State and local governments are important if not senior partners with the federal agencies in designing and putting into effect the kinds of land-use institutions needed for guiding land uses toward long-run objectives.
>
> As we proceed with the task of ascertaining and implementing solutions to land-water-use problems, we seek a balance of the following: (1) research to provide ideas and facts, interpretations of facts, and creative means for achieving peoples' wants; (2) education to disseminate these ideas and facts and to encourage discussion and decision by the nation's citizens and their representatives in the legislative and executive branches of government; (3) institutional change to encourage and guide land-use adjustments towards desired objectives; and (4) money payments to help facilitate land-use changes toward objectives in the public interest.
>
> Inasmuch as the science and art of predicting needs for lands well into the future are imperfect, the probabilities of uncertainty warrant the concept of a "contingency reservoir" of cropland which does not get committed irrevocably to other uses.
>
> Upon this concept, the objective would not be just idling land from the farm plant but instead the objective would be a positive one in terms of prudent provision for an uncertain future. Thus, the objective would possess value to our nation in serving a positive purpose of insuring the nation's future food and fiber needs. Public investments in this purpose would constitute insurance premiums paid for insuring the nation's food and fiber into the future.
>
> Under this concept, other uses which might not conflict with the "contingency reservoir" objective such as certain recreational, forestry, and grazing uses could be tolerated.
>
> No doubt the secretary will continue and expand the role of the Land and Water Policy Committee as a continuing central core of integration and vision within that department. The committee might well become interdepartmental in light of the joint responsibilities mentioned by both USDA and USDI secretaries.

In 1966, the secretaries of the Departments of Housing and Urban Development (HUD) and Agriculture initiated a conference to explore the opportunities of providing improved services to people when land is in transit from rural to suburban and other nonfarm uses. In 1967, this first National Conference on Soil, Water, and Suburbia was held in Washington, D.C. Taking part were planners, engineers, architects, investors, conservationists, and public officials representing all levels of government. Most represented organizations and agencies directly involved in the transition of land in the nation's growth process.

The secretary of agriculture pointed to the unending tragedy of developing and building on land unsuited to the selected use and added that the problem calls for "broad comprehensive planning on an area or regional basis . . . and for public understanding." "I cannot emphasize this enough," he declared. "The individual citizen and his community have everything to gain if soil and water resources are managed properly. They have a great deal to lose if they aren't."

In light of this extensive history, it was unbelievable that as land-use legislation was debated in Congress in the late 1960s and early 1970s USDA was not involved. This long history of land-use experience within USDA and the land-grant universities was simply ignored.

Even more crucial was that under the early reorganization plan of President Nixon, USDA was to be eliminated and the Department of Interior was to be the nucleus for a proposed Department of Natural Resources. Interior thus became the focal point for land-use legislation.

Interior saw the issue of land use as one of inadequate federal, state, and local regulation. Misuse of land could be cured by better regulations, often meaning regulation by a larger unit of government. Local government, historically the only level involved in land-use controls, would be subjected to a state overview, operating under federal guidelines.

USDA's constituency, the owners and users of most of America's land, found this to be the wrong concept of the issue and the wrong prescription for curing the nation's land-use problems. This constituency mounted heavy opposition to land-use bills. The land-use legislation passed the Senate but was defeated in the House in the waning days of the Nixon administration.

USDA's Concept of the Land-Use Issue

Land-use problems and issues did not go away. The nation needed to improve the use of its land base to meet ever-pressing demands. The question was how to accomplish this.

USDA had been active in developing a concept of the land-use issue and establishing a way to actually improve land-use decision making. The concept is essentially one of informed citizen input into decisions. These decisions involve conflicting social goals. They also require complex tradeoffs among values. Land-use questions are seldom absolute. It is not a matter of whether or not you can build the subdivision on prime farmland, or whether or not you can fill in the swamp for an airport, but whether or not you should do these things. Such issues become the battleground where citizens determine the direction of growth and change in our society. Land-use decisions are not so much rational designs as social and political expressions of what people perceive as good or bad for the present and the long-term future.

USDA saw the proper federal role in this process as a limited but vital one. Federal investments in such things as roads, schools, airports, or power plants are often the "growth shapers" that overpower all local determinations. Federal lands, most of which are in the western states, make up one-third of the nation. Federal guidelines and regulations on everything from air and water pollution control to airport safety either limit or demand local actions. The federal programs, functional in nature, often produce unintended side effects that pave over prime lands, limit productive land uses, or encourage inefficient growth patterns.

A key federal responsibility is to improve this process and reduce the harmful effects of major federal actions. USDA, particularly in regard to prime farmlands, had been working to see that this was done, but the effort was uneven in its intensity over the last 50 years.

Development of a Secretary's Memorandum on Land Use

With this background, a small committee set up by the secretary in 1972 determined that USDA needed a secretary's policy memorandum on land use. The committee had representation from the Forest Service, Economic Research Service, Agricultural Stabilization and Conservation Service, Extension Service, and Soil Conservation Service. It was chaired by Norman A. Berg. The drafting process began. It also became apparent that a central focal point on land use was needed. Therefore, a draft supplement to the policy memorandum establishing a USDA Land Use Policy Committee was prepared.

To formalize a secretary's numbered memorandum is a formidable task, unless the secretary or one of his top staff initiates the process. Policy takes many shapes and sizes, depending on the issue. At the same time the committee was working to establish the need for a policy on land use, the secretary issued numbered memorandums on subjects as diverse as equal employment opportunity coordinators, rural development, food and nutrition research, remote sensing user requirements task force, and earth resources survey committee.

Land-use policy was viewed, of course, as having many facets ranging across many interests. It attracted people who wanted something in it for public lands as well as private lands; for extension as well as research; for technical assistance as well as financial assistance; for the role of each level of government; and for special land uses, such as cropland, woodland, grassland, wetland, rural land, or urban land.

Finally, many constituents of USDA programs viewed land-use issues with concern. Some even questioned why the topic was discussed in Washington, D.C.

With the cooperation of key agency representatives and guidance from the assistant secretary for conservation, research, and education, the policy draft reached the desk of the secretary for his consideration in November 1972. In February 1973, the committee had the proposed policy back on its agenda with a memo from the secretary. That memo suggested that the draft be used as a basis for further study and development of a broader land-use policy statement. In addition, the secretary proposed a broadening of the representation on the committee that prepared the draft statement.

Encouraged by the secretary's interest in the proposed policy, the committee took immediate steps to respond by separating the proposed supplement to the policy statement. It rewrote that document and sent it to the secretary as a memo creating a "Committee on Planning and Policy for Land Use and Land Conservation." This was quickly signed by Secretary Earl Butz, becoming Secretary's Memorandum No. 1807, dated March 26, 1973 (USDA 1973a).

This breakthrough led to an eight-agency USDA committee chaired by an assistant secretary named by the secretary. The committee function included policy and legislative strategies, program coordination, surveillance, education and information, and program review. This committee was to advise the secretary and his staff on land-use issues related to policy, programs, and needed executive and legislative action.

A priority task was to rewrite the policy document, obtain committee support, and to again ask for the secretary's signature. On October 26, 1973, Secretary's Memorandum No. 1827 was approved by the secretary and became USDA's statement on land-use policy (USDA 1973b). In a note to the assistant secretary, the secretary commented, "Sorry this took so long for me to get to it. It's fine."

It was strong position for USDA to take in 1973 while land-use legislation was being debated in Congress. The statement recognized that major responsibility for land-use policy (planning and regulation) rests with local and state governments. USDA also recognized the rights and responsibilities of landowners and users in making decisions within this framework. It dramatized that through its agencies USDA administers some 80 programs that influence private as well as governmental land holders' decisions, urban as well as rural.

The statement attempted to define land-use policy for the first time as:

> Land-use policy is a facet of our general decision-making process on the use of our resources. It is a tool to carry out governmental development policies evolving from decisions on interrelated policies arising from economic, social, or environmental problems. Land-use policy and its consequences provide a focal point to identify and resolve conflicts growing out of competing land uses. Land-use policy is the expression of society's determination of how its resource land is used. Land-use policy refers to the total of all those national, state, and local laws, ordinances, and attitudes affecting the short-term or long-term uses of land, private or public, through such mechanisms as ownership, inheritance, taxation, condemnation, zoning, redevelopment, building regulation, master planning and legislative fiat.

Policy guidance itself was quite specific, stating that USDA would:

— Adapt present pertinent programs to help enhance and preserve prime agricultural, range, and forest lands for those uses.

— Promote and help influence the management of rural lands to assure adequate sources of high quality water.

— Intensify establishment of permanent soil and water conservation on the erosion-vulnerable lands returned to cultivation to help increase production of crops and livestock.

— Further coordinate the work of USDA. Agencies at the state level to make all its land use efforts relevant and harmonious.

— Provide timely information and assistance, including nonfarm interpretations of soil surveys, small watershed hydrologic data, and economic information to local, county, and state land-use decision-makers.

— Help protect rare and endangered plant and animal species and their ecological systems as well as historic, cultural, scientific, and natural systems.

— Help conserve and develop significant waterfowl habitat lands.

— Assist in the reclamation of land surfaces used for the extraction of nonrenewable resources, such as coal, minerals, oil, and gas.

— Expand USDA's efforts to assure wider understanding of how its programs and responsibilities contribute to improved land uses.

— Cooperate fully with other departments in terms of responsibility for policy and leadership.

USDA agencies were directed to emphasize, to the extent possible, including redefinition of modification of their policies, that their programs will

— Increase production of detailed soil surveys.

— Establish land capability criteria to help direct the flow of urbanization to land areas least suited to crops and forests.

— Help guide urban growth to preserve prime farmlands, minimize fragmentation of land holdings, provide adequate water supplies, equalize taxes, dispose waste properly, and provide adequate public health, recreation, and safety services.

— Plan and guide effectively land use in the rural-urban fringe areas and in recreation or second-home subdivisions

— Control erosion and reduce sedimentation.

— Minimize the impact of surface mining on rural land uses.

— Locate sites for solid waste disposal as an increasingly important land use.

— Give attention to the need for small watershed, flood plain, wetlands, and coastal zone management programs, based on comprehensive land-use planning incorporating ecological considerations.

An early result of the committee and policy memoranda was improved communication. In 1974, USDA held regional workshops for its state-level officials. There followed a request that each state establish a land-use committee to help state and local officials deal with land-use questions. Committees have since been established in every state, with varying organizational structures and ties to existing USDA mechanism, such as rural development committees. In most states, the USDA Land Use Committee quickly established itself as the best source of technical assistance available to state and local officials concerned with agricultural land-use questions or programs.

Seeking a USDA Focus on Land Use

But the land-use issue, by itself, was not a particularly attractive one for USDA's focus. There were several reasons for this. If the problem was land use, then what was to be the solution? The land-use bill sponsored by Senator Henry Jackson and Congressman Morris Udall was under active consideration, and most of USDA's clientele felt that was not the way to go. If USDA, with its expertise and field delivery system, was to do something constructive, it would have to be on a more clearly focused issue.

There were problems with turf also. USDA did not simply want to replace the Department of Interior as the federal agency with the lead role in a Jackson–Udall type land-use program. But if attention was stirred up in USDA about the land-use issue, that would be seen by many observers as the real motive.

Politically, the term "land use" was becoming inextricably tied to land-use regulation and federal regulation at that. The longer the Jackson—Udall bill continued, the more politically damaging it became to be associated with anything that could be labeled "land use." (That problem exists to this day, prompting at least one observer to suggest that the Department of Interior bill set back the cause of proper land management and conservation by 10 years or more.)

Finally, there were too many issues in land use that were outside USDA's main focus of interest. Urban growth problems, inner-city decay, facility siting, and similar issues concerned USDA because they affected agricultural land, but they were not issues primarily within USDA's scope. The one issue that clearly was and that showed promise of becoming an issue of national concern was the protection of agricultural land.

Reconciling Two Schools of Thought on Agricultural Land

Even the agricultural land issue was not without its problems in USDA. The major agricultural policy problem for two decades had been crop surpluses and the major farm program efforts had been land retirement. To suggest that farmland was a limited valuable resource that should be protected or even preserved was to fly in the face of the experience of some USDA scientists and policy makers.

Two schools of thought existed within USDA, and they caused conflicting signals to emerge about the agriculture land situation. The conservation point of view held that farmland, particularly prime farmland, was a national asset that should be protected. On this basis, concern was expressed about the continued loss of agricultural land. The economic point of view looked at the land as a factor in production, evaluated the productive capability of U.S. agriculture, estimated probable supply and demand, and came forth with assurances that America had an abundance of good land for the foreseeable future.

So in 1974, when the attention of the USDA committee shifted to the issue of retaining agricultural land, these points of view remained to be reconciled. A task force of the committee planned and conducted a national seminar on the retention of prime lands in July 1975. Both the background papers for that seminar and the findings and recommendations of the seminar were published (USDA 1975a, b).

The seminar brought together representatives of the many points of view. The 80 participants, experts from across the nation in many professional disciplines, were to settle on some conclusions and recommendations. A consensus emerged after 2 days of work: "The continued conversion of prime production lands to other land uses is a matter of growing concern that will require a great deal of attention in the future."

Although carefully couched in bureaucractic language, the summary of findings and conclusions from the seminar contained the following statement that represented a sharp turn in USDA policy thinking: "The demand for food, fiber, and timber from United States production lands is expected to increase to the point where that production capability of the nation will be tested. Although it is not certain when or with what degree of urgency this will occur."

To implement what they suggested was a national policy issue, the participants recommended: "Public interest will be served by maintaining a maximum flexibility of options with respect to future land use needs in a changing and uncertain world. Extreme caution should be exercised in approving actions that result in irreversible conversions of prime farmland to other uses. In some states, problems must be faced now, or significant options for the future will close. USDA should be concerned with any actions that will diminish the nation's ability to produce food, fiber, and timber."

The recommendations from the seminar were not USDA policy, but the die was cast. Agricultural land was a national policy issue in a new sense, and USDA had embarked on a new venture in national land-use policy leadership.

Actions in Response to the Prime Lands Seminar

USDA's Land Use Committee undertook several actions in response to the seminar. A specific policy statement on prime lands was published on June 21, 1976, as supplement No. 1 to the Secretary's Memorandum No. 1827 (USDA 1976). The policy statement called for USDA agencies to make special provisions in their programs and services for the recognition and retention of prime farm land.

Meetings between USDA and the Council on Environmental Quality (CEQ) resulted in an August 30, 1976, memorandum to the heads of federal agencies from the chairman of CEQ. That memorandum called for the heads of all federal agencies to include an analysis of the impact of their action on prime lands in the preparation of environmental impact statements.

The CEQ memorandum directed federal agencies to seek assistance from USDA in the definition of delineation of prime agricultural lands. USDA had development of a nationally consistent definition underway at the time and, following substantial local, state, and interest-group input, published its final definition on January 1, 1978, in the *Federal Register*.

To date, little attention has been given the CEQ memorandum. Recent studies show that few environmental impact statements contain any recognition of the effects of a proposed action on agricultural lands, and still fewer actions are modified in deference to their impacts on agricultural lands.

USDA also began an intensive effort to complete workable definitions of prime and unique farmland and to initiate a mapping program so that local, state, and federal decision makers could better understand the facts. Participants in the prime lands seminar had complained that "a frustrating lack of data prevents a clear picture of either the current situation or the probable future amount of land available or needed for agricultural production."

As a result, the Soil Conservation Service issued Land Inventory and Monitoring (LIM) Memorandum 3 on October 15, 1975. This memorandum not only defined prime and unique farmlands, but also established additional categories of important farmlands that could be defined by agenices of government at the state and local levels. It inaugurated a program of mapping these lands on a county-by-county basis that will result in the production of about 500 county maps by the end of fiscal year 1981 and a target of 1200 counties mapped by 1987. Most importantly, it provided a working definition of prime farmland that could be used in conjunction with other monitoring efforts in order to begin the process of inventorying the national supply of important farmland, identifying some of the trends in its use, and beginning to fill that frustrating lack of information.

One of the payoffs in this effort occurred during legislative consideration of the Surface Mining Control and Reclamation Act of 1977. The new act set forth special standards for soil reconstruction after mining on prime farmlands, to the end that agricultural productivity would be restored to the extent technically possible. That focus could not have occurred without the definition of prime farmlands and the newly acquired information about their amount and use.

An Updating of USDA Policy on Land Use

In 1977, it became apparent that USDA needed an updated policy. The assistant secretary convened the USDA Committee on Planning and Policy for Land Use and Conservation to solicit agency views on organizational arrangements for defining and implementing land-use policy in the new administration. There was concurrence on the continued need for a land-use committee within USDA.

On December 17, 1977, the secretary signed a revision of Secretary's Memorandum No. 1827, creating the USDA Committee on Land Use (USDA 1977). This memorandum named as members of the committee the seven agencies of USDA having programs that affect land use in any significant way. The memorandum assigned the committee responsibilities for making recommendations and assisting in actions to help USDA establish and implement departmental and federal land-use policies.

The committee then developed a revised departmental policy statement. In 1978 a series of five multistate workshops were conducted on land use, rural development, and energy. Nearly 40 Washington-based departmental officials, agency administrators, and their top staff met and interacted with more than 600 state-level USDA agency heads, regional office administrators, and other top staff members in USDA state and regional offices and land-grant universities.

The draft land-use policy statement, a major agenda item for the regional workshops, was thoroughly discussed. The statement was revised to reflect the recommendations of these workshop participants, who interact daily with local and state governing officials, with individual farmers, businessmen, industrialists, homeowners, and other landholders.

Secretary Bob Bergland signed Secretary's Memorandum No. 1827 (Revised) on October 30, 1978. In response to the Executive Orders of May 24, 1977, on the protection of wetlands and the regulation of flood plains, the secretary signed, on the same day, Supplement No. 1 to Secretary's Memorandum 1827 establishing USDA's policy for implementing those Executive Orders (USDA 1978b).

The statement was essentially a codification of USDA's responsibilities that evolved between 1972 and 1978. For example, with respect to prime farmlands, it dealt explicitly with USDA policy in fulfilling requirements under the CEQ letter of August 30, 1976, on this issue.

The secretary of agriculture and the chairman of CEQ, in 1979, signed an agreement to provide joint leadership in conducting a national study on the retention of agricultural lands, the National Agricultural Lands Study (NALS) (see Chapter 19). The goal of the study was to determine the nature, rate, extent, and causes of these losses; evaluate the economics, environmental, and social impacts of these losses in both rural and urban areas; and recommend administrative and legislative initiatives necessary to minimize these losses. The NALS report was delivered to the president in January 1981. Eight other federal departments or agencies, including the Departments of HUD, Transportation, Energy, Commerce, and Defense, EPA, and the Office of Management and Budget assisted through their cooperation in staffing and funding the activity. The NALS was a complete, well-documented report, which was well received by federal agencies, state and local governments and the public in general. It utilized extensive land-use data from the 1977 National Resources Inventory conducted by the Soil Conservation Service. That inventory concluded that of all the rural land converted to urban and water uses between 1967 and 1975, about one-third was prime farmland. The annual rate was about 1 million acres of prime farmland converted to nonagricultural uses. Prime farmland is defined by USDA as that land having the best combination of physical and chemical characteristics for producing food, feed, forage, fiber and oilseed crops. The prime farmland must meet extensive technical criteria and also be available for agriculture—by not being already committed to a nonagricultural use. Two-thirds of the land meeting the standard of prime farmland was being cropped in 1977. Of the 116 million acres of prime farmland not being cropped in 1977, SCS estimated that 45% (52 million acres) could feasibly be shifted into crop production under certain conditions. This acreage is our national reserve of prime farmland, about 2% of our nation's total area of 2.36 billion acres.

The conclusions of NALS stimulated the Congress to include a Farmland Protection Policy Act as Section 1539 of the Agriculture and Food Act of 1981, P.L. 97—98. The Act was signed by the president on December 22, 1981.

The Act established a national policy to "minimize the extent to which federal programs contribute to the unnecessary and irreversible conversion of farmland to nonagricultural uses, and to assure that federal programs are administered in a manner that, to the extent practicable, will be compatible with state, units of local government, and private programs and policies to protect farmland."

The state and local governments are given the opportunity to define farmland of statewide or local importance which, if endorsed by the secretary of agriculture, is given the same protective considerations as prime and unique farmland. The secretary of agriculture is given the authority to develop criteria, which all federal agencies are then directed to use in considering the effects of their programs on conversion of farmland. The secretary of agriculture has designated SCS as the agency with primary responsibility to administer the law.

Even before the Farmland Protection Policy Act was passed, SCS had developed a technique for evaluating the agricultural quality of farmland and determining the justification for converting a specific site from agriculture to nonagricultural uses. The technique is called the Land Evaluation and Site Assessment (LESA) system. The basic information for Land Evaluation is derived from the soils information of a cooperative soil survey. SCS can supply this. The Site Assessment is derived from a state or local government's knowledge about existing and proposed community facilities, growth patterns and the supporting systems for agricultural activities. LESA was originally designed to help state and local governments decide which land should be protected and which land would be converted.

When USDA tackled the job of drafting the criteria to be used in administering the Farmland Protection Policy Act, it was concluded that the LESA technique could be adapted for use by federal agencies as they carried out their responsibility to avoid the unnecessary conversion of farmland. On July 12, 1983, the proposed rule for implementing the Farmland Protection Policy Act was published in the *Federal Register*, incorporating the concept of LESA to be used by all federal agencies.

There is a sound basis for current optimism within USDA that the efforts to develop a land-use policy that would protect farmland and conserve our soil and water resources are beginning to pay off. The USDA land-use policy is now in the form of a permanent Departmental Regulation 9500-3 with full support from Secretary John R. Block. The federal government is now providing a model of governmental land-use policy that state and local governments can follow.

References

Public Law 97—98 1981. Agriculture and Food Act., Subtitle I, Farmland Protection Policy Act (December 22).

USDA. 1923. "Yearbook of Agriculture." U.S. Department of Agriculture, Washington, D.C.

USDA. 1938. "Soils and Man—Yearbook of Agriculture." U.S. Department of Agriculture, Washington, D.C.

USDA. 1940. "Farmers in a Changing World—Yearbook of Agriculture." U.S. Department of Agriculture, Washington, D.C.

USDA. 1958. "Land—Yearbook of Agriculture." U.S. Department of Agriculture, Washington, D.C.

USDA. 1973a. Secretary's Memorandum 1807, U.S. Department of Agriculture, Washington, D.C. (March 26).

USDA. 1973b. Secretary's Memorandum 1827, U.S. Department of Agriculture, Washington, D.C. (October 26).

USDA. 1975a. Perspectives on Prime Lands. U.S. Department of Agriculture, Washington, D.C.

USDA. 1975b. Recommendations on Prime Lands. U.S. Department of Agriculture, Washington, D.C.

USDA. 1976. Secretary's Memorandum 1827. U.S. Department of Agriculture, Washington, D.C.

USDA. 1977. Secretary's Memorandum 1807, revised. U.S. Department of Agriculture, Washington, D.C. (December 17).

USDA. 1978a. Secretary's Memorandum 1827, revised. U.S. Department of Agriculture, Washington, D.C. (October 30).

USDA. 1978b. Secretary's Memorandum 1827, revised, Suppl. No. 1. U.S. Department of Agriculture, Washington, D.C. (October 30).

USDA. 1983. Land Use Policy, Departmental Regulation 9500-3, U.S. Department of Agriculture, Washington, D.C. (March 22).

19

The National Agricultural Lands Study (NALS)

Robert J. Gray

When Secretary of Agriculture Bob Bergland and Chairman of the President's Council on Environmental Quality Charles Warren jointly signed a memorandum of agreement on June 14, 1979, the National Agricultural Lands Study (NALS) was officially underway. The actual signing of a cooperative agreement by the two lead agencies marked the culmination of several months of intensive efforts on the part of both the U.S. Department of Agriculture (USDA) and the Council on Environmental Quality (CEQ) to commit the Carter administration to agree to a national study. There were times during the winter and spring of 1979 when it seemed the study would never receive the official blessing from the White House. An earlier proposal by the USDA and CEQ to form a presidential commission on agricultural lands was rejected by the White House as being too highly visable and adding additional bureaucracy at a time when public opinion was opposed to continuing growth in government.

A compromise was struck when the proposal was modified to an interagency study in which ten other major federal agencies would be asked to participate within the availability of their existing resources. USDA agreed to commit half of the necessary funding and staff for the 18-month $2.2 million effort.

Although USDA and CEQ provided the initial leadership in establishing NALS, there were a number of developments that pressured the administration to take some kind of action. The most disturbing of these was the very sharp acceleration in the conversion rate of agricultural land to nonagricultural uses. When the Department of Agriculture completed the National Resource Inventory in 1977, it showed an annual rate of conversion of 3 million acres (1,215,000 ha) of agricultural land to nonagricultural uses. This was double the rate of the previous decade.

In response to these alarming figures, legislation had been introduced in both the 95th and 96th sessions of Congress. Congressman Jeffords of Vermont and Senator Magnuson of Washington introduced legislation that called for both an in-depth federal study on the causes and consequences of agricultural land conversion and provided for pilot programs to encourage state and local governments to develop new techniques to protect farmland. Later versions of the legislation also called for the development of a federal policy to curb the effects of various federal programs on the conversion of farmland. This proposed legislation was called the Agricultural Land Protection Act.

In addition to the information and resulting Congressional concern, Secretary Bergland and Chairman Warren were personally interested in the issue and had heard from a growing number of state and local officials who were concerned as well. All of these forces were instrumental in the final decision to proceed with a national study. The purpose of the study as outlined in the June 14 memorandum of agreement was fairly straightforward:

1. Determine the nature, rate, extent, and causes of agricultural land conversion

2. Evaluate the economic, environmental, and social consequences of agricultural land conversion and various methods to attempt to retard this conversion

3. Recommend administrative and legislative actions, if found necessary, to reduce the losses suffered by the nation as a result.

The memorandum called for issuance of a final report to the president in January of 1981 containing the study's findings and recommendations.

The Program of Study

The very first order of business confronting NALS was the preparation of a detailed research agenda, a budget showing a complete breakdown of major expenditures, and staff organization. This was prepared during late June and July, and was presented to Secretary Bergland and the new chairman of the Council of Environmental Quality, Gus Speth, on July 27, for their approval.

In developing the research agenda the staff, which at that time consisted of three agricultural specialists from USDA plus the executive director and a research director, drew on various comments and suggestions from farm, governmental, and environmental organizations and from many other federal employees as well. The areas of specific research were outlined into seven primary topics of investigation. These seven areas included: (1) U.S. agricultural lands as a national and global resource; (2) America's agricultural land base; (3) competing demands for U.S. agricultural lands; (4) the allocation of agricultural lands among competing demands; (5) the interplay between agricultural land availability and the rural community; (6) state and local actions affecting agricultural land availability and; (7) impacts of federal programs and policies on agricultural land availability.

The research into each of these areas would result in a series of NALS interim and special reports, technical papers, and case studies. All of this information would serve as the basis for the final report. It was clear from the beginning of NALS that the three most crucial areas of research involved the adequacy and accuracy of the current USDA land data, the effects of federal policies and programs on the conversion of agricultural lands, and the effectiveness of the various state and local programs being used to protect agricultural land.

The National Resource Inventory (NRI), which is USDA's land inventory data base, had been under a great deal of criticism regarding the methods used to collect the information and its resulting accuracy. The Agricultural Census, another source of data on cropland, pasture, range, and forestland, did not reflect similar figures on the land base when compared to the NRI. These differences had formed the basis for ongoing dispute within USDA on the magnitude of the conversion rate and the actual size of our cropland base. The Soil Conservation Service (SCS) and Economic Research Service (ERS), both USDA agencies, had long been at odds over the whole question of data reliability.

NALS automatically stepped into that argument as a result of its basic charge. Other thorny questions would need close attention. How much land currently in pasture, range, and forest had potential to be more intensively cropped? Could the Agriculture Census data and the NRI somehow be reconciled? Was it possible to identify the major factors relating to a higher rate of conversion during the 1970s, and would in fact these trends continue into the year 2000?

All of these questions had extremely important implications on other competing demands for U.S. agricultural land. Export demand would be a major factor in determining our total land base needs, and protecting these requirements would be much more difficult than determining domestic needs.

Competition for housing, economic development, rural transportation, and other nonagricultural uses would also have to be carefully considered. Strip-mining for coal, synthetic fuel plant development, and the overall question of water availability in the West would have to be taken into account. The seven primary areas of research as outlined earlier attempted to focus on each of these issues. All of the areas were interrelated to some degree.

During the debate in Congress on the Agricultural Land Protection Act, the question of the impact of federal programs on farmland conversion came up again and again. Did the federal government through its various programs have a major impact on conversion and if so, which programs could be identified as contributing to the problem? NALS would need to provide the answers.

At the onset of the study it was clear that an in-depth evaluation of state and local agriculture land protection programs was strongly needed. Although inventories on various county and state programs had been conducted, no one had previously attempted to evaluate their overall effectiveness in terms of political acceptance, administrative problems, and costs. It seemed that the opportunity was there for NALS to make a significant contribution to state and local governments by preparing a reference guidebook that would contain such an evaluation.

Staffing the NALS was a very difficult and time-consuming process. Final staffing was not complete until November 1, 1979. Although most of the 12 participating federal agencies were willing to contribute funding, the idea of detailing a top staff specialist at the GS-14 or 15 level was not as appealing. In a number of instances agencies contributed additional financial resources allowing NALS to find a suitable candidate elsewhere.

The staff consisted of a wide range of specialists including agricultural economists, public policy specialists, a demographer, an attorney, several planners, a public involvement specialist, a forestland and range conservationist, a fish and wildlife specialist, and a resource inventory and monitoring specialist. During the height of the research effort the professional staff reached 18 in number. The value in terms of in-kind contribution for staffing the NALS was approximately $1 million.

Public Participation and Information

One of the first major undertakings of NALS was the organization of 17 public workshops throughout the country. The purpose was to gauge public concern for the issue of agricultural land conversion and to solicit comments and suggestions on the approach NALS was taking in conducting its research. The public was asked to identify examples of competition for agricultural land within their community and to offer solutions to mitigate these conflicts. More than 1,500 farmers, ranchers, developers, real estate agents, and interested citizens attended these sessions. The information collected at the workshops was tabulated and analyzed and later became an excellent source of reference during the preparation of the final NALS recommendations.

In addition to the workshops, a series of regional conferences was held with state officials during the entire course of the study. Agricultural commissioners, departments of natural resources, state planning offices, and staff from governors' offices took part in these meetings. The whole thrust of NALS's research was discussed in detail, and suggestions regarding content, areas of emphasis and the recommendations were all part of these important meetings.

During the summer of 1979 the need to produce a basic informational piece on what NALS was all about was readily apparent. Inquiries from various farm, governmental, environmental organizations, and the media suggested the importance a beginning publication would have on giving the study some national visibility. The danger of NALS being cast as a "Federal Land Use" stalking horse made the production of such a publication even more important. In the middle of September, just prior to the start of the 17 workshops, a brochure entitled "Where Have the Farmlands Gone" was released by NALS. Initially 100,000 copies were printed. The reaction to this brochure was completely unexpected. In less than 3 weeks after its release, over 200,000 requests were received. Four reprintings were required and a total of 500,000 copies of the brochure were actually produced. Total requests for the publication came to almost one million, an amount much greater than NALS could afford from its small budget. It was clear that the public was both interested and concerned over the loss of farmland.

On the other hand, the reaction by a number of economists in USDA and a few members of the NALS research staff was highly negative. "The study had been compromised," was a typical reaction or, "the brochure was too slanted toward an advocacy position" was another form the complaints often took. The brochure was written in a manner and style that would hold one's attention. It also explained why the study was established and what it hoped to accomplish. In a public relations sense it was a masterful piece of work, which did more than any other single thing to put NALS on the map. Continuous grumbling both from within USDA and from certain NALS staff members persisted as the document became more and more popular. The difficulty of mixing a public information effort with a suitable research climate was never more apparent.

Providing a proper balance for both was a key element in making NALS a success.

Findings, Conclusions, and Recommendations

As the spring and summer of 1980 wore on the NALS findings started to take shape. However, when the initial set of findings were put forth in early September, several major gaps were quickly discovered. Projections regarding the amount of cropland needed for both export and domestic demand were based primarily on out-dated information that failed to account for the very rapid transition that had taken place in these key areas. Also, the information collected on strip-mining requirements and synthetic fuel production was totally inadequate. In addition, the preliminary information from the 1978 Agricultural Census showed sizeable increases in the "Land in Farms" category in practically every state. A great deal of work remained to be done and time was growing short. The study was slated for completion by January 1981, and its funding for the most part would be depleted by that time as well.

As this extra work proceeded, the completed portions of the research pointed to some very interesting results. The high conversion rate of the

Fig. 19.1 This garden subdivision was built on Class I and Class II prime farmland in Maryland. Courtesy of USDA, Soil Conservation Service.

1970s was brought about by a significant shift in population migration to the rural areas of the country. Over 40% of the housing constructed during the 1970s was built in rural areas. Rural economic opportunities both in trade-related jobs as well as manufacturing increased at a much higher rate than in metropolitan areas. In fact, the one hundred most agriculturally productive countries in the U.S. grew at twice the national average during the period of the 1970s. Much of it took place outside of the cities and incorporated villages, a trend that consumed a great deal of good agricultural land. The federal government's impact on these trends was broad and far reaching. About 90 federal programs contributed to conversion. Economic development programs, capital improvement programs, housing programs and environmental protection/natural resource development programs were the main contributors to agricultural land conversion. Only 2 out of 37 federal agencies reviewed had explicit policies to consider the effect of their programs on agricultural land. It was evident that the conversion rate of the 1970s was not an atypical occurrence but the result of major demographic shifts and a decentralization of industrial development, two trends that would continue on through the 1980s and well into the 1990s. The South and West received the most significant pressure on their land bases during this period and would also continue to feel these effects in the future.

The NRI when fully analyzed by NALS was consistent with the information on migration patterns and economic development. The agricultural cropland base totaled out at 413 million acres (165,265,000 ha). Additionally, there were 127 million acres (57,435,000 ha) of land currently in pasture, range, and forest that had soils suitable for more intensive cropping. However, the potential cropland was not idle land waiting to be plowed. The range and pasture land provided necessary forage for both dairy and meat production. In the case of the forestland, the potential for timber production was significant. If it became necessary to push the existing agriculture from this land in order to crop it, the impact would be felt most heavily by the dairy, red meat, and timber industries.

The reconciliation of the NRI data with the Agriculture Census did not occur until late in the study. The manner in which it occurred was largely the result of one state, Illinois, refusing to accept at face value the preliminary Agricultural Census data. The Illinois Department of Agriculture did not agree with earlier released figures showing an increase in "Land in Farms." Upon questioning the census data collected in both 1969 and 1974 the statistics showed that a measurable undercount in the number of farms had been made. NALS immediately investigated this further. The results represented an important breakthrough in the differences between the two data sets. After adjusting for the undercount in 1969 and 1974 the ag-census showed an annual loss of 9 million acres (3,645,000 ha) yearly from the "Land in Farms" category. Not all of this decrease could be attributed to conversion; however, it clearly demonstrated that the trend line of 3 million acres (1,215,000 ha) per year as shown by the NRI was not only accurate, but probably very conservative. Differences in definitions and inventory time periods accounted for discrepancies in actual acreages of cropland, pasture, range, and forestland.

The information on the Agricultural Census was developed at about the same time the projections for export demand became available. The Department of Agriculture had updated all of its most recent information on exports and NALS was given access to the economic model and

USDAs computer system to finalize its projections. Taking into account the rapid increase during the 1970s, an increase of about 10% per year, the projection for the year 2000 showed a tripling in export volume over the 1980 level of 164 million tons (148,780,800,000 kg).

Domestic demand was expected to rise steadily, but not in the dramatic fashion exports would. The ability to project future growth in ethanol production was extremely difficult. The NALS staff, with the help of outside consultants, was able to determine to some degree the growth of this new industry. After discussion, the projections, with both government and private analysts, NALS estimated a 4 to 6 billion gallon (15.1 to 22.7 billion litre) ethanol industry by 1990.

Exports and domestic consumption were the key factors in determining agricultural land needs in the future. To meet all of these demand requirements, the U.S. by the year 2000 would have to bring practically all of its potential cropland into production. The range of somewhere between 77 million and 113 million acres (31,185,000 and 45,765,000 ha) in addition to the current cropland base (413 million acres or 167,265,000 ha), would be needed to keep up with the level of overall demand. These findings stand out as one of NALS's most significant conclusions.

The transition of agricultural surpluses was over. The United States had entered a period of intensive use of its cropland base. This new information, when coupled with the prospect for continuing high rates of agricultural land conversion, demonstrated the critical importance of acting now to develop farmland protection programs.

As the work on the guidebook for state and local governments was completed, it pointed out in great detail the increased interest and response to agricultural land conversion at the state and local level (Coughlin and Keene 1981). Over 270 counties and municipalities and 13 states had devised and implemented agricultural land protection programs. A variety of approaches have been utilized. Agricultural districting, zoning, tax incentives and credits, right-to-farm laws, purchase of development rights, and comprehensive growth management techniques were all part of the growing number of very innovative and, in some cases, far-reaching programs. The major conclusion reached from this intensive effort was that any single approach by itself would not be successful. Combinations of various techniques were needed to address the problem adequately. Since the loss of farmland was the result of many factors, programs had to be many-faceted. The guidebook laid the foundation for continued farmland protection development around the country. It remains as NALS's finest product.

Summary

Like any federal study, NALS ran the very real risk of being ignored or discarded by the Reagan administration. Fortunately, that did not happen. Secretary of Agriculture John Block, formally the director of agriculture in Illinois, was throughly familiar with the contents of the NALS final report well before it was released in mid-January 1981. The NALS Regional Conference with state officials had paid off. Block and his staff had attended all of the Midwest conferences. At a major conference on the agricultural land issue held in early 1981, Secretary Block endorsed the findings of NALS. At the same time both Houses of Congress included agricultural land protection provisions in the 1981 Farm Bill.

NALS had given the issue of farmland losses national recognition and had provided a high amount of media visibility as well. The momentum was there to give the issue the kind of push and credibility it needed at a time when our national resources were under increased pressure.

Reference

Coughlin, R.E. and Keene, J.C. (Editors). 1981. "The Protection of Farmland: A Reference Guidebook for State and Local Governments." U.S. Government Printing Office, Washington, D.C.

20

SCS Important Farmlands Mapping Program

Raymond I. Dideriksen

The Soil Conservation Service (SCS) has always been concerned with the quality of the nation's land resource base and its agricultural use and potential. Now, others concerned about the cost of production of food and fiber, energy supplies, changing land uses, and the quality of the environment have expressed an interest in the important farmlands of the nation. This interest was first expressed in legislation by the passage of the Rural Development Act of 1972. Section 302 of the Act directs the secretary of agriculture to carry out a program "for the identification of prime agricultural producing areas. . . ."

Given the leadership responsibility for Section 302, SCS worked with other agencies, land-grant colleges, interested groups, and individuals to provide criteria for describing and classifying land best suited for farming. This effort of more than 4 years resulted in a document stating policy and procedures for carrying out a national inventory of important farmlands. After 2 years of testing, the criteria were published in the *Federal Register* on January 31, 1978, as the final rule for the important farmland inventory program.

Important Farmland Classification System and Criteria

The classification system identifies two major categories of farmland for the national appraisal, prime and unique farmlands, and two other categories, farmlands of statewide importance and local importance, four categories in all.

Prime farmland is land that has the best combination of physical and chemical characteristics for producing food, feed, forage, fiber, and oilseed crops and is also available for these uses. It has the soil quality, growing season, and moisture supply needed to economically produce sustained high yields of crops when treated and managed according to acceptable farming methods.

233

There are specific technical criteria that farmland must meet in order to qualify as prime (Soil Conservation Service 1978). Most are related to soil characteristics that are identified by a soil survey. The remaining criteria are based on the use and management of the land. The criteria for soils and management are generally stable characteristics that do not change rapidly. They are used to facilitate the identification and inventory in a reasonable time. The intent was to select those lands that are (1) highly productive and energy efficient, (2) environmentally "safe" to crop over a long period of time, (3) the most responsive to management, and (4) not difficult to maintain.

Unique farmland is land other than prime that is used for the production of specific food or fiber crops of high value and quality. It has the special combination of soil quality, location, growing season, and moisture supply to economically produce sustained high yields of crops of high quality when treated or managed according to acceptable farming methods. The intent is to select those lands that are (1) committed to a special agricultural use, (2) a "one-of-a-kind" combination of location, use, and soil, and (3) growing crops that provided a variety in foods available for consumption. SCS works with other agencies and agricultural specialists in a state to designate special crop uses and identify and locate areas of unique farmlands.

During the early testing of the classification system, it was recognized that identifying and mapping prime and unique farmlands for the national appraisal did not provide states and counties the opportunity to inventory all the farmlands that are important (U.S. Department of Agri-

Fig. 20.1.   Evaluating fall field conditions prior to winter run-off season. Weighing surface residue on a farm near Colfax, Washington.

culture 1975). Thus, two additional categories of land that do not meet the criteria for prime and unique farmlands are included in the system. These are additional farmlands of statewide importance and additional farmlands of local importance. As in the case of unique farmlands, SCS works with others at state and local levels to designate soil or areas that are to be inventoried as important to agriculture. The intent is to identify additional farmlands that (1) produce or are capable of producing high yields of food, feed, forage, fiber, or oilseed crops; and (2) when cropped do not seriously degrade the environment.

Inventory Program Products

The inventory provides several products: (1) a list of soils that qualify as prime farmland, (2) important farmland maps, and (3) statistical data on prime farmlands.

The first and most necessary product is a list of soil mapping units that qualify as prime farmland. This list has been developed for each state and is coordinated with other states having like soils. It places each soil in alphabetical order and notes which soils qualify as prime farmland under natural conditions and which qualify when irrigated, drained, or protected from flooding. An example for the Washington State is shown in Table 20.1.

Such information can be used with a complete soil survey to show the location and extent of prime farmlands (Soil Conservation Service 1978). The list is available from state Soil Conservation Service offices.

Another inventory product is a county or survey area map of important farmlands. The map is usually prepared by contracting with mapmaking firms. For each county or area, SCS provides to the contractor (1) a completed soil survey, (2) a list of soil mapping units that fit the criteria for prime farmlands, (3) an outline of the unique farmland areas of a base map, (4) a list of soil mapping units or other guides for classifying additional farmlands of statewide and/or local importance, (5) an outline on a base map of urban and built-up areas and bodies of water greater than 10 acres (4.05 ha) in size, and (6) an intermediate scale base map for publishing the product (Dideriksen and Sampson 1976.)

While this work is going on, SCS arranges with the U.S. Geological Survey for a standard intermediate-scale base map. Finally, the materials from the contractor are reviewed and corrected, if necessary, and provided to a printing firm for publication. Several hundred copies are printed and made available to the public through a local conservation district office.

Another map product made is the state prime farmland map showing generalized areas with a high, medium, low, or very low percentage of prime farmland. This map provides a visual estimate of where most of the prime farmland occurs in a state. For example, the prime farmland map for Indiana shows areas that have 75% or more prime farmland, 25–75% prime farmland, and less than 25% prime farmland.

The final inventory product consists of statistical data showing the areas and use of prime farmland for each state and how much is irrigated or dry farmed (Soil Conservation Service 1978b). The computer tapes that contain the statistical data on prime farmlands and other resource data are available from SCS and the Iowa State Statistical Laboratory at Ames.

Table 20.1. Prime Farmland Soils of Washington[a]

Record no.	Soils series name	Textural phase	Other phase criteria	Slope phase (%)	County	Acres[b] (× 0.405 ha)
1	Aabab	Silt loam			Grays Harbor	
2	Aabab	Silt loam			Pacific	2,792
3	Aeneas[c]	Fine sandy loam		0–3	Okanogan	
4	Aeneas[c]	Fine sandy loam		3–8	Douglas	
5	Aeneas[c]	Fine sandy loam		3–8	Okanogan	
6	Aeneas	Fine sandy loam	Gravel Substatum	3–8	Douglas	
7	Agnew	Silt loam			Clallam	
8	Agnew	Silty clay loam		0–8	Jefferson	1,180
9	Ahtanum[c,d]	Loam		0–2	Kittitas	
10	Ahtanum[c,d]	Loam		2–5	Kittitas	
11	Alstown[c]	Very fine sandy loam	Gravel substatum	0–8	Douglas	
12	Alvor	Silty clay loam			Lewis	2,989
13	Anders[c]	Silt loam		0–5	Adams	
14	Anders[c]	Silt loam		0–5	Lincoln	
15	Antilon[c]	Gravelly sandy loam		0–3	Chelan	474
16	Antilon[c]	Gravelly sandy loam		3–8	Chelan	257
17	Antilon[c]	Gravelly sandy loam	Deep	0–3	Chelan	363
18	Antilon[c]	Gravelly sandy loam	Deep	3–8	Chelan	275
19	Arta	Silt loam		0–3	Grays Harbor	
20	Arta	Silt loam		0–3	Pacific	3,463
21	Ashue[c]	Loam		0–2	Yakima	19,110
22	Astoria	Silt loam		3–8	Grays Harbor	
23	Astoria	Silt loam		3–8	Pacific	5,361
24	Athena	Silt loam		0–5	Spokane	864
25	Athena	Silt loam		0–7	Garfield	13,370
26	Athena	Silt loam		0–7	Lincoln	
27	Athena	Silt loam		0–8	Columbia	6,569
28	Athena	Silt loam		0–8	Walla Walla	8,570
29	Athena	Silt loam		3–7	Whitman	16,527
30	Babcok[c]	Fine sandy loam		2–5	Grant	
31	Babcock[c]	Silt loam		0–5	Grant	
32	Bagdad	Silt loam		0–5	Lincoln	
33	Beckley[c]	Very fine sandy loam		0–5	Lincoln	
34	Belfast	Sandy loam		0–3	Mason	356
35	Belfast	Fine sandy loam			Jefferson	390
36	Belfast	Loam			Kitsap	530
37	Belfast	Silt			Jefferson	860
38	Belfast	Silt loam		0–3	Mason	134
39	Belfast variant	Silt loam	Heavy		Jefferson	860

[a]Soil Conservation Service 1978c, USDA 1978.
[b]Absence of an acreage figure indicates soil survey still in progress or information not available.
[c]In irrigated areas only.
[d]Mapped as a reclaimed phase.

The national summary printed from the tape shows that Washington State, for example, ranks thirtieth in the nation in the amount of prime farmland. It has 2.01 million acres or 814,050 hectares, of which 1.45 million (72%) acres (587,250 ha) are cropland. Slightly over one-half of the prime cropland is irrigated. Acres of prime farmland for all states except Alaska are shown in Table 20.2.

Statistical data on the acres of prime farmland, how they are used, and their potential for conversion are the only available information that can be put together for analyses at state, regional, or national levels. Sampling is a cost-effective way to look at the total prime farmland picture and detect changes that may be taking place. In addition, the statistical data are being used in resource models to determine possible impacts on total crop production, foreign trade and the balance of payments, needs of conservation investments, and estimates for alternative uses of the land resource base.

Table 20.2. Prime Farmland in 1977, in State, in 1000 Acres

State	Cropland Irrigated	Cropland Nonirrigated	Native pasture and pastureland	Rangeland	Forestland	Other land	Total
Alabama	22	2,891	1,976	0	2,799	148	7,836
Arizona	1,085	1	5	25	0	45	1,161
Arkansas	2,072	4,561	2,138	41	4,224	214	13,250
California	6,103	442	311	417	56	476	7,805
Colorado	1,261	352	44	61	0	42	1,760
Connecticut	8	125	43	0	112	106	394
Delaware	17	259	11	0	47	16	350
Florida	23	381	252	7	742	12	1,417
Georgia	380	3,275	1,190	0	2,740	182	7,767
Hawaii	121	63	25	0	8	10	227
Idaho	2,415	583	267	180	4	63	3,512
Illinois	37	19,063	1,141	0	599	560	21,400
Indiana	85	11,430	1,035	0	1,091	521	14,162
Iowa	67	16,808	1,339	0	288	625	19,127
Kansas	2,545	16,975	1,850	5,135	319	494	27,318
Kentucky	4	3,330	1,607	0	799	254	5,994
Louisiana	1,092	4,175	1,403	49	2,429	205	9,353
Maine	5	319	79	0	352	98	853
Maryland	31	783	130	0	223	95	1,262
Massachusetts	3	158	25	0	199	63	448
Michigan	126	5,569	312	0	1,768	607	8,382
Minnesota	88	15,214	940	23	2,508	740	19,513
Mississippi	306	4,894	1,781	0	3,023	223	10,227
Missouri	715	8,829	4,040	23	1,147	313	15,067
Montana	504	385	124	176	3	48	1,240
Nebraska	4,093	6,996	779	1,068	73	384	14,203
Nevada	243	0	10	34	0	16	303
New Hampshire	0	86	10	0	37	11	144
New Jersey	119	383	87	0	512	148	1,249
New Mexico	501	3	16	0	0	4	524
New York	54	2,232	283	0	824	607	4,000
North Carolina	160	2,569	524	0	2,117	236	5,606
North Dakota	15	12,686	398	460	83	273	13,915
Ohio	38	9,178	803	0	837	424	11,280
Oklahoma	385	8,005	3,781	2,866	393	192	15,622
Oregon	1,075	748	258	8	173	111	2,373
Pennsylvania	0	2,351	269	0	1,518	310	4,448
Rhode Island	0	23	6	0	39	16	84
South Carolina	24	1,519	474	0	1,393	74	3,484
South Dakota	139	4,173	339	243	0	177	5,071
Tennesee	21	3,057	1,722	0	1,453	194	6,447
Texas	5,672	11,959	5,854	11,235	2,274	504	37,498
Utah	641	0	3	0	0	6	650
Vermont	0	128	82	0	138	26	374
Virginia	32	1,476	467	0	2,172	177	4,324
Washington	742	711	234	80	166	83	2,016
West Virginia	10	275	100	0	84	33	502
Wisconsin	82	6,393	781	0	2,539	524	10,319
Wyoming	224	0	35	0	0	0	291
Caribbean	20	106	138	3	4	11	291
Total	34,224	95,922	39,521	22,134	42,309	10,701	344,811

Inventory Program Status

A pilot test of the SCS important farmland inventory program was started in 1975. After successful completion of the test, SCS set a goal of completing 1300 counties in the United States by 1983. The counties selected had significant acres of prime farmland and were under pressure to convert farmland to other uses. Typical of such areas are those near urban centers and those underlain by coal that can be surface mined.

Funding for the program began with the 1977 budget year. By mid-1978, only 100 county important farmland inventories were published. Because of this limited progress, the goal was revised to complete the 1300 high priority counties by 1986.

As of September 1980, over 500 county important farmland maps were published and made available to the public. A number of county maps were completed because data such as soil survey were available. Some of the counties completed are not subject to rapid urbanization and are not underlain by coal that can be surface mined. Thus, they would not qualify as some of the 1300 priority counties to be completed by 1986. Even so, the target for inventorying the 1300 high-priority counties can be met.

About eight states have made generalized prime farmland maps. Other states are making plans, but there is no firm schedule to complete one for each state. The need for such maps is determined by agricultural officials and others in each state.

Statistical data provide estimates of prime farmland acres. New resource inventories are underway. Some will provide county statistical data. Most will furnish data for major land resource areas (MLRAs) or aggregated subareas (ASAs—hydrologic units). These new inventories are to be completed by the end of 1982 and the data released to the public later in 1983.

Prime Farmland Contributions to Food and Fiber Production

Few, if any, technical studies have been published on the value of prime farmlands. However, considerable data are available that can be used for estimating a value of the contribution of prime farmlands to food and fiber production.

Prime farmland accounts for a large share of the cropland acreage of the United States. About two-thirds of the prime farmland, 230 million acres (93,150,000 ha), was cropped in 1977. This is more than one-half of the 413 million acres (167,265,000 ha) of cropland in the country (Soil Conservation Service 1978b). The share of prime farmland varies greatly by region. For example, the Corn Belt has 22% of the nation's cropland. Of this, 74% is prime farmland. By contrast, the Mountain Region, which includes Colorado, accounts for 10% of the total cropland and 21% is prime.

Prime farmland not only makes up most of the cropland but is also more productive than nonprime farmland. For example, in Black Hawk County, Iowa, 44 of the 79 soil mapping units qualify as prime farmland (Soil Conservation Service 1978d, USDA 1979). The prime farmlands are very well suited for growing two major crops in Iowa, corn and soybeans.

These high-quality lands have an average corn yield of 106 bushels per acre (0.405 ha) and an average soybean yield of 40 bushels per acre (see Chapter 11).

Another 35 soil mapping units in Black Hawk County do not qualify as prime. Thirty-one of the nonprime farmlands are also suited for growing corn and soybeans but the yields are much lower: an average corn yield of 66 bushels per acre (0.405 ha) and an average soybean yield of 25 bushels per acre (Soil Conservation Service 1978d, USDA 1979).

Knowing the yield difference for prime and nonprime farmland, the amount of cropland in each class, and the total production of corn and soybeans, makes it possible to estimate the percentages and amount of production for prime and nonprime farmland. Recent data show that 64% of Iowa's cropland is prime farmland (Soil Conservation Service 1978b). Iowa produced 1.46 billion bushels of corn in 1978 (Economics, Statistics and Cooperatives Service 1979). Applying the Black Hawk County percentages to the total production shows that 1.08 billion bushels were produced on prime farmland and 380 million bushels were produced on nonprime.

About 30% of the nation's corn crop is exported as grain (Economics, Statistics and Cooperatives Service 1978). Iowa's share of this export market would amount to 438 million bushels of corn. Nearly three-fourths of this (324 million bushels) came from prime farmland in Iowa and was valued at $684 million. This contrasts with 114 million bushels of corn valued at $240 million that was exported from nonprime farmland.

Using a similar approach for estimating how much of the 1978 soybean production of 287 million bushels grown in Iowa came from prime farmland, we find that 212 million bushels were grown on prime farmland and 75 million bushels on nonprime. About 56% of the domestic soybean crop was exported in 1978 (Economics, Statistics and Cooperatives Service 1979). Applying the percentages of prime and nonprime crop production shows that about 119 million bushels of soybeans having an export value of nearly $791 million came from prime farmland in Iowa. About $279 million came from nonprime.

Estimates from other states such as Indiana show that prime farmland produces the largest share of the nation's total crop production and a large part of the commodities that are exported.

Summary

It is Soil Conservation Service policy to make and keep current an inventory of important farmlands.

The program to produce inventory maps that show the location and extent of these important rural lands is about on schedule. Also, there are soil surveys of about 70% of the nation's farmland and each local conservation district office has a list of soil mapping units that qualify as prime. Thus, units of government and the public can obtain information on prime farmlands for resource programing, planning, and assessment.

Statistical data gathered in 1977 clearly show that the supply and use of prime farmland differ widely among farm production regions. Relating the acreage data to yields of prime farmlands used for crops emphasizes the value of prime farmland for growing crops. A look at production shows that this land not only feeds much of the nation but also feeds many people abroad and significantly reduces the foreign trade deficit.

The important farmland inventory program furnishes much of the technical resource information needed to assess the prime farmland issue and examine the choices.

References

Dideriksen, R. I., and Sampson, R. N. 1976. Important farmlands: A national view, *Journal of Soil and Water Conservation* **31**, 195–197.

Economics, Statistics and Cooperatives Service. 1979. Crop Production, 1978 Annual Summary, pp. 1–17. U.S. Department of Agriculture, Washington, D.C. (January 16, 1979).

Economics, Statistics and Cooperatives Service. 1978. Foreign Agricultural Trade of the United States. U.S. Department of Agriculture, Washington, D.C. (February 1978).

Soil Conservation Service. 1978a. Important Farmland Inventory, Land Inventory and Monitoring Memorandum-3 (Rev. 2). U.S. Department of Agriculture, Washington, D.C.

Soil Conservation Service. 1978b. 1977 National Resource Inventories (unpublished). U.S. Department of Agriculture, Washington, D.C. (April 1979).

Soil Conservation Service. 1978c. Prime Farmland Soils of Washington. Information from SCS State Office. U.S. Department of Agriculture, Spokane, WA. (October 24, 1979).

Soil Conservation Service. 1978d. Soil Survey of Black Hawk County Iowa. U.S. Department of Agriculture, Washington, D.C.

USDA. 1975. Recommendations on Prime Lands. From the seminar on the retention of prime lands, July 16–17, 1975. U.S. Department of Agriculture, Washington, D.C.

USDA. 1979. Appraisal 1980 Review Draft Part 1, RCA. U.S. Department of Agriculture, Washington, D.C. (April 1979).

Part V

International Farmlands Protection Efforts

21

Canadian Provincial Farmland Protection Programs

C. E. Bray

Privately owned land traditionally has been treated as a commodity bought and sold and utilized in combination with capital and other inputs in a way that attempts to achieve the maximum return possible from its use in Canada as in the United States. It is being realized, increasingly, that land is a finite natural resource. Agricultural land in particular can be viewed as a natural resource of importance not only for the economic determinants of the quality of life but for life itself. Decisions on land use made now, irrevocably allocating land to nonagricultural uses, will have implications for world food production in a future of burgeoning world population (Bray 1980).

Land-use allocation is determined by the interaction of a complex web of factors. These include (1) economic forces, which allocate available supplies of land among competing demands at a given price in the market place, (2) political forces, which complement or redirect the economic forces depending on whether or not the market place is perceived to be allocating land appropriately (with appropriate allocation often being defined on the basis of other than economic criteria), and (3) historic social traditions, which provide the framework within which the economic and political forces operate (Bray 1980).

Since 1970 several Canadian provinces (Ontario, Manitoba, Saskatchewan, Alberta, and British Columbia) have developed policies regulating the use and ownership of agricultural land. These programs reflect an increased concern in Canada over the loss of prime agricultural land to nonagricultural uses, as well as concern over changes in farm land tenure patterns. They are designed to preserve agricultural land for future agricultural production, maintain the family farm, and perpetuate owner-operated rather than tenant-operated farming. Each of these programs is tailored to fit the perceived needs of the provinces, and as such, they illustrate the interaction of economic, political, and social forces affecting land in Canada. They also provide case studies of the type of policy instruments that can be used to deal with problems related to agricultural land.

243

These five provinces account for a major proportion of agricultural production for domestic and export markets. The prairie provinces (Manitoba, Saskatchewan, and Alberta) are Canada's major producers of grain and oilseeds. Ontario contains one-third of the entire Canadian population. Ontario and British Columbia produce a wide range of agricultural products which cannot be reproduced as efficiently elsewhere in Canada. Therefore, the loss of agricultural production in these areas has significant implications for Canada's ability to meet domestic and export demand for agricultural commodities.

Areas with moderate climate and level terrain conducive to both agriculture and human habitation in Canada are limited. They are located in a long narrow strip along the U.S.–Canadian border with particularly heavy concentrations along the lower Great Lakes and the St. Lawrence River in Ontario and Quebec provinces, and along the coast and intermontane valleys of British Columbia. This congruity in area for agriculture and population results in a direct competition for use of land, much of which is classified as Canada's best for agricultural production. This competition is perceived to be affecting the allocation of agricultural land to nonagricultural uses particularly in those areas of urban growth such as the Niagara peninsula in Ontario and the Vancouver area of British Columbia. A full assessment of the implications of Canada's urban growth for agricultural production, however, cannot be made without understanding how much land is being lost from agricultural production and analyzing the significance of this loss for Canada's total agricultural productive potential.

Agricultural Land Production Potential

Two sources of information can be used to determine the productivity of Canada's land: the Canadian Land Inventory (CLI) and the Canadian census of agriculture. The CLI, undertaken as a federal/provincial cooperative program in 1963 to document the land potential of settled areas of Canada, provides an extensive picture of the country's national and regional land base.

The CLI rates soils according to their capability for agriculture, wildlife, recreation, and forestry. It covers 1 million square miles (2,589,000 km^2) and encompasses all regions of Canada with agricultural capability. Areas outside CLI boundaries are generally considered not capable of sustaining agriculture, due to climate or topography (Environment Canada 1976). Soils are classified into seven categories according to their capacity for agricultural use (Beaubien and Tabacnik 1977). Classes 1–3 are considered capable of producing commonly cultivated crops. Class 4 can be used for crops but has marginal capability. Under present economic conditions, land with class 4 capability is considered the break-even point for commerical agriculture; class 5 is capable of growing improved pasture and hay; class 6 can sustain native pasture (Geno and Geno 1976).

Preliminary CLI data provide information on 424,668,000 acres (172 million hectares), or 19% of total Canadian land area. When data are compiled for British Columbia and Newfoundland, the inventory is expected to cover 29% of total Canadian land area. According to available CLI data, 89% of Canadian land cannot sustain any type of agriculture.

The remaining 11% falls within classes 1–6 and has some agricultural potential. Less than 1% of Canada's potential agricultural land is classified as class 1, and 1% is classified as class 6 (Table 21.1).

Ontario accounts for only 12% of the country's total potential agricultural land area (classes 1–6) but comprises 52% of its total class 1 land area, or most of Canada's prime agricultural land. The prairie provinces (Manitoba, Saskatchewan, and Alberta) in comparison make up 73% of Canada's potential agricultural land but only 47% of Canada's prime (class 1) agricultural land. The majority of land in the three prairie provinces is either class 5 (22 million hectares or 54,318,000 acres) or class 3 (18 million hectares or 44,442,000 acres) (Environment Canada 1976).

There are several characteristics of the CLI which make it difficult to use in assessing Canada's actual agricultural productive potential. Differences in regional climates are not incorporated into the inventory. Prime agricultural land in both Ontario and Alberta, for example, is classified as class 1. Agroclimatic conditions in Ontario, however, are conducive to the production of a much larger range of crops than can be produced on the same class of land in Alberta. If the CLI fully accounted for the differences in climate in these two provinces, class 1 land in Ontario would have a higher rating than class 1 land in Alberta.

Although socioeconomic factors were explicitly excluded from the CLI, economic factors do appear implicitly. Land was classified on the basis of its ability to produce given benchmark crops at the time the inventory was taken in the 1960s and early 1970s. Conceivably, changes in economic conditions can alter the quantity or mix of inputs that can be economically utilized for production. This would result in a change in the kind of "benchmark" crop that could be produced and consequently the land's productive capability would have to be reconsidered.

The CLI lists soils according to their physical capability for production. It does not, however, indicate how land of any given potential is presently being used. The lack of correlation between land capability and use is one of the major problems in conducting research on Canada's productive potential at a macro level.

Present land use can only be estimated indirectly by comparing CLI land classes with the Canadian census of agriculture for land in farms. Census measurements are broken down in terms of improved and unimproved land rather than CLI class capability. It is, therefore, necessary to assume that land presently used for farms, as indicated by the census, falls within the 424,668,000 acres (172 million ha) covered by the CLI, and that land presently used for crops falls within classes 1–4.

A comparison of census farm area with the quantity of potential agricultural land covered by the CLI indicates that the amount of improved and unimproved land in farms is about equal to the amount of land in the first four CLI classes. Most of Canada's best agricultural land, therefore, is probably already in farms. An additional 93,822,000 acres (38 million ha) of agricultural land could be incorporated into farms if all six CLI classes are considered.

Although most class 1–4 land is in use, there is evidence that not all is used for crop production. Area in crop and summer fallow combined amounts to 39 million ha, or about 58% of land classes 1–4. Analysis of the total production potential of Ontario, Manitoba, Saskatchewan, and Alberta if all CLI class 1–4 land were utilized for crop production indicates that the greatest potential for crop expansion exists in Ontario,

TABLE 21.1 Potential Agricultural Land and Land in Farms, 1976 (in thousands of hectares)

Province	Total land area	Area covered by the CLI[b]	Potential agricultural land				Land in farms, 1976		
			Prime agricultural land class I	Arable land classes 1–4	Marginally arable land classes 5–6	Other land in the CLI[c] area	Total area in farmland	Improved farmland	Unimproved farmland
Newfoundland	37,048	—[a]	—	—	—	—	30	10	20
Prince Edward Island	563	563	0	452	76	34	278	194	81
Nova Scotia	5,296	5,296	0	1,573	96	3,627	400	148	253
New Brunswick	7,145	7,145	0	3,346	1,712	2,087	402	172	231
Quebec	135,667	30,221	20	4,795	1,670	23,756	3,654	2,245	1,409
Ontario	89,118	27,530	2,157	9,909	3,056	14,565	5,967	4,333	1,634
Manitoba	54,894	19,277	163	7,524	4,325	7,430	7,611	5,182	2,129
Saskatchewan	57,026	34,455	1,000	20,075	11,442	2,938	26,433	18,896	7,537
Alberta	64,438	47,894	787	20,019	15,034	12,840	20,040	11,791	8,219
British Columbia	93,052	—	—	—	—	—	2,352	736	1,615
Yukon[b]	53,185	—	—	—	—	—	—	—	—
Northwest Territories[b]	324,634	—	—	—	—	—	—	—	—
Canada	922,030	172,381	4,125	67,695	37,410	67,276	67,167	43,707	23,461

Sources: Environment Canada 1976; Statistics Canada 1976.
[a]Not available
[b]Yukon and Northwest Territories are not covered by the CLI.
[c]Includes class 7 land, organic soils, and unclassified land in the CLI area which comprised urban areas. Also includes provincial parks, national parks and forest reserves.

where production could more than double (Bray 1979). Currently, land used for farms in Ontario is equivalent to about 60% of class 1–4 land for the province. Ontario, with a much milder climate than the prairie provinces, has the greatest number of frost-free days. Also, since the majority of class 1 land is located in Ontario, the province's productive potential is high in terms of yields and range of crops.

Potential for increases in crop production is also quite high in Alberta. Although production of wheat, oats, barley, rye, flaxseed, and rapeseed could more than double, climate factors limit the range of production to small grains, oilseeds, and forage. Saskatchewan accounts for about two-thirds of Canadian wheat production and has the lowest potential for crop expansion of the four provinces. Production of wheat, oats, and barley, for example, could increase only by about half, indicating that a large proportion of the available agricultural land in the province is already being used for crops.

If all class 1–4 land were allocated to crop production under existing cropping patterns, total Canadian wheat production could expand to 32 million tons (29,030,400,000 kg) (a 92% increase over the 1969/1970 to 1978/1979 10 year average production level), oat production could increase to 7.7 million tons (6,985,440,000 kg), or 78%, and barley to 18.8 million tons (17,055,360,000 kg), or 63%. These rates could change if cropping patterns are altered (Bray 1979). In addition, a change in technology resulting in a decline in the use of summer fallow in the prairie provinces, for example, would mean a much larger increase in wheat production (Shields and Ferguson 1975).

Loss of Agricultural Land through Urbanization

Urbanization influences agricultural land use (1) directly through actual incorporation of former agricultural land into expanding urban centers and (2) indirectly through changes in the economic environment of urban fringe areas which result in a transition from agricultural to urban-oriented land uses. Urban "commutersheds" and their concomitant highways, housing developments, and recreational facilities, for example, exert influence on land-use patterns some distance from the boundaries of the urban center. The growing demand for land puts pressure on land prices to reflect urban values instead of the value derived from agricultural capability. When the return from other uses exceeds that derived from farming, the agricultural use of the land is no longer considered justified on economic grounds and the land is allocated temporarily or permanently to alternate uses. This phenomenon often means abandoned farms, land left idle under speculation, or serious financial difficulties for those who continue to farm (Manning 1977).

D. M. Gierman has determined that during 1966–1971, 12,801 ha (31,620 acres) of class 1–4 agricultural land were irretrievably converted to urban use annually in Canada. The highest rates of conversion occurred in Ontario and Alberta, where an average of 6199 and 2046 ha (15,305 and 5,052 acres), respectively, of class 1–4 agricultural land were converted annually. Over 80% of the land converted was formerly classified class 1–4 for agriculture. The converted land, however, represents less than 1% of total class 1–4 land in those two provinces.

Analysis of the losses in potential production due to the direct incorporation of land into cities in the short term (1 year) and in the long run (20 years) assuming constant 1966–1971 rates shows them to be relatively small in the three prairie provinces (Bray 1979). Loss of potential production due to land-use changes in Ontario, however, is fairly substantial. If the current rate of losses continues, then declines in production of the major crops in Ontario by 1996 could range from almost 4% of average production of tame hay to over 6% of rye.

The above analysis gives some indication of the direct influence of expanding urban centers on agricultural production potential. Urban-oriented pressures for use of the land, however, are exerted well beyond the actual bounds of the city. Land use in these urban fringe areas is in a state of transition and the allocation of land to agricultural or nonagricultural use is a dynamic process. Pressures on land use are generated by a combination of agricultural and nonagricultural demand for the land which is generally reflected in upward trending land prices. Farmers in fringe areas may respond to the opportunity costs of keeping capital invested in land for agriculture in several ways: (1) selling the land for nonagricultural use, investing their capital elsewhere, (2) intensifying agricultural production, (3) reducing the intensity of land use and working part-time in nonfarm employment, and (4) maintaining land (either idle or in production) for speculative purposes (Manning 1977). Thus, some farmers may be taking land out of production alongside others who are not. Even if the land is actually taken out of production it may not be permanently lost to agriculture. As long as it is not radically altered physically it may be recouped when economic conditions become more favorable.

For these reasons it is extremely difficult to pinpoint the extent of production lost in urban fringe areas. Manning and McCuaig (1977), however, have quantified the amount of CLI class 1–4 agricultural land likely to be affected by urbanization by looking at CLI class 1–4 land within a 50-mile radius of 19 of Canada's major Census Metropolitan Areas. Census Metropolitan Areas, as designated by Statistics Canada, are urban areas with over 100,000 inhabitants. The areas are Edmonton, Calgary, Saskatoon, Regina, Winnipeg, Thunder Bay, Sudbury, Windsor, Toronto, Kitchener, St. Catherines, Hamilton, London, Ottawa, Montreal, Quebec, Chicoutini, St. John, and Halifax. Fifty-four percent of Canada's class 1 land and 21% of Canada's class 1–4 land is within 50 miles (80.45 km) of the specified areas. Approximately 4.5 million ha of class 1–4 land are located within the fringe areas of urban centers in Ontario.

The productive capacity of the urban fringe area in Ontario exceeds present production levels for the province and is over 50% of the total production potential on all CLI class 1–4 land in the province (Bray 1979). This means that a substantial quantity of agricultural land in Ontario is subject to change from agricultural to urban-oriented use. Although the potential for increased crop production in Ontario is substantial due to the combination of good land and favorable climate, this potential is affected by competition between agriculture and urban development. The situation in the prairie provinces is considerably different. The amount of land located in the fringe area of cities in Manitoba, Saskatchewan, and Alberta equals 1.4, 3.0, and 2.7 million ha (3.5, 7.4, and 6.7 million acres), respectively (Manning 1977). The productive potential of this land is equal to about one-fourth to one-half of present production in Manitoba, one-fourth in Saskatchewan, and one-third in Alberta. It represents one-fifth of the total productive potential of Manitoba, and one-sixth in Saskatchewan and Alberta.

Legislative Initiative

Despite its limitations the CLI does provide information on Canadian agricultural land capability which can be used to formulate land-use policy. In fact, as will be demonstrated in the next section, several provinces have used the CLI as a basis for their land-use programs. By using CLI as a determinant of what land should be maintained for agriculture these programs make land capability, not economic factors, the criteria for land use (Raciti and Lemay 1980).

Analysis of the CLI also illustrates that the provinces discussed can be broken into two categories: those that are facing severe competition for nonagricultural use of the land (Ontario and British Columbia) and those that are not (the prairie provinces). As may be expected, land regulation programs developed by these two groups of provinces reflect this dichotomy. Before discussing these differences, however, it is necessary to understand the underlying, constitutional framework that shapes the way in which land regulation has developed in Canada.

Federal versus Provincial Jurisdiction

Land-use and tenure programs in Canada fall under the jurisdiction of the provincial governments. The provinces maintain extensive powers for implementing land control measures under the British North America Act (BNA Act). As the act is generally interpreted, the provinces are constitutionally empowered to (1) develop laws concerning the purchase or expropriation of land for public recreational use, (2) implement differential tax structures so that local landowners using land for specific purposes such as agriculture do not bear the burden of increased property assessments resulting from nonresident purchases, (3) establish land-use and zoning controls, and (4) require disclosure of the place of residence, citizenship, and other pertinent information concerning persons owning or purchasing land in the province.

Determinants of Policy Orientation

Since land regulation is under provincial control the provinces have developed programs tailored to their individually perceived needs. The range of programs developed, therefore, is probably more diverse than if a single land regulation program had been developed at the national level.

The economic resource base of the province in large part determines whether the policies regulate land use or land tenure. In provinces where agriculture is the primary land use and competition for alternate uses is not severe, such as Manitoba, Saskatchewan, and Alberta, contention revolves around who will have access to land as an input for agriculture. Under these conditions land tenure not land use is the major focus of land regulation (Bray 1980). Land tenure programs concern owner versus tenant and family versus corporation farming. They seek to maintain the family farm in a rural social infrastructure and perpetuate the owner-operated rather than tenant-operated farm (Bray 1979). The programs implemented by the predominantly agricultural prairie provinces are tenure oriented. Land-use legislation either does not exist or focuses only on those areas surrounding a major metropolitan area such as Winnipeg in Manitoba.

In those provinces where agriculture is not the primary land use and the urban/industrial mix makes competition for nonagricultural use of the land severe, programs are developed to regulate not only land tenure but also the allocation of land between competing uses. The policies implemented by the more industrial provinces, British Columbia and Ontario, are land-use oriented, regulating the allocation of land between agricultural or nonagricultural purposes.

The philosophical orientation of the party in power in large part determines whether the government regulates land use and tenure within the parameters established by the operation of market forces or whether it adopts a more active role, actually entering the market itself and assuming ownership control of land. If private property ownership is considered inviolable, the government's role in regulation of land use is constrained. In Saskatchewan where the New Democratic Party (NDP), a "Socialist" party, is in power, the government assumes an active role in implementing the Saskatchewan Land Bank. It buys land that it then rents to applicant farmers who want to begin farming, but do not have the heavy capital backing needed to purchase land themselves. Through this program the government influences tenure arrangements in the province. With the Progressive Conservative Party in power in Ontario, the Ontario Planning Act allows land-use allocation to be determined through operation of market forces to the greatest extent possible (Bray 1980). Details of the land-use and land-tenure programs in effect in the five provinces are discussed in the following sections.

Land-Use Programs

British Columbia

British Columbia's agricultural land-use program implemented by the Land Commission Act was one of the first comprehensive attempts on the part of a province to redirect the process of agricultural land allocation to nonagricultural uses. British Columbia consists of a series of north–south mountain ranges with 90% of the land mountainous and nonarable. Agriculture is limited to the narrow fertile valleys between the mountains. The agroclimatic characteristics of the valleys, however, are conducive to producing such specialized crops as soft fruits, grapes, and tobacco (Manning 1978). Because crops are produced in the intermontane valleys to which access is restricted by mountains or sea, British Columbia farms are relatively small, highly specialized, and faced with major transportation constraints (Hudson 1977). The average farm size is 126 ha (311 acres), compared to an average of 201 ha (496 acres) for total Canada and 374 ha (924 acres) for Saskatchewan. Rapid population growth has led to competition for use of the same topographically limited land; this competition has resulted in land prices rising higher than is warranted by the land's agricultural productive potential (Hudson 1977).

The provincial government became increasingly concerned about the province's ability to produce food on a very narrow land resource base that was being affected by urban development during the early 1970s. British Columbia is highly dependent on imported food to meet local demand. The government, recognizing the province's high dependency on outside supply, became more sensitive to keeping future land-use options open. It soon sought a way to plan urban land uses in a more orderly way while preserving remaining farmland (Ward 1976).

In December 1972, the provincial government placed a moratorium on all future use of certain agricultural land for purposes other than farming. Two Orders-In-Council, one in December 1972 and one in January 1973, prohibited changes in use of land over 0.81 ha (2 acres) classified as farmland for taxation, zoned for agriculture, or designated as having Canadian Land Inventory (CLI) capability of 1−4 (Manning 1978). Land did not have to be in actual agricultural production to be affected by the moratorium, only to fit into one of the categories (Ward 1976). Bill 42, the Provincial Land Commission Act, as introduced in February 1973, aimed to preserve agricultural land for farm use and establish and maintain the family farm. Farm use was defined as the occupation or use of agricultural land for genuine farm purposes as well as certain other uses compatible with the preservation of land for farm use (Rees 1977).

Section 2 of the Land Commission Act created the Land Commission, a five-member board which would establish agricultural land reserves (ALR) in the 28 regional districts of the province. The land reserves were to include all land capable of sustaining agriculture, that is, all CLI class 1−4 land that had not been irreversibly developed. If nonagricultural land was not immediately available for urban expansion, land sufficient for 5 years of urban growth was excluded from the reserve. Lower capability land was included in the reserve where there was evidence that it could be used successfully in conjunction with class 1−4 land. Class 7 land was included in those instances where excluding it would result in nonagricultural use of an otherwise agricultural area (Manning 1978). Land was also exempt from the reserve if it had been continuously used for a nonagricultural purpose 6 months prior to December 21, 1972 (Beaubien and Tabacnik 1977).

The provincial government maintained review and veto power over the ALRs developed by the regional districts. As the provincially approved ALR plans came into effect, they replaced the previous moratorium on land use (Manning 1978). Land designated as part of an ALR could not be used for any purpose other than farming except as permitted by the Land Commission Act or by order of the Land Commission (Government of British Columbia, no date). Procedures were established for appealing an ALR designation. All ALR plans were completed by 1975, and as of Janaury 1, 1978, the total area within the ALRs was 4.7 million ha (11,604,300 acres) (Ontario Ministry of Agriculture and Food 1977).

By limiting use of land to agricultural purposes, the provincial government was denying farmers the opportunity to cash in on the increased value of their land (Hudson 1977). Land sales often served as a form of farm retirement pension. On the other hand, it was argued that farmers should make a living from farming, not land speculation, and that proceeds from that living should permit them to retire on a decent income (Beaubien and Tabacnik 1977).

The British Columbia Farm Income Assurance Program (FIAP) was introduced in November 1973. It provides income protection for farmers operating under an ALR plan, with producers contributing one-third and the provincial government two-thirds of the premiums to an assurance fund. Indemnities are paid out of the fund when market returns fall to a specified percentage of the basic cost of production, which is calculated to include labor, management, depreciation, interest on investment, and cash operating costs (Hudson 1977). The programs, which are effective for 5 years, have operated for fruit trees, beef, dairy, hogs, field tomatoes, greenhouse vegetables, table eggs, broiler hatching eggs, sheep, blueberries, and potatoes (Jean 1976). As of September 1977, $89 million had been paid under the program to about 5000 producers, representing average payments of $17,800 per producer.

The British Columbia land-use program has been in effect long enough to make an assessment of its impact on land allocation to urban and agricultural uses. Manning and Eddy (Manning 1978) found that the British Columbia ALR did bring about a major shift in the location of new residential and commercial development. The ALR also prevented much change in land use within its boundaries. The rate of subdivision within the ALR, for example, was considerably lower than in undesignated areas.

The designation of land as agricultural within an ALR plan, however, was not enough to assure that the land was actually used for agricultural production. In the short-term period of the study, much of the ALR land was left idle because returns from farming were insignificant in relation to the costs of capital investment on land purchased at prices reflecting demand for the land for urban subdivisions (Manning 1978). If economic conditions are not conducive to allocating land to agricultural production, opportunity costs are incurred by keeping land in agriculture and even more by leaving it idle. Both the British Columbia and Ontario agricultural land-use programs incorporate farm income stabilization programs, which in effect represent a social payment to farmers for not reallocating their land to alternative uses. The British Columbia program has apparently been successful in keeping land for agriculture, although at $17,800 per producer, it has not been without some cost.

Ontario

Ontario is the home of a major part of the Canadian population and is the country's industrial center. It is similar to British Columbia in its agroclimatic capability of producing a wide range of speciality crops, including corn, soybeans, soft fruit, and tobacco, which cannot be produced elsewhere domestically as efficiently. Ontario, however, does not face the constraints imposed on British Columbia by its rugged topography. Most of Canada's prime agricultural land is located in Ontario, and transportation to markets and sources of input is not a major cost of production as in British Columbia. The province does experience intense competition for use of prime agricultural land. Speculation and nonfarm investment stemming from urban-oriented population pressures are identified as major factors driving up the price of land, making it difficult for farmers in the province (Manning 1977).

The Ontario government has not placed the kinds of restrictions on use of farmland as did British Columbia (Ward 1977). Like the latter, however, one of the motives for Ontario's developing a land-use program to preserve agricultural land was to reduce future dependence on other nations for those commodities that can be produced within the province (Ontario Ministry of Agriculture and Food 1977).

Ontario's agricultural land-use programs were developed on the premise that (1) land use will be determined by the operation of the marketplace to the greatest extent possible, (2) that tradeoffs will be made between economic growth and desired land-use patterns, (3) that land-use programs will be conducted and enforced at the local municipal level, and (4) that the Provincial Planning Act would be the main vehicle used to direct the allocation of land between agricultural and nonagricultural uses (Ontario Ministry of Agriculture and Food 1976).

Under the Provincial Planning Act, a designated planning area (which may be a single municipality, groups of municipalities, or a region) may draw up an official land-use plan, a statement of the development policies of the region. It may include a map and text showing land-use allocations. The plan by itself does not indicate how any piece of property may be used. Zoning and other bylaws, however, which state specifically what may or may not be done on individual parcels of property, must conform to an official plan. The province maintains ultimate review and veto authority over the regional official plans (Ontario Ministry of Housing, no date).

The Ontario Planning Act was originally devised to solve urban problems and was used as the province's primary vehicle for dealing with problems of agricultural land use. The Ontario Ministry of Agriculture has been working to develop a more comprehensive agricultural land-use program and guidelines under which agricultural considerations can be incorporated into local plans under the Planning Act. The ministry released a policy statement (Ontario Ministry of Agriculture and Food 1976) in March 1976, specifying the government's commitment to preserve better agricultural land to maintain the economic feasibility of using such land for agricultural purposes (Ward 1977).

The preservation of better agricultural land would also be achieved by encouraging municipal development on poorer soils, and channeling recreational and industrial development to lands less suited for agriculture. The Ontario Ministry of Agriculture also developed guidelines that apply agricultural interests to official regional plans (Ontario Ministry of Agriculture and Food 1976).

The guidelines presented in 1977 (Ontario Ministry of Agriculture and Food 1977) specify that the CLI could be used to identify prime agricultural land. Once the land capabilities are identified, the allocation of land among land uses should be evaluated. This distribution of land should reflect the priority of agriculture, however, if agricultural capabilities exist. If land is designated as agricultural, it should be incorporated into the official plan of the region and its supporting land-use map. High capability lands should be given the greatest protection, and uses compatible to its long-term retention for agriculture should be specified. Once agricultural land is incorporated into the official plan, it can be used only for agricultural or agriculturally compatible purposes. The agricultural use specification can be changed only if the official plan is amended. Thus, it is the ease or difficulty with which the official plan can be altered which determines whether or not land remains agricultural.

Two kinds of policy instruments are being used to preserve agricultural land in British Columbia and Ontario: agricultural land reserves and zoning. Under the British Columbia program a policy decision was made that market forces were not allocating land between competing uses appropriately. The government addressed the issue directly by intervening to manage the effect of market forces. The ALR specify that land of an identified agricultural capability will be used for agricultural purposes. The Bureau of Municipal Research stated that farmland cannot be saved by saving the farmer because government cannot afford to raise farm prices and incomes to a level sufficient to compete with land prices that other nonfarm uses can command (Bureau of Municipal Research 1977). The British Columbia land-use program attempts to save farm land not only by regulating how land of agricultural capability is used but also by saving the farmer. Evidence indicates that land-use programs such as the one implemented by the British Columbia Land Commission Act apparently can stop the reallocation of agricultural land to urban uses. If the general economic environment is not conducive to the allocation of agricultural land to production, however, maintaining that land for future agricultural use may require a substantial social investment.

Ontario so far has chosen not to develop a program along the lines of the British Columbia prototype. It is acknowledged that market forces may not be allocating land appropriately between competing uses, yet there is a reluctance to directly intervene in market operations to socially redirect present trends. This, combined with the fact that the provincial legislature represents an agricultural/industrial mix and that agriculture is not the primary resource base of the province results in a program that realistically reflects the conflicting actualities of the situation but that may not categorically assure the preservation of agricultural land. Competition for agricultural and nonagricultural use of the land will continue both in the market place and in planning session negotiations. The preservation of land with agricultural capability is not as specifically assured in Ontario as it is in British Columbia. The costs of the Ontario program may not be as high as the costs of the British Columbia program in the short run. They may increase in the long run as additional agricultural land is reallocated to nonagricultural use (Bray 1980).

Land Tenure Programs

Land tenure is an issue closely related to land use because land use combines human and land resource inputs. Land-use programs control how the land is to be used. Land-tenure programs control who is to use the land. Their effect on land use therefore is indirect. It is the owner who most frequently determines how the land will be utilized. If ownership of a certain quality land is restricted to farmers, it is expected that the land will likely be used for agricultural production.

Programs implemented by the prairie provinces deal with perceived problems relating to land tenure. The provincial governments have chosen to control the amount of land an individual may own in order to assure that one of Canada's basic resources, land, remains in the hands of Canadians, particularly farmers for whom it is a major input of production. An underlying theme inherent in these land tenure programs is the maintenance of the owner-operated family farm so embedded in North American tradition. Programs perpetuating the family farm prevent the development of a tenant peasantry more traditional to the countries from which North American settlers emigrated. The range of government involvement in these programs is fairly extensive. Under the Saskatchewan Land Bank program the provincial government buys land to aid young farmers who if left to deal with the market system for land allocation might not be able to compete.

Ownership Control

Canadian settlement policies established the owner-operated family farm as the predominant form of agricultural production (Parlby 1974). Recently, however, technological changes in agriculture resulted in an increase in the scale of farming, and a shift from single proprietorship to partnerships or family corporations. These changes have caused concern about the economic survival of family farms, their ability to compete with commercial corporations or communes, and the effect of their decline on the rural community (Alberta Land Use Forum 1976).

There are three traditional forms of tenancy: full owner, part owner, and tenant (Boylen 1975). The full owner has the most security and freedom for decision making of the three tenure forms. Full ownership facilitates the adoption of improved farming practices and effective long-range farm plans necessary for efficient use of farm resources.

Part owners and tenants rent or work on shares for others. This type of tenure involves a lease in which the landlord conveys rights of use and possession of a given property for a definite period of time in return for payment. Rental contracts are based on custom and tend to be fairly rigid. Insecurity in rental tenure, which results in the movement of operators from farm to farm, often affects the efficiency of farm resources use. Rental tenants typically do not make the long-term decisions necessary for continued efficient agriculture, such as those decisions relating to soil maintenance. Consequently, rental tenancy conflicts with social goals concerning the long-term existence of agriculture (Boylen 1975).

When nonresidents, foreigners, or commercial corporations own the land, they often act as absentee landlords, renting the land to farmers. Foreign, nonresident, and commercial corporate ownership of agricultural land has thus been a focus of land tenure programs in Canada. Foreign investors and commercial corporations, with access to capital not available to Canadian family farmers, are investing in land as a hedge against inflation. Since they can use their capital resources to buy land at prices unrelated to the return from agricultural production, they are perceived to be driving up the price of agricultural land (Brown 1978). Family farmers with a smaller capital base thus find it increasingly difficult to compete for land resources needed for efficient agriculture or to transfer land to the next generation of young farmers. Saskatchewan, Manitoba, and Alberta have developed legislation to control foreign, nonresident, and commercial corporation ownership of land.

Saskatchewan

The Saskatchewan Farm Ownership Act of 1974, as amended, was developed on the premise that provincial residents who were involved in day-to-day agricultural operations and who spend a major part of their time and agricultural income in the province should control agricultural resources. In addition, they should be protected to some extent from capital resources accumulated in other industries or countries (Saskatchewan Farm Ownership Board 1975).

Under the Farm Ownership Act, implemented by the Farm Ownership Board nonresidents and nonagricultural corporations are prohibited from owning more than 65 ha (160.485 acres) or a quarter section. (A resident is defined as one who lives in Saskatchewan for 183 days or more a year, or within 20 miles (32.18 km) of the Saskatchewan border. This includes United States citizens who may own land on both sides of the border. An agricultural corporation is defined as a corporation primarily engaged in farming where at least 60% of both the voting and nonvoting stock is owned by resident farmers.) Nonresidents did not have to dispose of land held prior to 1974 or of holdings acquired between March 31, 1974, and September 15, 1977, if the assessed value of the holdings for taxation is not greater than $15,000 (Government of Saskatchewan, no date).

A nonresident holding land in excess of the amount stipulated in the act has 5 years from the date of becoming a nonresident to dispose of the excess land unless he or she is a former farmer in which case the land may continue to be held regardless of residence status. (A former farmer is defined as someone who at some time in the past lived in Saskatchewan and farmed the land for 5 years.) Former farmers may also transfer their land to direct relatives: spouse, child, grandchild, brother, sister, nephew, niece, or spouse thereof, regardless of their residence status (Government of Saskatchewan, no date). Nonresidents intending to become a resident within 3 years may, with the permission of the Farm Ownership Board, acquire more than 65 ha (160.5 acres) during the 3 year period.

Nonagricultural corporations with holdings in excess of 65 ha prior to March 31, 1974, must dispose of the excess land by January 1, 1994, and submit a land holding disclosure statement to the Farm Ownership Board once a year (Government of Saskatchewan, no date).

The act is enforced by the Farm Ownership Board, which may conduct investigations into land ownership. The board may also order nonresidents or nonagricultural corporations to divest of any land over that amount permitted (Government of Saskatchewan, no date).

A computer land registry system, based on a survey of municipalities providing information on 5000 nonresidents and 1000 corporations, is the basis of a continuing registry used to monitor land transfer (Saskatchewan Farm Ownership Board 1975). Legislation is being formulated requiring residence to be declared as part of a land transfer.

Manitoba
Under the Manitoba Agricultural Land Protection Act of June 1977, as amended and administered by the Agricultural Lands Protection Board, nonresidents may own no more than 8 ha (19.752 acres) of land. A nonresident can own land in excess of 8 ha if it was owned prior to April 1, 1977, or if right to the title for the land arose prior to that date (Government of Manitoba, no date).

If a corporation becomes a nonresident through the sale of shares, or if a nonresident corporation acquires land in excess of 8 ha (19.752 acres) through a legal settlement, it has 2 years to dispose of the excess land. The board may take legal action to dispose of land acquired by a nonresident in excess of the amount stipulated if the nonresident has not already done so (Government of Manitoba, no date).

Alberta
Foreign ownership of land in Alberta is controlled by the Foreign Ownership of Land (temporary) Regulations established by an Order-in-Council under Section 33 of the Citizenship Act on 26 April 1977. These temporary regulations will eventually be supplanted by the Foreign Ownership of Land Regulations passed under the dual authority of the Agricultural and Recreational Land Ownership Act and Section 33 of the Citizenship Act

(Alberta Department of Energy and Natural Resources, no date). (As of October 1978, Bill 40 was not yet in effect. Regulations under Bill 40, however, will not differ in intent from the temporary regulations but will be more detailed.)

Under the regulations, ineligible persons (non-Canadians and temporary residents) and corporations with 50% or more of their shares or memberships held by ineligible persons cannot own more than 8 ha (19.752 acres) of controlled land. Controlled land is defined as any land outside the boundaries of a city, town, new town, village, or summer village.

Enforcement of the regulation is ensured by sworn declaration attached to land transfers and by investigative procedures carried out by the Foreign Ownership of Land Administration with use of information supplied by the Land Titles Branch. Land that is acquired in contravention of the law may be sold by judicial sale. Proceeds from the sale are used to cover sale expenses and any remaining funds up to the amount originally paid for the land are returned to the individual. Any proceeds exceeding the amount originally paid for the land are put into the General Revenue Fund of Alberta (Alberta Department of Energy and Natural Resources, no date).

Transfer of Ownership

The transfer of agricultural land from one generation to the next is an integral part of maintaining the owner-operated family farm, ensuring that future farmers are available to utilize the land of agricultural capability (Saskatchewan Land Use Policy Committee, no date). A start in farming, however, requires substantial capital resources. As land prices continue to increase, the need for capital for young farmers entering the industry becomes increasingly acute.

Saskatchewan

The Saskatchewan Land Bank, established in 1972 by the Land Bank Act and administered by the Land Bank Commission, was developed to alleviate some of the problems associated with the generational transfer of land. Its objectives were to develop a viable agricultural industry in Saskatchewan and provide for a transfer of farms from generation to generation rather than have family farms absorbed by large farm units.

The Land Bank Commission, a government agency, purchased land, thereby absorbing the capital costs associated with land transfer. It then rents the land to applicant farmers. The land bank program provides continuing sales opportunities to Saskatchewan farmers and enables individuals to begin farming independently of substantial family assistance. It also encourages the perpetuation of viable family farm units through the transfer of land to direct descendants (Saskatchewan Land Bank Commission, various dates).

Although the land bank program involves the transfer of land through rental tenancy, efforts have been made to eliminate this type of transfer's detrimental effects on efficient resource utilization. Saskatchewan Land Bank leases, for example, are long term, and the commission reimburses the lessee for capital improvements made during tenure which (it is expected) would provide the security necessary to make long-term investment decisions to use resources efficiently.

Under the program, the Saskatchewan Land Bank Commission may purchase land from anyone wishing to sell. In instances where the commission must allocate available funds among several offers for sale it will purchase by order of priority from farmers who (1) want to retire and transfer their land to a direct descendant, (2) are selling land that can be used to establish a viable farm unit, (3) have large tracts of land on which two or more operators can be supported, (4) have parcels of land constituting full units, or (5) have no other sale alternative (Saskatchewan Land Bank Commission 1978).

The commission purchases land at market value. This is determined through an appraisal process in which the productive value of the cultivated portion of the sale property is correlated with the productive value and sale price of cultivated properties of similar soil quality in the same area. The productive value is determined through tax assessment data. Thus, the commission price is essentially determined by the relationship between prices of recent land sales in the area and the assessed value of the land for taxation purposes. A similar process is used to determine the market value of grazing land. Assessments are also made of the value of buildings and other improvements on the property.

Land purchased by the commission is allocated to lessees on the basis of a point competitive system if there is more than one applicant for a given piece of land. Applicants are scored on their income potential, skill, age, vendor's preference, and potential disruption of existing farming enterprises. The applicant must declare an intention to make farming the principal occupation, and be of legal age, a resident at the time of leasing and during tenure, and a Canadian citizen or immigrant. The applicant's and spouse's combined average annual income for the preceding 3 years must not exceed an amount annually determined by the commission. The applicant's and spouse's net worth may not exceed $121,000 in 1979. Applicants gain or lose points if their projected net income, projected land base in work units, or age is outside the optimal range established by the commission. Points are gained for education, experience, and for an indication from the vendor that the applicant is the preferred recipient of the land. Points are lost for the average distance in miles that the piece of land applied for is from other land units the applicant is farming.

Applicants scoring highest are then interviewed to assess their motivation, management ability, and other characteristics, all of which are also numerically scored. The applicant with the highest cumulative point score, unless otherwise determined by the commission, is awarded the lease (Saskatchewan Land Bank Commission 1978).

The lease remains in effect until the lessee reaches the age of 65 or dies. The lessee may stipulate in writing if the lease is to be passed on to a direct descendant. After the age of 65, short-term leases may be granted under certain circumstances.

Since June 1978, rent is based on the production value of the land which is calculated from the prices of oilseeds, wheat, and barley, and the long-term yield of equal quality land in the area. Prior to that time, rent was based on a percentage of the land's market value. The lessee is responsible for the payment of taxes (Saskatchewan Land Bank Commission, various dates).

Lessees have the option to purchase land after leasing from the commission for 5 years. The land is sold to lessees at its market value at the time of sale. Lessees purchasing land are entitled to an earned "homestead quarter" refund made by the commission on the purchase price of a quarter section of land. If the lessee lives on the rented land, the inhabited quarter section is the section on which the refund is paid. If the lessee does not live on the rented land, a quarter section is designated as the homestead quarter on which the refund is paid. The refund is 20% of the price paid by the purchaser for the quarter section, to a maximum of $5000, paid over a period of 5 years following the land transfer. In order to receive the refund, the purchaser must be actively engaged in farming and remain a resident of Saskatchewan during the 5 years, or the balance of the refund is forfeited.

Buildings and improvements on the property are sold under a long-term agreement to the lessee. When the lease expires, the commission purchases the lessee's earned equity based on the market value of the improvements, thus ensuring that lessees receive the benefits of their investment decisions. This, combined with the homestead refund means that the lessee builds equity while renting from the commission (Saskatchewan Land Bank Commission 1978).

Experience of the Land Tenure Programs

During 1972–1977, the Saskatchewan Land Bank Commission acquired 354,000 ha (874,025 acres) of land for a total cost of $81 million. This land as of December 31, 1977 was being leased to 1912 lessees through 2009 leases (Saskatchewan Land Bank Commission, various dates).

In Alberta, the amount of land purchases by non-Canadians and foreign corporations during 1976–1977, as monitored under the Foreign Ownership of Land Regulations, declined 60%. During January–August 1978, foreign purchases were running 89% behind purchases for the same period in 1977. In 1977, foreign purchases accounted for 2% of total area of rural sales, compared to 5% of total rural sales in 1976 (Alberta Department of Energy and Natural Resources, no date).

Conclusions

The policies developed by the five provinces discussed in this chapter fall into two main categories: those regulating land use and those regulating land tenure. The perceived problems and the instruments used to deal with them vary among the provinces, reflecting the combined influences of the economic resource base of the constituency and the philosophical orientation of the political party in power.

These land-use programs were developed at the provincial rather than the local municipal or federal level, reflecting the degree of autonomy granted the provinces under the Canadian Constitution in the BNA act. The extent of government activity in the preservation of agricultural land depends on the general attitude of the constituency concerning the inviolability of private ownership. Under the Canadian programs the provincial governments exercise a wide range of powers. They control the amount of land nonfarmers or non-Canadians may own; they enter the market and purchase land, which is then rented to private citizens; they also specify how privately owned land may be used. The Canadian approaches can provide considerable flexibility in controlling land-use patterns, and ownership of land, but it also means that the government involvement in land ownership is much greater than may be expedient in another country such as the United States.

As illustrated in the case of British Columbia, a comprehensive land-use program can stop the reallocation of agricultural land to nonagricultural uses. If the general economic environment is not conducive to the allocation of agricultural land to production, however, maintaining that land for future agricultural use may require a substantial social investment.

A significant aspect of the British Columbia program is that land use is determined by the capability of the land for agriculture rather than economic factors. Once it has been determined that capability rather than economic return should be the basis for land allocation, programs can be developed to fit within the political and historic framework operative in the country.

References

Alberta Department of Energy and Natural Resources. No date. The Agricultural and Recreational Land Ownership Act. Explanatory bulletin, Edmonton, Alberta.

Alberta Department of Energy and Natural Resources. No date. Foreign Ownership of Land Administration. Unpublished data. Edmonton, Alberta.

Alberta Land Use Forum. 1976. Report and Recommendations. Edmonton, Alberta (January).

Beaubien, C. and Tabacnik, R. 1977. People and Agricultural Land. Science Council of Canada, Ottawa, Ontario (June).

Boylen, D.M. 1975. Rural Land Tenure. Tech. Rep. No. 6B. Alberta Land Use Forum, Edmonton.

Bray C.E. 1979. Canadian Land Use, Foreign Agricultural Economic Rep. No. 155. Economics, Statistics, Cooperatives Service, United States Department of Agriculture, Washington D.C. (August).

Bray, C.E. 1980. Land Regulation in Several Canadian Provinces, *Canadian Public Policy* **VI**(4).

British Columbia, Government of. No date. Land Commission Act, Vancouver.

Brown, J. 1978. Our home and native land, extent and implications of foreign land ownership, *The Agrologist* **71**.

Bureau of Municipal Research. 1977. Food for the Cities, Disappearing Farmland and Provincial Land Policy. Ontario, Canada (June).

Environment Canada, 1976. Land Capability for Agriculture Canada Land Inventory Preliminary Report. Lands Directorate, Ottawa, Ontario (April).

Esau, A.A.J. 1974. Land Ownership Rights, Law and Land, an Overview. Alberta Land Use Forum, Edmonton. Summary Rep. 9.

Federal/Provincial Committee on Foreign Ownership of Land. 1974. Report to the First Minister's Conference. Canadian Intergovernmental Conference Secretariat, Ottawa, Ontario (Aug.).

Geno, B.J. and Geno, L.M. 1976. Food Production in the Canadian Environment. Science Council of Canada, Ottawa, Ontario (December).

Hudson, S.C. 1977. A Review of Farm Income Stabilization in British Columbia, A Report to the Minister of Agriculture. Ministry of Agriculture, Ottawa (October).

Jean, C.V. 1976. Land use, income assurance linked in British Columbia, *Foreign Agriculture*, March 22.

McFadyen, S. 1976. The control of foreign ownership of Canadian real estate, *Canadian Public Policy*, **II**, I (winter).

Manitoba, Government of. No date. Agricultural Land Protection Act. Winnipeg.

Manning, E.W. and Eddy, S. 1978. The Agricultural Land Reserves of British Columbia: An Impact Analysis. Fisheries and Environment Canada, Lands Directorate, Ottawa, Ontario (November).

Manning, E.W. and McCuaig, J.D. 1977. Agricultural Land and Urban Centres, an Overview of the Significance of Urban Centres to Canada's Quality Agricultural Land. Ministries Fisheries and Environment Canada, Land Directorate, Ottawa, Ontario (July).

Ontario Ministry of Agriculture and Food. 1976. A Strategy for Ontario Farmland, Ontario (March).

Ontario Ministry of Agriculture and Food. 1977. Green Paper on Planning for Agriculture, Food Land Guidelines, Ontario, Canada.

Ontario Ministry of Housing. No date. A Guide to the Planning Act, Ontario.

Parlby, G.B. 1974. The "Family Farm" in Alberta, Its Origins, Development, Future. Summary Rep. 1. Alberta Land Use Forum, Edmonton.

Raciti, S.J. and Lemay, J. 1980. Farmland Preservation in Quebec and New Jersey. Ramapo College of New Jersey, Mahwah, NJ.

Rees, W.E. 1977. The Canadian Land Inventory in Perspective. Fisheries and Environment Canada, Lands Directorate, Ottawa, Ontario (March).

Saskatchewan, Government of. No date. Farm Ownership Act. Regina, Saskatchewan.

Saskatchewan Farm Ownership Board. Various dates. Unpublished data. Saskatoon, Saskatchewan.

Saskatchewan Farm Ownership Board. 1975. First Annual Report. Saskatoon.

Saskatchewan Land Bank Commission. Various dates. Annual Reports. Regina.

Saskatchewan Land Bank Commission. 1978. Saskatchewan Land Bank Regulations. Regina (June).

Saskatchewan Land Use Policy Committee. No date. Land Use in Saskatchewan Agricultural Land, Fact Sheet NO. 7. Regina.

Sheilds, J.A. and Ferguson, W.S. 1975. Land resources, production possibilities and limitations for crop production in the prairie provinces, *Oilseed and Pulse Crops in Western Canada*. Western Cooperatives Fertilizers Limited, Calgary, Alberta.

Statistics Canada. 1976. Census of Agriculture, Ottawa.

U.S. Department of State. Various reports from U.S. Embassy, Ottawa. Washington, D.C.

Ward N.E. 1976. Land Use Programs in Canada, British Columbia. Fisheries and Environment Canada, Lands Directorate, Ottawa, Ontario (July).

Ward, N.E. 1977. Land Use Programs in Canada, Ontario. Fisheries and Environment Canada, Lands Directorate, Ottawa, Ontario (September).

22

The European and International Experience with Farmland Protection: Some Inferences[1]

Dallas Miner, Martin Chorich, and Mark B. Lapping

Agricultural land outside North America faces most of the same development pressures felt in the United States and Canada. Many nations undergoing the sort of urban sprawl common in North America have taken measures to preserve agricultural land. This sprawl owes to a number of factors, most important of which is the fact that many countries continue to urbanize. In 1946, 55% of the French population resided in cities. By 1968 the figure had risen to 70%.

Not only has the number of urban residents increased, but their per capita living space has grown as well. Higher living standards have led to construction of more single-family homes in American-style suburbs.

Many countries also have adopted regional development schemes in order to shift new industrial development to outlying and depressed regions. British attempts to locate new industry in North England and Wales, French moves to develop the Midregion, and continuing Italian efforts to reduce the economic disparities between the industrial North and less-developed South all fall into this category.

Urban growth adversely affects agriculture in several ways. The flight of people to the cities results in smaller rural populations. Urban growth both consumes land and drives up the price of farmland adjacent to the urban area, rendering many continuing agricultural land uses economically untenable. In West Germany, for example, agricultural land in outlying areas sold for an average price of $15,000 per hectare ($6,075 per acre) in 1975, while farmland adjacent to major metropolitan regions averaged $26,000 per hectare ($10,525 per acre).

The traditional advantage of farmland close to urban areas in supplying city markets with high-value specialty crops also has eroded because of lower tariff barriers and improved transportation. Israeli oranges com-

[1]This chapter was adapted from Miner and Chorich. 1979. The European experience with farmland protection: Some inferences" in "Food, Farmland, and the Future," Max Schnepf (Editor). Soil Conservation Society of America, Ankeny, Iowa, and Mark B. Lapping. 1980. Agricultural land retention: Responses, American, and foreign in "The Farm and the City." Archibald M. Woodruff (Editor). Prentice-Hall, Inc., Englewood Cliffs, New Jersey.

pete with Spanish oranges in Madrid in the same way that California tomatoes compete with New Jersey tomatoes in New York City. Further complicating all of this is the tendency for urban areas to expand on the most fertile lands.

No Common Approach

Despite the similar problems faced by agriculture in the industrial West, policies and approaches in managing urban growth vary considerably from nation to nation. The great geographic, sociological, and economic differences among countries in Europe preclude all but the most rudimentary generalizations concerning any common "European approach" or an "international approach" to land-use management.

Although some European nations have population densities far greater than the United States, others remain more sparsely populated than America. Norway, Finland, and Sweden all have small populations and abundant open space, although much of this open space is in forests and mountains. Other countries, such as West Germany, Great Britain, and the Benelux (Belgium, the Netherlands, and Luxembourg) nations, have population densities comparable to the most highly urbanized regions of the United States. Despite extremely dense populations, some countries, such as Great Britain, France, and West Germany, have high proportions of arable land in comparison with their total land areas.

Much European farmland lies close to urban areas. In Belgium, for example, all of the country's farmland lies within so-called peri-urban areas. West German officials have classified 27% of their country's land area as peri-urban.

Not surprisingly, attitudes and policies on protecting farmland from urban encroachment vary considerably from nation to nation. Generally speaking, countries with low overall population densities, one or two large urban areas, and abundant open space do not place a high priority on controlling rural land use. They restrict planning activities to urban regions. Other nations have adopted specific policies to preserve agricultural land. Still others view urban encroachment as a natural consequence of industrialization and rely on foreign sources for agricultural products.

Even where the problems of peri-urban agriculture receive official recognition, approaches to solving these problems differ. Some countries take regulatory approaches to control rural land use, whereas others attempt to maintain agriculture as a land use competitive with industrial and urban uses. Policies that fall into the latter category include measures to increase the size of individual holdings, the provision of urban style cultural and social services in rural areas, and special tax benefits designed to keep farms in a family after the retirement or death of a generation of proprietors.

France, for example, places little emphasis on regulatory approaches. Instead, government-sponsored private corporations (SAFER's) buy and resell farmland to farmers interested in increasing the size and economic viability of their holdings. SAFER's have the right of first refusal in all land sales within this jurisdiction. They operate as revolving funds, buying and selling land, and paying nominal dividends to their investors. Because SAFER's historically have attempted to conserve their funds by purchasing lower cost rural land, their influence in peri-urban areas has been somewhat spotty due to higher land prices in these areas (see Chapter 12).

On the whole, European officials have somewhat less regard for the sanctity of property rights than is common in North America. European planners often make decisions affecting owners' property rights without compensating for the financial consequences of those decisions.

A relationship apparently also exists between population density and stringency of land-use controls. The Netherlands, Great Britain, and West Germany all feature comprehensive land management schemes, whereas the less densely populated Scandinavian countries, despite their reputation for imposing bureaucratic solutions to social problems, follow almost *laissez-faire* policies for rural land use.

Some Pertinent Examples

The following examples of agricultural land-use policy in selected countries represent major tendencies found throughout the world. Although some of these countries are not large or densely populated, the examples illustrate variations in land-use policy through observation of some archetypes.

Finland

Finland presents a fairly typical example of a sparsely populated country with few urban areas and little agricultural land. Not surprisingly, the lion's share of planning activities occur in and near urban areas, most notable the Helsinki region. Helsinki has experienced rapid growth in recent years. Although much of Finland's open space is mountainous and most remains in forest, the amount of agricultural land has declined because of reductions in rural population and urban growth.

The country's Building Act and Statute of 1958 establishes a system of regional, master, general, municipal, town, rural, and shoreline plans. The first three present general goals and policies to be followed in individual land use decisions. The latter, more localized plans, resemble American-style zoning maps in their specification of permissible uses.

Overall, these plans emphasize economic development. They do not address the urban encroachment issue specifically. However, the Helsinki regional plan attempts to steer new growth to areas with existing infrastructures (roads, sewage, utilities, and so on) to minimize the cost of development. If anything, the plans place greater emphasis on preserving forests, which are generally privately owned.

With limited agricultural production, Finland relies on foreign trade to provide much of its food. But this may change soon. Pending changes in the Building Act before parliament may place new emphasis upon agriculture.

West Germany

West Germany has accomplished the feat of rebuilding a war-shattered economy and accommodating a population of 60 million people in a land area the size of Oregon, while maintaining 29% of its land in forest and 55% in agriculture.

Since German basic law (akin to American and English common law) takes special note of "the social obligations of private property," it is not surprising that the West German system relies on an array of planning objectives backed by economic incentives. The most significant aspect of this system is urban limit lines within which developers have unlimited right to build, whereas tracts outside these lines are almost permanently devoted to low density land use. Inside the development zones, property owners may subdivide and improve their lands. In turn, the government cannot downzone these lands without paying compensation for development rights cost. Owners outside the development zone receive no compensation for adverse changes in their land zoning status.

Additional features of the German system that work to preserve agriculture include low property taxes on farmland and regulations that limit farmland purchases to farmers or other agricultural interests.

Great Britain

The United Kingdom enacted its first land development controls in the Town and Country Planning Act of 1947. The Act established a land planning system that includes two types of plans: structure plans, with goals and policies followed by a jurisdiction in individual land-use decisions; and local plans, which specify permissible uses on a property-by-property basis.

All new developments must receive approval by local government. The British system does not compensate landowners adversely affected by planning decisions. In contrast to the United States, the British consider land-use decisions a political function of local government rather than an administrative function. Policies applied on both the local and national levels vary according to which political party controls the relevant decision making body. Indeed, the story of land planning in Great Britain since World War II corresponds closely to the ebb and flow of Conservative and Labour party control of government.

The courts play a minor role in the British planning system. They have no right to overturn a decision reached by a governmental body. Also, parliamentary legislation usually includes clear policy guidance to local officials, further reducing the opportunity for judicial interpretation.

A continuing controversy in British land planning is the degree to which the public holds land development rights. The Community Land Act of 1975, passed by the most recent Labour government, nationalizes the right to develop land. Under the Act, local governments buy up undeveloped land and sell it to developers at its development value. In this way the public realizes the capital gains inherent in land development.

The Conservative opposition attacked the system as unduly socialistic, and some analysts suspect that landowners have trimmed back plans to improve or update their land until the new Conservative government honors the party's pledge to repeal the Act. Other observers criticize the law because it does not specifically require local governments to conduct their development activities in accordance with their local land-use plans.

This emphasis on land-use planning as a political process necessarily implies a great deal of public participation in planning decisions. Britain does indeed have a strong public planning constituency. Groups, such as the Council to Protect Rural England (CPRE), closely monitor land-use decisions all over the country for compliance, in CPRE's case, with goals of protecting open space.

In practice, British planners have shown great care for protecting open space and agricultural land. London's greenbelt is world famous as an example of open space preservation and control of urban sprawl. Where urban development does occur, most notably in the nation's new towns program, British planners take pains to steer it to areas of marginal agricultural promise, close to existing service infrastructures.

Despite England's extensive planning efforts, a great deal of controversy exists as to their efficacy. Some analysts argue that planning has failed, noting a sharp rise in urbanization of agricultural land in recent years. Others point to figures that show while an average of 62,000 acres (25,110 ha) of agricultural land were converted to urban uses each year in the 1930s, the urbanization rate declined to 29,000 acres (11,745 ha) annually in the 1950s, and rose only to 40,000–43,000 acres (16,200–17,415 ha) a year during the boom years of the 1960s.

Israel

Though accounting for only 5% of Israel's gross national product in the late 1970s, agriculture played a preeminate role in the nation's life and identity. Farming occupied a fundamental role in the ideology of Zionism and thus helped shape the historical development of the nation since the inception of the Jewish National Fund in 1901. Agricultural areas in Israel were utilized as a process for the socialization and integration of immigrants into the fabric of modern Israeli life. Water resource planning and development investments reclaimed hundreds of thousands of acres of arid desert lands. And finally, in a nation almost constantly on a war footing since its establishment in 1948, rural communities formed the basis of a national defense policy and often contributed to the settlement of new regions. The protection and retention of agricultural land had been a critical concern of Israeli policy since the founding of the modern state. Well before World War I, the Jewish National Fund (JNF) began to acquire land for the purpose of establishing agricultural settlements throughout Palestine, although the fund avoided the purchase of lands close to urban areas. Over 30% of the present population occupies lands owned by the JNF. With the establishment of modern Israel, it became national policy aggressively to maintain the integrity of the country's farming communities.

Israel's effort to retain land have been successful for three fundamental reasons:

1. Land-use planning was done by the national government and adopted plans were considered legally binding. The lack of a tradition of home rule, together with a long history of immigration and military conflict, enhanced the role of strong central planning and policy making.

2. Over 90% of all land in Israel was publicly owned. Private lands were found in the major cities, Tel Aviv, Haifa, and Jerusalem, and along the coastal plain and were subject to land-use controls.

3. Landowners did not have the right to develop land in uses other than those authorized in officially adopted plans, and hence there was little conflict over the kinds of legal issues which were encountered in the United States. A different land-use ethic existed in Israel, and when tied to historical themes inherent in Zionism, agricultural lands and farming communities enjoyed significant levels of protection.

Israeli agricultural and rural land policy is epitomized by the example of the Lankhish region, which extends from the coastal plains eastward toward the Judean Hills. Approximately 200,000 acres (80,972 ha) are within the Lakhish, almost all of it state owned. Though composed of some very rich soils farm development was not really possible until the construction of the Yarkon–Negev irrigation system. Intensive crop agriculture flourished in the well-irrigated central and western areas. The pasturing of beef and dairy cattle predominated in the less fertile and less irrigated eastern areas, as did small grain production. In all, nearly 45% of the Lakhish was farmed. A system of differentiated new communities was created to serve the population of the region, and many are still maturing. A typical area within the Lakhish is the "Nehora Block," which was composed of an urban center, Kiryat Gat; two smaller rural centers, Nehora and Even Shemu'el; several *moshavim* (small holder's cooperative villages), Zohar, Sede Dawid, Kakhav, Uza; and several *kibbutzim* (rural collectives) and *moshavas* (colonies of privately owned and operated small farms). Together these communities and settlements were organized to be mutually supportive in terms of services and amenities. They illustrate the high level of regional cooperation which Israeli planners had sought to achieve.

Israel imports considerable amounts of meat, vegetable oil, and grains, but self-sufficiency has been achieved in fruit and vegetable cultures, poultry, eggs, and dairy products. This sector has the capacity of producing substantial exports, which in the 1970s amounted to some 13% of all Israeli exports. This helped a generally negative trade balance. Israel's agricultural economy is quite strong, buttressed by major national investments in training, irrigation, technology, export policy, and based on a relatively secure farmland base.

Sweden

Sweden is a predominantly urban nation with only 10%, roughly 7.5 million acres (3,037,500 ha), of its land mass of arable quality. Agricultural production varies with climatic zone change. In the heavily urbanized south, where development pressures were strongest, soils are most favorable to farming. This region produces significant amounts of wheat, sugar beets, peas, and other field crops. In central Sweden the production of bread grains is predominant, and farther north, with a shorter growing season, fodder production assumes a larger role. Perhaps as much as 80% of all farm income in Sweden is derived from animal production, with dairying accounting for nearly one-third.

Farms in Sweden were decreasing in number, growing in size, and producing more per unit in the 1970s than in previous decades. Swedish agricultural policy in the 1970s encouraged these trends, though national planners were seeking to stabilize the number of farming units throughout the nation.

December 1977 was something of a watershed for Swedish agricultural policy. During that month the Swedish Parliament promulgated a number of new programs which have had important impacts on the structure of the nation's farming industry. National agricultural goals were established to create efficiency of farm size, assure favorable economic returns for farmers, and guarantee the Swedish consumer a reasonable supply of food at reasonable prices.

To achieve these results, the following programs were initiated or continued:

1. Domestic production was protected through tariffs on imported products.

2. Consumer prices were subsidized by the national government.

3. Credit guarantees were made available to farmers to help them expand their units and buy machinery to reach greater economies.

A system of County Agricultural Boards (CABs) was created to aid local farmers within their jurisdictions. Working under the Land Acquisition Act of 1965, the CABs operated directly with local farmers to consolidate local farms into more efficient units. Utilizing monies in the National Land Fund, approximately $73 million was spent by 1980 for this purpose. Each purchase had to be approved by the local CAB. Moreover, under other provisions of the law, the CAB monitored the sale of farmland and could refuse to permit a sale if there was reason to believe that the land would be taken out of farm use or be held for speculation. If the CAB refused to allow the sale, it had to purchase the land at the price agreed on by the farmer and the would-be purchaser. The CAB then held the land until it could sell to a local farmer. Rarely were lands held for a period longer than 2 years. The loan program developed in the 1977 legislation was one of the key mechanisms to retain Swedish farmland.

Yet some farms were purchased for investment, causing a rise in farmland prices, and a Land Purchase Commission was established to evaluate this problem. It is expected to develop proposals to restrict the purchase of farmlands to those who demonstrate the ability and desire to farm. A strong capital gains tax (Realisationsvinst), implemented in 1967, is a further mechanism to discourage speculation.

In the 1970s the average age of the Swedish farmer was 54 but increased steadily when young people chose high-paying positions in the country's urban areas. Because it was national policy to sustain family farming, loan guarantees were established to promote the entry of younger farmers. A deferred interest program, with loans payable over a 15 year period once farming was fully established, was the key to this program.

As Sweden's population grew, new land was needed for urban development. The CAB system provided for some preemption by urban development. This was especially important in the central and southern regions where growth was sustained, particularly in the suburban areas around such older central cities as Stockholm, Örebro, Gothenburg, and Malmö. Here lands were largely controlled by public land banks operated by urban municipalities. Sweden had a long tradition of municipal planning and local control, and land banking was a major element. The expansion of the metropolitan areas of these cities often meant that farmland was purchased by the municipality to prepare for eventual development. Around Stockholm, 135,000 acres (54,675 ha) were purchased for such development since the beginning of its land banking system in 1904.

An effort to consolidate urbanization and halt the spread of cities occurred during the 1970s. A location policy for Sweden was established which created 26 primary growth centers. It was anticipated that restricting development and growth within these areas would bring a degree of stability to farmland near urban areas, as well as regions where farming predominated.

Republic of China (Taiwan)

The Republic of China on Taiwan was, in the late 1970s, a highly urbanized and industrialized country and one of the most densely populated in the world. With a land mass smaller than the combined areas of Rhode Island, Connecticut, and Massachusetts, Taiwan had over 17 million people, and over half the land area is mountainous. Yet the nation substantially fed itself and exported considerable amounts of food.

Efforts to stabilize agriculture began with the transfer of the Nationalist government from the mainland to Taiwan in 1949. Following the original precepts of Dr. Sun Yat-sen, founder of modern China, the Nationalists, under General Chiang Kai-shek, initiated a major land reform program which vested land title in the peasants. The peasants purchased this land on terms they could easily manage out of the prior level of farm income.

Taiwan's land reform program consisted of three elements. First, rent control with written leases was established on all privately owned farmlands with rent limited to three-eighths of the rice crop in a given year. Second, lands in the public domain, a large area of arable land that the Japanese had acquired during their 50 years of occupation, were sold to the tillers in 7.5 acre (3.0375 ha) parcels on mortgage terms designed to keep payments also at three-eighths of the annual rice crop. Finally, the central government purchased all rental lands above 7.5 acres (3.0375 ha) and sold them to tillers at equivalent to three-eighths of the rice crop.

The landlords were compensated for their land through bonds, which carried a clause to protect the bondholder in case of inflation, and shares of stock in one of four corporations that had been left by the Japanese. Through this land reform, bona fide small family farmers got land on manageable terms and with it a degree of security which encouraged them to cultivate rice intensively (two annual crops) and also diversify into vegetable production between rice crops. From 1949 to 1955, when the program was substantially completed, the percentage of farmers who owned their lands increased from 57 to 80%, while tenant farmers decreased correspondingly. At the same time, efforts by the Joint Commission on Rural Development, a Sino-American agency, encouraged more efficient farming and better conservation. Improvements were made to the rural irrigation system. The result of these programs was a rice yield of approximately 1 metric ton per acre, one of the highest in the world. The production of bananas, sugar, and vegetables also increased significantly to the point that export markets were developed. Internally the government developed a system of farmers' cooperatives to market produce, supply fertilizer, and extend credit. Rather than creating a new mechanism, the government utilized formerly underground farmers' cooperatives, which had grown up during the Japanese occupation. These associations had played a key role during the Japanese times as sub-rosa bankers, and their credibility served the farmers and the Nationalist government well during the land reform.

In the 1970s a system of land-use planning and zoning was established to protect farmlands and to halt urban sprawl. This program was partly effective. As industrialization progressed, sprawl became more and more evident, and farmlands were idled along highways near rapidly growing areas. In 1973 the federal government passed an Agricultural Development Act in an effort to stop the conversion of agricultural lands to other uses. This law required permission of the central agricultural authorities for any conversion of high-grade farmland to other uses. The Regional Planning Act was passed in 1974 and refined the original Chinese Land Act. It remained the principal basis of land-use control. It required the classification of all land into one of 26 grades and stipulated that

1. Municipal governments (*Hsien*) designate all farmlands of grades one through twelve as agricultural lands that must be used for farming purposes unless changes were officially authorized.

2. All farmlands above the grade of eight should not be utilized for any construction except farmhouses, which must receive prior authorization.

3. Lands between grades nine and twelve should not be converted to industrial uses without the joint approval of the authorities of industry, agriculture, food, and land administrations.

4. Any deviations from these designations without approval would be regarded as illegal constructions and subject to heavy penalty.

A heavy windfall tax (unearned increment tax) was imposed in the 1940s to take for the government a substantial part of any profits from rising land prices. This, incidentally, softened the effects of the land control program.

Industrial development expanded throughout Taiwan, and attempts in the late 1970s to direct it onto lands without agricultural potential were relatively successful. The government encouraged the creation of industrial parks and sought to locate them in foothill areas, and it assumed the cost of road construction and also water pollution control. Public facilities, e.g., schools, hospitals, and government offices, were generally developed on public lands, and this further helped the government control the location and timing of development in fringe areas.

A second phase of the Regional Planning Act was implemented in the late 1970s with a pilot program in the southern Taiwan region, containing the cities of Kaohsiung, Tainen, and their rural hinterlands. Under this program, lands were zoned for certain uses, and these would be permanent, single-purpose classifications. The zones to be created included special agriculture, general agriculture, industrial, village, forest, scenic, slope conservation, and special use.

Taiwan also had a most successful program of land consolidation. Rice paddies, for reasons of irrigation, had to be precisely level and have hand-built terraces. The dikes followed contour lines. The result was a patchwork of small fields, and many farmers owned several, sometimes widely scattered. Furthermore, few fields had road frontage, and access was by narrow footpaths along the dikes. The process of consolidation involved the deeding of the small plots to the government, leveling large areas by heavy machine, and reparceling the land back to the former owners, but now in contiguous, rectangular blocks, each with road frontage. Additional benefits were better irrigation and better drainage. The government kept about 10% of the land to cover its cost. The value and productivity of the 90% returned were better than the small fields given up.

The system worked so well with farmland that it was later extended to city land, and large areas of small holdings were consolidated into lots large enought for apartment projects.

The government of the Republic of Korea (South Korea) implemented a system modeled closely on the successful elements of the Chinese experience on Taiwan.

Conclusion

It is difficult to draw general conclusions from the variety of experiences with agricultural land issues in Europe and around the world. As in the United States, where counties and states are adopting different programs, there is no single approach to farmland preservation in Europe or elsewhere in the world. At this time there is no clear national policy in the United States on farmland protection. In contrast, a few European governments have adopted strong policies, which they are implementing through direct land-use controls.

On the second point, land in the United States is regarded more as a market commodity than as a national resource. The rights of individual property owners are a dominant concern in any retention program. In several European nations property owners have much less discretion in changing from agriculture to another land use. In fact, it simply cannot be done in some instances. Agriculture is the established land use.

The likelihood of such a strong, national approach to agricultural land retention in the United States is uncertain. Open to serious question is the desirability of this deep an intervention into the traditional relationship between government and the landowner. But this relationship is certainly changing, and many would argue that government already has intruded deeply into the domain of private property rights.

In time a national posture or policy probably will emerge in this country on the maintenance of our most productive agricultural lands. It is not likely to be patterned in any purposeful way after any particular European experience, however. Rather, it will undoubtedly be general in scope, place the burden of emphasis on state and local governments, and, most importantly, acknowledge the need for equity in dealing with the private landowner.

References

Chassagne, E. 1977. Community of land use: Historical development and limitations and corrective mechanisms—the French system as an example. Organization for Economic Cooperation and Development, Paris, France.

Coughlin, Robert E. 1977. Saving the garden: The preservation of farmland and other environmentally sensitive land. Regional Science Research Institute, Philadelphia, PA.

Duerksen, Christopher J. 1976. England's Community Land Act: A Yankee's view, *Urban Law Annual* **12**, 49–76.

Ikaheimo, E. 1977. Peri-urban agriculture of the Helsinki region. Organization for Economic Cooperation and Development, Paris, France.

Lapping, M. B. 1980. Agricultural land retention: Responses, American and foreign, *in* "The Farm and the City," Archibald M. Woodruff (Editor). Prentice-Hall, Englewood Cliffs, NJ.

Lapping, M. B. and Forster, V. D. 1982. Swedish Agriculture and Land Policy: An Integrated Approach, *International Regional Science Review* 7:3, 293–302.

Lassey, W. R. 1977. "Planning in Rural Environments." McGraw-Hill Book Co., New York.

Miner, D. and Chorich, M. 1979. The European experience with farmland protection: Some inferences, *in* "Food, Farmland, and the Future," Max Schnepf (Editor). Soil Conservation Society of America, Ankeny, IA

Mrohs, E. 1977. Peri-urban agriculture in the Rhein-Ruhr region. Organization for Economic Cooperation and Development, Paris, France.

Organization for Economic Cooperation and Development. 1978. Agriculture in the planning of areas-synthesis report. Paris, France.

Organization for Economic Cooperation and Development. 1976. Land use policies and agriculture. Paris, France.

Reilly, W. K. 1976. Thoughts on the second German miracle, *CF Letter*. The Conservation Foundation, Washington D.C.

Shroad, M. 1976. Does planning check the rate of farmed land loss— arguments for and against? Council for the Protection of Rural England, London, England.

23

Farmland Protection in the Netherlands[1]

Frederick R. Steiner

The Netherlands is the most densely populated country in Europe. Some 14 million people live on 33,734 km² (13,177 square miles) of land, an area roughly the size of the states of Connecticut and Massachusetts combined (Fig. 23.1). Yet Dutch agriculture ranks as one of the most productive in the European Economic Community. While world famous for their bulb production, the Dutch are also active in other horticultural commodities, animal husbandry, and arable farming. For many commodities, Dutch farmers are able to feed their own people, but some agricultural products must be imported. However, on the balance, Dutch farmers actually produce a surplus of farm products.

Exports of agricultural products from the Netherlands exhibit a clear surplus over imports. According to the Ministry of Agriculture and Fisheries, agricultural products in 1978 accounted for about 24% of total exports and 16% of total imports. In 1978, exports totaled 26.5 billion guilders and imports 18.2 billion guilders, so that the agricultural export surplus amount to 7.7 billion guilders. (The exchange rate between Dutch guilders and U.S. dollars, of course, fluctuates daily. FAO's Trade Yearbook-1978, reported imports of 10.61 billion dollars and exports of 13.03 billion dollars, yielding a surplus of 2.42 billion dollars. Since 1978, the guilder has lost against the dollar which means the surplus would now be slightly lower in dollars.) The principal agricultural products imported from other countries are new materials for livestock, farming, and the food industry, largely grain from North America. Principal export products include poultry and eggs, livestock and meat products, dairy products, fruit and vegetables, and flowers, plants, and bulbs (Ministry of Agriculture and Fisheries 1979).

This ability to export agricultural products is astounding, given the country's population density of 415 inhabitants per km² (1062 people per square mile) compared to 23 per km² (59 per square mile) in the United States, excluding Alaska. With this population density, the pressure to convert agricultural land is, and has for decades been, intense. The

---

[1]This chapter was adapted from an article of the same title that appeared in the *Journal of Soil and Water Conservation* **36**(2), 71–76.

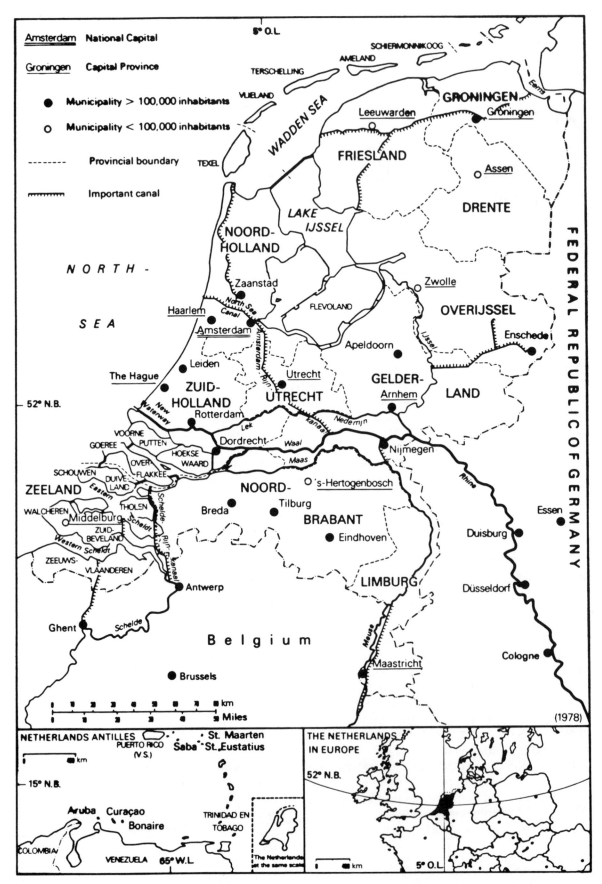

Fig. 23.1 Location of the Netherlands in Europe. (Courtesy of the Information and Documentation Centre for the Geography of the Netherlands, Utrecht.)

Dutch protect farmland in three ways: comprehensive physical planning, land reallotment programs, and the reclamation of new land.

Framework for Physical Planning

The Dutch define physical planning as "the guiding of a process of physical development of an area in order to promote the formation of an overall pattern best suited to the community" (Ministry of Housing and Physical Planning, no date, p. 5). Housing, transportation, agriculture, recreation, and natural areas all compete for space and each has its own constituency that lobbies for its interest. In addition, there is a special concern for the "landscape." The landscape includes housing, transportation, agriculture, recreation, and natural areas, and is given its own status in the physical planning process. To mitigate these various and often conflicting demands, it has been the national government's policy to encourage comprehensive physical planning. Because of high demand of often conflicting uses of the land, planning has evolved from "passive land-use planning to the active guidance of physical development" (Witsen 1977, p. 101).

Physical planning is an integral part of the national policy in the Netherlands. It has existed for about 100 years, developing from the improvement of housing to a complex system in which government agencies act in spontaneous developments within society, taking carefully formulated rules into consideration (van Mourik 1977). The first planning legislation, the Housing Act of 1901, was a result of slum housing conditions in urban areas. In addition to addressing housing, this initial law included provisions that made it possible to reserve land for laying out street, squares, and canals. So this early legislation only addressed the townscape or urban areas. By 1931, regional planning authority was incorporated into the act, which continued to undergo refinement. In 1962 a physical planning bill was passed with a new housing act. This legislation authorized national-, regional-, and town-scale land-use planning (Ministry of Housing and Physical Planning, no date; van Mourik 1977).

Physical planning in the Netherlands, then, is done on three levels: the national, provincial, and municipal, each with its own politically responsible bodies, which are at the same time the planning bodies. There are 11 provinces and approximately 800 municipalities. A fourth level exists in between the provinces and municipalities in some regions, such as the area around the city of Rotterdam. There is a hierarchical arrangement for decision making. Each level of administration is free to conduct its own policy as long as it is not in conflict with the policy of the higher level. The higher levels of government have the power to enforce their policy, if it is not adhered to by the lower levels. However, planning officials stress coordination and cooperation rather than coercion between the levels of governments and within each level (Ministry of Housing and Physical Planning, no date).

Making National Policy

Physical planning policy is established on the national level. It is important to note, however, there are differences between the organization of the national governments in the Netherlands and the United States. One major difference is that the Netherlands is a constitutional monarchy. The Crown is entrusted with the executive power of government. The Crown is comprised of the queen and the ministers, who are selected by the majority party, or a coalition of parties, in Parliament. The Dutch constitution establishes that the queen shall be inviolable and that the ministers shall be responsible. All acts and royal decrees are signed by the queen and countersigned by the minister responsible for their formulation and implementation. The minister responsible for physical planning is the minister of housing and physical planning (Ministry of Housing and Physical Planning, no date). The long standing existence of a monarchy, as a symbol of strong central control, is a marked contrast to the traditional American distrust of centralized government, even in the new federalism of the past several decades.

Although the minister of housing and physical planning is responsible for the preparation of physical planning policy, this policy is not developed in the vacuum of a single government department. The Dutch have developed an elaborate organization for interdepartmental cooperation. First, there is a cabinet-level committee comprised of various ministers, those from agriculture and conservation. At the provincial level, there is also a professional physical planning agency which conducts research and submits recommendations concerning regional planning (Ministry of Housing and Physical Planning, no date).

Information for the decisions made at the cabinet level is prepared by another interdepartmental committee comprised of staff from various departments, again including the Ministry of Agriculture and Fisheries. Alongside this committee of largely high-level civil servants, there is an advisory council comprised of technical experts from universities and the private sector and representatives from various special interest groups, including agricultural and conservation associations. This council has several task forces that study various physical planning issues and make recommendations.

Official supervision of the established planning policy is by the National Physical Planning Agency. This agency constitutes the administrative link between the central government on one hand and the provinces and municipalities on the other (Ministry of Housing and Physical Planning, no date).

The Provincial Role in Planning

Provincial governments are responsible for establishing regional plans and regulations and approving provincial policy in regard to physical planning. The executive branch of provincial government prepares such plans and policy, and it is approved by the legislative branch. The executive branch is also responsible for implementation of policy and reviewing municipal plans.

Each province also has a Provincial Physical Planning Committee, whose task it is to consider matters concerning physical planning and to submit recommendations to provincial authorities on how to perform the tasks entrusted to them pursuant to the Physical Planning Act. This committee is comprised both of regional governmental officials and members of special interest groups, including recreation and conservation. There is also a professional physical planning agency at the provincial level that conducts research and submits recommendations on regional planning (Ministry of Housing and Physical Planning, no date).

Municipal-Level Planning

The organization of planning responsibilities is similar at the municipal level where the strongest mechanisms for physical planning rest. Again, the legislative branch approves, thereby establishes, policy and the executive prepares planning alternatives and is responsible for implementation. Municipal-level planning must conform to national and provincial policy but may be modified for local conditions.

The Dutch municipal-level legislative branch would be analogous to the American county commission, city council, or township trustees. Since Dutch municipalities often include many towns and villages, their municipal councils are rather large bodies. The Dutch municipal executive branch, the aldermen and burgomaster, would be similar to the American mayor and city manager. Only the larger municipalities have their own professional town planning department. The majority of the municipalities use planning consultants (Ministry of Housing and Physical Planning, no date).

The planning at the municipal level most directly affects land owners and land users. Municipalities have two instruments of physical planning: the "structure plan" and the "allocation plan." The structure plan is similar to the American master or comprehensive plans. In the Netherlands, it consists of a description of the municipality's future development, the phasing of such development, and maps showing where the development will take place. The structure plan is accompanied by technical reports. Structure plans must be reviewed at least once every 10 years. There is a catch, however. Municipalities are not required to have a structure plan, so very few do. In any case, the actual planning power rests in the allocation plan (Ministry of Housing and Physical Planning, no date).

The municipalities have the power to establish allocation plans for their built-up areas and for those areas adjacent to built-up areas. These plans specify land-use allocations and regulations concerning the purpose for which the land and buildings on it may be used. They also give restrictions on developments. So if one wants to change the land use, he needs a permit.

The allocation plan is the only mechanism of physical planning which is binding on the citizens. A building permit is only granted if the project concerned is in agreement with the allocation plan. The same applies when the municipality decides a construction permit is required for works other than buildings (Manten 1975). Allocation plans are similar to the American mechanism of zoning, only it is much more difficult to change allocation plans in the Netherlands than it is to rezone property in the United States.

Provincial governments must approve municipal plans. They have the authority to direct changes in the municipal plans. This authority is exercised from time to time. Likewise, the national government, through the minister of housing and physical planning, can direct changes in provincial and municipal plans. This happens, but only once every 4 years or so.

Protecting Farmland

Now, how does this rather complex system of physical planning work to protect farmland? That depends on with whom one speaks. From the perspective of a tourist, or someone on a quick visit to the Netherlands, reading official reports, and speaking to top-level government officials, it is easy to surmise that everything is working excellently. This conclusion is especially easily reached when it is compared to American efforts to protect farmland. In reality, things are not quite that rosy.

The Netherlands is a lively democracy with numerous political parties ranging from monarchists to Marxists. Included are ecology and farmers' parties. Debates concerning planning issues are thorough and well informed at all levels of government. Local governments are given quite a bit of discretionary power concerning allocation plans. For example, the minister of agriculture may argue at the national level that a policy to protect farmlands should be adopted. But, this policy can be superseded, at the municipal level, if alternate uses for the land are deemed more important. In comparison with most American cases of local planning, agricultural land is indeed highly valued. It is not seen as undeveloped land ripe for conversion to other uses, but as land developed for agriculture. For instance, in one recent case, there were two alternatives for an extension of a town, that is, the building of a new town. One alternative was on a good farmland whereas the other was on more marginal land both for agriculture and building construction. The marginal land was chosen in the allocation plan, even though construction costs were double. It should be noted here that the extension of all urban areas is done through coordinated new towns. This results in a substantial savings in the cost of the construction and maintenance of utilities, transportation systems, and other urban services.

Are the farmers, the other land users, and professionals happy with the existing system? The common answers are "No, but . . ." and "Yes, but. . . ." Some people feel that regulations have gone too far, whereas others feel that regulations have not gone far enough. One farmer that I talked with, for instance, complained about all the governmental "red tape" necessary to build an additional house for his son. "Of course," he continued, "if we allowed all of them to build wherever they pleased, then we would have no ground left for farming. So, I guess, it's okay for him to live in the village, there's plenty of houses available there anyway."

Farmland-Related Problems

The Dutch face other problems in rural areas which they are attempting to address through physical planning. Many of these issues are similar to those being faced in the United States. The Dutch have identified several of these issues, all of which are interrelated to each other and each has some bearing on the protection of farmland. These issues include the following (van Mourik 1977, p. 140):

1. Rural centers generally face the problem of deteriorating amenities. In the smallest centers the cohesion of the social structure is endangered, while in centers of varying sizes, differences in the way of life give rise to tension.
2. The claims on space for all kinds of purposes as a result of urbanization occur at the expense of the rural area. In addition to the loss in a narrower sense, this increases uncertainty and the stability of the existing order.
3. Flows of people wishing to indulge in outdoor recreation lay a claim to space of a specific nature (large-scale aquatic sports for example) and create such problems as traffic congestion, air pollution and damage to nature reserves.
4. Roads, waterways, overhead high-voltage lines, pipelines, as well as purification installations, water reservoirs, etc., often have a disturbing visual effect.
5. Agriculture is experiencing difficulties because of the constant demands being made on agricultural land. At the same time farmers must increase production, without harmful consequences for the natural environment and the landscape.
6. The problem areas mentioned threaten to have an adverse effect on essential functions, more especially on ecological functions.
7. The landscape as the bearer of socio-historic characteristics and orientation elements of human scale is constantly being endangered.

These problems have been addressed by the minister of housing and physical planning and a number of his colleagues, including the minister of agriculture. From these discussions have come proposals of national policy alternatives, presented in the "Report on Rural Areas." The alternatives presented in this report are a series of models in which different land-use demands (urbanization, agriculture, nature/landscape) are each arranged in different mutual relationships over time. The basic question that is asked is should these land uses be segregated or integrated?

The problem is that changes in urbanization, agriculture, recreation, and nature occur at different rates. Urbanization occurs fast and is often irreversible. Changes in nature proceed gradually. Agriculture occupies a position somewhere in between. The report's authors concluded that, in view of these different rates of change, "complete intermingling of land uses is undesirable. Nature and landscape would soon be ousted by urbanization and agriculture" (Ministry of Housing and Physical Planning 1978, p. 13).

As a result, it was concluded that

> quite a lot of changes are taking place in the rural area. What these changes amount to is that stronger elements are pushing out the weaker ones. Urbanization forces back agriculture and nature. The developments in agriculture can have adverse effect on nature and landscape. The result is that variety in the rural area diminishes. The policy of the government, therefore, aims to protect nature and landscape against the adverse effect of urbanization and agriculture. Agriculture will in turn be protected against the unfavorable influences of urbanization (Ministry of Housing and Physical Planning 1978, pp. 16–18).

Again, this policy may be modified on the regional and municipal levels in response to local conditions. However, the Dutch government has taken the necessary steps to establish a coordinated policy concerning rural areas within its existing physical planning framework.

Agriculture land may also be affected by a voluntary government easement program. Certain areas have been specially designated by the national government as important for nature conservation and/or landscape values. These areas may eventually include some 200,000 ha (480,000 acres) or 10% of the agricultural ground in the Netherlands. In such areas, farmers are compensated for refraining from extensive agricultural development. In return for this compensation, which may vary from 500 to 1000 guilders per hectare ($100–$200 per acre), farmers refrain from such activities as digging deeper drainage systems, mowing intensively, applying certain amounts of fertilizer, or cutting hedgerows. In other words, farmers are encouraged with financial incentives to use traditional, low-technological agricultural practices. As might be expected, this program has not been enthusiastically embraced by many farmers. But it is a new program that offers a way to integrate nature conservation and landscape values with agriculture.

The Land Reallocation Program

A second program that is used to protect agriculture in the Netherlands is an extensive land reallotment or consolidation program. This program might be characterized as a Humpty Dumpty program. For several historic and physical reasons, parcel sizes in some areas of the Netherlands are too small for modern agricultural practices. These reasons include the dividing of land due to inheritance over centuries, the former reallotments of common areas, the smaller size of a landholding needed to farm in prior times, and the canal projects historically necessary to drain the land that created small islands for farming. As a result, it is necessary to reorganize farm regions so that farmers have a suitable amount of land to farm. It can be characterized as a Humpty Dumpty program because it is much easier to keep an entity together than it is to try to put the pieces back together once it has been broken apart.

The first Dutch Land Reallotment Act was passed to promote agricultural development in 1924. It was preceded by similar acts in other European states, such as Prussia, which were facing the same problems of small farm sizes. A modest budget was allocated by the 1924 act and the work started. The initial planning efforts by the government to reorganize farmholdings was predictably greeted by "many false notions and much mistrust and fear on the part of landowners and farmers" (Manten 1975, p. 200). By 1935, a government agency, the Service for Land and Water Use (formerly *Cultuurtechnische Dienst*, now *Landinrichtingsdienst*) was created in the Ministry of Agriculture and Fisheries to manage land reallotment programs, and in 1938 a second Land Reallotment Act was passed.

A description of the professionals who are largely responsible for the Service of Land and Water Use may be helpful because there is no direct American equivalent. They are called *cultuurtechniek* engineers and have their professional roots in the science of agronomy. In addition, they freely use the techniques of the disciplines of soil science, hydrology, regional planning, resource economics, and civil engineering, though each of these disciplines also exists independently in the Netherlands. *Cultuurtechniek* engineers are also active in Germany and Switzerland. In France the term *génie rural* is used.

The 1938 act simplified formation of a land consolidation project. As few as one-fifth of the landowners in an area could initiate a project, as could agricultural organizations and municipal governments. The 1938 act also widened the possibilities for the types of work that could be undertaken. In addition, to the construction, improvement and displacement of canals and roads, soil improvement, drainage, and reclamation works could also be executed. There were substantial government subsidies for much of this work. As a result, the number of applications for projects grew rapidly and the size of the Service for Land and Water Use steadily increased (Manten 1975).

World War II proved destructive both to Dutch cities and the landscape. Because of this massive destruction, there was an increased interest from farmers and some necessary modifications were adopted after the war. The Walcheren Land Consolidation Act of 1947 was passed to help reconstruct the island of Walcheren, which was nearly inundated during the war following the bombing of its sea dikes. The act added a number of new elements to the land consolidation process. These included the displacement of farm buildings, extension of the size of farms, construction of utility works, tenure regulations, and special attention to landscaping measures (Manten 1975).

The reconstruction of Walcheren served as a model for newer land consolidation developments. Land reallocation programs, which began as developments involving a relatively simple redistribution of land parcels, accompanied by improved drainage and soil improvement, soon became much more complicated, aimed at integrating the interests of agriculture, outdoor recreation, landscape management, public housing, and nature conservation (Ministry of Housing and Physical Planning, no date). These new purposes were incorporated into the third Land Reallotment Act of 1954, and the responsibilities were amended further in 1975. Further revisions have been made in a fourth act, discussed by Parliament during the early 1980s.

The Land Consolidation Process

Land consolidation projects do not occur overnight. A project may take from 15 to 25 years to complete. Each project has three phases: preparation, execution, and conclusion. The preparation phase may take anywhere from 3 to 15 years (10 years is average). It starts with an application to the provincial government. This application can be generated by an agricultural organization, by the national government, a provincial or a municipal government, by a water-control board, or one-fifth of the registered landowners in the area (van Lier and Taylor 1982). (Water has been and still is one of the major factors in Dutch history. Proper river and sea defenses and good water management were necessary for people to live and work in large parts of what is now the Netherlands. Water-control boards fulfilled this function. Many water-control boards have their origins as far back as the twelfth century, and their function has evolved ever since. Currently, they can be described as public bodies that are responsible for carrying out duties with respect to water control. Their jurisdictional boundaries are not necessarily coterminous with provincial or municipal borders.)

The application is then reviewed and ranked in relation to other requests by provincial and national officials from the Service of Land and Water Use. An inventory of the proposed project area is conducted and close contact is established with the preparatory committee from the community. The preparatory committee consists mainly of farmers and landowners, some officials, various representatives from government agencies as advisory members (such as extension agents), and some members of special interest groups (such as conservation organizations). The inventory includes detailed ecological, social, land-use, and economic data.

Once all the information is analyzed, a provisional plan is published. This provisional plan consists of an agricultural development plan, a landscape plan, suggestions for outdoor recreation, and suggestions for nature conservancy. This plan is then made available for public review and comment (van Lier and Taylor 1982). From experience, the Dutch have learned that it is best to coordinate planning efforts between government agencies. As a result, the plans of land consolidation projects are coordinated with the physical plans for consistency.

During the public review and comment period, representatives of the Service for Land and Water Use conduct numerous meetings in the community to explain the plan. Newsletters are printed announcing these meetings, and various aspects of the plan are described in simple, easy-to-read Dutch. Misunderstandings and objectives are aired and debated. Once governmental officials have attempted to incorporate the public's suggestions into the plan, the plan is put to a vote. All registered landowners and farmers are entitled to vote. The resolution to proceed with the land consolidation scheme is approved if the majority of the voters and/or the number of landowners who together hold more than 50% of the land in the proposed area are in favor (van Lier and Taylor 1982).

In the execution phase, which may take from 4 to 10 years, a local committee is appointed to be responsible for the implementation of the plan. Landowners, especially farmers, are appointed to the committee, which is assisted by a land surveyor and one or more experts, depending on the project's size. The district court appoints an examining magistrate to see that the law is properly observed and applied. The Service for Land and Water Use maintains control of the project during this phase. It oversees such matters as the assessment of the property values of land traded between farmers, the time planning of the project, and the construction and administration costs (van Lier and Taylor 1982).

The concluding phase varies in length depending on the project's size it usually is shorter than the two previous phases. During this concluding phase, all land transfers are made final with new deeds, project costs are levied, and regulations are developed for the new facilities. These may include roads, ditches and canals, utilities, farm houses and buildings, outdoor recreation facilities, and nature preserves (van Lier and Taylor 1982).

Extent of Land Consolidation

Land consolidation has been extensive in the Netherlands. Over 25% of the total area of cultivated land has been transformed since 1940 as a result of land consolidation legislation. Currently, between 40,000 and 45,000 ha (99,000–111,000 acres) per year are affected.

Land reallocation projects help to preserve Dutch farmland by developing the structure of the agricultural community. The approach is comprehensive and the Service for Land and Water Use has built a reputation for success over decades. This success has fostered trust and respect in the farming community. For Dutch farmers to remain competitive in the European and world markets, they must use their land and water resources wisely. Land consolidation projects, however, are expensive. This should provide a warning to the American agricultural community that it is much easier and less expensive to keep agricultural communities together than it is to try to piece them back together after they have been broken apart. Indeed there is some question whether all the king's (or queen's) men (and women) ever can put it together again.

Reclamation of New Land

The Dutch landscape is a result of human intervention; it is largely a made environment. An excellent history of the process is provided in English by Lambert (1971). Without human intervention, large tracts of land would be periodically or permanently under water (Fig. 23.2). The earliest inhabitants of the Netherlands built rudimentary mounds to which they could retreat with their livestock during periods of flooding. With a more developed social organization from the Middle Ages on, the Dutch adopted more elaborate means of protecting their lands against the water. They formed the water-control boards and built a system of dikes (earthen walls) to hold back the water. With the aid of windmills, they were thus able to drain the enclosed tracts of land, making them available for farming. These lands reclaimed from lakes or the sea are called polders. Polders initially encompassed small areas but eventually the reclamation techniques were extended to larger regions (van Lier and Steiner 1982).

The largest polders are those that have been built on the former Zuider Zee (Sea). The Zuider Sea was an extension of the North Sea into the heart of Holland. At one time, it must have been a large inland lake based on accounts by Roman historians. As early as 1667, the Dutch speculated on damming the Zuider Sea and reclaiming it. But the technology of the seventeenth century was not advanced enough to tame the tempestuous inland sea of nearly 400,000 ha (approximately 1 million acres). By the late nineteenth century, however, serious plans were developed by Cornelis Lely, an engineer (van Lier and Steiner 1982; Ministry of Transport and Public Works, no date).

Lely's plans were given serious consideration through a concurrence of several events. First, Lely became a politician of considerable stature, becoming the minister of public works. This put him in the position of being able to lobby for his plan in Parliament. Second, during World War I, the Dutch became painfully aware of how dependent they were on foreign countries for food. The third and perhaps a decisive factor was a massive storm in 1916 which caused extensive flooding in the area adjacent to the Zuider Sea (van Lier and Steiner 1982; Ministry of Transport and Public Works, no date).

In 1918, the Zuider Zee Act was passed by Parliament. In this act, the Dutch established three goals:

1. To provide a greater security against flooding
2. To form a freshwater reservoir
3. To enlarge the amount of existing agricultural acreage (van Lier and Steiner 1982, and Ministry of Transport and Public Works, no date)

The first two goals were realized by the completion of the Barrier Dam

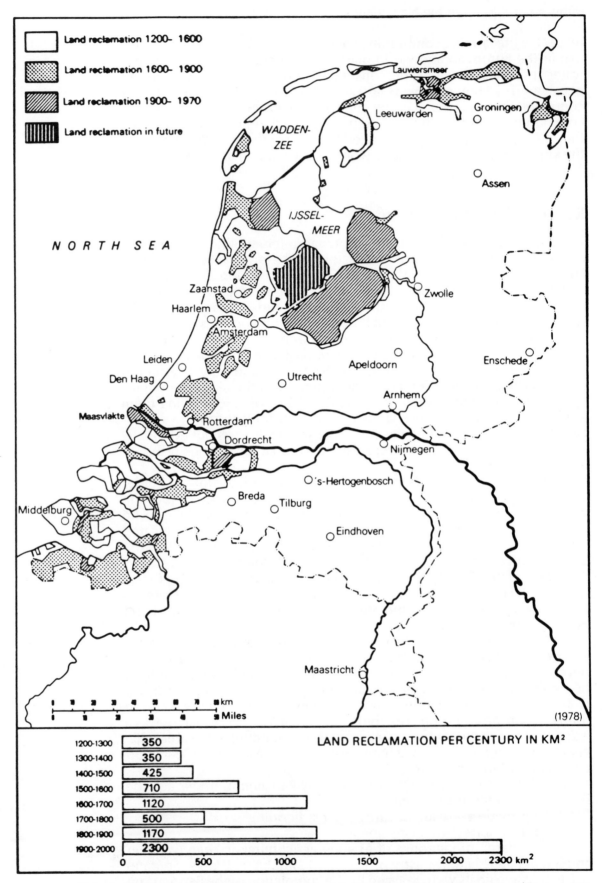

Fig. 23.2 Land gained in the Netherlands from lakes and the sea. (Courtesy of the Information and Documentation Centre for the Geography of the Netherlands, Utrecht.)

in 1932 which separated the Zuider Sea from the North Sea. The Zuider Sea then became a lake known as the IJsselmeer. The Barrier Dam provided a much shorter road connection between the western and northern regions of the Netherlands. The third goal was to be met by building five large polders: Wieringermeer, Northeast Polder, Eastern Flevoland, Southern Flevoland, and Markerwaard (Fig. 23.3). The first four of these polders have been constructed. The scale of agriculture in these polders is similar to that in North America, and the success of agricultural development in these areas contribute to the Dutch capacity to export farm products.

The first two polders were devoted almost entirely to agriculture. But the allocation of land use in the polders has changed over time. After World War II, the people in the Netherlands became much more acutely aware of the problems created by the shortage of space coupled with a rapidly growing population. The newer polders of the former Zuider Sea were in close proximity to Amsterdam. As a result, other purposes were incorporated into the planning of these polders, though agricultural interests were considered paramount. Other uses included complete new cities, new forests, recreation facilities, and even created "natural" areas for wildlife. So, as with their experience in physical planning and reallotment programs, the Dutch have adopted a comprehensive approach for the development of new lands reclaimed from the sea.

The final polder first proposed by Lely, now almost a century ago, is currently being debated. Opponents of the final polder, Markerwaard, argue that it creates superfluous space and can be developed only at the cost of the disappearance of a unique water body. Supporters regard the Markerwaard as important for the housing problems of the Amsterdam region and for the national food supply. Other options have also been discussed for the Markerwaard, such as a second national airport and a military base. The Dutch have taken considerable time, since 1972, discussing this issue and seem willing to air all the options before making a decision (Ministry of Transport and Public Works, no date).

However this debate is resolved, it is important to emphasize that the Dutch are willing to take time before reaching important planning decisions, and they are willing to listen to all sides of an issue. When decisions are reached, they seem to be willing to pull together and work for whatever the mandate is.

Lessons from the Dutch Experience

So the Dutch protect farmland in three ways. First, the use of land for agriculture is carefully weighed against other uses by comprehensive physical planning nationally and on the provincial and municipal levels. Second, the structure of agriculture is enhanced through extensive reallotment schemes. Third, new land is created for agriculture and other uses. What can be learned from the Dutch experience that may be helpful in North America?

The Dutch physical planning system is an excellent example of national land-use planning that allows local flexibility. However, the scale of the Netherlands is much different than that of the United States, Canada, and Mexico. It is doubtful if the Dutch national planning system could be adapted by any nation in North America, or even if such an adaptation is

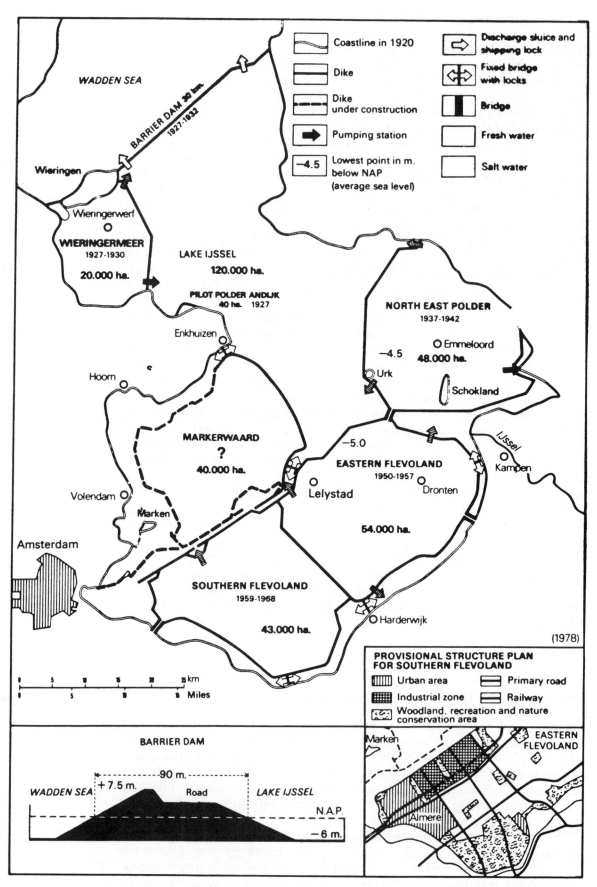

Fig. 23.3 The IJsselmeer polders. (Courtesy of the Information and Documentation Centre for the Geography of the Netherlands, Utrecht.)

Fig. 23.4   Dutch polders.   Courtesy of IJsselmeerpolders Development Authority, Lelystad, The Netherlands.

necessary or desirable. The Dutch have developed a system especially well suited for the ecology and geographic location of the Netherlands. However, the example of a nation adopting a policy that recognizes the importance of farmland to its people is one that could be followed.

Furthermore, some mechanisms for physical planning the Dutch have developed may be applicable at the state or provincial level. In fact, the Dutch system is similar in many respects to the programs land that have been developed in Oregon and Hawaii. These two states have adopted state-level land-use planning that recognizes the various, competing demands for space. In these states, agricultural needs are weighed against those of urbanization, recreation, and transportation. Both states have strong controls over local decisions, yet allow local flexibility.

There is a key lesson in the land reallotment program also: it is easier and less expensive to keep agricultural communities together than it is to reconstruct them once they have been broken apart. And there are further lessons in the process the Dutch use for consolidation programs. They take their time. Governmental officials talk to farmers, provide the farmers with facts, and listen to what the farmers have to say. Governmental employees spend a lot of time in the field and maintain close contact with local communities. As a result, there is a sense of cooperation and trust between farmers and governmental employees. There is also a good deal of intragovernmental cooperation. Plans are well publicized and suggestions from many groups are incorporated into plans.

Time is also an important factor in the reclamation of new land, much of it required to convert a water body to a muddy area, mud to a reed area, and reeds to farmable, livable land. Cooperation again is important. The scale of work involved in the Zuider Sea polders requires a high degree of intragovernmental cooperation which, in turn, requires a long-term commitment by the national government. Still, the government remains flexible and willing to incorporate the new suggestions and air new debates. As a result, the Zuider Sea polders have evolved multiple land uses, with the importance of farmland held high.

One important lesson that the Dutch learned from all their experience is that planning cannot solve all problems; it merely creates a framework for decision making. Several events have dramatically affected Holland this past century: World War II, the entrance into the European Economic Community, the changing status of former colonies, and sudden natural disasters. Although the Dutch have coped with these changes, some problems persist. Housing, for instance, remains a problem. Two-thirds of the housing in the Netherlands has been built since World War II. Yet, because of the massive destruction during the war, the population growth afterwards, the liberal immigration policy toward people from former colonies, and the ever-present problem of the scarcity of land and the abundance of water, a continual housing shortage remains. To their credit, the Dutch have not tried to solve this problem by needlessly paving over good farmland.

Over time, the delicate balance between the forces of nature and the needs of people in the Netherlands has created a social democracy based on cooperation. One gets the feeling that the Dutch are not a people mindlessly drifting from one crisis to another. Rather, they are willing to link knowledge to action.

References

Lambert, A. M. 1971. "The Making of the Dutch Landscape." Seminar Press, London.

Manten, A. A. 1975. Fifty years of rural landscape planning in the Netherlands, *Landscape Planning* **2**(3), 197–217.

Ministry of Agriculture and Fisheries. 1979. Aspects of Dutch Agriculture and Fisheries. The Hague, The Netherlands.

Ministry of Housing and Physical Planning. 1978. Summary of Rural Areas Report. The Hague, The Netherlands.

Ministry of Housing and Physical Planning. No date. The Rules of Physical Planning in the Netherlands. The Hague, The Netherlands.

Ministry of Transport and Public Works. No date. Room at Last. IJsselmeer Development Authority, Lelystad, The Netherlands.

van Lier, H., and F. Steiner. 1982. A Review of the Zuiderzee Reclamation Works: An Example of Dutch Physical Planning, *Landscape Planning* **9**(1), 35–59.

van Lier, H., and P. Taylor. 1982. Land reallocation and rural landscapes: the Dutch experience, *Landscape Architecture* **72**(2), 66–71.

van Mourik, W. J. G. 1977. Physical planning in rural areas, policy resolutions of the Netherlands government 1977, *Planning and Development in the Netherlands* **9**(2), 135–148.

van Mourik, W. J. G. 1978. Development of Planning in the Netherlands. Paper presented at a summer course in environmental science. The Agricultural University, Wageningen, The Netherlands.

Witsen, J. 1977. Crucial physical planning decisions, *Planning and Development in the Netherlands* **9**(2), 99–114.

Annotated Bibliography

The Issue of Agricultural Land
Protection-Overviews

Beldon, J., Edwards, G., Guyer, C., and Webb, L. (Editors). No date. New Directions in Farm, Land and Food Policies: A Time for Local and State Action. Conference on Alternative State and Local Policies, Washington, D.C. 319 pp.

This publication presents a progressive agenda on farm, land, and food policies for state and local action. Each of the seventeen chapters includes innovative approaches and policy alternatives that have been proposed and/or implemented in states, counties, and cities; several articles and reprints describing the most exciting of these new proposals; and a reference bibliography and a listing of key organizations. There is a resource and contact section of the book that contains additional references; newsletters; a listing of relevant federal, state, and local agencies; and organizations to contact for further information, publications, and technical assistance.

Blobaum, R. 1974. The Loss of Agricultural Land. Citizen's Advisory Committee on Environmental Quality. Washington, D.C. 30 pp.

This report looks at agricultural preservation and the increasing amount of land taken out of production. The major topics reviewed are a national inventory of soil and water conservation needs, the amount of land being planned for development through conversion of productive farmland to urban uses, the recreation home land boom, energy-related land demands, the economic impact of conversion, and planning techniques.

Cotner, M.L., Skold, M.D., and Krause, O. 1975. Farmland: Will There Be Enough? ERS-584. U.S. Department of Agriculture. Economic Research Service, Natural Resource Division, Washington, D.C. 15 pp.

This illustrated report presents 1974 statistics regarding cropland production, the amount of land added to and lost from agricultural production, the amount of land in SCS capability classes I–III, and an outlook for future land conversion.

Dideriksen, R.I., Hidlebough, A.R., and Schmude, K.O. 1977. Potential Cropland Study, Statistical Bull. No. 578. U.S. Department of Agriculture, Soil Conservation Service, Washington, D.C. 104 pp.

This SCS report is illustrated with charts, tables, and figures. The report is a result of an extensive survey concerning the amount of land available for conversion to agriculture. Also discussed are the general reasons why some land cannot be converted. These include climate, slope, the size of parcels, and other physical and socioeconomic reasons.

Fletcher W.W. 1978. Agricultural Land Retention; An Analysis of the Issue. A Survey of Recent State and Local Farmland Retention Programs and a Discussion of Proposed Federal Legislation (78-177 ENT). Congressional Research Service, Library of Congress, Washington, D.C. 52 pp.
This excellent brief synopsis of the agricultural land issue covers recent state and local farmland retention programs and a discussion of proposed federal legislation. The Congressional Research Service is the division of the Library of Congress which studies various issues for Congress.

Fletcher, W.W., and Grenfell, A.G. 1978. Preservation of Agricultural Land—An Annotated Bibliography (78-238 ENR). Congressional Research Service, Library of Congress, Washington, D.C. 55 pp.
This annotated bibliography includes such topic areas as nationwide estimates of present and future trends, the conversion of farmland to urban use, the conversion of farmland to nonurban use, limiting factors affecting agricultural production and land needs, and state and local programs and studies.

Fletcher, W.W. and Little, C.E. 1982. "The American Cropland Crisis." American Land Forum, Bethesda, MD. 193 pp.
This book describes how American farmland is being lost and what people are doing to protect it; why the protection of American cropland is an urgent strategic priority for the nation; and what must be done in the future, with special emphasis on new approaches to preservation adapted from Canada, France, and the private land trust efforts in the United States. Complete with illustrations, this paperback is meant for wide readership by all those concerned with farming and the use of land.

Frey, H.T. and Otte, R.L. 1975. Cropland for Today and Tomorrow, Agricultural Economic Rep. No. 291. U.S. Department of Agriculture, Economic Research Service, Natural Resource Division, Washington, D.C. 17 pp.
This illustrated report presents data on the nation's actual and potential cropland resources. The present cropland base is examined mainly in terms of cropland uses in 1973–1974 compared with 1969. Potential cropland is examined in terms of the characteristics and distribution of land physically suitable for crop use but now in noncropland uses, primarily pasture and forestry. A bibliography is included.

Isberg, G. 1973. Controlling growth on the urban fringe, *Journal of Soil and Water Conservation* **28**(4),155-161.
This article discusses the problem of urban expansion into areas of agricultural or environmental importance. Patterns of urban growth are

presented with several methods of controlling development. These methods include utility extension policies, large-lot or agricultural zoning, parks and open space policies, and improving communications between urban and regional planners and agriculturalists.

Lee, L.K. 1978. A Perspective on Cropland Availability, Agricultural Economic Rep. No. 406. U.S. Department of Agriculture, Economics, Statistics and Cooperatives Service, Washington, D.C. 23 pp.

This illustrated study analyzes the amount, location, and quality of land with cropland potential by region. Declines in the cropland base through irreversible land-use changes as well as the issue of prime farmland are investigated. In addition, future research needs are outlined.

Little, C. 1976. Shifting Ground: New Priorities for National Land Use Policy. Congressional Research Service, Library of Congress, Washington, D.C. 18 pp.

The shifting to new more finely tuned land-use planning issues provides the focus for this CRS report. These issues include energy development and conservation, worldwide food demand, the growth of community consciousness, an increasing demand to protect high-quality landscapes near metropolitan areas, and concern of the federal program comprehensiveness being overwhelmingly influential on land-use decision making. Explanations about the failure of early attempts in national land-use planning are also presented in this report. New approaches are discussed for effective land-use legislation.

Little, C. (Editor). 1979. Land & Food. The Preservation of U.S. Farmland. American Land Forum, Washington, D.C. 63 pp.

This well-written, illustrated publication provides an excellent overview of the issue; reports on the cropland squeeze, buckshot urbanization, and the policy gap are included. Several leading authorities offer their viewpoints.

National Agricultural Lands Study. 1981. "Agricultural Land Retention and Availability: A Bibliographic Source Book." U.S. Government Printing Office, Washington, D.C. 47 pp.

This annotated bibliography is one of the fine series of reports produced as part of the National Agricultural Lands Study.

National Agricultural Lands Study. 1981. Final Report. U.S. Government Printing Office, Washington, D.C. 108 pp.

This is the final report that resulted from an extensive eighteen month, interagency study initiated by former President Jimmy Carter. The study was charged with determining the nature, rate, extent, and causes of conversion of agricultural land to nonagricultural use; evaluating the economic, environmental, and social consequences of agricultural land conversion and methods used to attempt to restrain and retard conversion; recommending administrative and legislative actions to reduce potential loses that might result from continued conversion of agricultural land to other uses; and presenting a final report on findings and recommendations.

National Agricultural Lands Study. 1980. The Program of Study, Interim Rep. No. 1. U.S. Department of Agriculture and Council on Environmental Quality, Washington, D.C. 20 pp.
This report of the National Agricultural Lands Study describes the origin of the study, the problems it addressed, and the research design it followed.

National Trust for Historic Preservation. 1979. Rural Conservation, Info. Sheet No. 19. Washington, D.C. 28 pp.
This report discusses the importance of relating conservation and preservation efforts. An annotated bibliography and a list of resources are included.

Soil Conservation Society of America. 1975. Land Use: Food and Living, Proceedings, 30th Annual Meeting Soil Conservation Society of America August 10-13, 1975, San Antonio, Texas. Ankey, IA.
Subjects presented within this proceedings report include soil resources, air resources and land-use planning, environmental education, outdoor recreation, land use, food-fiber production potential, plant resources and fish and wildlife resources, erosion and sedimentation, waste management, environmental quality for living, and water resources.

Soil Conservation Society of America. 1976. Retention of Agricultural Land, Special Publication No. 19. Ankeny, IA. 30 pp.
This collected series of articles includes the topic areas of the overall issue of agricultural land retention, state and local programs, and planning methods for preservation. Professional planners, soil scientists, and other interested parties will find this publication helpful.

U.S. Department of Agriculture, Committee on Land Use. 1975. Perspectives on Prime Land, Seminar on Retention of Prime Land. Soil Conservation Service, Information Division, Washington, D.C. 257 pp.

These are the background papers from the Department of Agriculture's 1975 two-day seminar on the retention of prime lands. The topics covered by these papers include land-use trends, competing uses with agriculture, future agricultural land requirements, future forestry land needs, prime and unique lands criteria, the political and economic aspects of agricultural land retention, and the relationship of the states to the issue.

U.S. Department of Agriculture, Committee on Land Use. 1975. Recommendations on Prime Lands, Seminar on Retention of Prime Lands. Soil Conservation Service, Information Division, Washington, D.C. 54 pp.
This summary report from the Department of Agriculture's 1975 two-day seminar on the retention of prime lands includes findings, conclusions, and recommendations reached by the seminar participants.

Urban Land Institute. 1975. Agricultural retention: An emerging issue, *Environmental Comment*, No. 21. Research Division, Washington, D.C. 17 pp.
This *Environmental Comment* is devoted to farmland retention. Topics of the articles include the overall issue of agricultural land preservation,

use-value farmland assessments, legal aspects, and alternatives for rural development.

Yannaconne, V.J., Jr. 1975. Agricultural lands, fertile soils, popular sovereignty, the trust doctrine, environmental impact assessment and the natural law. *North Dakota Law Review* **51,** 615-653.

This important article discusses the legal aspects of agricultural land preservation, with special attention paid to constitutional law. Although land-use attorneys and planners will find this article most helpful, it is well written and accessible enough to be interesting to others.

Local and Regional Programs

Bureau of Environmental Planning. 1978. Exploring the Use of TDR in Pennsylvania, Conference Proceedings, Environmental Planning Inf. Series Rep. No. 2. Department of Environmental Resources, Harrisburg, PA. 102 pp.

This report was developed as a result of a southeastern Pennsylvania conference among several state and local planning agencies and commissions where the Transferable Development Rights (TDR) concept was discussed. Three case studies of the use of Transfer of Development Rights in Chester County, Pennsylvania, are included.

Conklin, H.E. 1967. Property Tax Incentives to Preserve Farming in Areas of Urban Pressure, No. 76-2. Cornell University Agricultural Experiment Station, Department of Agricultural Economics, Ithaca, NY. 7 pp.

This paper discusses the issue of agricultural land retention along the urban fringe with case studies of two counties in the state of New York: Orange County (a semirural area) and Suffolk County (a semisuburban area). Land retention methods of agricultural districts with farm-value assessments and property tax incentives are discussed as present attempts to preserve the agricultural livelihood of these two counties. The paper is helpful to both administrators and those interested in farmland retention strategies.

Gale, D.E. and Yampolsky, H. 1975. Agri-zoning—How they're gonna keep'em down on the farm, *Planning* (October).

This short article reviews the Suffolk County issue of decreasing agricultural land due to farmers selling to developers and the methods used in the county to combat this problem. Discussed briefly as methods for retaining agricultural lands are preferential tax schemes and the transfer of development rights. Most academic libraries carry *Planning*.

People for Open Space. 1980. Endangered Harvest. The Future of the Bay Area Farmland. San Francisco, CA. 80 pp.

People for Open Space is a San Francisco Bay Area-wide nonprofit citizen conservation organization. The report was a result of a two-year farmlands conservation project.

Toner, W. 1978. Saving Farms and Farmlands: A Community Guide Rep. No. 333. American Planning Association. Chicago, IL. 45 pp.

This down-to-earth report reviews both the purpose of saving farm-lands and how to approach solving the problem of agricultural land conversion. Illustrated with photographs and graphics, the case studies reviewed include Walworth County, Wisconsin; Columbia County, Wisconsin; Black Hawk County, Iowa; and Tulare County, California. This practical and well-written report should be of interest both to professional planners and concerned citizens.

Toner, W. 1981. Zoning to Protect Farming, A Citizens Guidebook, National Agricultural Lands Study. U.S. Government Printing Office, Washington,D.C. 32 pp.

This publication is for citizens interested in using local zoning ordinances to protect farming. It explains reasons people give for protecting farms and farmland, describes how farms are converted to nonagricultural uses, explains zoning tools available to protect farmland, and includes some reference case studies of farmland protection.

Steiner, F. and Theilacker, J. 1979. Locating feasible areas for rural housing in Whitman County, Washington, *Journal of Soil and Water Conservation* **34**, 283-285.

This article is a review of a natural resource inventory and rural housing feasibility study conducted in Whitman County, Washington. This study was an effort to identify lands feasible for rural housing in a county where the preservation of the agricultural economy is the primary goal. The study was conducted in concurrence with the newly adopted guidelines for rural home site selection as adopted in the 1978 county comprehensive plan.

State Programs

Barrows, R. 1978. Wisconsin's Farmland Preservation Program (Circ. G2890). University of Wisconsin Extension Circular. Madison, WI. 4 pp.

This concise circular provides an excellent explanation of Wisconsin's Farmland Preservation Program by its first administrator. Planning standards are explained for both the first and second phase of the program. Wisconsin's program seeks to stimulate local initiative and to combine tax incentives with local planning and zoning and with conservation practices.

Conklin, H.E. and Bryant, W.R. 1974. Agricultural Districts: A Compromise Approach to Agricultural Preservation, No. 74-22. Cornell University, Department of Agriculture Economics, Ithaca, NY. 7 pp.

This paper reviews briefly the rural land use situation in the state of New York, and then discusses the state Agricultural District Law. New York's Agricultural District Law contains a series of interrelated programs designed to encourage the continuance of agriculture under conditions of urban sprawl and its associated problems. Other states with similar rural land-use problems may find this approach helpful.

Hunt, M. and Smith, C. 1977. Deciding the future of Pennsylvania's farmland, *Facts and Issues*, League of Women Voters of Pennsylvania. 6 pp.

This short article contains a very extensive review of two agricultural preservation laws used in Pennsylvania: Act 515 of 1966 and Act 319 of 1974. Differential assessment, the assessment of the value of land in its current use rather than its market value, is discussed as the major emphasis of both these Acts. The effectiveness of these Acts in preserving farmland and open space as seen through public participation in the programs is evaluated. Though written for Pennsylvania citizens, others may find this article helpful.

Land Conservation and Development Commission. 1977. Oregon's Agricultural Land Protection Program. Salem, OR. 3 pp.
This is a brief explanation of Oregon's land-use policy of 1973 and its older Greenbelt Law of 1961 and how each relate at the protection of farmland. Like Wisconsin, Oregon links its tax policies to local comprehensive planning and zoning. Oregon goes one step further and requires all local governments to comply with statewide goals. For agricultural preservation, Oregon specifies that lands with low SCS soil capability ratings be placed in exclusive farm use zones.

Land Conservation and Development Commission. 1978. Statewide Planning Goals and Guidelines. Salem, OR. 24 pp.
This newsprint circular clearly explains all of Oregon's 19 statewide planning goals and guidelines, including goal No. 3, Agricultural Lands, and goal No. 14, which deals with the establishment of urban growth boundaries. This circular should be of interest to anyone interested in agricultural preservation or planning in general.

Mitchell, J.B. 1978. An Analysis of Land Use Legislation in Selected States, Research Bull. No. 1100. Ohio Agricultural Research and Development Center, Wooster, OH. 25 pp.
The major purpose of this bulletin is to examine land-use legislation and policies of selected states and organizational structures involved in implementing these policies, plus related observations concerning the effectiveness of the programs.

Pease, J.R. and Jackson, P.L. 1979. Farmland preservation in Oregon, *Journal of Soil and Water Conservation* **34,** 256-259.
This article provides an excellent review of Oregon's farmland preservation program.

Wilson, L. U. 1979. State Agricultural Land Issues. The Council of State Governments, Lexington, KY. 75 pp.
This publication provides a comprehensive introduction to agricultural land issues and related problems: farmland preservation, foreign investment, agricultural water problems, erosion, and other concerns. It attempts to bring these matters together into a single perspective to stimulate thinking on state roles and responsibilities present and prospective.

Federal Programs

Jeffords, J.M. 1979. Protecting farmland: Minimizing the federal role, *Journal of Soil and Water Conservation* **34,** 158-159.

In this editorial, Congressman Jeffords stresses the importance of protecting farmland from two equally important enemies, erosion and competing land use. Jeffords believes that time is of the essence in protecting farmland at the local level, before this resource is affected by federally managed land use planning. Two congressional bills, the Agricultural Lands Protection Bill and a bill centered at the prevention of erosion (Soil Conservation Bill), are explained as to their contribution to farmland protection programs managed by local officials, farmers, and all citizens concerned about their individual rights.

U.S. Congress. 1978. Agricultural Land Retention Act, *Congressional Record* **124** (February 23).
The Agricultural Land Retention Act was proposed by Vermont Representative James Jeffords in the 95th Congress. Though the measure did not pass then, a similar bill was introduced by Representative Jeffords in the 96th Congress. The Act proposed the formation of an Agricultural Land Review Commission and the establishment of demonstration programs.

U.S. Congress. 1979. Farmlands Protection Act, *Congressional Record* **125** (March 27).
The Farmlands Protection Act was proposed by Washington Senator Warren G. Magnuson in the 95th Congress. The act proposed a national farmland policy and research and technical assistance programs.

U.S. Congress. 1980. Agricultural Land Protection Act, *Congressional Record* **126** (February 6 and 7).
The Agricultural Land Protection Act was proposed by Vermont Representative James Jeffords in the 96th Congress. The Act lost by a narrow margin.

U.S. Department of Agriculture. 1978. Statement on Land Use Policy, Secretary's Memo. No. 1827, revised. Washington, D.C. (October 30). 5 pp.
The purpose of this policy was to coordinate USDA programs as they affect the preservation of agricultural land.

U.S. Environmental Protection Agency. 1978. EPA Policy to Protect Environmentally-Significant Agricultural Land, Memo. and related appendix from Administrator Douglas Costle. Washington, D.C. (September 8). 37 pp.
The purpose of this policy was "to establish EPA policy that will recognize the food production and environmental value of agricultural land and the necessity to protect them." This policy is anticipated to affect EPA's construction grant program for municipal sewage treatment works, which has been criticized by many for contributing to urban sprawl.

International Programs

Best, R. 1979. Land-use structure and change in the EEC, *Town Planning Review* **50**, 395-411.
This article reviews land-use structure and change in the European

Economic Community (Common Market). Major attention is paid to the inconsistencies of data between the various European countries.

Bray, C.E. 1979. Canadian Land Use, Foreign Agricultural Economic Rep. No. 155. Economics, Statistics, and Cooperative Service, U.S. Department of Agriculture, Washington, D.C. 34 pp.
This study examines the potential of Canada's prime agricultural land, the loss of agricultural land through urbanization, determinants of farmland prices, and land-use and tenure programs in five provinces.

Government of Ontario. 1978. Food Land Guidelines: A Policy Statement of the Government of Ontario on Planning for Agriculture. Ministry of Agriculture and Food, Food Land Development Branch, Toronto, Ontario. 28 pp.
This statement explains Ontario's agricultural planning policy, the methods used for identifying agricultural resource lands, and implementation guidelines for achieving the policy. Ontario's policy should be interesting to those approaching agricultural preservation on the state level.

Manten, A.A. 1975. Fifty years of rural landscape planning in the Netherlands, *Landscape Planning* **2**, 197-217.
Rural planning in the Netherlands dates back to 1924. Its primary original purpose was the improvement to agricultural land use. In recent years many other developments have affected the rural areas, and the need for integrated rural planning is continuously increasing. The problems with adopting to these changing demands are reviewed in this article.

Ministry of Housing and Physical Planning. No date. The Rules of Physical Planning in the Netherlands. The Hague, The Netherlands, 36 pp.
This report reviews the structure and process of physical planning in the Netherlands. Physical planning is a highly developed art in the Netherlands. Dutch planners delicately balance the demands of various land uses, including agriculture.

Ministry of Housing and Physical Planning. No date. Summary of Rural Areas Report. The Hague, The Netherlands. 36 pp.
This report summarizes in English a larger report conducted to review the problems facing rural areas in the Netherlands. Many of the problems are familiar to those in North America; others are specific to the Netherlands.

Ministry of Housing and Physical Planning. No date. Summary of the Report on Urbanization in the Netherlands. The Hague, The Netherlands. 14 pp.
The flip side of the protection of farmlands is the accommodation of growth in urban areas. This report summarizes in English a larger report conducted to review the problems facing urbanization in the Netherlands.

Strong, A.L. 1980. "Land Banking, European Reality, American Prospect." Johns Hopkins University Press, Baltimore, MD.

Land banking is a normal municipal activity in much of Western Europe. Cities bank land so that their development will occur in accord with plans and when infrastructure is ready, and so that gains in land value due to public development decisions will be shared by the public.

Methods for Protecting Agricultural Land

Barron, J.C. and Florea, B. 1973. Open Space Taxation: Guidelines for Assessing Open Space Property Values; (E.M. 3426. Washington State University, College of Agriculture, Cooperative Extension Service. Pullman, WA. 19 pp.

This circular discusses the use of the Open Space Taxation program for assessing the true and fair value of farm or open space lands in the state of Washington. The major issue discussed is how to determine the value of land by using land classification systems. The second issue discussed is methods for determining the net income of the classified groups along with an estimation of the land value by capitalizing income.

Block, W.J. 1969. Rural Zoning: People, Property and Public Policy. E.B. 600. Washington State University, College of Agriculture, Cooperative Extension Service, Pullman, WA. 32 pp.

This circular discusses the differences between (urban) metropolitan and nonmetropolitan (rural) zoning. The potential and limitations are presented as well as public misconceptions and misunderstandings about rural zoning. Also discussed in this report are the zoning incentives (suburban growth, highways, infringements) and techniques and processes to bring about effective zoning plans.

Boyce, D.E., Kohlhase, J. and Plaut, T. 1978. The Development of a Planning-Oriented Method for Estimating the Value of Development Easements on Agricultural Land. Regional Science Research Institute, Philadelphia, PA. 54 pp.

This paper presents a method that can be used to estimate the value of development easements on agricultural land for general planning purposes. The paper discusses a method for estimating the market value of land, then addresses the problem of estimating agricultural use values, and concludes by combining these two sets of estimates to determine the value of development easements.

Conklin, H.E. (Editor). 1980. Preserving Agriculture in an Urban Region, Northeast Regional Project 90 Rep. Cornell University, Ithaca, NY. 30 pp.

This is the final report of the major findings of a Northeast regional project that studied rural land-use policy in an urbanizing environment.

Coughlin, R.E. and Keene, J.C. (Editors). 1982. "The Protection of Farmland: A Reference Guidebook for State and Local Government," National Agricultural Lands Study. U.S. Government Printing Office, Washington, D.C. 284 pp.

The intent of this guidebook is to provide a reference guide to programs currently used to protect agricultural land: to identify their elements, document the experience that state and local governments have had with them, identify their intended and unintended costs, and comment on their long- and short-term effectiveness. The authors accomplish these goals masterfully.

Gray, W.H. 1975. Methods of Agricultural Land Preservation, E.M. 3906. Washington State University, College of Agriculture, Cooperative Extension Service, Pullman WA. 8 pp.

This circular reviews several methods for retaining productive agricultural lands including property taxation programs and agricultural and flood plain regulations. The circular includes a matrixed comparison of policy tools designed to preserve agricultural land.

Jacobs, P. 1971. Landscape development in the urban fringe. A case study of the site planning process, *Town Planning Review* **42**, 342-360.

The author proposes a method for evaluating the impacts associated with urban growth. A case study of an area near Halifax, Nova Scotia, is used.

National Agricultural Lands Study. 1981. "Case Studies on State and Local Programs to Protect Farmland." U.S. Government Printing Office, Washington, D.C.

This exhaustive, detailed volume reviews case studies of various methods for farmland protection. Studies include agricultural districting, zoning, purchase of development rights, growth management, state programs, and the siting of public facilities. Examples are included from throughout the United States.

Reganold, J.P. and Singer, M.J. 1977. Defining Prime Agricultural Land in California, Environmental Quality Ser. No. 29. University of California, Davis, CA. 45 pp.

This report discusses the issue of urban encroachment on prime agricultural land in California and the need for preserving farmland. Methods for identifying those lands to preserve and a discussion of implementation possibilities are included. The methods reviewed for defining prime agricultural lands are the USDA Capability Classification System and Land Inventory and Monitoring System, the Storie Index, Black Hawk County's Corn Suitability Rating System, Canada's Land Capability System, California's legislative definitions, and those methods employed in Tulare County and the city of Visalia. The report is illustrated with tables and includes an extensive bibliography.

Stockham, J. and Pease, J.R. 1974. Performance Standards. . . A Technique for Controlling Land Use, Special Rep. 424. Oregon State University Extension Service. Corvallis, OR. 50 pp.

This report examines various land-use control techniques available to the planner as supplements or alternatives to zoning for implementing plans. Emphasis is placed on the performance standard as a tool for determining proper land-use decisions. Case studies of performance zoning include Franklin County, Massachusetts; Gay Head, Massachusetts; Knoxville, Tennessee; Chicago, Illinois; New York, New York; and Duxbury, Massachusetts.

Trudel, P.A. (Editor). 1980. *Gonzaga Law Review* **15**(3), 621-956.

Most of this issue of the *Gonzaga Law Review* is devoted to agricultural land preservation. Articles by John C. Keene and Richard W. Dunford are included. There are also other interesting pieces on the various legal aspects of farming.

U.S. Department of Commerce. 1975. Zoning for Small Towns and Rural Counties. Economic Development Administration. Washington, D.C. 97 pp.

This report for county and local administrators, planners, and officials discusses community development problems and how they may be solved through zoning. The report, presented in a "handbook" format, includes a section on agricultural zoning.

Washborn, W.E. 1976. A new way to place money back into our farmlands, *Planning,* 25-27.

This article discusses the agricultural land preservation method, Transfer Fee Plan (TFP), for discouraging the conversion of reserve land to a nonfarm use. This approach proposes the creation of prime farmland reserves in counties with commercial food or fiber production, provisions for jurisdiction over the reserves by county prime land preservation boards, and distribution of penalty payments to those landowners in the TFP program as compensation for lost development rights.

Other Helpful References

Barron, J.C. 1972. Economics of Environmental Management, E.M. 3654. Washington State University, College of Agriculture, Cooperative Extension Service, Pullman, WA. 24 pp.

This publication describes the conceptual framework of economics as it relates to environmental management. The basic tool kit of the economist is inventoried in a simplistic manner and applications are made to environmental issues. A list of references for empirical information on specific effects and control systems is provided.

Beatty, M.T., Peterson, G.W. and Swindale, L.D. (Editors). 1979. "Planning the Uses and Management of Land." Society of Agronomy, Madison, WI. 1028 pp.

This is an excellent, comprehensive review of land-use planning. Major topics include the present status of land uses and land-use planning, data bases, planning cultivated uses, planning range land uses, planning forest and woodland uses, planning metropolitan uses, planning for transportation systems and utility corridors, planning for waste disposal, planning diverse land uses, and integrated land-use, planning, and plan implementation.

Beek, K.J. 1978. "Land Evaluation for Agricultural Development." International Institute for Land Reclamation and Improvement. Wageningen, The Netherlands. 333 pp.

K. J. Beek is a scientist at the International Institute for Land Reclamation and Improvement at Wageningen, The Netherlands. This book explores land evaluation for agricultural development with a special emphasis on land-use systems analysis for Latin America. The major topics include the purpose of land evaluation the land utilization type concept, approaches to land evaluation, and a systems approach in specific purpose land evaluation. A Spanish language summary is included.

Berry, W. 1970. "A Continuous Harmony, Essays Cultural and Agricultural." Harcourt Brace Jovanovich, New York, 182 pp.
Kentucky poet Wendell Berry's theme in this collection of essays is the relationship of humanity to the earth. The essays help to form an ethical, ecological basis for land uses and farming.

Berry. W. 1977. "The Unsettling of America Culture and Agriculture." Sierra Club Books, San Francisco, CA. 228 pp.
Here Berry takes on what he terms "orthodox, agricultural policy" and former Secretary of Agriculture Earl Butz.

Bosselman, F., Callies, D. and Banta, J. 1973. "The Taking Issue: An Analysis of the Constitutional Limits of Land Use Control." Council on Environmental Quality, Washington, D.C. 329 pp.
This publication presents an in-depth examination of the constitutional parameters within which land-use regulation must operate. As land-use regulation is implemented in the United States as a response to environmental problems, the "taking" issue, that is the issue of the constitutional legality of land-use regulation, is foreseen by the authors to become a key issue. This book takes a close look at this "taking" issue, cites many previous court decisions, presents an overview of current land-use problems, reviews the historical development of the "taking" issue, reviews current U.S. laws relating to these issues, and discusses likely future trends in the interpretation of this law. The book is thus intended for planners and specialists in environmental law who may well expect to encounter legal actions that question the constitutionality of land-use planning regulation.

Bosselman, F. and Callis, D. 1971. "The Quiet Revolution in Land Use Control." U.S. Government Printing Office, Washington, D.C. 327 pp.
The Council on Environmental Quality commissioned this report on the innovative land-use laws of several states in order to learn how some of the most complex land-use issues are being addressed. This is basic reading for those with an interest in land-use issues.

Delafons, J. 1969. "Land-Use Controls in the United States." MIT Press, Cambridge, MA. 203 pp.
This is an account of the American system of land-use controls as seen by a British observer in 1960.

Fletcher, W. W. 1980. Farm Land and Energy: Conflicts in the Making, National Agricultural Lands Study, Interim Rep. No. 3. U.S. Government Printing Office, Washington, D.C. 35 pp.
This report describes the possible future effects of energy development on agricultural lands. It addresses some of the conflicts that may

arise as the nation's energy demands evolve. Suggestions are made concerning how to integrate energy and agricultural policy so that they are as mutually supportive as possible.

Getzels, J. and Thurow, C. (Editors). 1979. "Rural and Small Town Planning." The Planners Press, Chicago, IL. 326 pp.
This book was based on a report prepared for the Old West Regional Commission of Billings, Montana, by the American Planning Association of Chicago. Using mostly Western examples, the authors review planning techniques most applicable to rural areas and small towns.

Hagman, D.G. and Misczynski, D.J. No date. Windfalls for Wipeouts: Land Value Capture and Compensation. The American Society of Planning Officials. Chicago, IL. 660 pp.
This report discusses the benefits (windfalls) and losses (wipeouts) to land and real estate often as a result of governmental projects and regulations. The report discusses windfall recapture techniques including special assessments, sale of development permission, land-value taxation, and several others.

Lapping, M.B. (Guest editor). 1975. Agriculture and urbanizaiton, *Journal of the American Institute of Planners* **41** (6), 369-396.
This symposium volume contains three thoughtful articles about agriculture and urbanization. These articles include: "Urban Threats to Rural Lands: Backgrounds and Beginnings" by Phillip M. Raup; "Differential Assessment as Land Use Policy: The California Case" by Gregory C. Gustafson and L.T. Wallace; and "New Farmland Preservation Programs in New York" by William R. Bryant and Howard E. Conklin.

Lassey, W.R. 1977. "Planning in Rural Environments." Mc-Graw Hill Book Co., Inc. New York. 257 pp.
This book describes the issues and elements with which rural planners must deal. Methods and procedures for improving the rural planning process are discussed, including strategies for the improvement of human services in rural regions. Planning concepts and methods are illustrated through a series of case examples and diagrams are used to integrate the key issues and variables discussed in each chapter. The text concludes with a critical discussion of education for planning and presents and adapted organizational structure for rural regions to support improved planning mechanisms and processes.

McHarg, I.L. 1969. "Design with Nature." Natural History Press, Garden City, New York.
A classic. For McHarg's foresighted comments concerning the protection of farmland see the chapter "A Response to Values," which was based on work he did with his former partner David Wallace for the Valleys Region of Maryland.

Meyer, P. 1979. Land rush: a survey of America's land, who owns it-who controls it, how much is left, *Harpers* (January).
This report is a very thorough review of America's land, through ownership, including private, federal, state, local, and Indian trust land, who profits from the harvest, the price of the land, and the changes in

major uses of land. A review of land legislation and a presentation of land rush examples conclude this well-researched article. Complete with charts, tables, and illustrations, the article is useful to those interested in the issue of land preservation, specifically agricultural land retention.

Moss, E. (Editor). 1977. "Land Use Controls in the United States," A Handbook on the Legal Rights of Citizens by the Natural Resources Defense Council, The Dial Press, New York. 362 pp.

This excellent book reviews federal, state and local laws dealing with land-use issues. Included are discussions on basic constitutional issues, the National Environmental Policy Act, the Clean Air Act, the Federal Water Pollution Control Act, the Coastal Zone Management Act, the National Flood Insurance Program, the Wild and Scenic Rivers Act, consumer and investor protection, transportation facilities, public lands, and state, local, and regional land-use controls. Many of these topic areas are relevant to agricultural preservation.

National Association of Conservation Districts. 1980. Soil Degradation: Effects on Agricultural Production, National Agricultural Lands Study, Interim Rep. No. 4. U.S. Government Printing Office, Washington, D.C. 56 pp.

Number four of the NALS interim reports, this report presents in nontechnical terms what is known about the whole process of soil degradation, and identifies what still needs to be learned. Topics presented include soil erosion; soil compactation and physical deterioration; soil–water problems affecting agricultural productivity; air pollution; and soil problems in urbanizing areas. Also presented in the appendices are the Land Capability Classification System; the Universal Soil Loss Equation; the National Resources Inventories; and USDA RCA "Acre Equivalent" Approach. Complete with tables, figures, and bibliography.

Sampson, R.N. 1981. "Farmland or Wasteland: A Time To Choose." Rodale Press, Emmaus, PA. 422 pp.

This worthy contribution to the overall philosophy of farmland preservation ties together situations of growing competition for water; a high rate of loss of good farmland to other uses; an emerging shortage of land for forest and range uses; and severe soil erosion to present an emerging national problem. Data and ideas form fifteen chapters plus a useful series of appendices on land capability classification, national resource inventories, the cropland resource pool, measuring soil loss, and American's land base in 1977. Complete with notes and references.

Schnepf, M. (Editor). 1979. "Food, Farmland and the Future." Soil Conservation Society of America, Ankeny, IA. 214 pp.

This compendium of papers by some of the leading authorities concerned with farmlands protection attempts to answer three general questions: (1)What are the important facts and trends involved? (2) What are the issues and how important are they? (3) What are people doing about these issues?

Vink, A.P.A. 1975. "Land Use in Advancing Agriculture." Springer-Verlag, New York. 394 pp.

A. P.A. Vink is a professor of physical geography and soil science at the

University of Amsterdam. His book explores the relationship between agricultural land use and land resources. The major topics covered include some of the historical aspects of land use, land-use surveys, land utilization types, land resources, landscape ecology and land conditions, land evaluation, and the development of land use in advancing agriculture.

Woodruff, A.M. (Editor). 1980. "The Farm and the City." Prentice-Hall, Englewood Cliffs, NJ. 184 pp.
This book is a product of the American Assembly at Columbia University. It explores the process and implications of disappearing farmland and seeks to answer important related questions. Contributions are drawn from several related disciplines.

Index

A

Acid rain, 47
Agins v. City of Tiburon, 29
Agricultural Census
    Canada, 244–245
    United States, 227, 229–230
Agricultural districting, 135–137, 164,
        176–177, 180, 188–189, 231,
        295–296, 301
Agricultural economics, 163–164, 198
Agricultural exports, 184, 189
Agricultural Land Development Act,
        Taiwan, 271
Agricultural Land Protection Act,
        226–227, 298
Agricultural land reserve, 251–253
Agricultural surpluses, 200, 219, 231
Agricultural zoning, 16–17, 56, 73–80,
        99, 144, 147, 149–150, 154,
        161–171, 190, 192–195, 293, 302
Agricultural and Food Act of 1981,
        202–203, 222–223, 232
Agronomy, 282
Air rights, 22–23
Alabama, 38, 187, 237
Alaska, 38, 187, 237
Albany, New York, 99
Alberta, Canada, 243–249, 255–257, 259
Allocation plan, 279
American Assembly, 306
American Farmland Trust, 140
American Land Forum, 131
American Law Institute, 39
American Planning Association, 304
American Society of Planning Officials, 79
Ames, Iowa, 118, 126, 236
Amish, 131
Amsterdam, 276, 286–288
Andrus v. Allard, 26–29
A-95 review, 69
Annapolis, Maryland, 99

Annexation, 68, 85, 124
Antitrust laws, 31–33
Appraisals, 88–89
Arizona, 38, 187, 237
Arkansas, 187, 237

B

Baker v. City of Milwaukie, 17
Baltimore, Maryland, 97
Barley, 247, 258
*Bass v. General Development
        Corporation*, 37
Belgium, 264
Benelux, 264
Berenson v. Town of New Castle, 35
Bergland, Bob, 198, 205, 221, 225–226
Billings, Montana, 304
Big Horn County, Wyoming, 79
Black Hawk County Board of Supervisors,
        112, 119
Black Hawk County, Iowa, 109–127, 202,
        238–239, 295, 301
Block, John R., 223, 231–232
Boise, Idaho, 82, 92
Boston, Massachusetts, 139
Boulder, Colorado, 41
British Columbia, Canada, 135, 140,
        243–244, 246, 249–254, 260
British North America Act, 249, 259
Bucks County, Pennsylvania, 78
Burlington County, New Jersey, 40
Butz, Earl L., 205, 217, 303

C

Calgary, Alberta, 248
California, 16, 20, 28–29, 76, 131,
        133–135, 187, 189, 201, 237, 264,
        295, 301

Coastal Commission, 133–136,
        140–141, 143
    legislature, 21
    Supreme Court, 20, 34
Canada, 131, 135–137, 243–261, 263, 287,
        292, 299, *see also* specific pro-
        vinces
    Constitution, 259
    Land Inventory, 244–247, 249, 251, 301
Capital gains tax, 176, 269
Capital improvements, 42–43
    plan, 68, 70
Caribbean, 237
Carter administration, 204, 225
Carver County, Minnesota, 74
Cascade Mountains, 81
Cedar Falls, Iowa, 109, 111, 125
Cedar River, 109–111
*Ceder-Riverside Association v. United
        States*, 32
Chester County, Pennsylvania, 295
Cheyenne, Wyoming, 59
Chiang Kai-shek, 270
Chicago, Illinois, 110, 301, 304
Chicoutini, Quebec, 248
China, 270–272
Circuit-breaker tax credit, 148, 150, 152, 186
Citizens, 84, 88–90, 212, 296–297
Citrus groves, 37
*City of Lafayette v. Louisiana Power and
        Light Co.*, 31–33
Civil Rights Acts, 30–31
Clayton Antitrust Act, 31
Clean Air Act, 204, 305
Clean Water Act, 31
Climate, 98, 110, 115, 118, 198, 244–246,
        248, 250, 268, 292
Coastal zone management, 133–136,
        161–162, 206–207, 209
Coastal Zone Management Act of 1972,
        206–207, 209, 305
Colfax, Washington, 92, 234

Colorado, 38, 41, 187, 237–238
  Supreme Court, 41
Columbia County, Wisconsin, 295
Columbia University, 306
Common law, 266
Common Market, see European
  Economic Community
Community Land Development Act of
  1975, United Kingdom, 266
Comprehensive plans, 16–17, 41–43, 79,
  84, 91–95, 118, 125, 161, 166,
  296–297
Connecticut, 37–38, 40, 58, 174–175,
  178–180, 187, 201, 237, 270, 275
  legislature, 175
Conservation districts, 142, 213, 235, 239
Conservationists, 215, 227
Conservative party, 226
Consumers, 55–57, 60–61
Corn, 56, 60, 110, 115, 173, 238–239, 252
Corn Belt, 142, 203, 238
Corn Suitability Ratings, 109–127, 301
*Corstiaan Van Vugt v. Zoning Hearing
  Board of Springfield Township*,
  106
Council to Protect Rural England, 267
County Agricultural Boards, Sweden, 269
Covenants, 132, 189
Cultuurtechniek, 282
Current use taxation, 36–38, 85, 185,
  187–188

D

Dade County, Florida, 7
Dairy, 56, 58, 82–83, 230, 252, 268, 275
Deed restrictions, 131–133
Deferred taxation, 175, 186–189
Delaware, 38, 97, 174–175, 179, 187, 237
  legislature, 175
Des Moines, Iowa, 110
Des Moines Register, 126
Developers, 56, 61, 84, 228, 295
Development rights, 22, 25, 81–90,
  131–132, 134, 139, 144, 176–177,
  266, 302
Differential assessment taxation, 25,
  36–38, 185, 201, 296, 304
Dikes, 271, 283, 285
Dover, Delaware, 99
Due process, 22, 30, 44, 180
Dutch Land Reallotment Act(s), 282–283
Duxbury, Massachusetts, 301

E

Eagle Protection Act, 26
Earth Day, 8
Easements, 98, 134, 300
Eastern Flevoland, 287–288
Ecology, 19–20, 45, 51, 218, 281, 289,
  303, 306
Economics, 46–47, 49–50, 147, 243, 265,
  282, 302

Economists, 227–228
Edmonton, Alberta, 248
Education, 66, 87, 153, 155, 157–158, 167,
  193, 214, 294
Edward Golla v. Hopewell Township, 106
Eggs, 252, 268, 275
Eminent domain, 18, 134, 140–141, 144,
  176, 179, 189
Energy, 3–4, 12, 45–46, 55, 59, 83, 98, 173,
  200–201, 218, 233, 291, 293, 303
England, see Great Britain
Engineering, 282
Engineers, 215, 282, 285
Environment, 183–184, 201, 217–218
Environmental Comment, 294
Environmental impact statements,
  204–206, 220
Environmentalists, 84
Environmentally significant lands, 206
Equal protection, 44, 75
Ethics, 45–53, 84, 303
Euclidian zoning, 164
Europe, 263–265, 272, 275–276, 300
European Economic Community, 275,
  290, 298–299
Exclusionary zoning, 33–36, 43, 93, 107
Exclusive farm use zone, 161–171, 297
Extension agents, 66, 213, 284
Extension service, 112, 153, 156–157,
  161, 216

F

Family farms, 13, 141, 243, 249, 251,
  254–255, 269–270
Farm Bureau, 66, 126
Farmers, 3, 10, 13, 24–25, 38–39, 45–46,
  50–51, 55–60, 65–67, 75–76,
  84–87, 98, 106, 111–112, 131,
  136, 141, 147–149, 156, 164, 166,
  175–176, 201, 207, 213, 221, 228,
  248, 251, 254, 256–258, 269–270,
  282–283, 289, 295
  cooperatives, 270
  party, 280
Farmers Home Administration, 203, 208
Farmland, 141, 221, 233–240
Farmland conservancies, 131–145
Farmland Protection Policy Act of 1981,
  202–203, 205, 208, 222–223
Federal Energy Administration, 201
Federal Register, 220, 223, 233
Federal Water Pollution Control Act,
  204–205, 305
Fertilizer, 56, 60, 282
Finland, 264–265
Flood plain, 94, 110, 204, 207, 221, 301
Florida, 37–38, 55, 187, 202, 237
  Supreme Court, 37
Ford Foundation, 139
Forest land, 21, 217, 244, 265–266, 287, 302
Fox Indians, 111
France, 131, 135, 137–138, 143, 263–265,
  282, 292

Franklin County, Massachusetts, 301
*Fred F. French Investing Co. v. City of
  New York*, 20
Freedom of Information Act, 10
Fruits, 55, 57–60, 82–83, 176, 268, 270, 275

G

Gay Head, Massachusetts, 301
Génie rural, 282
Geology, 91–92, 94, 109–110
Georgia, 38, 186–187, 237
German law, 266
Glaciers, 110, 124
Gonzaga Law Review, 302
Grain, 55–56, 58, 110, 200, 239, 244,
  247, 275
Grange, 65
Great Britain, 10, 179, 264–267
Great Lakes, 244
  states, 202, 207
Greenhouses, 57, 59, 82–83, 252
Growth management, 42–44, 57, 154, 157,
  231, 301

H

Haifa, Israel, 267
Halifax, Nova Scotia, 248, 301
Hamilton, Ontario, 248
Harrisburg, Pennsylvania, 97, 99
Hawaii, 16, 186–187, 190, 202, 237, 289
Hawkeye Institute of Technology, 109
Health official, 94, 119
Helsinki, Finland, 265
Highways, 173, 176, 193, 197, 200, 247, 300
Hoffman v. Clark, 36
Holland, see Netherlands
House Agriculture Committee, 202–203
Housing, 14, 39, 70, 75–78, 83, 161, 165,
  173, 197, 200, 205, 247, 277, 283,
  287, 290
Housing Act
  of 1901, Netherlands, 277
  United States, 30
Horticulture, 82, 275
Howard County, Maryland, 40, 73
Humboldt County, California, 134
Hydrology, 282

I

Idaho, 47, 82, 187–188, 237
IJsselmeer, 286–288
Illinois, 16, 38, 187, 203, 230–231, 237
  Department of Agriculture, 230
Indiana, 187, 237
Industrial Revolution, 9–10, 111
International Institute for Land
  Reclamation and Improvement,
  Netherlands, 302

Iowa, 32−33, 109−127, 187, 203, 237−239, 295
  Northland Regional Council of Governments, 112, 125
  State Agricultural and Home Economics Research Station, 115, 118
  State Statistical Laboratory, 236
  State University, 214
  State Zoning Enabling Act, 11
Israel, 267−268

J

Jerusalem, 267
Jewish National Fund, 267
John Deere and Company, 109, 124
Johnson County, Iowa, 126
Just v. Marinette County, 20, 29

K

Kaiser Aetna v. U.S., 27
Kansas, 38, 186−187, 203, 237
Kaohsiung, Taiwan, 271
Kentucky, 38, 187, 237
Kibbutzim, 268
King County, Washington, 40, 56, 73, 81−90
  Office of Agriculture, 88−89
Kiryat Gat, Israel, 268
Knoxville, Tennessee, 301
Kohler Act, Pennsylvania, 18−19

L

Labour party, 266
Lancaster County, Pennsylvania, 131−133, 140−141
  Agricultural Preservation Board, 140−141
  Planning Commission, 133
Land Acquisition Act of 1965, Sweden, 269
Land banking, 39−40, 136, 179, 257−259, 269, 300
Land Commission Act, British Columbia, 250−252, 254
Land Evaluation and Site Assessment system, 223
Land-grant colleges, 213, 215, 233
Land reallotment, 271, 282−285, 287, 289
Landscape, 110, 118, 179, 277, 280, 282−284
  plan, 284
Lands Directorate, Canada, 136
Land tenure, 243, 249, 254−260, 299
Land trusts, 139−140, 179
Land Use Board of Appeals, Oregon, 162
Lankhish region, Israel, 268
Large-lot zoning, 66, 100, 293
Latin America, 303
Lewiston, Idaho, 92
Lincoln, Massachusetts, 139

Lincoln Rural Land Foundation, 139−140
Livestock, 55−56, 58, 60, 82, 167, 199, 252, 268, 275, 285
London, England, 267
  Greenbelt, 267
London, Ontario, 248
Louisiana, 187
Louisiana Purchase, 11
Low and moderate income housing, 33−36
Luxembourg, 264

M

Madison, Wisconsin, 110, 112
Madrid, 264
Maine, 174−175, 187, 237
Malmö, Sweden, 269
Manitoba, 243−250, 255−256
  Agricultural Land Protection Act of 1977, 256
  Agricultural Lands Protection Board, 256
Marginal lands, 163, 165−166, 280
Markerwaard, 287
Maryland, 16, 38, 40−41, 98, 177, 179−180, 186−187, 201, 229, 237
Mason City Center Association v. City of Mason City, 32
Mason City, Iowa, 32
Massachusetts, 40, 59−60, 139, 174−175, 178−179, 185, 187, 201, 237, 270, 275
  Department of Food and Agriculture, 139
  Farmlands Trust, 139−140, 142
Metropolitan Council of the Twin Cities Area, 193
Mexico, 287
Michigan, 6, 38, 69, 186−187, 189, 237
Middle Ages, 285
Midwest, 33, 60, 115, 173, 203, 231
Migration Bird Act, 26
Minimum lot size, 16−17, 66, 68, 74, 93, 162−164, 166
Minneapolis, 32, 193
  twin city region, 16, 193
Minnesota, 16, 38, 66, 109−110, 136, 187, 193, 237
Miracle Mile Association v. City of Rochester, 32
Mississippi, 38, 187, 237
Mississippi River, 109
Missouri, 38, 187, 203, 237
Model Land Development Code, 39
Monell v. Department of Social Services, 30
Monkton Landing, Vermont, 7
Mona County, Iowa, 48
Montgomery County, Maryland, 41−42
Montana, 38, 187, 237
Montreal, Canada, 248
Morris County Land Improvement Co. v. Township of Parsippany-Troy Hills, 19
Morro Valley, 134

Moshavas, 268
Moshavim, 265
Mount Weather, Virginia, 213

N

Nashville, Tennessee, 59
National Agricultural Lands Study, 65, 69, 124, 186, 204, 222, 225−232, 293−294, 305
National Association of Counties, 126
National Conference of State Legislatures, 186
National Conference on Land and People, 214
National Conference on Land Utilization, 211
National Conference on Soil, Water and Suburbia, 215
National Farmers Organization, 126
National Flood Insurance Program, 204, 207−208, 305
National Environmental Policy Act of 1969, 10, 204, 305
National Land Fund, Sweden, 269
National land-use legislation, 215, 217−219
National Land Use Planning Committee, 211
National Oceanic and Atmospheric Administration, 207
National Park Service, 139
National Physical Planning Agency, Netherlands, 278
National Resources Inventory, 222, 227, 230, 305
National Resources Planning Board, 211−212
National Wildlife, 126
Nature Conservancy, 139
Nebraska, 187, 237
Netherlands, 264−265, 275−290, 299
  Constitution, 278
  Housing Act of 1901, 277
  Ministry of Agriculture, 280−281
  Ministry of Housing and Physical Planning, 278
  Ministry of Public Works, 285
  Parliament, 278, 283, 285
  Water Control Board, 285
New Brunswick, Canada, 246
New Democratic Party, 135
New England, 6, 55, 142, 178
Newfoundland, Canada, 244, 246
New Hampshire, 40, 174−175, 178, 186−187, 189, 237
New Jersey, 16, 33−35, 40, 43, 58, 81, 98, 174−175, 179, 185, 187, 201, 237
  Department of Agriculture, 58
  Supreme Court, 19, 34
New Mexico, 38, 187, 237
New towns, 267, 280, 287
New York City, 16, 22−23, 42, 264, 301

Landmarks Preservation Law, 22–23
New York State, 16, 20, 22, 32–33, 35, 38,
    43, 69, 76, 98, 164, 174–178, 180,
    185, 187–189, 201, 237, 264,
    295–296
  Court of Appeals, 20, 35, 41, 43
  New Town Law, 42
Nevada, 187, 237
Niagara peninsula, 244
North America, 254, 263, 265, 275, 287, 299
North Carolina, 187, 237
North Dakota, 38, 187, 237
Northeast Polder, 287–288
Northeast United States, 33, 55, 58, 142,
    173–181, 188
Northern Illinois University, 124
North Hopewell Township, Pennsylvania,
    103–104
North Sea, 285–287
Northwest Territories, Canada, 246
Norway, 264
Nova Scotia, Canada, 246, 301
Nuisance liability, 166
  ordinances, 132
  suits, 94, 180

O

Oahu, Hawaii, 27
Oakwood at Madison, Inc. v. Township
    of Mt. Laurel, 34
Oats, 60, 110, 247
Ohio, 187, 237
Oklahoma, 187, 237
Olympia, Washington, 82, 92
Old West Regional Commission, 304
Omaha-Council Bluff SMSA, 60
Omnibus Budget Reconciliation Act of
    1981, 203
Ontario, Canada, 243–250, 252–254, 299
  Ministry of Agriculture, 253
  Planning Act, 250, 253
Open space, 21, 29, 39, 61, 87, 139, 147,
    163, 167, 176, 183–184, 191, 198,
    265, 267, 293
Orange County, New York, 295
Orebro, 269
Oregon, 16, 20–21, 33, 38–39, 69, 76–77,
    82, 161–171, 186–187, 190, 202,
    237, 266, 289, 297
  Court of Appeals, 165
  Land Conservation and Development
      Commission, 21, 161–171
  legislature, 21, 164–165
  Senate Bill 100, 161–162
  Supreme Court, 17
Ottawa, Ontario, 248
Owen v. City of Independence, 30

P

Palestine, 267
Palouse, 91–92

Peach Bottom Township, Pennsylvania,
    16, 104–105
Penn Central, 22–23, 25
Penn Central Transportation Co. v. City
    of New York, 22–23, 26, 28–29
Pennsylvania, 16, 33–35, 43, 97–108, 131,
    139, 174–175, 177, 179, 187, 237,
    296–297
  House of Representatives, 132
  Supreme Court, 18, 24, 106
  Turnpike, 35
Pennsylvania Coal Co. v. Mahon,
    18–19, 25
People's Republic of China, 198
Petaluma, California, 42–43
Philadelphia, 35, 97
Physical planning, 277–282, 284, 287,
    289, 299
Physical Planning Act, Netherlands,
    278–279
Planners, 9, 13–14, 66–67, 112, 155, 215,
    227, 267–268, 294–296, 299,
    301–302
Planning, 295
Polder, 285, 287–290
Police power, 16, 19, 179
Pollution, 204, 207, 216, 271, 281
Poultry, 56, 82, 252, 268, 275
Prairie provinces, 244–246, 248–250, 254
Preferrential taxation, 56, 173, 186–188
Prince Edward Island, Canada, 135–137,
    140, 246
  Development Corporation, 136–137
Prince George's County, Maryland,
    41–42
Prime agricultural land, 20, 25, 46, 56, 66,
    69, 86, 101, 109, 112, 124–125,
    141–142, 162, 164, 176, 198, 203,
    205, 208, 217, 219–222, 233–240,
    243, 245, 252, 299, 301–302
Progressive Conservative Party, 250
Project Independence, 201
Property, 266
  rights, 17–30, 44, 272
  tax, 184–193
Proposition 20, 133
Prune Yard Shopping Center v. Robbins,
    28
Prussia, 282
Public health, safety, and welfare, 19–21,
    23, 34, 166
Public hearing, 119, 188
Puget Sound, 81
Pullman, Washington, 92–93
Purchase of development rights, 25, 40,
    56, 73, 81–90, 99, 131, 144, 158,
    176–178, 231, 301

Q

Quarter/quarter zoning, 16, 68, 74,
    102–107
Quebec City, Quebec, 248
Quebec, Canada, 246

R

Railroads, 111
Ramapo, New York, 42–43
Ranchers, 65–67, 228
Reagan administration, 231
Realtors, 84, 228
Reclamation, 218, 277, 283, 285–289
Regina, Saskatchewan, 248
Regional food plans, 57–61
Regional planners, 94, 198, 293
Regional planning, 278–279, 282
  agencies, 69, 155
Regional Planning Act, Taiwan, 270–272
Regional plans, 57–61, 253, 265, 277–278
Regional Science Institute, 192, 201
Republic of China, 270–272
Republic of Korea, 272
Rhode Island, 40, 174–175, 187, 237, 270
Rice, 270–271
Richmond, Virginia, 49
Right-to-farm legislation, 179–180, 231
Robinson v. City of Boulder, 41
Roden v. K & K Land Management, Inc., 37
Roosevelt, Franklin D., 84, 142
Rotterdam, 276–277, 286
Rural Development Act of 1972, 233
Rutgers University, 179
Rye, 247–248

S

Salem, Oregon, 82, 92
San Francisco, 42
  Bay, 20, 29, 295
San Louis Obispo County, California, 134
Santa Monica Mountains, 134
Saskatchewan, Canada, 135–136,
    243–246, 248–250, 254–259
  Farm Ownership Act of 1974, 255–256
  Land Bank, 250, 254, 257–259
  Land Bank Act of 1972, 257
  Land Bank Commission, 257–259
Saskatoon, Saskatchewan, 248
Saturday Review, 126
Sauk Indians, 111
Scandinavia, 265
Scott County, Iowa, 126
Seal Beach, 134
Seattle, Washington, 55, 82–83, 90, 92
Seminar on the retention of prime lands,
    219–221, 294
Service for Land and Water Use, 282–284
Sherman Antitrust Act, 31
Sliding scale zoning, 16, 68, 74
Snake River, 94
Snoqualmie National Forest, 81
Socialism, 250, 266
Sociétés d'Aménagement Foncier et
    d'Éstablissement Rural (SAFERs),
    137–138, 140, 143, 264–265
Soil, 5, 7, 94, 98, 110–126, 135, 199,
    233–240, 268

Soil and Water Resource Conservation
	Act of 1978, 207
Soil Conservation, 126
Soil erosion, 25, 46−47, 115, 197−198,
	206−207, 212, 218, 297−298, 305
Soil science, 282, 305
Soil scientists, 66, 94, 118, 294
Soil surveys, 233−240
Soil types, 113−117, 119, 236
South Carolina, 187, 237
South Dakota, 187, 237
*Southern Burlington County NAACP v.
	Township of Mt. Laurel*, 34
Southern Flevoland, 287−288
Soybeans, 60, 110, 115, 238−239, 252
Speculators, 24, 51, 58, 175
Spokane, Washington, 92
Springfield, Illinois, 110
Standard Zoning Enabling Act, 15, 33
State programs, 69, 75−77, 139, 147−194
State income tax, 148, 152
Statistics Canada, 248
St. Catherines, 248
Steward Snyder v. Railroad Borough, 106
St. John, New Brunswick, 248
St. Lawrence River, 244
Stockholm, 269
Storie Index, 301
Story County, Iowa, 126
St. Paul, Minnesota, 110
Structure plans, 266, 279
Subdivision regulation, 79, 97, 161
Successful Farming, 126
Sudbury, 248
Suffolk County, New York, 40, 73, 176,
	202, 295
Surface mining, 203, 229, 238
Surface Mining and Control Act of 1977,
	203, 211
Surrick v. Zoning Hearing Board, 34−35
Susquehanna River, 97
Sweden, 264, 268−270
	Parliament, 268−269
Switzerland, 282

T

Taiwan, *see* Republic of China
Taking issue, 17−30, 44, 303
Taxing powers, 23, 36−39
Tax programs and policies, 55, 69, 75−76,
	98, 141, 158, 163, 173, 175−176,
	183−193, 201, 208, 217, 231, 251,
	264, 269, 295, 297, 300−301
Tax Reform Act of 1976, 38
Tel Aviv, 267
Tennessee, 38, 187, 237
Texas, 55, 187, 237
Thunder Bay, 248
Tiburon, California, 29
Tobacco, 250, 252
Tomatoes, 252, 264
Topography, 109−110, 244, 250, 252
Toronto, Ontario, 248

Town and Country Planning Act of 1947,
	United Kingdom, 266
Transfer of development rights, 25, 73, 99,
	144, 158, 178−179, 295
Transportation, 55, 57, 277, 280, 288,
	302, 305
Trenton, New Jersey, 99
Trust for Public Land, 139−140
Tulare County, California, 295, 301

U

Udell v. Haas, 17
Unique farmlands, 203, 220−221, 233−240
United Kingdom, *see* Great Britain
United Nations, 28
United States, 81, 110, 131, 133, 135−136,
	144, 198, 213, 231, 238, 243, 255,
	260, 266, 268, 272, 275, 278−280,
	287, 292, 301, 303
	Agricultural Stabilization and
		Conservation Service, 156, 216
	Army Corps of Engineers, 27, 94, 212
	Congress, 7−8, 136, 197, 202−204,
		208−209, 212, 215, 222,
		225−227, 232
	Constitution, 17−31, 37, 43
		fifth amendment, 17−30
		fourteenth amendment, 22
	Council on Environmental Quality, 48,
		201, 204, 220, 222, 225, 303
	Department of Agriculture, 5, 60, 78,
		112, 142, 197−200, 202−205,
		208, 211−223, 230, 294, 301, 305
		Land Use Policy Committee, 216,
			220−221
		Office of Land Use Coordination,
			211−212
	Department of Commerce, 207, 222
	Department of Defense, 222
	Department of Energy, 201, 222
	Department of Housing and Urban
		Development, 207, 215, 222,
	Department of Interior, 212, 214, 215,
		218−219
	Department of Natural Resources, 215
	Department of Transportation, 222
	Environmental Protection Agency, 93,
		205−206, 208−209, 222, 298
	Economic Research Service, 216, 227
	Forest Service, 216
	Geological Survey, 119, 235
	Office of Management and Budget, 222
	Secretary of agriculture, 198, 202, 205,
		212, 214−217, 221−223,
		225−226
	Secretary of housing and urban
		development, 215
	Secretary of interior, 26, 214
	Senate Agriculture Committee, 202
	Soil Conservation Service, 58, 94, 97,
		112, 115, 118−119, 149, 156,
		163, 192, 198, 200, 216,
		220−223, 227, 233−240

	soil classification system, 21, 83, 97,
		112−114, 155, 163, 223, 229,
		235−236, 291, 297, 301, 305
	Supreme Court, 18−19, 22−31
U.S. News and World Report, 126
University of Amsterdam, 306
University of Northern Iowa, 109
University of Pennsylvania, 137
University of Washington, 84
University of Wisconsin, 111
Urban development, 69−70
Urban growth boundaries, 165−167, 297
Urban-rural fringe, 24, 29, 36, 40, 55−61,
	158, 184−185, 198, 247−248
Urban sprawl, 86, 111, 147, 153−154,
	183−185, 198, 201, 263, 267,
	270−271, 298
Urbanization, 82, 111, 144, 183, 238, 247,
	281, 289, 293, 299
Utah, 38, 187, 237
Utrecht, Netherlands, 276, 286

V

Vallejo, California, 6
Valleys region of Maryland, 304
Vancouver, British Columbia, 244
Visalia, California, 301
Vegetables, 55, 57−60, 82−83, 176, 268,
	270, 275
Vegetation, 94, 110, 124−125, 218, 244
Vermont, 37−38, 59, 174−176, 179, 181,
	187, 202, 237, 298
	Supreme Court, 38
Veterans Administration, 208
Village of Euclid v. Amber Realty Co., 23, 26
Virginia, 16, 38, 187, 213, 237
Voluntary restrictive agreement,
	186−187, 189

W

Wageningen, Netherlands, 302
Walcheren, 283
	Land Consolidation Act of 1947,
		Netherlands, 283
Wales, 263
Walla Walla, Washington, 92
Walworth County, Wisconsin, 112, 295
Wapsipinicon River, 110
Washington, D.C., 4−5, 7−8, 51, 57, 143,
	215−216, 221
Washington State, 6, 38, 81−95, 187−188,
	235−237, 298, 300
	Open Space Taxation Act, 188, 300
	Planning and Community Affairs
		Agency, 81
	Supreme Court, 88−89
Washington State University, 81
Waste recycling, 57, 60−61
Water and sewer facilities, 22−23, 25, 36,
	41−43, 68, 75, 121, 176, 189, 200,
	205−206, 265, 298

Waterloo, Iowa, 109–111, 125
Ways and Means, 126
Weather Bureau, 213
Western Pennsylvania Conservancy, 139
West Germany, 263–266, 282
Wheat, 95, 173, 247, 258, 268
Whitman County, Washington, 75,
      91–95, 296
   Board of County Commissioners,
      92–93, 95
   Planning Commission, 92–93, 95
Wieringermeer, 287–288
Wild and Scenic Rivers Act, 305
Wildlife, 94, 119, 133, 244, 287, 294
Williamette River, 161, 165
Williamson Act, 76, 189, 192
Windsor, Ontario, 248
Winningham v. Department of Revenue,
   39
Winnipeg, Manitoba, 248, 250
Wisconsin, 16, 20, 69, 76–77, 110, 147–159,
   186–187, 189–190, 201, 237,
   295–297
   Department of Administration, 152–153
   Department of Agriculture, Trade and
      Consumer Protection, 152
   Department of Development, 152–153
   Department of Natural Resources, 152,
      156
   Department of Revenue, 153
   Farmland Preservation Act, 147
   Farmland Preservation Program,
      147–159, 296
   Land Conservation Board, 150, 152–153
   legislature, 152
   Supreme Court, 120
Wisconsin glacier, 110
World War I, 267, 285
World War II, 82, 111, 173, 183, 200, 214,
   266, 283, 287, 290
Wyoming, 187, 237

Y

Yakima County, Washington, 79
York County, Pennsylvania, 97–108
   Planning Commission, 98
York, Pennsylvania, 97
Yukon, 246

Z

Zionism, 28, 267–268
Zoning, 16–17, 19–20, 21, 23–25, 27, 29,
   31–33, 35–36, 65–66, 68, 73–80,
   85–86, 92–93, 97–108, 111–112,
   119, 125, 131, 135, 141, 144,
   148–150, 153–154, 161, 166,
   186–187, 190–192, 217, 231, 249,
   251, 253, 265, 270–271, 279, 293,
   296–297, 300, 302
   administrator, 119
   ordinance, 118, 125, 157
Zuider Sea, 285, 287, 290
   Act of 1918, 285